THE PROMISE AND PERILS OF LAW

THE PROMISE AND PERILS OF LAW

LAWYERS IN CANADIAN HISTORY

Constance Backhouse & W. Wesley Pue
CO-EDITORS

The Promise and Perils of Law: Lawyers in Canadian History
© Irwin Law Inc., 2009

All rights reserved. No part of this publication may be reproduced, stored in a retrieval system, or transmitted, in any form or by any means, without the prior written permission of the publisher or, in the case of photocopying or other reprographic copying, a licence from Access Copyright (Canadian Copyright Licensing Agency), 1 Yonge Street, Suite 800, Toronto, ON, M5E 1E5.

Published in 2009 by

Irwin Law Inc.
14 Duncan Street
Suite 206
Toronto, ON
M5H 3G8
www.irwinlaw.com

ISBN: 978-1-55221-166-3

Library and Archives Canada Cataloguing in Publication

Law Society of Upper Canada Symposium on the History of the Canadian Legal Profession (2007: Toronto, Ont.)

The promise and perils of law : lawyers in Canadian history / Constance Backhouse & W. Wesley Pue, co-editors.

Papers presented at the symposium, Law Society of Upper Canada Symposium on the History of the Canadian Legal Profession, held October 12, 2007 at Osgoode Hall, Toronto, Ont.
Includes bibliographical references and index.
ISBN 978-1-55221-166-3

1. Lawyers—Canada—History—Congresses. 2. Practice of law—Canada—History—Congresses. 3. Law—Study and teaching—Canada—History—Congresses. I. Backhouse, Constance, 1952– II. Pue, W. Wesley III. Title.

KE330.L38 2009   340.023'71   C2009-901730-X
KF297.A2L39 2009

The publisher acknowledges the financial support of the Government of Canada through the Book Publishing Industry Development Program (BPIDP) for its publishing activities.

We acknowledge the assistance of the OMDC Book Fund, an initiative of Ontario Media Development Corporation.

Printed and bound in Canada.

1 2 3 4 5   13 12 11 10 09

Contents

Acknowledgments vii

1 **Introduction** 1
W. Wesley Pue

2 **An Introduction to Osgoode Hall on Its 175th Anniversary: More than Bricks and Mortar** 13
Deidré Rowe Brown

PART 1
HISTORICAL PERSPECTIVES ON LEGAL EDUCATION 29

3 **Slamming the Door on Brains: Two Early Twentieth-Century Law Schools and the Narrowing of Educational Opportunity** 31
David G. Bell

4 **"Good Government, without Him, is Well-nigh Impossible": Training Future (Male) Lawyers for Politics in Ontario, Quebec, and Nova Scotia, 1920–1960** 49
Mélanie Brunet

PART 2
HISTORICAL REFLECTIONS ON THE PRACTICE OF LAW 73

5 **Stratification, Economic Adversity, and Diversity in an Urban Bar: Halifax, Nova Scotia, 1900–1950** 75
Philip Girard and Jeffrey Haylock

6 **Megafirm: A Chronology for the Large Law Firm in Canada** 103
Christopher Moore

PART 3
QUEBEC: A DISTINCT LEGAL HISTORY 127

7 **Civil Law, Legal Practitioners, and Everyday Justice in the Decades following the *Quebec Act of 1774*** 129
Jean-Philippe Garneau (translated by Steven Watt, Ph.D.)

v

8 The Legal Profession and Penal Justice in Quebec City, 1856–1965: From Modernity to Anti-Modernity 141
  Donald Fyson

PART 4
THE RULE OF LAW, IMPEACHMENT, AND BUREAUCRATIC REGULATION 159

9 The Court and the Legal Profession: Loyalist Lawyers and the Nova Scotia Supreme Court in the 1780s 161
  Jim Phillips

10 "Guardians of Liberty": R.M.W. Chitty and the Wartime Idea of Constitutional Rights 173
  Eric M. Adams

PART 5
RACE ISSUES: DIVERSIFYING THE BAR AND ITS LEGAL STRATEGIES 191

11 Ethelbert Lionel Cross: Toronto's First Black Lawyer 193
  Susan Lewthwaite

12 If Your Life Is a Leaf: Arthur Eugene O'Meara's Campaign for Aboriginal Justice 225
  Hamar Foster

PART 6
GENDER ISSUES: THE IMPACT OF WOMEN ON THE PROFESSION 243

13 "Into the Rough of Things": Women Lawyers in British Columbia, 1912–1930 245
  Dorothy E. Chunn and Joan Brockman

14 "A Revolution in Numbers": Ontario Feminist Lawyers in the Formative Years 1970s to the 1990s 265
  Constance Backhouse

List of Contributors 295

Index 299

Acknowledgments

ON 6 FEBRUARY 2007, the Law Society of Upper Canada celebrated the 175th anniversary of the opening of Osgoode Hall, at the corner of what is now Queen Street and University Avenue, in the heart of downtown Toronto. One of the city's architectural treasures, the enduring majestic beauty of Osgoode Hall has captivated lawyers and the public alike for one and three-quarter centuries. A beacon of pride and stature for members of the legal profession, Osgoode Hall also consistently takes top honour for the most-visited site during Toronto's annual "Doors Open" event, when members of the public are invited to tour the city's most interesting buildings. For those who are not personally familiar with the site, in her chapter later in this volume, Deidré Rowe Brown, a doctoral history student and executive assistant to the Treasurer of the Law Society of Upper Canada, provides an introductory description of Osgoode Hall, its history, and its significance to the legal profession.

To mark the auspicious 175th anniversary, and to celebrate a building that can claim to be the oldest, continuously-used home for a professional regulatory legal body in Canada, the Law Society of Upper Canada generously provided funding to host a day-long symposium on the history of the legal profession in Canada. On 12 October 2007, the symposium unveiled a program of oral presentations from interdisciplinary scholars and lawyers whose interests touched the history of the legal profession in a variety of ways. They presented their research before an engaged and remarkably diverse audience composed of judges, lawyers from Bay Street megafirms, lawyers from mid-sized "boutique" firms, lawyers from small firms and sole practitioners, historians, archivists, and individuals who fit none of these categories but were simply drawn to learn more about the history of the legal profession. The range of background and expertise was quite unprecedented, both within the group of those who presented papers and the audience, who participated with vigour. All of those involved in the event came away with a high regard for the intensity of interest that this topic attracts. Whatever people may say about the strengths and weaknesses of the legal profession, its history is magnetic.

This volume of essays has emerged from the marvellous range of papers presented at the Osgoode Hall symposium. It is not intended to be a strictly scholarly or academic volume, although some of the papers clearly qualify as such. Nor is it intended to be a publication that caters solely to a popular audience. And although lawyers and judges may make up the lion's share of its readers, it is not aimed exclusively at members of the profession. Rather, our objective has been to put together a book of essays that aims to be accessible while also making a scholarly contribution. It lies at the midpoint of a triangle representing "popular," "academic," and "professional" writing. As such it fits into no neat category, and we hope that readers will be open and generous in approaching its diversity.

We are indebted to the staff at the Law Society of Upper Canada, who assisted with the many details required to bring the symposium to such a successful conclusion. We are indebted to the benchers of the Law Society of Upper Canada, who agreed to fund the symposium, and to the members of the Law Society whose fees contributed to the project. We are indebted to Jim Phillips, editor-in-chief of the Osgoode Society, who generously donated his time as one of the co-organizers of the symposium. We are indebted to the authors of the papers, who produced written texts in accordance with strict timetables and guidelines. We are indebted to the law publisher Irwin Law, and its very capable staff, who assisted us in bringing this manuscript to fruition. And we are equally indebted to the magnificent old Osgoode Hall itself, in recognition of which we have published this book. We hope that this project may contribute in some small way to the enduring legacy of a building that houses Canada's largest legal and professional regulatory body.

Constance Backhouse & W. Wesley Pue
Ottawa & Vancouver
April 2008

CHAPTER 1

Introduction

W. WESLEY PUE

LAWYERS.
　　Everyone loves them; or hates them. Only physicians and cops compete for domination of prime-time television. From *Perry Mason* through *Rumpole of the Bailey*, *L.A. Law*, *Night Court*, *Street Legal*, *Ally McBeal*, and *Court TV*, television portrayals of lawyers seem ubiquitous. Our cultural obsession with the profession is also reflected in a seemingly unending array of movies, books, talk-radio, news reports, and other media. The cumulative cultural impact of even these few, high-impact TV shows is enormous. TV lawyers are, to varying degrees, smart, principled, eccentric, beautiful, or goofy, but always interesting. Some of the wealthiest and most powerful, it seems, are also witty, attractive, and relatively unencumbered by the tedium of work. Motion picture lawyers and those in novels more frequently reveal a darker side. News coverage reveals the good, the bad, and the ugly. Not infrequently, one person's hero is another's villain. Accountants, engineers, dentists, and mechanics just do not seem to capture the popular imagination in the same way.
　　A sort of lawyerly omnipresence in popular consciousness is also revealed in the wide proliferation of lawyer jokes. Rarely as complimentary as television portrayals, these circulate at a great rate of speed. Some spoof the ethical standards of a profession duty-bound to represent repulsive individuals or unpopular causes; for example:

> The devil visited a lawyer's office and made him an offer. "I can arrange some things for you," the devil said. "I'll increase your income five-fold. Your partners will love you; your clients will respect you; you'll have four months of

vacation each year and live to be a hundred. All I require in return is that your wife's soul, your children's souls, and their children's souls rot in hell for eternity." The lawyer thought for a moment. "What's the catch?" he asked.[1]

Others play on the gap between law and common sense:

> A man went to a brain store to get some brain to complete a study. He sees a sign remarking on the quality of professional brain offered at this particular brain store. He begins to question the butcher about the cost of these brains. "How much does it cost for engineer brain?"
>
> "Three dollars an ounce."
>
> "How much does it cost for programmer brain?"
>
> "Four dollars an ounce."
>
> "How much for lawyer brain?"
>
> "$1,000 an ounce."
>
> "Why is lawyer brain so much more?"
>
> "Do you know how many lawyers we had to kill to get one ounce of brain?"

Marc Galanter, who wrote a scholarly tome on the topic, told the *Wisconsin Lawyer* that "lawyer jokes often mock lawyers as being arrogant, shifty, pushy, and so on," emphasizing "the flip side of lawyers' virtues: their focus, resourcefulness, persistence." Recurrent themes, he says, portray lawyers as "liars, economic predators, allies of the devil, fomenters of strife, and enemies of justice" or as "betrayers of trust, morally deficient, objects of scorn," and, ominously, "targets for extinction."[2] Though there is a high degree of interchangeability with jokes aimed at politicians (frequently lawyers in any event) and with ethnic jokes (where the humour in speaking of 6,000 people at the bottom of the sea as a "good start" is much less apparent), the urge to satirize lawyers or to spoof them has been surprisingly persistent over the centuries.[3]

---

1   Entire websites are dedicated to lawyer jokes. This joke and others can be found online: www.lawyer-jokes.us/modules/mylinks/viewcat.php?cid=3.
2   "'What's up with that?' Lampooning Lawyers" (March 2007) 80:3 Wisconsin Lawyer, online: www.wisbar.org/am/template.cfm?section=wisconsin_lawyer&template=/cm/contentdisplay.cfm&contentid=63864. See also Marc Galanter, *Lowering the Bar: Lawyer Jokes & Legal Culture* (Madison: University of Wisconsin Press, 2005).
3   David Sugarman and W. Wesley Pue, "Introduction: Towards a Cultural History of Lawyers" in W. Wesley Pue and David Sugarman, *Lawyers and Vampires: Cultural Histories of Legal Professions* (Oxford: Hart, 2004) at 1–24.

Lawyers are at least as interested in themselves as are other people. The profession of law predates all other professions, excepting only the clergy and the profession of arms. Lawyers have often found themselves at or near the centre of the defining struggles of their era. Some, though rarely the majority, have found themselves cast in heroic roles in defence of enduring ideals such as constitutionalism, fair play, the rule of law, and civil or human rights. Lawyers contributed much to the historic struggles that wrestled constitutional government from the shadow of absolute monarchy in the United Kingdom. Their ideals gave definition to the American Revolution, shaped the movement from which Indian independence was born, and played significant roles in the emergence of liberal constitutionalism throughout Europe. Canada's founding prime minister was a lawyer, and so were many of the great protagonists of Canadian history. The *Canadian Bill of Rights*[4] was ushered in by a prime minister who was a Saskatchewan barrister, the *Canadian Charter of Rights and Freedoms*[5] was conceived and brought into being by a Montreal lawyer, and the *North American Free Trade Agreement*[6] (*NAFTA*) was implemented by yet another lawyer/prime minister. Lawyers opposed Stuart despotism, sought responsible government in British colonies, defended individuals from oppression by kings, dictators, and overbearing prime ministers, and have been present in great moments of constitutional transformation. Around the world today lawyers risk status, wealth, life, and limb in order to defend the unpopular, assert the values of the rule of law, and resist the drift to authoritarianism, corruption, or despotism.[7] Less gloriously — and less celebrated by the legal profession — some lawyers have also always worked against all of these causes. Corrupt lawyers, authoritarian lawyers, servile lawyers, and unprincipled lawyers also exist — and always have.

The 175th anniversary of the opening of one of Toronto's landmark buildings provides an opportunity for reflection on the history of the legal profession in Canada. Toronto's Osgoode Hall — not to be confused with York University's Osgoode Hall Law School — has provided a home for the Law Society of Upper Canada and an important locus of legal education since 6

---

4   S.C. 1960, c. 44.
5   Part I of the *Constitution Act, 1982*, being Schedule B to the *Canada Act 1982*, c. 11, s. 33.
6   *North American Free Trade Agreement between the Government of Canada, the Government of Mexico and the Government of the United States*, 17 December 1992, Can. T.S. 1994 No. 2, 32 I.L.M. 289 (entered into force 1 January 1994).
7   See, for example, W. Wesley Pue, "Death Squads and 'Directions over Lunch': A Comparative Review of the Independence of the Bar" in Lorne Sossin, ed., *In the Public Interest: The Report and Research Papers of the Law Society's Task Force on the Rule of Law and the Independence of the Bar* (Toronto: Irwin Law, 2007).

February 1832, as well as a home for Ontario's courts since the 1840s.[8] Ontario's Law Society, still known as the Law Society of Upper Canada, dates back another thirty-five years, to its creation by *An Act for the Better Regulating the Practice of the Law* in 1797. Though a good deal younger than its English counterparts (by some 400 to 500 years in the case of the English bar, and many years younger than the antecedents of the Law Society of England and Wales[9]) the Law Society of Upper Canada and its home are an important part of the historic fabric of Ontario. Indeed, in the time scale of British-Canada, 1797 is almost prehistoric.

Northrop Frye famously had it that we "move in time with our backs to what's ahead and our faces to the past, and all we know is in a rear-view mirror ... and in fact all our really urgent, mysterious and frightening questions have to do with the burden of the past and the meaning of tradition."[10] Parsing the burdens of the past and discerning the meaning of tradition for the legal profession turns out to be a difficult task. Though the importance of the inquiry seems obvious, things quickly become more complex. What are we to make of the antiquity of the legal profession, its historic importance, and its contemporary cultural resonances? Is long history in and of itself a source of pride or, perhaps, embarrassment? Or, contrary to Frye, is history irrelevant to contemporary circumstances? Should this anniversary be cause for celebration, for earnest reflection, for affirmation, or for rupture? There seems to be something important here, if only because lawyers have a special relationship to the idea of law and to legal ideals, both of which define our political culture. The fact that a very high proportion of political leaders, intellectuals, activists, opinion-makers, business leaders, and rabble-rousers has been drawn from or strongly influenced by the legal profession shows, at a minimum and for good or ill, that the legal profession has mattered immensely to Canada.

---

8   Deidré Rowe Brown, "An Introduction to Osgoode Hall on Its 175th Anniversary: More than Bricks and Mortar" (Paper presented at 175th Anniversary Celebration of Osgoode Hall, Law Society of Upper Canada Symposium on the History of the Canadian Legal Profession, Osgoode Hall, Toronto, 12 October 2007), see Chapter 2 of this book for the full text of this paper.

9   See Philip Girard, "The Independence of the Bar in Historical Perspective: Comforting Myths, Troubling Realities" in Lorne Sossin, ed., *In the Public Interest: The Report and Research Papers of the Law Society's Task Force on the Rule of Law and the Independence of the Bar* (Toronto: Irwin Law, 2007); W. Wesley Pue, "Legal Profession, History of" in Peter Cane and Joanne Conaghan, eds., *New Oxford Companion to Law* (Oxford: Oxford University Press, 2008).

10 Northrop Frye, "The Rear-View Mirror: Notes toward a Future" in Northrop Frye, *Divisions on a Ground: Essays on Canadian Culture* (Toronto: Anansi, 1982) 181 at 183.

The phrase "the legal profession" points, ambiguously, to the organized legal profession in the form of provincial law societies or their equivalents, and the activities or actions of individual lawyers or groups of lawyers working in their professional roles. "The legal profession" is simultaneously a trade organization, a corporate ideology, an important cultural actor, and an aggregation of individuals known both for their zealous pursuit of their clients' interests and for their assertive individualism. This book offers essays that seek to add to the understanding of Canada's legal profession and its historic role in each of these aspects.

Scholars who have sought to understand the legal profession as a collectivity or as an institutional structure have found themselves torn between two powerfully competing interpretations. This mainstream, through most of the twentieth century, emphasized the positive role of an autonomous legal profession in maintaining professional standards of competence and ethics, thereby creating the conditions allowing lawyers to zealously advance the interests of their clients without doing damage to the public good. This interpretation was more or less inverted in a powerful body of scholarship emerging in history, sociology, and the law during the 1970s and 1980s. The very traits of professionalism celebrated in the one approach were cast in a negative light as markers of a "monopoly," cleverly structured so as to dupe the public, restrict competition, inflate prices, and pad the pockets of lawyers.[11] Everything the legal profession collectively takes pride in, from its antiquity through self-regulation, an ethic of service, enforced ethical codes, and high educational attainment was presented as further evidence of a conspiracy against consumers. Curiously, the literature of this era focused almost exclusively on economic monopoly, overlooking the much more important "cultural" monopoly that lawyers sought to create. More recent scholarship that emphasizes the alignment of professional practices relating to admission, training, and ethics enforcement with the world view of cultural elites (in English Canada, often Conservative or Liberal, British, middle-class males) has brought sharp focus to issues relating to cultural authority. The exclusions of women, First Nations peoples, minority groups, and people from less advantaged backgrounds arise from larger cultural projects. Canada's most energetic and transformative leaders of the legal profession in the early twentieth century, for example, sought to restrict entry to individuals pre-adapted by class background, ethnicity, or in

---

11   The contours of this scholarly debate are outlined in W. Wesley Pue, "Trajectories of Professionalism: Legal Professionalism after Abel" in Alvin Esau, ed., *Manitoba Law Annual, 1989–1990* (Winnipeg. Legal Research Institute, 1991) at 57–92 (reprinted from (1990) 19 Man. L.J. 384–418).

some other way, to their own mental world. Manitoba's distinguished jurist, H. A. Robson, for example, approved the "pious fraud" by which one USA law school used the argument for higher admissions standards with the explicit, though hidden-from-view, objective of deterring men of "an undesirable class" from entering the profession.[12] Such currents recur in a wide array of literature focusing on "cultural history" approaches to the legal profession.[13] Deidré Rowe Brown's contribution to this volume provides a framework for understanding the organized legal profession in Canada, while the essays in the "Historical Perspectives on Legal Education" section emphasize the relationships between the legal profession and legal credentialing processes with notions of public service, on the one hand, and with exclusions of women and disadvantaged individuals on the other. Paradoxically, as David Bell points out, the meritocratic criteria that elevated the legal profession, made it better qualified for public service, and opened the door (eventually) to female enrollment in law school *simultaneously* had the effect of "slamming the door on brains" — creating barriers to the profession that individuals from less advantaged backgrounds found almost insurmountable.

Cultural practices of exclusion are also revealed in the section on "Historical Reflections on the Practice of Law," but these essays open up another important area of inquiry in the history of the legal profession. The relationship of the practice of law to the market and to market principles presents one of the thorny issues in interpreting professional history. On the one hand, lawyers earn an income from the provision of professional services in an open market and in return for the payment of fees. On the other hand, the ideals of law have it that justice is available to one and all without regard to ability to pay, that the provision of legal services is a high calling, and that the mere pursuit of profit is unseemly. So pervasive is this ethos that it finds reflection in the formal dress of lawyers to this day. Canadian barristers' gowns incorporate the remnants of a pouch, located at the middle of the back, safely outside of the barrister's range of vision. Its original was there to provide a means by which clients could discretely provide payment of an honorarium, *not* a fee, without causing affront or embarrassment: a professional man would never be so crass as to exchange his services for payment. Though this seems impossibly quaint and unrealistic from the perspective of the twenty-first century's most market-oriented continent, the culture of legal practice

---

12   Memo, Robson to MacLean (22 April 1914), Manitoba Legal Archives (UA20, Box 10, Folder 5).
13   See, for example, W. Wesley Pue and David Sugarman, eds., *Lawyers and Vampires: Cultural Histories of Legal Professions* (Oxford: Hart, 2003).

has traditionally been shot through with an anti-commercial ideology expressed in the etiquette of the English bar, the codes of professional conduct of Canadian legal professions, and long-standing traditions of *pro bono* (free) legal services to the disadvantaged, participation in legal aid schemes, value-billing practices, and so on. In this volume, Philip Girard and Jeffrey Haylock explore the corrosion of cultural monopolies and the evolving economic structures that transformed the Halifax legal profession in the first half of the twentieth century. Christopher Moore's article on "megafirms" picks up the story of the economic transformation in another city and another time. Whereas Girard and Haylock treat as "large" firms with four or more partners, Moore reports an average of sixteen lawyers in Canada's ten largest firms in 1952. By 1992 this had grown to 241 lawyers, and the most significant changes in scope and structure of practice were yet to come. The profound tension between the market and professionalism is well captured by Moore in questioning the extent to which "professional ethics and professional independence of the lawyer can endure in [a] ... legal environment in which law firms become businesses like any other."[14]

The legal profession's relation to markets traces, to some extent, larger transformations in the political economy of Europe and its colonies. Highly regulated premodern economies, in which guilds played significant cultural and economic roles, gave way to liberalized trade principles during the period, conveniently labeled the "industrial revolution," that produced Adam Smith, John Stuart Mill, and the transformations wrought by ideas such as theirs. The subsequent overlay of mega-industries and monopoly capital on the riotously democratic competitive environment Smith imagined ultimately produced its corollary in the megafirm and the challenges to inherited professional traditions that it represents. It is important to recall that there is a *political* economy here, not an economy innocent of politics. The corollary of a liberal market economy was the development of a liberal state, understood as involving moderate government, regularity and transparency of law, guarantees of some minimal civil rights, and, eventually, democracy. Legal professions were central in these great historic transitions, sometimes dramatically and deliberately, but sometimes merely incidentally, as an inevitable consequence of legal representation.[15] The chapters in this book entitled "Quebec: A Distinct Legal History" and "The Rule of Law, Impeachment,

---

14 See Chapter 6, "Conclusion."
15 Terence Halliday and Lucien Karpik, eds., *Lawyers and the Rise of Western Political Liberalism: Legal Professions and the Constitution of Modern Politics* (Oxford: Oxford University Press, 1997).

and Bureaucratic Regulation" each pick up on themes related to this larger transformation. In each case, some portions of the legal profession found themselves aligned with the political transformations that "modernization" (the creation of a liberal political economy) seemed to require. R.M.W. Chitty's defence of property rights and conventional civil liberties in the face of wartime authoritarianism cast him in the role of a rear-guard defender of a previously assumed principle, in opposition to lawyers "who don't give a damn about the law, just want to get things done."[16]

The final two sections of this book simultaneously address questions related to the cultural monopoly asserted over the legal profession by certain types of lawyers, and the fundamental principle of the rule of law that the profession should be open to "all the talents."[17] Shocking manipulations of state authorities designed to deny even elementary legal rights of representation to First Nations peoples — all the while flouting the virtues of "British Justice"[18] — are documented by Hamar Foster. The effect is to locate Canada's colonial practices much closer to those of British colonists in Africa than we might like to think.[19] The subject of Foster's study, however, gave "a damn about the law." Arthur Eugene O'Meara's heroic, even quixotic, efforts to hold British-Canadian authorities to the standards that the rule of law demands in their treatment of Canada's original sovereign peoples is a stunning tribute to his values as both priest and lawyer. This marked him as an "outsider."

Lionel Cross too was an outsider who sought to uphold principles of British justice in interwar Toronto. The fourth black man known to be called to

---

16 Joseph Schull, *The Great Scot: A Biography of Donald Gordon* (Montreal: McGill-Queen's University Press, 1979) at 56; cited by Eric Adams in Chapter 10 of this book.
17 Dean George Curtis, as cited by W. Welsey Pue in *Law School: The Story of Legal Education in British Columbia* (Vancouver: Continuing Legal Education Society of British Columbia & Faculty of Law, University of British Columbia, 1995) at 223.
18 The concept of "British justice" and its meanings to a previous generation of Canadians is well captured in Greg Marquis, "Doing Justice to British Justice: Law, Ideology, and Canadian Historiography" in W. Wesley Pue and Barry Wright, *Canadian Perspectives on Law and Society: Issues in Legal History* (Ottawa: Carleton University Press, 1987). See also Carolyn Strange, "Discretionary Justice: Political Culture and the Death Penalty in New South Wales and Ontario, 1890–1920" in Carolyn Strange, ed., *Qualities of Mercy: Justice, Punishment and Mercy* (Vancouver: UBC Press, 1996) at 134.
19 Chidi Oguamanam and W. Wesley Pue, "Lawyers' Professionalism, Colonialism, State Formation and National Life in Nigeria, 1900–1960: 'The Fighting Brigade of the People'" (2007) Social Identities 769–785; Grace Li Xiu Woo, "Canada's Forgotten Founders: The Modern Significance of the Haudenosaunee (Iroquois) Application for Membership in the League of Nations" in "Postcolonial Legal Studies" (April 2003) Journal of Law, Social Justice & Global Development (Symposium Issue), online: www2.warwick.ac.uk/fac/soc/law/elj/lgd/2003_1/woo.

the Ontario bar, Cross was prominent in defence of those on the outside of Ontario's power elite until he was disbarred in 1937. The pattern of individuals who are outsiders, in one fashion or another, playing significant roles in sustaining the legal system's integrity is a common one in professional history. Indeed, on reflection, the point is so obvious as to be almost tautological. Insiders, by definition, never challenge the power elites they serve. The languages and institutions of law are powerful, however. Unlike purely political fora, they are bound by standards of integrity, procedure, consistency, and propriety that render them particularly susceptible to influence by outside demands calling, in one form or another, for consistency with articulated principle, or pointing to system failures.[20] It is no surprise, then, that organized legal professions have often sought to exclude from their membership individuals whose identity makes them suspect, whether on grounds of political belief, racialized background, class, "foreignness," faith, or gender.

Participation in the legal profession is a matter of civil liberties and career advancement for individuals and is one factor, among many others, that determines the evolving contours of the legal system as a whole. The chapters on gender bring this into focus. "Into the Rough of Things" addresses the pioneering first cohort of women in the legal profession in British Columbia, in the years between 1912 and 1930, emphasizing both the resilience of a vanguard generation and the challenges they faced, not only because of misogyny, and there was some, but also, more subtly, as they confronted a "historically male mould of legal education and practice."[21] It was to be another four decades before the number of women entering legal education approached a critical mass. It is salutary to recall the very different gender environment that prevailed even at the dawn of that new age:

> When I started law school in 1970, I was one of (I think) 16 women in a first year class of 240. It had only been a year or two since female students were allowed to use the student Common Room. Sixteen was an all-time high for admissions. I was an active and open feminist, and spent a fair amount of time either fighting certain issues or suppressing my feelings about them. Fortunately I had one classmate who could be counted upon to erupt like a volcano (that is, with an inexorable, fiery flow of words) if a professor or a

---

20 See Terence C. Halliday and Lucien Karpik, "Politics Matter: A Comparative Theory of Lawyers in the Making of Political Liberalism"; L. Karpik, "Builders of Liberal Society: French Lawyers and Politics"; W. Wesley Pue, "Lawyers and Political Liberalism in Eighteenth- and Nineteenth-Century England"; all found in *Lawyers and the Rise of Western Political Liberalism*, above note 13.
21 See Chapter 13, "Formal Gender Equality and the Legal Profession."

guest speaker crossed certain lines of insult or belittlement of women. I shall forever be in her debt. When I was in first-year, two women (one of then me) attended the annual law students' retreat at Harrison Hot Springs. I believe it was the first time that any women had attended. It was not a pleasant experience in some ways, although I enjoyed the opportunity to meet some of my classmates in a social setting. My female classmate, I recall, refused to give her room key to a drunken third-year male student, who then poured a bottle of beer over her head. The fact that others found this amusing did not startle me at the time. Neither she nor I had any notion that there might be norms of conduct to be invoked in that situation. That recognition startles me now.[22]

Constance Backhouse's contribution to this volume traces the history of a second vanguard generation of women lawyers, who found community in the sense of their difference, and who knew they constituted a vanguard. Their motivations were diverse. One was inspired by the nuns who taught her in a Catholic school, while another engaged feminist lawyering *in reaction to* her Catholicism. Nonetheless, as a group they had the confidence to believe they could make a difference, and they acted accordingly.

The tale of inclusions and exclusions — the *difference* that difference makes — is not concluded as we approach the second decade of the twenty-first century. Neither are the other stories that pervade a history of the legal profession. Lawyers, as a group, have probably always been, and always will be, divided between those for whom law is an intensely important ideal and those who "don't give a damn for law" and just want to get things done. The seesaw pulls of integrity against the urge towards authoritarianism, self-interest, or corruption are constant themes in human history.

Throughout this volume there are stories of more or less heroic individuals who stood up against powerful structures and powerful personalities in order to uphold enduring legal values. It is troubling that, more often than not, the organized legal profession as such has seemed incapable of acting on the side of the gods. Zealous advocates and heroic individuals have often been able to pursue their work only in the shadows of the organized profession. One does not, apparently, look to venerable institutions for heroic leadership. Nonetheless, the structures, cultures, and traditions of legal professionalism are such as to provide some institutional protection for idealistic

---

22 Lynn Smith, "Gender Equality — Professional and Ethical Issues" (Paper presented at "Gender Equality — A Challenge for the Legal Profession," Conference of the Canadian Bar Association's Continuing Education Committee and Task Force on Gender Equality, Toronto, 29–31 October 1992).

individuals within the fold. Even on the matter of outsider access to careers in law, there have always been a few established lawyers willing to sponsor and mentor newcomers, whatever the challenges. There is an immense difference here between a self-governing profession, whatever its flaws may be, and one regulated directly by state authorities. History's lesson may simply be that we should be grateful for small mercies and, perhaps, not expect too much.

There is heroism too associated with business law and corporate practice. Such lawyers play instrumental roles in the history of the country, as the essays discussing their work show. These are contributions of a different sort. Corporate law megafirms are a new vanguard in professionalism. This vanguard, however, mimics the structures and values of other large, economic entities more than those conventionally associated with the highest ideals of professionalism. The bulk of megafirm work derives from solicitors' practice, a branch of professional work profoundly disconnected from the advocates' profession and the historic struggles that have defined it. Just as the single category "capitalist enterprise" captures imperfectly commonalities of eighteenth-century cottage-industry weavers and Bombardier Inc., so too an expanding gulf separates legal aid lawyers or storefront real estate practices, for example, from the life and work of the mega-law firm.

We end then, as we began, with questions rather than answers. History is both good at interpreting the past and helpful in casting key issues in relief. It is, however, notoriously flawed at prognostication. O'Meara, the priest-advocate for First Nations entitlements, seems prescient now. That he was viewed as dangerous during his lifetime and, even by those he sought to help, as something of a flake for much of the next half-century, provides a lesson in humility for all of us.

What is to be valued within the legal profession and how its future should be shaped ought to be informed by a historical appreciation and an understanding of the glory and the blemishes associated with professional tradition. While this volume provides a background to inform conversation about the "really urgent, mysterious, and frightening questions" concerning "the burden of the past and the meaning of tradition"[23] within the legal profession, it does so in order to open, not to foreclose, discussion.

---

23 Northrup Frye, "Notes toward a Future" in Northrup Frye and James Polk, *Divisions on a Ground: Essays on Canadian Culture* (Toronto: House of Anansi, 1982) 181–90 at 183.

CHAPTER 2

An Introduction to Osgoode Hall on Its 175th Anniversary: More than Bricks and Mortar

DEIDRÉ ROWE BROWN

ON 6 FEBRUARY 2007, Osgoode Hall celebrated its 175th anniversary. Since opening its doors in 1832, it has been the residence of the Law Society of Upper Canada, the governing body of the legal profession of what is now Ontario. The profession's history has transpired within its walls, and as a result, Osgoode Hall has become a leading symbol of legal tradition in Ontario. To celebrate the building's anniversary, the Law Society's Heritage Committee, chaired by bencher[1] and law professor Constance Backhouse, planned a number of events and initiatives to be undertaken in 2007.

On the evening of February 6, the celebrations were opened with a reception in Osgoode Hall hosted by Law Society Treasurer Gavin MacKenzie. At that reception, Lieutenant Governor James Bartleman opened two historical exhibits about Osgoode Hall, one of which was created by Law Society curator Elise Brunet. The other, a virtual exhibit, was designed in partnership with the Archives of Ontario.

On October 12, the Law Society hosted a symposium entitled The History of the Canadian Legal Profession, the final event in conjunction with Osgoode Hall's anniversary celebrations. Chaired by Constance Backhouse, Jim Phillips, and W. Wesley Pue, the symposium showcased a number of academics from across the country who presented important papers on a variety of topics relating to the history of the legal profession in Canada. An abbreviated version of the following paper was presented at the symposium.

---

1   The term "bencher" refers to a director of the Law Society of Upper Canada.

Legal historians have recreated the history of the profession in Ontario through careful examination of the practices and the policies adopted by convocation[2] within the walls of Osgoode Hall.[3] Architectural historians have meticulously recorded the building's construction,[4] and are now beginning to study it as a visual phenomenon of social and political influences of various time periods. This paper traces the architectural evolution of Osgoode Hall from the opening of its original wing in 1832 to its present form, linking its physical changes to the Society's continuing efforts to fulfill its legislated mandate and protect its entitlement to self-governance. In doing so, this paper attempts to show that Osgoode Hall is not only an admired structure inside whose walls legal history has occurred, but also a visual history of the defining moments in the Society's and the profession's evolution.

Prior to 1797, the colony's legal profession was in a complete state of disarray. Although the population of Upper Canada was close to 14,000 in 1792, the legal profession consisted of only one lawyer, Walter Roe, who had any legal training and a number of untrained lay advocates.[5] Trained lawyers, well versed in the ways of the court, were desperately needed. A statute enacted in 1794 attempted to address this problem. It gave the Lieutenant Governor the authority to grant licences to British subjects he deemed the best qualified to act as advocates and attorneys in the conduct of all legal business in the province. The number of these licences was not to exceed sixteen. Unfortunately, licences were not usually issued to those who were qualified, but rather to those who had roles in the provincial government, were leaders of local communities, or belonged to wealthy, established families.[6]

In 1797, *An Act for the Better Regulating the Practice of the Law* came into effect. The Act authorized the legal practitioners of Upper Canada to gather and form the Law Society of Upper Canada "for the purpose of securing to the Province and the Profession a learned and Honourable body to assist their fellow subjects as the occasion may require and to support and maintain

---

2   The term "Convocation" refers to the monthly meetings of the Law Society of Upper Canada's governing body of benchers.
3   For a detailed history of the Law Society of Upper Canada, see Christopher Moore, *The Law Society of Upper Canada 1797–1997* (Toronto: University of Toronto Press, 1997) [Moore].
4   For a detailed architectural history of Osgoode Hall, see Angela Carr, The Architecture of Osgoode Hall from 1829 to 1984 (research paper, Department of Architecture, University of Toronto, 1984) [Carr]. This research paper is available through the Law Society Archives.
5   C.H.A. Armstrong, *The Honourable Society of Osgoode Hall* (Toronto: Clarke, Irwin & Company, 1952) at 17–18.
6   John Honsberger, *Osgoode Hall: An Illustrated History* (Toronto: Osgoode Society for Canadian Legal History, 2004) at 81–87 [Honsberger].

the constitution of the said Province."⁷ It gave the Society the right to control admission to its ranks and to regulate and discipline its members. The entitlement to self-regulation was unusual in this era. Philip Girard writes, "Neither in England itself nor in any other British colony had the bar been created by statute, and in the colonies the bar was usually under the supervision of the judges of the superior courts, who arranged for admission and, if necessary, discipline of local lawyers."⁸ The Law Society of Upper Canada was unique in this respect but the power of its members was not absolute. Although the Act stipulated that the Society should form rules for its own government, the final approval of those rules was to rest with the judiciary.⁹

The Law Society of Upper Canada was also unique in that it was authorized to admit both barristers and attorneys to its membership.¹⁰ In England, practitioners of the law had always been divided into two distinct branches, barristers who specialized in litigation, and solicitors and attorneys who focused more on procedural steps and document drafting. The two branches were further separated by training, certification,¹¹ and status. Cross-membership was strictly prohibited. In Upper Canada, different qualifications and requirements were imposed for barristers and solicitors but membership in the Law Society was required of both.¹² The sheer size of Upper Canada often made it necessary for lawyers to perform the work of barristers and attorneys, thus cross-membership was permitted by the Society.

The first meeting of the Law Society of Upper Canada was held at Wilson's Tavern in Newark, now Niagara-on-the-Lake, in July 1797. After a brief

---

7   Moore, above note 3 at 15.
8   Philip Girard, "The Independence of the Bar in Historical Perspective: Comforting Myths, Troubling Realities in Law Society of Upper Canada" in Lorne Sossin, ed., *In the Public Interest: The Report and Research Papers of the Law Society of Upper Canada's Task Force on the Rule of Law and the Independence of the Bar* (Toronto: Irwin Law, 2007) at 19.
9   Michael J. Trebilcock, Carolyn J. Tuohy, and Alan D. Wolfson, eds., *Professional Regulation: A Staff Study of Accountancy, Architecture, Engineering and Law in Ontario*, Appendix B (Toronto: Research Directorate, 1978) at 6 [Trebilcock *et al.*].
10 Until the establishment of Court of Chancery in 1837, the title of solicitor did not exist in Upper Canada. The fact that solicitors were mentioned by name in the Act of 1797 implies that the government was drafting in anticipation of the elaboration of the court system in the colony.
11 "In England barristers were called by one of the four Inns of Court, attorneys admitted by the Courts of Common Law, solicitors admitted by the Court of Chancery, and proctors by the Admiralty and Ecclesiastical Courts." See Trebilcock *et al*, above note 9 at 2.
12 "From its formation in 1797, the Law Society recognized the distinction between barristers and attorneys or solicitors by allowing the latter two groups to practise with only three years on the rolls of the Law Society, whereas the former required five years on the rolls." See *ibid.* at 10.

discussion among the ten men present, a number of resolutions were unanimously approved:

- Six of those present were elected benchers or governors of the Society.
- John White was named the Society's first treasurer.[13]
- Fees were set for members of the Society.
- It was declared that anyone wishing to practise law in Upper Canada would now need to earn and retain the sanction of the Law Society.
- It was declared that the definition of lawyers' work would be the preserve of the Law Society.[14]

After this initial meeting the benchers did not assemble again until 1799 in the town of York,[15] and the Law Society conducted very little business except to admit students-at-law and to call them to the bar when they had completed their practical training. G. Blaine Baker has written that in the first fifty years of its existence, the Law Society believed its main responsibility to be the training and admission of aspiring lawyers and, as a result, 95 percent of its business involved legal education in that period.[16] It is not entirely clear from the existing records where Convocation was held between 1799 and 1803. It is known that the chambers of Attorney General Thomas Scott were used at times during this period, as well as the office of the Clerk of the Crown.[17] When the War of 1812 began, military service was compulsory for adult males in Upper Canada and so virtually all members of the legal profession were drawn into the militia.[18] Between 1812 and 1815, the benchers did not meet and the Law Society all but ceased to operate.

In the years immediately following the war, the benchers continued with their makeshift arrangements, utilizing the courthouse, as well as the chambers of Attorney General John Beverley Robinson, for their meetings.[19] It became increasingly apparent, however, that if the Society was to be taken seriously a permanent residence in which to house its offices was required. As early as 1815, a movement began to acquire property on which to build.

---

13   The term "treasurer" refers to the president and head of the Law Society of Upper Canada.
14   Moore, above note 3 at 15–16.
15   George A. Johnson, Q.C., "Osgoode Hall Lore" (Address given to the Lawyers' Club, Toronto, 14 April 1955).
16   G. Blaine Baker, "Legal Education in Upper Canada 1785–1889: The Law Society As an Educator" in David H. Flaherty, ed., *Essays in the History of Canadian Law: Volume II.* (Toronto: Osgoode Society, 1981) at 50 [Baker].
17   Honsberger, above note 6 at 88.
18   Moore, above note 3 at 56.
19   Honsberger, above note 6 at 89.

The project was costly, however, and as a result progress was slow. In 1822, the *Law Society Act* was amended to allow the Law Society of Upper Canada to become a corporation. The amendment gave the treasurer and the benchers authority to conduct the business of the Society and permitted them to purchase land upon which to build a permanent residence.[20] It also removed the Law Society's obligation to supervise the colony's attorneys, placing that responsibility firmly in the control of the judiciary. There is no evidence to suggest that either the profession at large or the public supported the increased separation of barristers and attorneys. Opponents of the amendments felt that this would only increase the elitism of the Law Society.[21] Christopher Moore suggests that it was the benchers, in their efforts to enhance the image of the legal profession, who desired the further separation of the higher and lower branches of the profession.[22]

Despite the fact that the Society could now purchase land, interest in the building project did not surface again in earnest until 1825. This may be attributed, in part, to the end of the economic depression that had plagued the colony from 1819 to 1822 and, in part, to the promotion of the construction of King's College by Bishop John Strachan. King's College was to be primarily a missionary college, but it was Strachan's hope that it would also include a faculty of law. In a petition to Lieutenant Governor Sir Peregrine Maitland, he wrote that it was his belief that it was in the colony's best interests that all of its learned professionals, including lawyers, receive a uniform education supervised by the Church of England that would instil British principles.[23] Although the Society's right to call students to the bar was never officially challenged, the benchers realized that by building Osgoode Hall they would be sending a strong message that the Society was not prepared to cede control over legal education, an integral component of its mandate.[24]

The strategy was effective and although King's College received a royal charter in 1827, it was not given the authority to grant law degrees and did not open its doors until 1843.[25]

It was due in large part to the continued efforts of Treasurer William Warren Baldwin and Attorney General and Treasurer John Beverley Robinson that Osgoode Hall was eventually constructed to provide the Society with a place to conduct its business, to maintain a library, and to provide for legal

---

20   Moore, above note 3 at 62.
21   *Ibid.* at 60.
22   *Ibid.* at 62.
23   Baker, above note 16 at 55.
24   Moore, above note 3 at 78–79.
25   *Ibid.* at 79.

education. They believed that the Society needed to firmly establish its authority. They understood that self-governance was a privilege, not a right, and that the continuance of this privilege was dependent upon the ability of the legal profession to fulfill the mandate that had been set for it. Despite the objections of some benchers that the construction of Osgoode Hall would prove to be too costly for the fledgling Society, Baldwin and Robinson successfully convinced the majority that the risk was not only worth taking, but also that it was imperative to do so. [26]

In 1828, the Law Society purchased the property it occupies today from John Beverley Robinson for £1000. Immediately after the purchase, convocation approved the construction of a great hall on the site and hired architect John Ewart to prepare a design and, once it had been approved, to supervise the project.

It is believed that Ewart based his plans on earlier drawings prepared by Treasurer William Warren Baldwin. Baldwin, an amateur architect, believed that the design of Osgoode Hall would play an important part in establishing the authority and power of the Law Society and commanding greater public respect for the legal profession.

The use of architecture to evoke a specific feeling or image was a well utilized concept. In his book, *An Imperial Vision*, Thomas Metcalf examines the relationship between culture and authority as expressed by architecture during European Colonization. In India, the British continually sought to remind the Indian people of their power and their imperial vision. In part, they were able to accomplish this through architecture by adopting the classical Palladian styles of ancient Rome in their design of public buildings thus reinforcing Britain's image of power, domination and authority.[27] Metcalf writes, "In India, and in the colonies elsewhere, the choice of styles, the arrangement of space within a building and, of course, the decision to erect such a particular building, all testified . . . to the vision of empire."[28]

In his final plan to Convocation, Ewart proposed the construction of three connecting pavilions. The first would house rooms and offices for the Society, the second would hold chambers for students and advocates, and the third would contain the King's Court.[29] The design would allow the building

---

26   Philip Girard, above note 7 at 21. Girard states, "insofar as the authority was based on statute, it was never completely free from the possibility of alteration against the wishes of the Society."
27   Thomas R. Metcalf, *An Imperial Vision: Indian Architecture and Britain's Raj* (Berkeley and Los Angeles, University of California Press, 1989).
28   *Ibid.* at 2.
29   Honsberger, above note 6 at 117.

to be completed in stages and provide for future expansion northward by the Society and the Court.

Concerned about the cost of erecting the proposed building, Convocation directed Ewart to proceed only with the construction of the east pavilion that would house the Society's offices. It would be a square, three-storey, red brick, Regency building devoid of architectural ornamentation save for plain pilasters.

Construction began in the summer of 1829, and on 6 February 1832, the benchers held their first Convocation in their new home. Heralded immediately as one of the city's most important buildings, Osgoode Hall created an impressive and imposing image of authority on the outskirts of the infant town of York. Thus, the building successfully achieved the original goal envisioned by its proponents — it provided the governing body of the legal profession with a permanent residence and emphasized the power of the Law Society and its authority to govern the province's legal profession.

It was not simply enough, however, for the Law Society to construct a symbol of its authority and a place to conduct its business. As Philip Girard has written, "there was certainly a good deal of anti-lawyer sentiment in colonial Upper Canada, based on an agrarian distrust of monopolies and a concern that lawyers held more than their fair share of remunerative provincial offices."[30] To earn the respect and trust of the public and the continued support of the government it was also necessary to implement initiatives and policies designed to better fulfill the Society's legislated mandate. Throughout the 1820s and 1830s the Society took important steps to accomplish this. Although the Law Society had, in 1797, been granted the authority to oversee legal education and control admission to the profession, until 1819 the benchers required little more than verification of good character to admit students to the Society's membership. Students learned through self-study and by articling with practising lawyers. Christopher Moore attributes this to the fact that "the early legal community of Upper Canada espoused what is referred to as Georgian professionalism, the belief that what defined a professional man was not skill or qualifications but status."[31]

In 1819, however, the benchers passed a rule that required a candidate for admission "to give a written translation in the presence of the Society of a portion of one of Cicero's Orations or perform such other exercise as may satisfy

---

30 Philip Girard, above note 7 at 22.
31 *Ibid.* at 43.

the Society of his acquaintance with Latin and English composition."[32] While no documented explanations for this change exist, one may deduce that the introduction of an admission examination was in keeping with the benchers' efforts to enhance and legitimize the professional image of the legal community. Despite the introduction of an admission examination, the number of students-at-law increased significantly throughout the 1820s. In response, the Law Society began to further develop its educational requirements. In 1828, for example, convocation instituted term-keeping, which required students-at-law to assemble together at York at least four times during their apprenticeship to observe the sittings of the Court of the King's Bench. And, in 1831, it approved the adoption of a rule requiring examinations to be successfully completed both before admission as a student member and before call.[33]

In addition to establishing educational requirements, the Law Society began to show greater interest in creating educational and reference resources for use by its members. In 1823, it began to provide law reports to the bar and the courts, and in 1827, Convocation unanimously approved the establishment of a law library. It resolved that Treasurer William Warren Baldwin, "the Attorney General, the Solicitor General, and Mr. Macaulay be a committee to determine what books shall be purchased for the Society — not exceeding the value of 200 pounds — and that said committee be directed as soon as convenient to procure the same."[34] In accordance with Convocation's instructions, Solicitor General Henry John Boulton purchased a number of books while in London, England later that year. As the Law Society did not yet have a permanent residence, the books were kept in a room in the York courthouse. They remained there until the doors of Osgoode Hall opened in 1832.

It was also during this period that the Society began to review its operating principles. Since the Society's creation in 1797, the benchers had never compiled a complete record of its rules, or determined which rules fell within the Society's sole jurisdiction and which rules required judicial approval. In 1831, a committee chaired by bencher Robert Baldwin was charged with the task of reviewing and revising the Society's existing rules and regulations. The committee recommended that the benchers repeal the existing regulations and replace them with a completely revised rulebook. The committee's recommendations were approved and the first effective constitution of the Society was born.[35] These new rules authorized the benchers to establish

---

32 William Renwick Riddell, *The Legal Profession in Upper Canada in Its Early Periods* (Toronto: Law Society of Upper Canada, 1916) at 15 [Riddell].
33 Moore, above note 3 at 89–90.
34 Honsberger, above note 6 at 108.
35 Moore, above note 3 at 69.

regulations or standing orders for internal matters and directed them to seek judicial approval only for matters dealing with the governance of the profession at large. Christopher Moore suggests that the definition of "internal matters" was purposely left largely undefined and, as a result, Convocation was able to gradually erode judicial control.[36]

When Osgoode Hall opened in 1832, it contained space in which to conduct the Society's business, house its law library, and provide accommodation for nine students-at-law. Then Treasurer William Warren Baldwin believed that residency for students not indentured in York would provide invaluable experience and knowledge.[37] In 1833, Convocation hired John Ritchie to build an addition that would extend the original building westward in a low range of chambers providing accommodation for twenty-four students in total, as well as additional office space. In the aftermath of the 1837 rebellions, however, the student housing experiment ended as the benchers vacated Osgoode Hall to allow troops to be housed there. When Convocation returned to the building in 1843, the students did not. The benchers evidently decided that the problems and costs associated with housing students far outweighed any benefit to their legal education.[38]

In the 1840s, the population of Upper Canada (now Canada West) increased dramatically due to an influx of predominantly British immigrants. Despite this increase, the population remained basically an agrarian one and many of those settling in the colony began to move even further into its interior. There were approximately 148 barristers actively practising in the colony and 119 students-at-law. Only one-quarter of the barristers were located in York.[39] Although the profession was growing, it could not match the population influx. Many in the colony were unable to secure the services of members of the Society and relied instead on the opinions and advice of educated laymen. Christopher Moore writes, "even as transactions became more sophisticated, farmers were more apt to turn to a non-lawyer notary (an unlicensed conveyancer) or a non-lawyer attorney than a member of the Law Society."[40]

The period also witnessed the birth of the university era in Canada West and the next challenge to the Law Society's monopoly over the provision of legal education. During the 1840s, King's College was opened in Toronto, Queen's College in Kingston, and Victoria College in Cobourg. In addition

---

36 Ibid. at 69.
37 Ibid. at 92.
38 Ibid. at 98.
39 Ibid. at 103.
40 Ibid.

to operating faculties of medicine, theology, and arts, each college was keen to develop faculties of law. To this end, King's College began formal academic lectures in law in 1843, although these lectures were discontinued in 1847.[41] Although the Law Society of Upper Canada developed a new entry classification for students with university degrees, it was unwilling to make special concessions for these students despite their higher education. However, at the insistence of the Legislative Assembly and the growing respect for university training among members of the public, the Society reduced the period of training from five years to three years for university graduates entering Osgoode Hall.[42] Once again, the Law Society had staved off the threat of competitors to its monopoly over legal education and underlined the fact that admission to the profession remained solely in its control.

Between 1844 and 1846, Convocation approved the reconstruction of the Baldwin Range (as it was known) by architect Henry Bower Lane to provide adequate space for the Society's growing law library and additional office space. It also constructed a west wing during this period, similar in design to the east wing, to house the courtrooms of the Court of Queen's Bench and the Chancery Court.[43] The residency of the courts in Osgoode Hall was neither a surprise development nor an unwelcome one. The original plan for the east wing had included a room to be used by the Court of the King's Bench. Shortly after the opening of Osgoode Hall, however, the courts moved to the Parliament buildings.[44] By renting space to the courts, the benchers hoped not only to offset the expense of their building, but also to further legitimize the standing of the legal profession in the eyes of the public.

During the occupation of Osgoode Hall by the troops, extensive damage was done to the building. The government refused to pay the full cost of the damage, and in 1843 the Society considered suing the government for the cost of the repairs. Ultimately, an agreement was reached in which the government paid for the expansion and complete renovation of Osgoode Hall in exchange for space to house its courts.[45] The benchers, it would seem, had achieved their original goals of enhancing the Society's stature and offsetting their expenses.

The establishment of the Chancery Court in Upper Canada in 1837 had resulted in legislation making all Upper Canadian attorneys solicitors of the

---

41 Ibid. at 114.
42 Baker, above note 16 at 76.
43 Ibid. at 100–1.
44 Ibid. at 84.
45 Ibid. at 101–2.

Chancery Court, and all barristers Chancery Counsel.[46] The result was a sudden transformation in the image and position of the attorney. Indeed, by 1840, 40 percent of the legal practitioners in Upper Canada were attorneys who had not qualified as barristers.[47] This trend continued in the 1850s with the appearance of railways that expanded the professional space of lawyers, and the birth of corporations that redefined the work of lawyers in Canada West. As the focus of the legal profession began to shift increasingly from courtroom work to client-based work, the duties and status of attorneys continued to evolve.[48]

The result of this increase in the number of attorneys who chose not to become barristers caused growing concern among the members of the legal profession and the public at large. An editorial in the *Canada Law Journal* in 1856 illustrates the reason for this discontent. "The attorney is subject to no examination whatever, preliminary or final. The barrister must have proved his fitness, the fitness of the attorney is presumed."[49] In 1857, convinced by arguments that unregulated solicitors were not in the public interest, the legislature restored the Law Society's control over this branch of the legal profession.[50] In response, the Society immediately imposed rigorous examinations upon attorneys, lessening the educational gap between the two branches of the profession and providing some control over the profession's increasing numbers. In 1854, facing increased pressure from the emerging liberal arts colleges and the public's growing belief that professionals required formal academic training, Convocation established its first lectures in law in 1854. It made attendance at twelve lectures per term compulsory, but the ability to pass the written examinations remained the essential criterion of entry to the profession.[51]

The centre portion of Osgoode Hall was enlarged again and renovated to its present state between 1857 and 1860 by Frederic William Cumberland and William G. Storm.[52] This addition allowed for the creation of a number of new courtrooms and office space for judicial administrators, as well as for the further expansion and elaboration of the Great Library. Over the next 112 years, the courts continued to expand northward and westward, as they required additional room to conduct their business effectively. The permanent residence of the courts at Osgoode Hall established the building as the cradle of the justice system in Ontario.

---

46 *Ibid.* at 111.
47 Riddell, above note 32 at 18.
48 Moore, above note 3 at 125.
49 Riddell, above note 32 at 20.
50 Moore, above note 3 at 110.
51 *Ibid.* at 116.
52 Honsberger, above note 6 at 178.

Designed to serve not only as a law library but also a banquet hall, the benchers unveiled the Great Library at a reception for the Prince of Wales in 1860. With the opening of the Great Library, Osgoode Hall became the building that William Warren Baldwin had envisioned. Its grandeur, classical design, and sprawling layout exuded power and knowledge. A newspaper article of the period stated, "There is not in America a more magnificent building devoted to law than Osgoode Hall. All that architecture can do to charm the eye or impress the mind with a sense of splendour is there."[53]

Osgoode Hall served as a permanent visual reminder of the Law Society's authority. That it elevated the status and public perception of the legal profession is undeniable. In 1873, the Reverend Dr. Henry Scadding, and early Toronto historian, wrote that

> great expense has been lavished by the Benchers on this Canadian *Palais de Justice*, but the effect of such a pile, kept in every nook and corner and in all its surroundings in scrupulous order, is invaluable, tending to refine and elevated each successive generation of our young candidates for the legal profession and helping to insure amongst them a salutary *esprit de corps*.[54]

During the 1860s, a sense of regionalism began to develop among the members of the Law Society. Those outside of Toronto felt that they were unfairly disadvantaged by their lack of proximity to Osgoode Hall. Access to the resources contained in the Great Library was not available to those outside of Toronto; despite the expansion and elaboration of the district courts, students were still required to fulfill their term-keeping requirements at Osgoode Hall; and the governing body continued to be populated by predominately city lawyers appointed to their positions based on their status and family connections.[55] The Law Society took marked steps to quash this growing discontent among its members. In the late 1860s, it eliminated term-keeping requirements and compulsory lectures. By doing this, it was able to argue that it treated all students equally as they were all required to write examinations to be admitted to the bar despite their geographical location. As Christopher Moore writes, "men could now study anywhere there were lawyers."[56] A voluntary lecture program was started in 1876, but it soon followed the fate of its predecessor. Examinations once again became the dominant factor in the Society's legal education program throughout the 1880s.[57]

---

53 *Ibid.* at 183.
54 *Ibid.* at 21.
55 Moore, above note 3 at 139.
56 *Ibid.* at 117.
57 *Ibid.* at 116–17 and 166–67.

In 1871, the principle of elective representation was an accepted fact in political spheres and many members of the legal profession believed that Convocation should also be an elected body. The membership was growing rapidly and spreading out from the urban centres and into the smaller communities. The Law Society was viewed by many as being unrepresentative of its membership. In the face of growing opposition on the part of the legal profession and the public who felt that the Convocation should be more transparent and geographically diverse, the government passed legislation that ended the life appointments of the current benchers (except those who were *ex-officio*) by capping terms at five years, increased the number of sitting benchers to thirty, and gave the profession the right to elect its governing body.[58] The first election was held in April 1871.

Out-of-town benchers and members of the profession complained that the resources contained in the Great Library were not readily available to them and, therefore, they were at a disadvantage from those who resided in Toronto. In 1879, Convocation agreed to support local libraries as well as the Great Library. It also agreed that if any of the local libraries incorporated into associations the Law Society would provide annual grants to ensure the libraries' maintenance and survival.[59] In 1880, Convocation approved the construction of a hall behind the original east wing of Osgoode Hall. Completed in two years, Convocation Hall served as an examination room for the Society's growing number of students-at-law.[60]

Throughout the late nineteenth century, the ideal of modern professionalism was spreading across North America. Harvard, Dalhousie, and McGill University developed three-year LL.B. programs, arguing that lawyers needed more formal, academic training. The three-year program soon became the norm.[61] In a bid to maintain its authority over the requirements for entry to the profession, the Law Society of Upper Canada began its own law school with a three-year compulsory non-degree program in 1889. To meet the law school's increased needs two classrooms, a reading room, and a student library were built immediately behind Convocation Hall.[62]

In the first half of the twentieth century, the wisdom of allowing the Law Society to maintain sole control over the education of its members was debated repeatedly. The case for a university education for those in the profes-

---

58   Ibid. at 132.
59   Ibid. at 139.
60   Honsberger, above note 6 at 201.
61   Curtis Cole, *A Learned and Honourable Body: The Professionalization of the Ontario Bar 1867–1929* (Ph.D. Thesis, University of Western Ontario, 1987) at 176.
62   Moore, above note 3 at 143.

sions became increasingly persuasive and, despite the numerous adjustments to and expansions of Osgoode Hall Law School's program, its effectiveness was continually challenged during this period. Despite the rising controversy over legal education, in 1938 the Society undertook a third law school addition. The student library was moved to the ground floor, the east side of the third floor was converted into a common room, and a large examination hall was constructed on the second floor. Accommodations for lecturers and the Law Society's secretary were also created.[63]

In 1949, the education issue reached a boiling point when the Law Society became embroiled in an internal battle as well as an external one. Osgoode Hall Law School's dean, Caesar Wright, vehemently disagreed with Convocation's conception of legal education. While the benchers continued to cling to the earlier model of part-time lectures with a strong focus on a period of articling consisting of practical training, Wright and his supporters advocated a full-time, three-year professional education, ideally in a university setting. Unable to change the minds of the benchers, Wright and his complete faculty quit and were immediately hired by the University of Toronto. There he set about creating his vision of a strong and modern law school.[64]

The defection of Wright and the Osgoode Hall Law School faculty created a public relations nightmare for the Society and undermined public confidence in its effectiveness. The incident could not, however, eliminate the right to control admission into the profession that the Society had been granted by the Legislature in 1797. In an effort to reach an acceptable compromise and repair the damage that had been done, the Society agreed to grant partial recognition to the university courses, but insisted that university students finish their studies at Osgoode Hall before being admitted as members of the Society. It also refused to discontinue its own law school, offering it as an alternative to university training.[65]

This compromise continued until the 1950s when the benchers came to the realization that it was no longer in the Society's best interests to compete with the universities. Public opinion firmly held that a professional education should be synonymous with a university education and the profession, facing a second fee increase in four years, also began seriously to doubt the wisdom of continuing the Osgoode Hall Law School.[66] The benchers also realized that as the number of lawyers increased, so too did the Society's obligation

---

63 Carr, above note 4 at 84.
64 Moore, above note 3 at 230–31.
65 *Ibid.* at 253–54.
66 *Ibid.* at 258.

to honour the other parts of its mandate — the regulation and discipline of members of the legal profession in the public interest. In 1957, benchers John Arnup and Park Jamieson acted as the Law Society representatives in negotiations that culminated in the "New Deal" in legal education and the creation of accredited university law schools and the Bar Admission Course. The Bar Admission Course, supervised by the Law Society, would provide practical training after the completion of an LL.B. program at an accredited university and a period of articling. Students would be called to the bar of Ontario only upon the successful completion of the Society's course.[67] A fourth addition to Osgoode Hall was constructed behind the east wing between 1956 and 1959 to provide additional lecture halls, reading rooms, and office space.

Faculties of law began to appear across the province. In addition to the already established University of Toronto law school, Queen's University, Faculty of Law opened its doors in September 1957, followed by the establishment of a common law program at the University of Ottawa. In 1968, realizing that it was fighting a losing battle in its attempts to continue to hold onto Osgoode Hall Law School as an alternative to university training, the Law Society ceded control of the school to the newly founded York University.[68] It continued, however, to retain control over the admission of students to its membership through the Bar Admission Course. In 1990, Convocation approved the final addition to Osgoode Hall, consisting of two and a half floors on top of the 1956 addition. This addition provided further classroom facilities and faculty offices for the Bar Admission Course.[69]

Since the 1990 addition was completed, no further expansions have been made to Osgoode Hall. Numerous renovations have been undertaken, however, to modernize the building and allow the Law Society to fulfill its mandate effectively. Today, Osgoode Hall no longer houses the Bar Admission Course, although the Law Society maintains its authority to admit students to its ranks. The licensing process, which has replaced the Bar Admission Course, is conducted off-site to provide more office space for the Society's staff. The lecture hall is now used to conduct continuing legal education programs to ensure the continued competency of Ontario's lawyers after the completion of their formal education, and the northeast wing houses a modern membership services division, including a call centre to deal with inquiries from the public and the Society's membership.

---

67 Ibid. at 258–62.
68 Ibid. at 263.
69 Honsberger, above note 6 at 262.

Although the Law Society of Upper Canada was created by an Act of Legislature in 1797 and charged with the mandate to govern the legal profession in the public interest, it was not until after the War of 1812 that the governing body actually began to take responsibility for the powers it had been granted. Throughout the 1820s, there was a marked movement to enhance the integrity, respectability, and professional nature of the Society. The construction of Osgoode Hall was part of that movement. It was envisioned not only as the Society's permanent residence, but also as a visual reminder of the Society's status, power, and evolving professionalism.

In the ensuing years, Osgoode Hall has been expanded to accommodate the increasing needs of the Law Society. As this paper shows, the building's physical form has been defined by the decisions of the governing body and thus the history of Ontario's legal profession. Osgoode Hall embodies the history and the spirit of the legal profession in this province. Its construction lent an air of respectability and professionalism to the Law Society in its early years. Today, the building's noble appearance and architectural impressiveness serve not only as a symbol of the strength of this province's legal profession, but also as a visual history of the Law Society's efforts to fulfill its mandate and ensure the continuance of its self-regulation.

PART 1

HISTORICAL PERSPECTIVES ON LEGAL EDUCATION

CHAPTER 3

Slamming the Door on Brains: Two Early Twentieth-Century Law Schools and the Narrowing of Educational Opportunity

D.G. BELL

IN 1922, AFTER YEARS of debating educational standards, the Canadian Bar Association (CBA) recommended that provincial societies set the threshold for entry into law study at the equivalent of two years of an Arts program. Shortly thereafter, in the midst of campaigning to promote this benchmark, the new dean of the Osgoode Hall law school saluted the dean of Dalhousie's law school as a comrade in what he called the "Battle of the Standard."[1] Ultimately, that battle to raise the standard of professional entry was won. The CBA's 1922 recommendation proved a watershed in defining which aspirants would be allowed access to legal education. This essay draws attention to an apparent casualty in this "Battle of the Standard" — educational accessibility — and speculates why scholars have chosen to overlook it. It tells the story in part within the context of two of Canada's oldest law schools, Dalhousie in Halifax and the King's College (now University of New Brunswick) School of Law, located then in Saint John.

TWO EARLY CANADIAN LAW SCHOOLS

THERE IS NO GENERAL history of Canadian common law education but its outline is clear. In whatever province, legal education begins with student

---

1   D. A. MacRae, "Legal Education in Canada" (1923) 1 Can. Bar Rev. 671; J. D. Falconbridge to D. A. MacRae (3 Nov. 1923), Halifax, Dalhousie University Archives and Special Collections (ms 1, C 3 Falconbridge).

mooting clubs, then moves to sporadic, and then institutionalized lectures, usually offered precariously at first. There is always tension between broad professional access and raising standards. Usually, there is a point at which practitioner-lecturers and the practitioner orientation are challenged for dominance and eventually supplanted by academic teachers and an academic perspective. That academic perspective is associated with the influence of teachers trained in the eastern United States. Canadian law schools become ever more prestigious and, by the 1960s, selective in admissions. Then legal academics chronicle the story of this progress and declare it a "good thing." In writing it up, the 1950s are identified as *the* revolutionary decade in Canadian legal education.[2]

The subject of this paper takes place between two other of those transformational decades, the 1880s, when continuous formal legal education began in the common law provinces, and the 1920s, when the "Battle of the Standard" was won and legal education turned decisively in a modern direction. It was in the 1880s that lectures at Toronto's Osgoode Hall settled onto what would become a permanent footing (1889), and that university-connected law schools opened in Halifax (1883) and — if one may extend the decade by two years — in Saint John (1892).[3] Both of the Maritime law schools were founded in response to a student demand that was evident as early as the 1860s. By the 1880s dozens of would-be Maritime lawyers had made the trek to the law schools of Boston or Harvard universities. Articling students unable to afford a Massachusetts sojourn formed self-improvement societies to sponsor lectures and moot courts. With the opening of local law schools, many members of Saint John's Law Students' Association (founded 1879), the Halifax Law Club (by 1880), and the St. John Law Students' Debating Club (by 1891) availed themselves of the opportunity to attend lectures presenting law systematically.[4] Initially, both institutions confined classes to

---

2   The best historical overview remains J.P.S. McLaren, "The History of Legal Education in Common Law Canada" in R.J. Matas and D.J. McCawley, *Legal Education in Canada: Reports and Background Papers of a National Conference on Legal Education held in Winnipeg, Manitoba, October 23–26, 1985* (Montreal: Federation of Law Societies of Canada, 1987) at 111 [McLaren]. Thoughtful observations prefatory to a history of legal education are offered by Wesley Pue in "Common Law Legal Education in Canada's Age of Light, Soap and Water" in D.J. Guth and W.W. Pue, eds., *Canada's Legal Inheritances* (Winnipeg: Canadian Legal History Project, Faculty of Law, University of Manitoba, 2001) 654 at 654–62.

3   At about the same time Acadia, Dalhousie, King's, Mount Allison, St. Francis Xavier, and the University of New Brunswick were introducing law courses for Arts undergraduates.

4   P.V. Girard, "The Roots of a Professional Renaissance: Lawyers in Nova Scotia, 1850–1910" in D. Gibson and W.W. Pue, eds., *Glimpses of Canadian Legal History* (Winnipeg:

early morning, late afternoon, and sometimes mid-evening, so as not to interrupt office attendance for either the students or the judges and practitioners who delivered most of the lectures. Conveniently, both schools opened their doors in the commercial heart of their respective downtowns.

In these respects the two Maritime law schools were alike in the era of their founding. By the 1920s they would come to differ greatly in ambition and outlook. While the Saint John school was becoming an educational backwater, Dalhousie was in the vanguard of common law legal education in Canada. Although Dalhousie's era of distinction dates from the 1910s, its advantages were evident already at the school's inauguration. The movement to open a law faculty in Halifax finally succeeded in 1883 because one of Dalhousie's New York partisans endowed the college with a chair in law. This funding, originally on a generous scale, of what was then the only full-time professor in common law Canada, brought a core of stability in finance and personnel to the precarious enterprise of opening a law school. The occupant of this chair of "constitutional and international law" and the faculty's dean from 1883 to 1914 was Richard Weldon. Although Weldon turned out not to be a scholar in the modern, publishing sense, the thirty-four-year-old dean boasted an American doctorate in political science and study in Germany, the intellectual capital of the nineteenth-century world. His acquaintance with the practice of law, and even knowledge of the common law, cannot have been great — he was not called to the Nova Scotia bar until 1884 and had no law degree — but Weldon the intellectual brought to the Dalhousie experiment a breadth of academic vision that endured through its early decades. His 1883 inaugural address offered a sustained defence of the study of international and constitutional law; in a single sentence he acknowledged that most student time would be taken up by the "more useful and practical subjects" that downtown practitioners would teach. Eventually this "cultural" approach to curriculum (as one of his successors styled it) would seem backward-looking, but in Weldon's own day Dalhousie's students and partisans accepted it enthusiastically and self-consciously as Canada's most distinguished experiment in common law education.[5]

Manitoba Law Journal Faculty Committee, 1991) 155 at 164 and 171–75. Minutes of the Halifax Law Club, 1880–82, are in Special Collections, Dunn Law Library, Dalhousie University. The two Saint John student organizations were written up regularly in that city's press. There had been proposals to open a Saint John law school (connected with the University of New Brunswick) in 1869 and a Halifax law school in 1874.

5   J.T. Bulmer, ed., *Inaugural Addresses... Delivered at the Opening of the Law School in Connection with Dalhousie University... at the Beginning of the First Term in 1883* (Halifax: n.p., 1884) at 52–55 [Bulmer]; J. Willis, *History of Dalhousie Law School* (To-

Meanwhile in 1892, Saint John's bar embarked on an experiment of its own. Lawyers and judges had already offered an annual program of lectures for a decade, sometimes as many as thirteen, to the city's Law Students' Association. Ten years later, the University of New Brunswick (UNB, located in Fredericton) inaugurated a series of "university extension" lectures in law in Saint John. Although touted as "solid" and "educational" rather than "popular," the lectures drew an average attendance of nearly 100. It is surprising, then, that the successful move to harness the talent of the Saint John bar to meet the demand of legal education in a more stable way came not from UNB but from King's College of Windsor, Nova Scotia. The King's initiative proved to be all that was needed to prompt the city's lawyers and judges to announce formation of a Saint John law school where students might earn a law degree that would be awarded through the ancient Anglican foundation at Windsor. All courses were to be offered by part-time lecturers. On the whole, the lecturers proved a distinguished lot. One held an American doctorate (in Mexican history), and another was a fellow of the Royal Society of Canada. Allen Earle, dean for the school's first decade, lacked any academic degree but was a revered "lawyer's lawyer." He edited law reports and several editions of New Brunswick's rules of court.[6] Rather more than Weldon, Earle was just what a nineteenth-century law dean should have been.

Yet, in time the fortunes of the Saint John school would differ greatly from those of its Halifax counterpart. Saint John was not a provincial capital and, under the impact of the federal tariff policies, was already a port in commercial and industrial decline. While the school's founders, several of whom might fairly be called intellectuals, did not lack for academic ambition, their institution had no philanthropist to fund the services of a full-time dean. More than this, the Dalhousie school was founded in the environs of a college and grew to be part of that college. From this connection the academic orientation evident in the inaugural speeches of 1883 was strengthened and safeguarded through the spiritually lean years that come in the history of any institution. This was not the case at Saint John, where the city had no local university and where the connection to the college at Windsor, replaced in 1923 by connection with the University of New Brunswick, was mostly a degree-granting convenience. While the founding vision of the Saint John

---

ronto: University of Toronto Press, 1979) at 7, 25–27, 31 [Willis]; P.V. Girard, "Richard Chapman Weldon" in *Dictionary of Canadian Biography*, vol. 15 (Toronto: University of Toronto Press, 2005) at 1064–67; D.M.M. Stanley, "Richard Chapman Weldon, 1849–1925: Fact, Fiction and Enigma" (1989) 12 Dalhousie L. J. 539.

6   D.G. Bell, *Legal Education in New Brunswick: A History* (Fredericton: Faculty of Law, University of New Brunswick, 1992) at 47–50 and 75–81 [Bell].

school is not without interest, as noted below, the idea of a law faculty within a larger community of learning was no part of that vision.

AN ERA OF EDUCATIONAL OPPORTUNITY

FOR DECADES AFTER THEIR founding, both Maritime schools accepted two classes of students: degree candidates called "undergraduates," who paid an annual tuition, and a class of general, partial, or, as they are called here, "special" students, who were assessed fees on a per course basis. As neither school required any college education of its applicants, both were effectively open to all who could afford the time and the fee.[7] The result was a student population that exhibited considerable diversity, especially in Saint John.

Special Students

STUDENTS REGISTERED IN INDIVIDUAL courses were once numerous. At Saint John's King's College law school between 1892 and 1923, the special students numbered about one-quarter of the student body; in some years they outnumbered degree candidates. In Halifax they were no less numerous, accounting for slightly more than 30 percent of the student body in the period up to 1925.[8] Who were these students? As John Willis notes of Dalhousie, some were enthusiastic, practising lawyers enrolled in a course of particular interest. There are also occasional instances of students taking individual courses in preparation for provincial bar examinations. This was so at the Saint John school, also.[9] In neither case is this phenomenon likely to have been large. In Saint John there must have been quite a few instances in which the special student was experimenting with law, or taking a course while accumulating

---

7   At both schools the minimum entry qualification was equivalent to about grade 11: Willis, above note 5 at 39; Bell, above note 6 at 83 and 90. Though much lower than the admission standard would become in the 1920s, such a barrier to access was not negligible: R.D. Gidney and W.P.J. Millar, *Professional Gentlemen: The Professions in Nineteenth-Century Ontario* (Toronto: University of Toronto Press, 1994) at 355.

8   Bell, *ibid.* at 93 and 131. For Dalhousie this percentage is generated by counting special students and regular undergraduates listed in the annual *Calendar of the Law School of Dalhousie University*, 1884–85 to 1924–25 [*Calendar*] supplemented by the manuscript "Law School Register," 1883–84 to 1897–98, in Special Collections, Dunn Law Library, Dalhousie University. Special students, even as a category, are unmentioned in C.L. Wiktor, ed., *Dalhousie Law School Register, 1883–1983* (Halifax: Dalhousie Law School, 1983) [Wiktor], but their presence is noted in P.B. Waite, *Lives of Dalhousie University: Lord Dalhousie's College* (Montreal: McGill-Queen's University Press, 1994) at 290 [Waite].

9   Willis, above note 5 at 36; Bell, *ibid.* at 93.

funds for the full law program because some special students became regular undergraduates. This was also the case (or at least attempted) at Dalhousie, for in 1912 the law school prohibited it.[10]

Existence of a category of non-degree students in the two Maritime law schools created the possibility that interested members of the Halifax and Saint John public might take law courses. In Halifax, for no reason that is obvious, this did not occur. On investigation, nearly all non-LL.B. candidates listed in the annual calendars prove to be Arts undergraduates taking one or more law school credits.[11] To be sure, this represented some broadening of educational access, for it was in the character of special students who were regular college undergraduates that the first seventeen Nova Scotia women were able to study law.[12] But what Dalhousie's apparently great number of special students does not represent is the dissemination of legal education within the general community. On the other hand, in Saint John the special students could not simply be undergraduates in other programs picking up a law course because there were no such undergraduates in the city, the school being physically remote from both King's College in Windsor and the University of New Brunswick in Fredericton. Who were these non-degree law students?

In proceedings inaugurating the Saint John law faculty in 1892, Dean Allen Earle had announced that the school would accommodate two types of students: not only those seeking to enter the legal profession, but also others such as "business men who desire to gain a general knowledge of law."[13] Perhaps he was alluding to the demand for legal education evident earlier that same year in the broad popularity of the University of New Brunswick's Saint

---

10   Instances are given in Bell, *ibid.* at 93. Dalhousie's preclusion of counting credits earned as a special student towards degree study appears first in the *Calendar*, above note 8, for 1912–13 at 9. Classification of Dalhousie students is elusive because some who appear in the university's registration records as what this paper calls special students are listed in the corresponding published law calendar as degree candidates.

11   For example, for the academic year 1912–13, when the twenty-one special students listed in the school's published calendar are cross-checked against their university registration, no fewer than seventeen are revealed as Arts students taking a law school course: *Calendar*, 1913–14, above note 8 at 22; Student Register (1912–13), Halifax, Dalhousie University Archives and Special Collections, UA-7. When the thirty-three special students listed for 1920–21 are checked against their university registration papers, only two appear to have been non-degree students.

12   The first Dalhousie woman to take a law course appears to have been Margaret Moody, a thirty-year-old Arts student, who enrolled for the year 1899–1900. Sixteen other women took courses (we do not know which law courses) prior to Frances Fish's arrival in 1915 as the first LL.B. candidate.

13   "The New Law School" [*Saint John*] *Daily Sun* (10 October 1892); *King's College Record* 17 (1895) 105; *King's College Record* 24 (1902) 83.

John extension lectures in law. In responding, the board of trade's president applauded Earle's intention, enlarging on the "complications and intricacies of a world wide interchange, and the great importance to commercial men of a broad knowledge of commercial law."[14] Soon, a plan to teach commercial law specifically to the "more intelligent of the young merchants and bookkeepers"[15] was mooted. In 1902, more than thirty bank clerks attended the first-year course on bills of exchange and promissory notes.[16] It would seem, then, that an aspect of the founding vision of the law school in Saint John was the idea that legal education should not be confined to intending lawyers. Rather, the institution might serve a wider community by making the law accessible to those who had a practical need of it. For at least a decade after the founding, there is evidence that this mission was carried into practice in various ways. Moreover, to the extent that one can track them down, there are indeed represented among special students such occupations as post office clerk, bank clerk, commercial clerk, printer, and a notable number of newspaper reporters.[17]

In the 1920s, in both Saint John and Halifax, special students all but disappeared from the law school ranks. In Dalhousie in 1921, they still numbered thirty-three; by 1928, non-LL.B. students were down to two. At Saint John the story was similar, though more complicated. Between 1923 and 1946 there were only fifteen special students, although this number excludes those who began as special students and then converted their status to undergraduate, something that was impossible at Dalhousie. Roughly, then, the 1920s is the moment when Dalhousie and King's College and UNB law schools become concerned almost wholly with educating future lawyers. It appears that this had been Dalhousie's vision from the outset, so that the special students — overwhelmingly Arts undergraduates rather than members of the wider community — must always have seemed an anomaly. In Saint John it marked, or perhaps completed, a reorientation away from the school's originally more catholic educational vision.

Undergraduates

THE PRESENCE OF SO many students at the Saint John school who were not candidates in any degree program marks a distant time when law schools

---

14   Ibid.
15   Ibid.
16   Ibid.
17   Bell, above note 6 at 93. The only requisite for admission as a special student was a certificate of good character.

might have a mission to offer legal education to the broader community. This theme of access is approached from a different perspective by considering how the relatively low admission standards of the late nineteenth and early twentieth centuries opened the legal profession to students from what a later time would regard as non-traditional backgrounds. Of these, the best-studied group is women. Mary Jane Mossman found significance in the fact that Canadian women, unlike their US counterparts, began entering the legal profession only when it became possible to study law in a school setting rather than solely through articling. The classroom, whatever its drawbacks, was a more respectable and meritocratic forum than mere clerkship. Perhaps as important, by proving an ability to tackle law academically, doors to articling positions might open that would have stayed closed otherwise.[18] Dalhousie Law School admitted its first three female LL.B. candidates in the period under discussion. The earliest arrived in 1915 although, as noted earlier, by that time the school had already admitted more than a dozen women as special students. At the Saint John school, a female undergraduate enrolled as early as 1893. She appears to have been the second female law student in Canada, following Clara Martin by two years. She was somewhat predictable in type, for her uncle was a judge and law school lecturer. Less typical was the next woman, who entered in 1896. She was a court stenographer and the daughter of a cobbler. Then came the now-famous Mabel French, who entered the Saint John school in 1902. She too was a stenographer, and the daughter of a process server. Unlike her two predecessors, French persisted in joining the bar and entering practice, though not before becoming a *cause célèbre* in both court and legislature.[19] Given French's victory, it is surprising that the next female undergraduate did not enroll until 1919, and that none of the many special students was female.

In reviewing paternal occupations for degree candidates at the two Maritime schools it is striking how many of the Saint John students were, like French, of an undistinguished social background. Dalhousie law students tended to be children of stockbrokers, manufacturers, merchants, engineers, contractors, and public servants, as well as the inevitable lawyers and farm-

---

18   M.J. Mossman, *The First Women Lawyers: A Comparative Study of Gender, Law and the Legal Professions* (Oxford: Hart, 2006) at 11 and 76. A more sanguine view of the articling system in mid- to late-nineteenth-century Ontario is offered in G.B. Baker, "Legal Education in Upper Canada, 1785–1889: The Law Society As Educator" in D.H. Flaherty, ed., *Essays in the History of Canadian Law*, vol. II (Toronto: University of Toronto Press for the Osgoode Society, 1983) 49 at 57–58 and 125.

19   Willis, above note 5 at 76–77; L.K. Yorke, "Mabel Penery French (1881–1955): A Life Re-Created" (1993) 42 U.N.B.L.J. 3 at 9–18; Bell, above note 6 at 95–100.

ers.[20] In contrast, Saint John law students were offspring not just of lawyers, politicians, and farmers, but also of fathers in comparatively humble situations: brakemen on the railway, carpenters, barbers, fishermen, and even "junk" dealers. Presumably this greater social diversity reflects the fact that tuition at Saint John was consistently 30–50 percent lower than at the Halifax school. Moreover, as late as the 1930s the lecture schedule at the Saint John school was still arranged so as to permit students to take paid employment for part of each day (in theory, by clerking in law offices); in that way, too, the Saint John law degree was more accessible than at Dalhousie, where decades earlier the schedule had changed to pre-empt the possibility of daytime employment. Cheap tuition brought Saint John a measure of ethnic as well as economic diversity. Among the students were the first Jewish individual to earn a law degree in the Maritimes, probably the first Japanese individual to receive a law degree in Canada, and a considerable number of New Brunswick Acadians. Strictly speaking, there were no blacks among the undergraduates but this was only because a technicality kept the school's sole black student within the ranks of special students.[21]

"SLAMMING THE DOOR ON BRAINS"

IT WAS IN THE first half of the 1920s when what J.D. Falconbridge would call the "battle" to raise law admission standards was fought across a broad Canadian front.[22] Its chronicle is the annual proceedings of the then recently founded Canadian Bar Association and its legal education committee. Agitation over admission standards coincided with parallel debates on adopting a canon of professional ethics, teaching a fairly standard law school curricu-

---

20   These are paternal occupations for the class of 1912–13, as recorded on their sons' university registration. The only apparently modest backgrounds represented were a mason and a "painter" (another's father was given as "seaman" but that was the student's surname): Student Register (1912–13), Halifax, Dalhousie University Archives and Special Collections, UA-7. The great preponderance of children of professionals and businessmen at Dalhousie Law School, albeit in the 1920s, is confirmed by the systematic analysis of M.P. Brunet, *Becoming Lawyers: Gender, Legal Education and Professional Identity Formation in Canada, 1920–1980* (Ph.D. dissertation, University of Toronto, 2005) at 85 and 137 [Brunet].
21   As described in Bell, above note 6 at 83, 92, and 94–95.
22   Note that the campaign was to raise the standard for admission to law "study," whether "study" at law school or solely through long attendance at a law office. The object of the CBA's campaign was to persuade provincial law societies to raise requirements for admission as a student-at-law, which was tantamount to raising law school admission requirements.

lum, making ethics part of that curriculum, imposing a character test on prospective students-at-law, recommending use of the case method of instruction, and clarifying the relationship between law school study and law office attendance. None of these analogous moves, even if successful (as some were), was as portentous as raising the admission barrier.

So far as one can tell, the movement began in Nova Scotia, though here the "battle" metaphor has no application. It was law students themselves, as early as the 1890s, who first raised the cry over admission standards. In 1914, after a nudge from the provincial Barristers' Society, Dalhousie Law School raised its minimum admission standard to one year of an Arts degree, with effect from 1915. No longer could one enter law study with a secondary school education. This was the highest standard in common law Canada.[23] In 1918, Donald MacRae, Richard Weldon's distinguished successor as dean of Dalhousie, urged the Canadian Bar Association, unsuccessfully, to recommend such a standard nationally. In this, its first national airing, the proposal for a one-year pre-law minimum attracted support from the West, where it was thought that sons of foreign-born parents needed the acculturation that college study would bring. But it also attracted opposition from John Baxter, a long-time lecturer at the Saint John law school, who thought it too soon to abandon the possibility of obtaining legal qualification purely through articling after high school.[24]

What members of the CBA rejected in 1918, they accepted in 1919 — almost without debate. Meeting in Winnipeg just weeks after suppression of the General Strike, perhaps they caught the mood of Sir James Aitkins, who used his presidential address to decry the notion that professional entry should be free to just anyone.[25] Within two years Dalhousie's Dean MacRae, now chair of the CBA's committee on legal education, could report that six of the nine provinces had adopted the one-year Arts prerequisite. The conspicuous foot-dragger was New Brunswick, whose admission standard was now the lowest in the dominion.[26]

---

23 Willis, above note 5 at 72; Waite, above note 8 at 228. At the school's inauguration, the idea of requiring collegiate education for entering law students had been dismissed as unrealistic: Bulmer, above note 5 at 32 and 38.
24 *Proceedings of the Third Annual Meeting of the Canadian Bar Association ... 1918* (Toronto: Carswell Co, 1918) at 22, 44, 47–48.
25 *Proceedings of the Fourth Annual Meeting of the Canadian Bar Association ... 1919* (Winnipeg: n.p., 1920) at 18, 86.
26 *Proceedings of the Sixth Annual Meeting of the Canadian Bar Association ... 1921* (Toronto: Carswell Company, 1922) at 242–43.

All of this was preliminary to the question, debated in 1922, of whether the CBA should recommend that the admission standard for law study be raised again, this time to the equivalent of *two* years of an Arts degree. This standard was already in place in Manitoba and, just months before the CBA annual meeting, Dalhousie had adopted it prospectively for the fall of 1924.[27] Dalhousie's dean, still chair of the CBA's legal education committee, predicted that this was the last rise that the committee would ever seek, for men who took two years of an Arts degree would likely persevere for the full degree anyway, before embarking on law study.[28]

The CBA embraced the two-year standard, but not without an equivocal speech from Saint John law school's John Baxter. Having just returned from the annual meeting of the American Bar Association, Baxter voiced his hesitation in distinctively American terms: higher admission standards would effectively bar from the profession the brilliant but poor Canadian counterparts of Abraham Lincoln. Yet by the speech's end Baxter had come round to reluctant support for the two-year proposal.[29] By the following year his thinking was clearer. Acknowledging how ineffectual it was for the profession to respond to an episode of ethical misconduct once it had occurred, Baxter agreed that the solution was, after all, to be found in the pre-law admission requirement:

> The great corrective ... is to close the gate very firmly and very resolutely to a certain class of applicants to the Bar, who never can become, and never will become, ethical in any respect. Instead of letting a man pass his final examination, the thing to do is to stop him at the outset.[30]

Note that Baxter's reliance on education to address the ethical problem had nothing to do with prescribing ethics lectures to law students. Rather, he

---

27 D. Gibson and L. Gibson, *Substantial Justice: Law and Lawyers in Manitoba, 1670–1970* (Winnipeg: Peguis, 1972) at 248; D.A. MacRae to J.D. Falconbridge (10 Apr. 1922), Halifax, Dalhousie University Archives (ms 1, C 3 Falconbridge); *Law Faculty Minutes* (12 June 1922), Halifax, Dalhousie University Archives (ms 13).
28 *Proceedings of the Seventh Annual Meeting of the Canadian Bar Association ... 1922* (Toronto: Carswell Company, 1923) at 262 [*Seventh Annual Meeting*].
29 Ibid. at 36–37. An Ontario delegate reported that the "Abraham Lincoln" argument was much heard in that province: ibid. 38–39. For more on Lincoln-ism in Canada, or what was termed "slamming the door on brains," see S. Denison, "Legal Education in Ontario" (1924) 2 Can. Bar Rev. 85 at 91; *Minutes of Proceedings of the Tenth Annual Meeting of the Canadian Bar Association ... 1925* (Toronto: Carswell Company, 1926) at 227 [*Tenth Annual Meeting*]; G.F. Henderson, "A Problem of Legal Education" (1925) 7 Can. Bar Rev. 371; *Minutes of Proceedings of the Fourteenth Annual Meeting of the Canadian Bar Association ... 1929* (Toronto: Carswell Company, 1930) at 100 [*Fourteenth Annual Meeting*].
30 *Proceedings of the Eighth Annual Meeting of the Canadian Bar Association ... 1923* (Toronto: Carswell Company, 1924) at 93–94 [*Eighth Annual Meeting*].

would "stop" the undesirable class at the "outset" by prescribing additional years of pre-law college study.[31] On this reasoning those who never could or would "become ethical" would be those students too dull, poor, or impatient to navigate two years of an Arts degree before proceeding to law study, whether in a law school or a law office.

At the time that Baxter spoke, New Brunswick still trailed the league tables in terms of its standard for professional entry, but pressure for change was afoot. In 1922 the lecturers at the Saint John law school had already urged the Barristers' Society to adopt at least the one-year standard, and the CBA's legal education committee engaged in a supportive letter-writing campaign.[32] By the end of 1923, Baxter himself was leading the law school's committee to investigate admission standards in terms of the CBA's then even-higher recommendation. By the CBA's annual meeting of 1924, the legal education committee could note with gratification that New Brunswick had moved out of last place and into the national vanguard in terms of the two-year standard, although in fact the new order was not operative until 1926 — coincidentally, the year that the CBA first met in Saint John.[33]

With Dalhousie Law School adopting the two-year standard in 1922 (effective from 1924) and the same occurring in New Brunswick in 1924 (effective from 1926), the two developments are properly regarded as minor variations on the same theme. Yet it cannot be overlooked that Dalhousie, and in particular Dean Donald MacRae, led the national charge for higher pre-law standards, whereas the Saint John lawyers, who dominated the New

---

31 *Ibid.* CBA deliberations on ethics are contextualized in W.W. Pue, "Becoming 'Ethical': Lawyers' Professional Ethics in Early Twentieth Century Canada" in Gibson and Pue, *Glimpses of Canadian Legal History*, above note 4 at 237. CBA debate over the relationship between academic and practical formation is rehearsed in C.I. Kyer and J.E. Bickenbach, *Fiercest Debate: Cecil A. Wright, the Benchers, and Legal Education in Ontario, 1923–1957* (Toronto: University of Toronto Press for the Osgoode Society, 1987) at c 2 [*Fiercest Debate*].

32 *Eighth Annual Meeting, ibid.* at 377. While minutes of the 1922 Saint John Law Faculty resolution do not survive, the matter is discussed in minutes for 5 Oct. 1923 and 31 Jan. 1924: Law Faculty minutes-book, Fredericton, University of New Brunswick Archives (RG 25, bk 1). The New Brunswick Barristers' Society approved the two-year standard in principle on 12 Feb. 1924, reciting a request to that effect from the University of New Brunswick law faculty: General Meeting minute-book, Fredericton, Provincial Archives of New Brunswick (Barristers' Society Collection, MC 288, ms 1).

33 *Minutes of Proceedings of [the] Ninth Annual Meeting of the Canadian Bar Association... 1924* (Toronto: Carswell Company, 1925) at 57; *Tenth Annual Meeting*, above note 29 at 223–25; *Minutes of Proceedings of the Eleventh Annual Meeting of the Canadian Bar Association... 1926* (Toronto: Carswell Company, 1927) at 360 [*Eleventh Annual Meeting*].

Brunswick Barristers' Society, came to the change reluctantly.[34] The CBA speeches of John Baxter, who was not just a long-time lecturer at the Saint John school but its future dean, reveal an allegiance to the new order that was equivocal. Moreover, although his fellow law lecturers joined Baxter in making the case for change to the Barristers' Society, they did not do so unanimously.[35] Evidently, some of them embraced more firmly than did Baxter what he had called the "Abraham Lincoln" argument.

GAIN AND LOSS

BY THE END OF the 1920s only Prince Edward Island held out against the national two-year pre-law standard, and the CBA's legal education committee pronounced itself content.[36] To be sure, higher entrance standards would weed out weak law school applicants but, as Dalhousie's dean (now John Read) advised, no longer was it necessary to fail one-quarter of the first year class, so the net effect on enrollment would be slight.[37] Actual experience at both Halifax and Saint John law schools suggests a somewhat different story. Dalhousie's largest graduating classes for the decade of the 1920s were in the early years. Its smallest graduating classes were in 1928 and 1930 and were less than half the size of the earlier years. In terms of total student enrollment, the highest numbers in the decade were for the academic years 1922 and 1923, exactly preceding the imposition of the new standard; for years at the end of the decade numbers were one-third lower.[38] The effect on Saint John was

---

34 However, one does note that both of Dalhousie's moves to raise admission requirements, first to the one- and then the two-year Arts standard, came after prodding from the NS Barristers' Society rather than the reverse: Law Faculty minutes (8 Apr. 1914), Halifax, Dalhousie University Archives (ms 13); *Seventh Annual Meeting*, above note 28 at 260. In New Brunswick, in contrast, it was the Barristers' Society that dragged its heels.

35 The faculty council minutes for 31 January 1924 recites that the "majority" of faculty had agreed to recommend to the Barristers' Society what it describes as the Nova Scotia/Manitoba standard; see *Eighth Annual Meeting*, above note 30.

36 From 1932 Ontario retreated to a one-year-college-or-equivalent requirement, maintaining it for thirty years: C. Moore, *Law Society of Upper Canada and Ontario's Lawyers, 1797–1997* (Toronto: University of Toronto Press, 1997) 218–19; B.D. Bucknall et al., "Pedants, Practitioners and Prophets: Legal Education at Osgoode Hall to 1957" (1968) 16:2 Osgoode Hall L.J. 137 at 196. This does not negate the reality that, from the mid-1920s, substantial pre-law education was the accepted Canadian model.

37 *Eleventh Annual Meeting*, above note 33 at 36. See also *Fourteenth Annual Meeting*, above note 29 at 329.

38 Admittedly, numbers for 1922 and 1923, the highest of the decade, might reflect some residual postwar crowding. Data on graduates are derived from Wiktor, above note 8, and those for all students from the yearly calendars.

more profound still. Higher admission standards together with more stringent examining brought the lowest attendance in the school's history, nearly extinguishing it.[39] Both Dalhousie and UNB reflected a trend that was Canada-wide, with national enrollment figures bottoming-out in 1930.[40]

For many who spoke in the 1920s at the CBA's annual debate on legal education, lower but better law student enrollments were just what was wanted. Of the many arguments that might have been made in favour of a heightened pre-law standard, the one that recurred was that medicine and dentistry had raised their educational bar in recent decades, diverting the academically weak into law. When John Baxter concluded his "Abraham Lincoln" speech in 1922 by acceding to the higher standard, the deciding factor for him was the comparison with medicine. Speaking for the legal education committee in 1925, the dean of Dalhousie deplored the luring of "hesitating youth into the profession of law, merely because it is the easiest and cheapest to enter."[41] A different dean of Dalhousie made the same remark the next year. In 1927 the CBA printed a paper by Donald MacRae (then teaching at Osgoode Hall) recalling that pre-law standards had been raised because the profession had become crowded with unsuitable types, lured in by the comparative ease of entry.[42]

---

39 A.B. Gilbert to C.C. Jones: Presidential Correspondence (23 Sept. 1927), Fredericton, University of New Brunswick Archives.
40 A.Z. Reed, *Review of Legal Education in the United States and Canada for the Year 1934* (New York: Carnegie Foundation for the Advancement of Teaching, 1935) at 63. Reed's numbers here and in earlier Carnegie Foundation annual reports are not completely useful for this purpose as they include Quebec schools, which had distinctive admission standards. In A.Z. Reed, *Present-Day Law Schools in the United States and Canada* (New York: Carnegie Foundation for the Advancement of Teaching, 1928) Reed did segregate enrollment in the "English-speaking" law schools, noting (at 359) that it had dropped over 45 percent between the academic years 1919 and 1926. As 1919 was the first year of the postwar bulge and the largest enrollment to that time and for many years after, the comparison is not of much value in terms of gauging the impact of higher admission standards. After 1930 enrollment began rising again owing to the economic crisis, a development that the CBA's legal education committee viewed with predictable dismay: *Minutes of Proceedings of the Eighteenth Annual Meeting of the Canadian Bar Association...1933* (Toronto: Carswell Company, 1934) at 219.
41 *Seventh Annual Meeting*, above note 28 at 36–37.
42 *Seventh Annual Meeting*, ibid. at 37; *Tenth Annual Meeting*, above note 29 at 59, 227; *Eleventh Annual Meeting*, above note 33 at 163, 359; *Proceedings of the Thirteenth Annual Meeting of the Canadian Bar Association...1928* (Toronto: Carswell Company, 1929) at 354. Debate over raising pre-law standards in Canada was stimulated by many of the same concerns, expressed more vividly, in the United States, especially the comparison with the state of medical education: R.B. Stevens, *Law School: Legal Education in America from the 1850s to the 1980s* (Chapel Hill: University of North Carolina Press, 1983) c. 6 [Stevens]; J.S. Auerbach, *Unequal Justice: Lawyers and Social Change in Modern America*

Falling enrollment at both Maritime law schools, for both degree candidates and special students, suggests that the 1920s was the period when bar societies and law schools combined to put a final stop to the educational possibilities of a generation earlier. In the era of the schools' founding, it was not quite clear in what direction legal education would move. Both had opened merely "in connection with" their respective colleges, half-way between free-standing establishments and university departments: Would their orientation be academic or vocational? Would their mission be confined to would-be lawyers? Would they aim to be part of a general liberal formation? Or, would they think it important to assist men of commerce and others to get along in their trades? Would they be accessible to students of ordinary social background or open only to those who could afford to attend a college first? Would they exclude women or Jews or blacks?

The polyphonous state of law schools and educational missions in the United States in the late nineteenth and early twentieth centuries suggests that in the 1880s and 1890s there was no set or predetermined answer to such questions.[43] If there is no sign of any broad educational mission at the founding of the law school at Halifax, there are hints, at least, of such multiple possibilities in the early days of the smaller institution in Saint John. The latter school did indeed make a professional credential accessible to men (and women) from the more humble classes. What seems to have happened in the 1920s is that these older possibilities were largely foreclosed for Canadian legal education generally. The CBA's success in raising pre-law standards signalled that the sole purpose of legal education was to prepare future lawyers for their profession, and that the lawyers of the future would be only those who could afford first to pass some years at a college.

HALIFAX, 1933

THIS CHAPTER BEGAN BY resurrecting the case of the special students not to claim for them particular importance, but because they represent what later generations would regard as law-school anomalies, on that account, to be forgotten. However they may have been viewed by the Halifax and Saint John

---

(New York: Oxford University Press, 1976) c. 4. Kyer and Bickenbach caution against assuming that CBA members were influenced to raise pre-law standards so that offspring of immigrants might be better acculturated: *Fiercest Debate*, above note 31 at 72–73 and 273–74. However, the concern is expressed unmistakably, if softly, in CBA debates.

43 Stevens, *ibid.* at c. 5. Admittedly, professional admission was always apt to be more constricted in the Canadian provinces than in the US because of the door-keeping role of provincial law societies. Note also, for Ontario, and *Fiercest Debate*, *ibid.* at 29.

schools at their nineteenth-century founding, by the 1920s they were survivors from a more primitive age. Their story does not fit the "whigish" pedigree that contemporary legal education still assumes as its institutional memory. This chapter has also pointed to indications of diversity of background among early students at the Saint John law school, though less obviously so at Dalhousie. While the entry of women into the legal profession has become a subject of interest, the contemporaneous diversity in class and ethnicity among early law students has not seemed worth remembering, presumably because it suggests the mongrel standards prevalent in Canadian legal education during its nascent age. Perhaps because no one has written a general history, we still regard our story, so far as the students go, as a progress from uniformity of background to the comparative diversity of more recent times. Indications that the true story is one of narrowed, rather than broadened, educational access comes as something of a surprise.

It is also part of collective memory that the principal tension in Canadian legal education has been between the Dalhousie or academic orientation on the one hand, and the Osgoode Hall model, emphasizing training, on the other.[44] The long resolution of this tension between the 1920s and the 1950s, marked by a climax of splendid drama, lends itself readily to depiction in terms of angels and demons. The importance of Dalhousie in Canadian legal education was never more evident than in the early 1920s, when its approach to curriculum and to pre-law study became the Canadian standard, promoted by the CBA's legal education committee, headed by Donald MacRae and his successor as dean, John Read. There were many influences in play in these developments, but the most visible hand was that of the two Dalhousie deans.

Not less important than the actual role of Dalhousie in the imagined history of Canadian legal education is the power of the *idea* that Dalhousie came to represent. For those arguing for a different sort of legal education in Ontario, and no doubt elsewhere, Dalhousie's example was a handy weapon in debate.[45] More influential still was the idea of Dalhousie, crystallized by the school's fiftieth anniversary celebrations in 1933. The Great Depression may

---

44 Without belabouring the point, this is indeed how the story is structured in McLaren, above note 2; *Fiercest Debate, ibid.*; and, not surprisingly, Willis, above note 5, which has this splendid index entry for Ontario: "falls in line with Dalhousie-Nova Scotia system," at 151–52.

45 Even Willis, who blushed at some of the claims associated with the Dalhousie name, could not resist citing a particularly good example from the editor of the *Canadian Law Times* as early as 1888: *ibid.* at 44–45. There is another fine specimen in *Tenth Annual Meeting*, above note 29 at 59: "We do need in Ontario to have the law schools of Ontario come into that [i.e., Dalhousie's] class."

have been an inauspicious time for rejoicing, but Dalhousie's law faculty presented a magnificent view to the world. Together the editor of the *Canadian Bar Review*, who had been a member of its first graduating class, and the assistant editor, who was also the school's dean, placed no fewer than five notices touting the school and its teachers in volume 11 of that journal.[46] By 1933 Dalhousie had one or more graduates on the bench of most superior courts in the country, notably in the West. But the propaganda centrepiece of the 1933 celebrations was the fact that Dalhousie had law graduates as premiers of Nova Scotia and New Brunswick and as prime ministers of Newfoundland and Canada. This, it was emphasized in the speechifying and transmission to the nation by the *Canadian Bar Review*, reflected the insistence of the school's founding dean that Dalhousie should be "not merely a law school," but also "a breeding ground for public service and public men."[47] Here was said to be the greatest proof of Dalhousie's success: it trained men for what, in the social gospel parlance of the day, was grandly called "public service." To fix these ideas on Dalhousie in 1933 is not to imply that Dalhousie invented the notion that a law school's success would be measured in the public influence of its graduates. In the wake of the rise of Progressive and socialist movements around World War I, Canadian lawyers as a class were keen to latch onto the prestige of specialized expertise and public service. The new CBA (1914) and its new canon of ethics (1920), proclaiming that a lawyer's first duty was to "the State," themselves reflect this perception that the profession should repackage its role.[48] In such a context Dalhousie's triumphalist fiftieth-anniversary celebration, headlined by the names of Prime Ministers Bennett and Squires and Premiers Tilley and Macdonald, is the moment when this vision

---

46 J.E. Read, "Fifty Years of Legal Education at Dalhousie" (1933) 11 Can. Bar Rev. 392 [Read]; editorial, "Jubilee of Dalhousie Law School" (1933) 11 Can. Bar Rev. 402; editorial, "Dalhousie's Quinquagenary" (1933) 11 Can. Bar Rev. 628; editorial, "Dalhousie's Quinquagenary" (1933) 11 Can. Bar Rev 690. The same number contained the editorial "Medical Jurisprudence at Dalhousie" (1933) 11 Can. Bar Rev. 201. There was also D.C. Harvey's centennial tribute to Beamish Murdoch, which managed to mention the law school: "Nova Scotia's Blackstone" (1933) 11 Can. Bar Rev. 339, and pieces from Dalhousie Law School faculty members unrelated to the anniversary. Fittingly, the same volume printed one of many protests from students of Osgoode Hall regretting the decision of the Law Society of Upper Canada to lower admission requirements beneath the two-year standard that Manitoba and Dalhousie had pioneered.

47 Read, *ibid.* at 629. Proceedings are summarized in Willis, above note 5 at 111–15, and P.V. Girard, "The Maritime Provinces, 1850–1939: Lawyers and Legal Institutions" in Guth and Pue, above note 2, 379 at 404–5. Similar Dalhousie rhetoric is highlighted in Brunet, above note 20 at 180–82.

48 *Proceedings of the Fifth Annual Meeting of the Canadian Bar Association 1920* (Winnipeg: n.p., 1920) at 261.

of a law school as a privileged training ground for the future elite crystalized in the imagination of Canadian lawyers, law teachers, and law students.

One might cite many specimens of this phraseology, especially from law deans. Typical are the observations of F.C. Cronkite, chair of the CBA's legal education committee and dean of the Saskatchewan law school, written in 1935. Cronkite's argument was that an academic approach to legal formation was the best sort of preparation for public service.

> [T]he legal profession has customarily been a recruiting ground for political leaders. There is still a great demand for leaders and the government services are becoming wider year by year. Does it not seem reasonable that every effort should be made to ensure that the level of education of members of the legal profession, particularly in matters of economic organization, should be at least a little higher than that of the man in the street?[49]

This was Cronkite's preface to a plea for raising pre-law standards beyond two years of an Arts program.

Dean Cronkite was a prophet. In the name of better preparation for better public service, educational standards would continue to be raised in Canadian law schools and, beginning in the 1960s, enrollment would be limited further by selecting students from among a pool of the qualified. The result of these ever-rising standards is that nowadays all law schools, not just Dalhousie, can feel that they are imparting royal jelly into the leaders of the future. But the raising of standards that began in the 1920s for the purpose of fitting future premiers and lesser "public men" for their station came at the cost of restricting the kind of person who could enter the legal profession. The early history of at least the Saint John law school suggests that Canadian lawyers and law teachers did not merely forgo broader access to the legal profession, they went to the trouble of leaving it behind. Having been sacrificed for the sake of a more prestigious profession and more influential law schools, the comparatively open access that was an early feature of organized legal education in Canada was deleted from collective memory as irrelevant to the mission, and perhaps slightly embarrassing.

---

49 F.C. Cronkite, "Legal Education — Which Trend?" (1935) 13 Can. Bar Rev. 375 at 382–84. Cronkite's argument is contextualized in *Fiercest Debate*, above note 31 at 130–33.

CHAPTER 4

"Good Government, without Him, Is Well-nigh Impossible": Training Future (Male) Lawyers for Politics in Ontario, Quebec, and Nova Scotia, 1920–1960

MÉLANIE BRUNET[*]

IT HAS BEEN OBSERVED that a disproportionate number of politicians are lawyers.[1] Since Confederation, just over 70 percent of Canadian prime ministers and more than 20 percent of members of Parliament have been lawyers,

---

[*] This paper is partly drawn from my dissertation, *Becoming Lawyers: Gender, Legal Education and Professional Identity Formation in Canada, 1920–1980* (Ph.D. dissertation, University of Toronto, 2005). I am grateful to Susan Lewthwaite at the Law Society of Upper Canada Archives; Kelly Casey and Kathryn Harvey at the Dalhousie University Archives; James Lambert at the Division des Archives de l'Université Laval; and Michel Champagne at the Division des Archives de l'Université de Montréal. Their assistance greatly facilitated my work. I also want to thank Ronda Ward for her comments and suggestions on an earlier version of this paper.

[1] This is especially true in the United States where social scientists have written extensively about the predominance of lawyers in American politics and their influence on the broader system of government. See, for example: William Miller, "American Lawyers in Business and in Politics: Their Social Backgrounds and Early Training" (1951) 60 Yale L.J. 1 at 66–76; Joseph A. Schlesinger, "Lawyers and American Politics: A Clarified View" (1957) 1 Midwest Journal of Political Science 1 at 26–39; David Gold, "Lawyers in Politics: An Empirical Exploration of Biographical Data on State Legislators" (1961) 4 Pacific Sociological Review 2 at 84–86; Heinz Eulau and John D. Sprague, *Lawyers in Politics: A Study of Professional Convergence* (Indianapolis: Bobbs-Merrill, 1964); Irvin H. Bromall, "Lawyers in Politics: An Exploratory Study of the Wisconsin Bar" (1968) Wis. L. Rev. at 751–64; Paul L. Hain and James E. Pierson, "Lawyers and Politics Revisited: Structural Advantages of Lawyer-Politicians" (1971) 19 American Journal of Political Science 1 at 41–51; and Mark C. Miller, *The High Priests of American Politics: The Role of Lawyers in American Political Institutions* (Knoxville: University of Tennessee Press, 1995). But the affinity between the legal profession and politics has

or possessed some background in law.² These lawyer-politicians were likely warned at some point during their training or early career that "the law is a jealous mistress," but it did not stop their professors and leading members of the bar from encouraging them to keep an eye on public affairs for the possibility of entering the political sphere. Between 1920 and 1960, discourses and activities in law schools clearly promoted this link between the legal profession and politics. In their student papers, future lawyers wrote of model parliaments, debates, and political clubs as essential components of their training, and reported on advice given by lawyer-politicians visiting their school. As a profession of service, legal practice was thought naturally to lead to public office. Furthermore, politics was associated with the formulation, adoption, and amendment of laws, thus making lawyers particularly suited for the task. Entering the political arena in order to guide the nation's destiny was even described as the lawyer's duty in a society built on the principles of peace, order, and good government.

Based primarily on reports in student newspapers, this chapter focuses on law schools in four institutions: Osgoode Hall (Toronto), Dalhousie University (Halifax), Laval University (Quebec City), and the University of Montreal. It examines the rhetoric and activities emphasizing lawyers' role in politics from the perspective of law students, their professors, and prominent members of the bar. Infused with masculine assumptions, these reports, addresses, and opportunities to train for politics excluded female students, thus reinforcing the image of the legal profession as a male preserve, and strengthening the relationship between power and masculinity.

NATURAL POLITICIANS: LAWYERS AS PUBLIC SERVANTS AND MAKERS OF LAWS

IN THESE FOUR LAW schools, professors and established lawyers went beyond the formal curriculum to discuss the social contributions of legal practice. They frequently described law as a profession of service. While addressing Convocation, guest speakers and deans advised law graduates of their "in-

---

    been neglected in Canadian academic circles, although it has been commented upon (and criticized) in popular culture.

2   Library of Parliament, "Prime Ministers of Canada: Biographical Information," *Parliament of Canada*, online: www2.parl.gc.ca/Parlinfo/Compilations/FederalGovernment/PrimeMinisters/Biographical.aspx?Language=E (accessed 14 September 2007); and Laura Carlin, "Canada Votes 2006 — Analysis & Commentary: Professions of the Politicians," *CBC News*, online: www.cbc.ca/canadavotes2006/analysiscommentary/professions.html (accessed 14 September 2007).

escapable social responsibility" to serve their community and society in general.[3] Agreeing with this premise, the editor of *Obiter Dicta* at Osgoode Hall wrote in 1948: "Every practicing lawyer, should in principle be, first and foremost a public servant. His duty is to society. His purpose is to serve."[4] In general, students writing in their school papers accepted the classic image of the lawyer as a courageous defender of the weak and the oppressed, a representation based at least partly on a perceived need for women to be protected.[5] However, while discharging his social responsibilities, he was warned to respect class boundaries and maintain his status as a member of the elite when helping the less fortunate. As a Montreal student explained: "instinctively, people prefer to not entrust their interests to equals."[6] As a learned individual, the lawyer was part of an "intellectual triumvirate" with the clergyman and the physician, quickly becoming identified with his community's elite, especially in smaller centres, and setting an example of responsible citizenship.[7] This type of commitment and service was distinctly masculine because of its public nature. In a society deeply influenced by the notion of "separate spheres," women were also expected to display such commitment and devotion, but usually in a private and familial context as wives and mothers.

To fulfill this role, the lawyer had to develop an ethic of service during his training, analyzing public questions with a view to helping others, thus preparing himself to serve society like a leader or a conscientious priest.[8] In line with the religious character of Laval University and the University of Montreal, francophone law students in Quebec tended to emphasize the spiritual

---

3   See, for example: Dean Vincent MacDonald's message in *Pharos 1938* at 39, see Dalhousie University Archives, *Pharos* [Dalhousie University Yearbook], 1938 and C.F.H. Carson, "Address to the Graduating Class" *Obiter Dicta* (Winter 1949) 38.
4   R.W.M., "Editorial: Legal Education — An Indictment" *Obiter Dicta* (Winter 1948) 8.
5   Paul Gérin-Lajoie, "La mission de l'avocat," *Le Quartier Latin* (25 October 1940) 6. On chivalric justice, see: Carolyn Strange, "Wounded Womanhood and Dead Men: Chivalry and the Trials of Clara Ford and Carrie Davies" in Franca Iacovetta and Mariana Valverde, eds., *Gender Conflicts: New Essays in Women's History* (Toronto: University of Toronto Press, 1992) at 149–88.
6   Gérald Morisset, "L'Élite professionnelle" *L'Hebdo-Laval* (14 February 1939) 1.
7   J. Alex. Edmison, "The Spotlight on Our Average Law Student: Searching Analysis in His Life, Actions, Inclinations, Hopes, and a Few Words Concerning His Probable Fate" *Obiter Dicta* (18 March 1929) at 1 and 4; A.M. Carter, "President Bids Osgoode Farewell" *Obiter Dicta* (April 1943) 4; and Roch Brunet, "Le notariat" *Le Quartier Latin* (14 March 1941) 4.
8   "October Luncheon" *Obiter Dicta* (16 October 1936) 4; Jacques Giraldeau, "Le sens de la profession" *Le Quartier Latin* (12 November 1948) 1; Dollar, "Pour occuper nos loisirs" *Le Béret* (1 April 1921) 1; and Jean Lebrun, "Les avocats" *Le Quartier Latin* (31 October 1935) 12.

aspect of their public duty.[9] Law was promoted as "a legal and social apostolate" for which a student had to prepare with perseverance, method, love, and passion.[10] In the Laval paper, Father Joseph-Papin Archambault, a Jesuit priest and teacher of Catholic social action, wrote that the Catholic lawyer had to be inspired by Church doctrine, which would give him a truly Christian mentality towards service.[11] As a good representative of Catholicism, he should be an example of "altruism at the service of others" and manifest the pleasure and satisfaction of helping his fellow man.[12] A lawyer's religious beliefs were considered central to his mission as a public servant and his understanding of society's needs.

Albeit from a secular perspective, Osgoode Hall graduates were also warned that such an ethic of service demanded effort and sacrifice but it would inevitably lead to success and satisfaction.[13] Indeed, the young lawyer

---

9 See Division des Archives de l'Université Laval, *Annuaire général de l'Université Laval pour l'année académique 1920–1921* (1921) at 39–40; and Division des Archives de l'Université Laval, *Annuaire général de l'Université Laval pour l'année académique 1953–1954* (1954) at 26; Jean Hamelin, *Histoire de l'Université Laval: les péripéties d'une idée* (Ste-Foy, QC: Les Presses de l'Université Laval, 1995); Guylaine Girouard, *L'admission des femmes à l'Université Laval, 1901–1945: un compromis entre des objectifs féministes et des objections cléricales* (Ste-Foy, QC: Groupe de recherche multidisciplinaire féministe, Université Laval, 1993); Hélène-Andrée Bizier, *L'Université de Montréal: la quête du savoir* (Montreal: Libre Expression, 1993); Nicole Neatby, *Carabins ou activistes? L'idéalisme et la radicalisation de la pensée étudiante à l'Université de Montréal au temps du duplessisme* (Montreal and Kinsgton: McGill-Queen's University Press, 1999) at 9–18; and Sylvio Normand, *Le droit comme discipline universitaire: une histoire de la Faculté de droit de l'Université Laval* (Quebec City: Les Presses de l'Université Laval, 2005) at 23.

10 J. Ls. Baillargeon, "Le rôle de l'avocat" *L'Hebdo-Laval* (12 October 1934) 3; "Law Notes" *Dalhousie Gazette* (11 January 1922) 5; Lomer Racicot, "Psychologie" *Le Quartier Latin* (14 March 1941) 2; and Gilles Dussault, "Les idéologies des professions libérales au Québec, 1940–1975" in Fernand Dumont, Jean Hamelin, and Jean-Paul Montminy, eds., *Idéologies au Canada français, 1940–1976 — Tome II* (Quebec City: Les Presses de l'Université Laval, 1981) at 53.

11 R.P. Archambault, S.J., "Le devoir professionnel" *Le Béret* (20 November 1928) 1.

12 Marcel Blais, "On n'en a pas conscience" *Le Carabin* (8 November 1950) 9; and Gérin-Lajoie, "La mission de l'avocat," above note 5 at 6. In the late 1950s, the Law Faculty at Laval University was still offering its students a course on professional ethics to discuss the responsibilities of the Catholic lawyer or notary, and a religion course to equip them with the knowledge necessary to defend their beliefs and teach them to others. The special course was established in 1934: Division des Archives de l'Université Laval, *Annuaire de la Faculté de Droit de l'Université Laval pour l'année académique 1958–1959* at 28–29.

13 Carson, "Address to the Graduating Class," above note 3 at 41. See also "Message du doyen," *Laval '56 : Album-souvenir de la vie étudiante pour l'année académique 1955–56* (Quebec City: Association Générale des Étudiants de l'Université Laval, 1956) at 36.

could not pretend to have received a full training for public service simply by attending law school. He was provided with a foundation there, but it was also his responsibility to become actively involved in public affairs as a "natural" community leader, and to take an interest in history, economics, and literature in order to "acquire that intangible and essential quality of human understanding."[14] In a free society, "qualified citizens" had a duty to serve and provide leadership. In an article on the lawyer and public life published in *Obiter Dicta* in 1954, Conservative lawyer-politician and future Finance Minister under John Diefenbaker, Donald M. Fleming, insisted that a "virile" democracy depended on the service of "able and devoted representatives."[15] His emphasis on virility may have been inspired by a fear expressed in some political circles in the United States that democracy had become "emasculated" by an increased feminine influence since women had begun to vote. His advice was also reminiscent of the political thought of Canadian imperialists in the late nineteenth and early twentieth century who counted on democracy to "produce a group of enlightened and educated leaders."[16]

At Dalhousie Law School, these principles were also at the heart of a tradition that originated with its first dean, Richard Chapman Weldon. The "Weldon tradition" inspired law students to be actively involved in their community and to use their training in public leadership "for more than mere money-making."[17] During his tenure, Weldon had been a federal member of Parliament for New Brunswick for nine years. Students were reminded of the words of this beloved dean who strongly believed that lawyers were among the most qualified individuals to lead the country: "In our free government we all have political duties ... and these duties will be best performed by those who have given them most thought."[18]

---

14   Donald M. Fleming, "Public Life and the Lawyer" *Obiter Dicta* (Winter 1954) 11 and "Extra-Curricula: Liberal Club" *Obiter Dicta* (19 March 1937) 5.
15   Fleming, "Public Life and the Lawyer," *ibid*. at 9–10.
16   K.A. Cuordileone, *Manhood and American Political Culture in the Cold War* (New York: Routledge, 2005) at 13 and Carl Berger, *The Sense of Power: Studies in the Ideas of Canadian Imperialism, 1867–1914* (Toronto: University of Toronto Press, 1970) at 207.
17   Marjorie Major, Lorne Yea, and John Braddock, "Dalhousie Law School — Training Ground for Premiers?" (1971) 62 The Atlantic Advocate 3 at 17; John Willis, *A History of Dalhousie Law School* (Toronto: University of Toronto Press, 1979) at 3 and 255–58 (Appendix II — The Weldon Tradition); and David MacDonald, "The Brainiest School in the Country" *Maclean's Magazine* (1 March 1954) at 21 and 40.
18   MacDonald, "The Brainiest School in the Country," *ibid*. at 21; and Major *et al*., "Dalhousie Law School — Training Ground for Premiers?" *ibid*. at 15. Graduates were reminded of these words by Dean Vincent MacDonald in his message in *Pharos 1936* at 30, see Dalhousie University Archives, *Pharos* [Dalhousie University Yearbook], 1936.

Osgoode graduate Donald Fleming essentially agreed with this premise, writing: "democracy ... needs the service of the ablest citizens in public office" and law school could train them for this task.[19] Students in Quebec and Ontario were also assured that "lawyers [were], as a result of their training, better equipped to assume a role of leadership in society, than any other group of individuals" and the public had come to expect their contribution.[20] Considering the number of lawyers entering politics, the editor of *Obiter Dicta* cautioned the Law Society of Upper Canada that it could not afford to fail to train its future members accordingly.[21] When the Ontario bar was under much pressure in the 1930s and 1940s to revamp the province's legal education system, it was reminded by a student that the "primary purpose [of a law school] should be to produce public servants of the highest professional standard, aware of their duty to the community and a knowledge of the leadership role they must play."[22]

Political office was often presented as the ultimate form of public service and leadership, if engaged for altruistic and non-financial motives.[23] Students were encouraged to enter politics, but only once they had a well-established practice warned J. Earl Lawson, Minister of National Revenue under R.B. Bennett, in a talk at Osgoode Hall. Laval students were given similar advice: if they were tempted by political life, they should at least wait until middle age to make the jump.[24] By then, they would have acquired the maturity, economic independence, and contacts necessary for a successful venture in politics. To those who believed such service brought generous financial rewards, Lawson bluntly stated: "You cannot earn a living in politics." He then added that when serving the state, the "perpetuity [of your country] must be a large part of your fee and retainer."[25] In his article, Fleming also stressed that public service "impose[d] heavy sacrifices and offer[ed] little in the way of material rewards."[26]

---

19 Fleming, "Public Life and the Lawyer," above note 14 at 9.
20 R.W.M., "Editorial: Legal Education — An Indictment," above note 4 at 8 and "Two Cabinet Ministers Address Osgoode Tories" *Obiter Dicta* (12 February 1931) 4.
21 R.W.M., "Editorial: Legal Education — An Indictment," *ibid*. at 8.
22 N. MacL. Rogers, "An Inquiry Into the Legal Education System" *Obiter Dicta* (Winter 1948) 43; and "Raising of Standards of Entrance and Full Time Law School Course Are Urged in Student Report" *Obiter Dicta* (15 March 1934) 1.
23 This is also reflected in letters of recommendation for the Sir James Dunn Scholarship at Dalhousie Law School. See, for example, Dalhousie University Archives, Faculty of Law, MS-1-13 (G-396), *Dean — Read, H.E. — Scholarships: Dunn, Sir James — Administration (1960/61)*, Letter from H.A. Hanson to Dean Horace Read (6 May 1960) 2.
24 Normand, *Le droit comme discipline universitaire*, above note 9 at 84.
25 "October Luncheon," above note 8 at 4 and 7.
26 Fleming, "Public Life and the Lawyer," above note 14 at 11.

However, as his own boss the established lawyer enjoyed a level of independence and freedom that made the risky business of politics more attractive and accessible.[27] Unlike businessmen or those engaged in routine occupations, he had more control over his daily agenda. When in partnership with another able lawyer, he could leave his practice for months certain that his clients would still be looked after. If politics turned out to be a short-lived engagement, he could return to his primary occupation. The lawyer also benefited from wider contact with the public than members of other occupations and was often called upon to interpret issues influencing the opinion of his fellow citizens. Such contacts at once made him more qualified for public service and reinforced his obligation to engage in such activities.[28]

Beyond being public servants, lawyers were thought to be especially qualified for political office because of their training. They had a fundamental role in politics as makers of laws and this required a thorough understanding of the constitution.[29] Lawson believed that legislatures dominated by non-lawyers adopted "unintelligible" laws, creating unnecessary "hardships and injustice." Speaking during the Depression years, he argued that in times of economic difficulties, the federal government could do more to help Canadians with laws on minimum wage, maximum working hours, and proper housing. But, given the division of powers, these measures could not be implemented without changes to the constitution, and "there is no group of men better fitted both by training and by intellect for this task, than are the lawyers."[30] According to another lawyer-politician, Liberal member of the Ontario Legislature Ian Strachan, lawyers in politics were often considered "'necessary evils' by their lay colleagues," but he insisted that drafting legislation was becoming an increasingly complex task with a high potential for error when handled by members not learned in the law. He pointed to the existence of a committee of the legislature "occupied in the dreary task of killing 'half-baked' legislation at its inception" as evidence of the importance of a thorough knowledge of laws. Furthermore, Strachan suggested that if there were more lawyers in legislatures, more time might be saved in the courts as judges would not have to deal with poorly conceived laws.[31]

According to Donald Fleming, beyond the training that makes him an interpreter of laws, the lawyer had the advantage of mastering a technique

---

27 George Scott, "The Lawyer & Politics" *Ansul* (September 1975) 7.
28 Fleming, "Public Life and the Lawyer," above note 14 at 11.
29 "October Luncheon," above note 8 at 4 and Fleming, "Public Life and the Lawyer," above note 14 at 10–11.
30 "October Luncheon," *ibid.* at 4 and 7.
31 "Osgoode Politics" *Obiter Dicta* (29 November 1937) 5.

similar to the parliamentary method: whether in court or in Parliament, he "prepares his case, examining its strengths and weaknesses, sifting and marshalling his evidence, setting forth his principles, and seeking to persuade the court of parliamentary and public opinion." This made the lawyer especially aware of the functions and responsibilities of Parliament and made him appreciate "the true significance of freedom" as well as its vulnerability.[32]

In every province, it was thought that lawyers had a duty to enter politics in order to guide the nation's destiny.[33] Because of his extensive knowledge of laws and procedures, "rarely can the lawyer stay out of politics and good government, without him, is well-nigh impossible."[34] At a luncheon in 1944, Wilfred Heighington, a Toronto lawyer serving as a Conservative member in the Ontario Legislature, advised "Osgoodians" to seriously think about "entering the public field for they are endowed with the knowledge of legal and public affairs by virtue of their training," which made them "leaders of the people."[35] Ten years later, Fleming stated that Ontario lawyers had been blessed with the "priceless heritage of freedom and British parliamentary institutions," making public service an inescapable obligation.[36] In Quebec, jurists were considered essential at all levels of government because those who used, modified, or replaced the laws had to know their origins, intentions, and deficiencies. If a legal education provided him with this basic knowledge, practice then gave the lawyer political wisdom by making him a conciliator with a sharp mind to weigh every side of a problem and suggest an adequate solution. His mastery of both official languages of the country, his knowledge of various legal systems, and his awareness of social issues made his participation in politics a duty he could not escape.[37]

Especially at Dalhousie, students were told of their predecessors' achievements in the public eye, at once a source of inspiration as well as a reminder of the hard work involved. R.B. Bennett was considered a success story in that regard. Of modest means, he graduated from Dalhousie Law School in 1893, moved to Calgary where he made his fortune, and went on to become Prime

---

32 Fleming, "Public Life and the Lawyer," above note 14 at 10–11.
33 "The Mock Parliament" *Dalhousie Gazette* (7 February 1935) 2.
34 R.G. Murray, "Law As a Profession; Combines the Interests of Many Other Vocations" *Dalhousie Gazette* (23 October 1951) 3.
35 "Heighington Urges Consideration for Politicians" *Obiter Dicta* (Spring 1944) 11.
36 Fleming, "Public Life and the Lawyer," above note 14 at 10–11.
37 Gérard Ally, "La défense de l'avocat" *Le Quartier Latin* (5 December 1941) 4; Jean-Pierre Houle, "Les carrières juridiques: la politique" *Le Quartier Latin* (14 March 1941) 4; André Montpetit, "Médecins et avocats de demain" *Le Quartier Latin* (7 November 1931) 1–2; Lebrun, "Les avocats," above note 8 at 12; and Gérin-Lajoie, "La mission de l'avocat," above notes at 6.

Minister of Canada. He was thought to be an inspiration for the poor but ambitious student wanting to make a difference in his country.[38] Addressing students during a visit to his *alma mater* in 1942, Bennett told them "the trained legalist was the most important instrument in the superb task of moulding the destiny of a nation."[39] A 1927 calendar supplement about Dalhousie Law School presented the legal profession as a stepping-stone to public life, the "surest way ... for the young man or woman of higher moral character and ability ... to devote his or her life to the service of the state."[40] Two law students who went on to lead their respective provinces as premiers recalled being regularly reminded that many leading politicians, businessmen, and judges had received their legal training at Dalhousie: "it was always impressed on us that great men came from Dal."[41] As a source of inspiration, the walls of the school were adorned with pictures of prominent male graduates, "bring[ing] to the student's mind the opportunity for public service which the law affords," but presenting role models that women could not readily identify with.[42] Students (including some women) also carved their initials in the benches next to those of their famous predecessors and dreamed about their own role in shaping Canada's future.[43] Dalhousie Law School enjoyed a nation-wide reputation as "a training school for great men" with politicians "its most notable byproduct."[44]

In Ontario, Osgoode Hall also sang the praises of "the great men it has produced whose names have been a light unto the Province and the Dominion

---

38 Dalhousie University Archives, Faculty of Law, MS-1-13 (F-20), *Dean: MacDonald, V.C. — Correspondence: Bennett, R.B.*, Letter from V.C. MacDonald to Prime Minister R.B. Bennett (21 November 1934).
39 "Lord Bennett Visits Law School" *Dalhousie Gazette* (30 October 1942) 1.
40 Dalhousie University Archives, *Calendar of Dalhousie University 1926–1927 Supplement "Law As a profession"* — Faculty of Law, Dalhousie University, Halifax, (1927) 1.
41 Gerald Regan of Nova Scotia and Richard Hatfield of New Brunswick in Major *et al.*, "Dalhousie Law School — Training Ground for Premiers?" above note 17 at 18.
42 "The Law School's Birthday" *Dalhousie Gazette* (22 February 1933) 3; "Law School Then and Now: An Interview with Dr. Moffat Hancock" *Ansul* (April 1974) 2; Dalhousie University Archives, Faculty of Law, MS-1-13 (F-47), *Dean: MacDonald, V.C. — Correspondence, general: D-I,* Letter from V.C. MacDonald to Hon. J.L. Ilsley (20 January 1947); and F.M. Covert, "In My Day at Dalhousie Law School" *Ansul: Special Edition* (13 January 1976) 42.
43 "Stereotypes of Students: The Law Student" *Dalhousie Gazette* (18 October 1934) 2; Gertrude Mills, "In My Day ... A Look Back to Life at Dalhousie Law School in the 20s" *Hearsay* (Summer 1982) 27; P.B. Waite, *The Lives of Dalhousie University: Volume 2, 1925–1980* (Montreal and Kingston: McGill-Queen's University Press, 1998) at 202; and R.A. Kanisberg, *Trials and Tribulations of a Bluenose Barrister* (Halifax: Petheric Press, 1977) at 1.
44 MacDonald, "The Brainiest School in the Country," above note 17 at 21.

at large." Students were advised that "it is at Osgoode that Canada expects to find her leaders learned in the law."[45] When explaining its mission to students and the opportunities it offered for public service, the Osgoode Conservative Club named a series of "leaders in the affairs of our country" as proof of these lawyers' importance and success.[46] In an open letter to Osgoode students in 1960, Conservative lawyer Arthur Maloney called upon them to continue the "outstanding public service [their predecessors] have rendered."[47] At Laval, public events promoting the institution were often a good occasion to recall the brilliant careers of graduates active in the political world.[48]

Public office often went hand in hand with nation-building, especially in the earlier decades of the twentieth century, and took the form of a patriotic duty by which men of law would bring "peace, order, and good government" to recently settled areas of the country.[49] Being called to a noble profession, lawyers should be inspired "to make law an instrument of civilization." As future leaders, law students were regularly made aware of the legal profession's central role in "the formulation and administration of just laws" ensuring order in the community.[50] Dalhousie Law School took pride in its contributions to the nation, especially in bringing the principles of British justice to newer parts of the country.[51] In 1933, Lt. Col. J. Keiller Mackay claimed in front of

---

45 "Invocation" *Obiter Dicta* (30 October 1931) 2.
46 "Osgoode Politics" *Obiter Dicta* (16 October 1936) 6.
47 Arthur Maloney, "An Open Letter to Osgoode Students" *Obiter Dicta* (New Series, 1960) 13.
48 Normand, *Le droit comme discipline universitaire*, above note 9 at 82.
49 "Shall I Take Law? A Survey of the Dalhousie Law School" *Dalhousie Gazette* (17 February 1932) 6.
50 Donald D. Carrick, "Wasting Three Years at Osgoode" *Obiter Dicta* (26 January 1933) 1; and "Law, the Preparation for Modern Business and Public Life: The First of a Series of Articles on Dalhousie's Little Law School 'the training school of a nation'" *Dalhousie Gazette* (14 November 1929) 5.
51 Willis, *A History of Dalhousie Law School*, above note 17 at 4; "Dalhousie Law School Completing 46th Year of Continued Activity" *Dalhousie Gazette* (15 March 1929) 4; "Editorial: Public Speaking and the Law School" *Dalhousie Gazette* (18 February 1931) 2. See also Dalhousie University Archives, Faculty of Law, MS-1-13 (E-4) — *Dean: Smith, S.E. — Clippings*, "Its Golden Anniversary" *Halifax Chronicle* (24 October 1933) n.p. It should be noted that Western Canada attracted many Dalhousie graduates forced to look outside the Maritimes if they wished to establish an independent practice. In the 1930s, the market for legal services in the Maritimes was thought to be crowded. Some also went to the United States. (E-1), *Dean: Smith, S.E. — Alumni questionnaire and responses*, Letter from W.N. Graburn to S.E. Smith (25 September 1930) 1; Letter from R.C. MacDonald to S.E. Smith (16 September 1930) 1; Letter from James H. Power to S.E. Smith (15 September 1930) 3; (F-41), *Dean: MacDonald, V.C. — Correspondence: Smith, S.E.*, Letter from V.C. MacDonald to S.E. Smith (19 June 1939); (F-169), *Dean:*

Conservative Club members at Osgoode Hall that the participation of lawyers in political affairs was "of the greatest possible value to our country and to mankind."[52] Like women, the nation also needed protection and lawyers were seen as ideal defenders of democracy and British civilization.[53]

In Quebec, nation-building and patriotism had a slightly different flavour. Legal education could foster a sense of patriotic duty as students were invited to take part "through action, speech, or the written word in the administration of their country."[54] An English-speaking student at the University of Montreal remarked that one of the first texts they had to read was about the responsibility of French-Canadian lawyers to safeguard the Code civil if they wished to preserve their national identity.[55] To help them achieve this objective, they were urged to read *L'Action française*, a monthly magazine published by the league of the same name led by l'Abbé Lionel Groulx. Students at Laval were reminded of jurists' important contribution to the nation since the British conquest of Canada: they had called for conciliation, national spirit, and patriotism under the military regime of 1760–64, during the adoption of the *Constitutional Act* of 1791, and after the rebellions of 1837.[56] Law professors at Laval and Montreal saw in their students more than future lawyers: they were to be leaders of a distinctly French-Canadian elite, an intellectual aristocracy, and a ruling class in opposition to British-inspired Canadian imperialists.[57]

MacDonald, V.C. — *Students* — *Correspondence:* G, Letter from V.C. MacDonald to Paul J. Gelinas (15 December 1933); (G-57), Dean: Read, H.E. — *Box of Miscellaneous Clippings* — *Law School, 1952–1961*, "Education Maritime 'First' but Grants Sticky Problem" *Financial Post* (16 June 1956); F.W. Bissett, "In My Day at Dalhousie Law School" *Ansul: Special Edition* (13 November 1976) 17; and Frank Rowe, "In My Day at Dalhousie Law School" *Ansul: Special Edition*, vol. 2 (December 1977) 15.

52   G.H.L., "Conservative Club" *Obiter Dicta* (13 November 1933) 3.
53   For more on the links among masculinity, nation, and Britishness, see: Paul Ward, *Britishness Since 1870* (London: Routledge, 2004) at 38–39.
54   Dollar, "Pour occuper nos loisirs," above note 8 at 1.
55   Emmett P. Maloney, "Impressions d'un Irlandais," *Le Quartier Latin* (14 March 1941) 8; and Dussault, "Les idéologies des professions libérales au Québec, 1940–1975," above note 10 at 50.
56   Dollar, "Pour occuper nos loisirs," above note 8 at 1; Blais, "On n'en a pas conscience," above note 12 at 9; and Baillargeon, "Le rôle de l'avocat," above note 10 at 3.
57   Dollar, "Pour occuper nos loisirs," *ibid.* at 1; Paul Lefebvre, "Chroniques universitaires: Droit" *Le Quartier Latin* (12 December 1929) 4; G.L.J.M.D., "Page des facultés: Droit" *Le Quartier Latin* (19 October 1933) 5; Division des Archives de l'Université de Montréal, Fonds du Secrétariat Général (D35) — Faculté de droit (C3), (C3.58), *Coupures de presses concernant la Faculté de droit et le droit en général, 1952–1964*, Gilles Duguay, "L'avocat: un civilisateur au service de la société" *Le Devoir* (6 December 1954) n.p.; and Normand, *Le droit comme discipline universitaire*, above note 9 at 23. Lawyers were

A good number of law students apparently responded to this call since more than one in five male members of the Quebec Legislative Assembly between 1948 and 1970 were lawyers.[58] At the House of Commons in Ottawa, from 1949 to 1971, almost 35 percent of members from Quebec were trained in the law.[59] At Laval, students could look to their own professors for examples of politically active lawyers: between 1902 and 1944, 42 percent of them also served in a political position during their career.[60] On the national scene (including all the provinces), from 1920 to the late 1950s, a consistent one-third of federal Members of Parliament were jurists (including lawyers and notaries), representing by far the largest occupational group.[61] In *The Vertical Mosaic*, John Porter estimated that between 1940 and 1960, 60 percent of federal cabinet members and 42 percent of provincial premiers were lawyers.[62] Finally, by 1971, Dalhousie Law School had produced one prime minister and twelve provincial premiers, with many more working for political parties or in the civil service, giving it a reputation as "a breeding ground for public service and public men."[63]

---

already part of the Montreal elite at the turn of the twentieth century. This elite was composed of both language groups, but it seems francophone jurists were more active in politics than their English-speaking counterparts. Dominique Marquis, "Une élite male connue: les avocats dans la société montréalaise au tournant du XXe siècle" (1995) 36 Recherches sociographiques 2 at 322.

58 The "Legislative Assembly" became the "National Assembly" in 1968. These numbers include one woman, Marie-Claire Kirkland, who was first elected in 1961. François Morneau, "L'influence du droit dans la société québécoise" (1984) 73 *L'Action nationale* 6 at 529; and Robert Boily, "Les hommes politiques du Québec, 1867–1967" in Richard Desrosiers, ed., *Le personnel politique québécois* (Montreal: Boréal Express, 1972) at 68.

59 Morneau, "L'influence du droit dans la société québécoise," *ibid.* at 529.

60 Normand, *Le droit comme discipline universitaire*, above note 9 at 91.

61 Based on data from Library of Parliament, Information and Documentation Branch, "Parliamentary Internet: Senators and Members — Occupations of Parliamentarians," online: www.parl.gc.ca (9 February 2004). See also Norman Ward, *The Canadian House of Commons: Representation* (Toronto: University of Toronto Press, 1950) at 135.

62 John A. Porter, *The Vertical Mosaic: An Analysis of Social Class and Power in Canada* (Toronto: University of Toronto Press, 1965) at 391–92. Also reported in Dennis Patterson, "Professionalism" *Ansul* (December 1972) 3; and Scott, "The Lawyer & Politics," above note 27 at 7.

63 Major *et al.*, "Dalhousie Law School — Training Ground for Premiers?" above note 17 at 10, 12, and 15. It is also estimated that between 1758 and 1983, lawyers consistently accounted for roughly 20 percent of the sitting members of the Nova Scotia Legislature. Bernard F. Miller, "The Legal Profession in Late Victorian Nova Scotia" (1991) 11 Nova Scotia Historical Review 1 at 74, note 54. However, it has been suggested that law schools do not necessarily produce politicians, but that individuals already thinking about politics will choose to study law because of a "natural affinity." See Scott, "The Lawyer & Politics," *ibid.* at 7.

LEARNING POLITICS BEYOND THE CLASSROOM

BEYOND THE KNOWLEDGE OF law they acquired in the classroom, students could prepare for a role in politics by taking part in a number of extra-curricular activities.[64] One of these was the "model" or "mock" parliament.[65] Instituted at Dalhousie Law School in 1886 by Dean Weldon with the objective of stimulating students' interest in public affairs, the mock parliament was considered "a kindergarten of Canada's leaders."[66] Held over three days, this event was open to the public, and spectators had a chance to see future political stars in action. In fact, it was said that Dalhousie's mock parliament "has been uncannily prophetic."[67] The school took this role very seriously: when the number of students dropped sharply during the Second World War, Dalhousie could not fail Canada by discontinuing this event for too long or else "who would guide her destiny?" asked the editor of the school paper.[68]

All four institutions regarded the model parliament as an integral component and "the most practical part" of a lawyer's training for public office.[69] Osgoode Hall established its first model parliament in 1928, also with the belief that it would train future political leaders.[70] Politicians and public officials were invited to take part. For example, the Speaker of the Ontario Legislature agreed to preside over the deliberations of the first session of the Osgoode par-

---

64 J.F. MacNeill, "In My Day at Dalhousie Law School" *Ansul: Special Edition* (13 January 1976) 32; Siraneau, "Chronique universitaire: Droit" *Le Quartier Latin* (8 October 1925) 7; and Darrell Lang, "Law, a Splendid Training for Modern Business and Public Life, Says Writer: Article Three" *Dalhousie Gazette* (18 February 1930) 2.

65 The term varied according to the institution. Dalhousie referred to it as the "mock" parliament, while Osgoode Hall called it the "model" parliament. In Quebec, both Laval and Montreal had a parlement "modèle."

66 "Editorial: The Mock Parliament" *Dalhousie Gazette* (7 February 1935) 2; Major *et al.*, "Dalhousie Law School," above note 17 at 16; Supplement *"Law As a Profession"* — Faculty of Law, Dalhousie University (1927), above note 40 at 3; *Pharos 1939* at 59, Dalhousie University Archives, *Pharos* [Dalhousie University Yearbook], 1939; Dalhousie University Archives, Faculty of Law, MS-1-13 (F-117), *Dean: MacDonald, V.C. — President's Annual Report*, Letter from V.C. MacDonald to Carleton W. Stanley (19 June 1936) at 1.

67 *Pharos 1948* at 68, Dalhousie University Archives, *Pharos* [Dalhousie University Yearbook], 1948; MacDonald, "The Brainiest School in the Country," above note 17 at 21; and *Pharos 1938* at 65, Dalhousie University Archives, *Pharos* [Dalhousie University Yearbook], 1938.

68 "Editorial: The Mock Parliament," above note 66 at 2; and *Pharos 1941*, n.p., Dalhousie University Archives, *Pharos* [Dalhousie University Yearbook], 1938.

69 "Editorial: The Mock Parliament,"*ibid.*; and "Law Notes" *Dalhousie Gazette* (19 February 1952) 3.

70 "W.B. 'Bill' Bates Will Lead First School Cabinet" *Obiter Dicta* (2 February 1928) 1; and "Parliament Will Develop Leaders" *Obiter Dicta* (2 February 1928) 2.

liament while the Lieutenant Governor delivered the Speech from the Throne.[71] The students behind this activity had high hopes for the inaugural gathering, which turned out to be more of a "mock" than a model parliament in the opinion of the editor of *Obiter Dicta*, who qualified it as a "grotesque exhibition."[72] It seems most participants either engaged in highly intellectual rhetoric or in humorous banter ("really saying nothing at all") and were more interested in the spotlight and the long-standing Liberal-Conservative rivalry than in "discussing the more important questions of the day."[73] This mitigated success was reflected in the attendance: there was a good turnout at the first session, but only a handful of spectators thereafter.[74] Despite these mixed results, the model parliament was held again in 1929 under the direction of the Osgoode Legal and Literary Society, but was then shelved until 1936, at which time the second attempt was interestingly remembered as "the most popular activity at Osgoode Hall."[75] By then, the parliament was said to have "received the wholehearted support of the Benchers and the Committee on Legal Education." After a seven-year absence, over 120 students, recruited by Osgoode political clubs or acting independently, sat as members and engaged in proceedings based on current issues affecting Canada. The gallery at Convocation Hall was filled to capacity with friends and fellow students, since participants were each obliged to invite one female spectator.[76] This rule made the model parliament a distinctly male activity while women were mostly relegated to the role of "cheerleaders" on the sidelines. The event was combined with a buffet-style dinner, giving some aspiring politicians a chance to mingle with prominent members of the bar and bench.[77] The quality of the speeches and the decorum may have been limited, but the student parliament had an undeniable value as a training tool for public speaking and parliamentary procedure.[78]

Only by preparing early through participation in the school parliament could future lawyers expect to survive "the rude contests in the Parliaments

---

71 "The First Speaker" *Obiter Dicta* (2 February 1928) 1 and "To Open Parliament" *Obiter Dicta* (2 February 1928) 1.
72 "Are They Leaders?" *Obiter Dicta* (3 April 1928) 2.
73 "The Parliament" *Obiter Dicta* (1 March 1928) 2.
74 "Are They Leaders?" above note 72 at 2.
75 "Mock Parliament Being Organized" *Obiter Dicta* (15 November 1935) 1.
76 "W.B. 'Bill' Bate Will Lead First School Cabinet," above note 70 at 1; "Conservatives, C.C.F., Independents Form Opposition," *Obiter Dicta* (15 January 1936) 1; "First Mock Parliament Holds Successful Sessions" *Obiter Dicta* (18 February 1936) 2; "Things to Come" *Obiter Dicta* (29 November 1937) 6.
77 "Things to Come," *ibid*.
78 "Osgoode Politics" *Obiter Dicta* (29 October 1937) 5 and "Things to Come" *Obiter Dicta* (15 January 1938) 8.

of the nation."[79] By 1953, the Osgoode model parliament was taking place at Queen's Park, but five years later it was starting to look like a mock parliament again; there was a 143-minute debate on a motion to establish a national lottery with profits going to charities, "sprinkled with dashes of poetry, a cue-card holding blonde model ... and a southern gambler complete with goatee."[80] By 1960 it had lost much of its attraction even as judges were invited to evaluate prepared speeches and award prizes.[81]

In Quebec, the model parliament was open to students of other faculties but was considered a complementary course permitting law students to overcome their nervousness and to practise the difficult art of speech, a quality required at the bar and in politics. It was an initiation to parliamentary rules and allowed students to debate current political issues. Through this significant tool, they were presumably training to steer their country to new heights of greatness and prosperity. The more talented orators might even have attracted the attention of prominent politicians in the audience.[82]

Despite the prevalent image of politicians as men, the small contingent of female law students at Dalhousie were involved in the model parliament as soon as they started attending the school in 1915, even comprising four cabinet members in 1924.[83] One of these was Grace Wambolt who acted as Minister of "Domestic Relations." She introduced a bill to tax bachelors for which she found little support, presumably because most of her classmates were themselves unmarried men.[84] At Osgoode female students were first involved in 1937 as speakers, but few made it to cabinet.[85] In 1953, Rainey Hunter acted as Master-at-Arms while, in 1956, Aileen Steel of the Conservative Party received a $25-award for presenting the best material during the divorce debate.[86] Noting the performance of three female representatives in

---

79 "Parliament Will Develop Leaders," above note 70 at 2.
80 "Osgoode News: Student Parliament, January 21, 1953" *Obiter Dicta* (Winter 1953) 41 and John Vojtech, "Model Parliament" *Obiter Dicta* (Spring 1959) 15.
81 "The Model Parliament" *Obiter Dicta* (New Series, 1960) n.p.
82 G.L., "Le Parlement Modèle" *Le Béret* (25 November 1921) 1; Achille Pettigrew, "Le Parlement Modèle" *Le Béret* (23 January 1920) n.p.; Yvan Beaudoin, "Parlement pour rire" *Le Quartier Latin* (12 March 1925) 6; Bizier, *L'Université de Montréal: la quête du savoir*, above note 9 at 77; and Normand, *Le droit comme discipline universitaire*, above note 9 at 82 and 117.
83 A.G. MaK., "Mock Parliament" *Dalhousie Gazette* (12 March 1924) 1.
84 M. Grace Wambolt, "In My Day at Dalhousie Law School" *Ansul: Special Edition, vol. 2* (December 1977) at 18.
85 "Extra-Curricula — Student Parliament" *Obiter Dicta* (19 February 1937) 2.
86 "Osgoode News: Student Parliament, January 21, 1953," above note 80 and Reginald Mori, "Osgoode Mock Parliament" *Obiter Dicta* (Winter 1956) 40.

1959, an *Obiter Dicta* reporter observed that none of them spoke during the debate, although one from the governing party spent the first hour of the session reading the program and the second sleeping.[87] At Laval and Montreal, women could attend as spectators to be charmed by the oratory talents of these budding politicians, some to the point of blushing purportedly to "the tip of their fingernails."[88] However, both schools' female law students were absent from the model parliament, presumably because of their very small numbers and the absence of a feminine tradition in party politics.

Debating was another activity that was strongly recommended for law students aspiring to a political career. At Dalhousie, because students were "aware of following in the footsteps of great men", they "[rated] brain-sharpening debates as a major sport."[89] At Osgoode Hall, they were advised that William Lyon Mackenzie King and Arthur Meighen, during their time at the University of Toronto, "had wisely prepared themselves for the future" by being active in debates and public speaking.[90] These activities helped students familiarize themselves with the clear delivery of their thoughts in front of an audience.[91] It taught them to express their views in a concise but forceful manner, one deemed essential for a lawyer's life in the public eye. They would have to deal with controversies and their special status in the community would require them to express their opinions on a variety of issues.[92] Women also participated in debates but in lower numbers, and their "feminine charms" seem to have attracted more attention than their eloquence.[93] During the Second World War when the level of activity had slowed down considerably due to a smaller student body, this kind of preparation was seen as a duty since "their presence as completely trained men of their profession will be essential to the era of reconstruction" after the war.[94]

---

87   Vojtech, "Model Parliament," above note 80 at 17.
88   Robbia, "Le Parlement Modèle" *Le Béret* (18 November 1927) 4; Amédée Caron, "La rentrée" *Le Béret* (9 January 1920) 1; and Margot, "Ils sont épatants!" *Le Béret* (29 October 1920) 3.
89   MacDonald, "The Brainiest School in the Country," above note 17 at 21.
90   "Parliament Will Develop Leaders," above note 70 at 2.
91   J.-Théo. Legault, "Chroniques des facultés: Faculté de droit" *Le Quartier Latin* (18 October 1928) 7.
92   R.L. Kayler, "Debating Activity Lacking at Osgoode: A Deplorable but Inevitable Fate" *Obiter Dicta* (December 1942) 2; Darrell Lang, "Law, a Splendid Training for Modern Business and Public Life, Says Writer: Article Three," above note 64 at 2; and "Editorial: Public Speaking and the Law School," above note 51 at 2.
93   "Débat en droit à St-Sulpice" *Le Quartier Latin* (19 February 1937) 3; "Debates" *Obiter Dicta* (29 February 1940) 5; and "Osgoode Hall Notes" *Obiter Dicta* (Spring 1944) 11.
94   R.L. Kayler, "Debating Activity Lacking at Osgoode," above note 92 at 2.

Involvement in school political organizations appeared to be another way students could prepare for politics. At Laval, both Jean Chrétien and Brian Mulroney were involved in such associations. The location of the law school close to the Legislative Assembly also facilitated meetings between students and Quebec politicians.[95] Osgoode Hall had Conservative, Gladstone (Liberal), and Mansfield (Cooperative Commonwealth Federation) clubs. Members were known for volunteering during elections, organizing, canvassing, appearing on platforms alongside candidates, or serving as clerks on election day.[96] All clubs also welcomed less politically inclined students looking to be "educated" by evaluating platforms and policies, but the primary goal was "to bring the students into intimate contact with the leading political stalwarts of the day."[97] Ontario Premier Howard Ferguson came to be known as the "patron saint" of the Osgoode Conservative Club, entertaining members with a reception at the Parliament Buildings. Although not created by the Conservative Party, Tory leaders were nonetheless said to hold the club in high esteem, presumably as a source of manpower at election time and also of possible future candidates.[98] Indeed, in its recruitment efforts, the club reminded students "that the young political enthusiasts of to-day are the members of Parliament and administrators of our countries [sic] affairs tomorrow."[99] Membership advantages included half-priced tickets for the Toronto Liberal-Conservative Business Men's Association luncheons and good seats at speaking events of prominent Conservatives in Toronto.[100]

At their monthly meetings, the Liberal and Conservative clubs invited prominent members of their respective parties (often politically active lawyers) to address various legal and current issues, including the role of lawyers in politics. For instance, Sir Thomas White, federal Finance Minister during the First World War "recommended the Bible, John Bunyan, and Bacon's Essays as the best training for public speech," suggested listening to good speakers, and advised members "to cultivate your own platform personality."[101]

---

95 Normand, *Le droit comme discipline universitaire*, above note 9 at 151–52.
96 "Tory Students Hear Leaders of Great Party" *Obiter Dicta* (23 January 1930) 3; "Gladstone Club Plans Activity for This Term" *Obiter Dicta* (23 January 1930) 1; "Conservative Club" *Obiter Dicta* (15 October 1934) 2; and "Clubs and Societies" *Obiter Dicta* (11 December 1939) 3.
97 "Tory Students Hear Leaders of Great Party," *ibid.* at 1 and "Osgoode Politics" *Obiter Dicta* (16 October 1936) 6.
98 "Osgoode Hall Conservative Club Non-partisan Organization" *Obiter Dicta* (13 November 1930) 3 and "Osgoode Politics," *Obiter Dicta* (16 October 1936) 6.
99 "Osgoode Politics," above note 97 at 6.
100 "Conservative Club" *Obiter Dicta* (15 October 1935) 2.
101 "Sir Thomas White at Albany Club" *Obiter Dicta* (1 March 1929) 3.

Speaking to Tory students in 1931, Charles McCrea, provincial Minister of Mines, urged them to do like him as an Osgoode graduate and participate in public life, either by running for office or working behind the scenes. At the annual dinner the same year, Leopold Macaulay, the new provincial secretary of the Conservative Party, stressed a similar message, inviting members of the audience to get involved in their riding associations. As future lawyers, they would be looked up to as members of a respected profession able to provide leadership and exercise influence on public opinion even if they were not the front men.[102] Addressing the Gladstone Club in 1934, future Ontario Chief Justice J.C. McRuer informed young Liberals that the party needed trained men to study the principles and policies of liberalism and maybe even force the party's leaders to adjust their views based on their discoveries.[103] There were women attending this meeting, but their gender apparently disqualified them for these tasks.

Indeed, Osgoode political clubs did have some female members and, although they were few in number, *Obiter Dicta* made a point of mentioning them. In 1928, it noted that Beatrice Van Wart was the new third-year representative for the Gladstone Liberals.[104] Of the first Liberal meeting of the academic year in October 1934, it observed that "even the feminine section of Osgoode Hall is represented, a fact worth of note in itself."[105] Then, in April 1935, another "tradition was broken" when Lola Boehmer attended a Conservative Club meeting. Finally, in 1938, the Gladstone Club elected Mary Gallagher as "ladies' representative," which was considered "an innovation" showing "the increased interest being taken by the fairer sex in Osgoode politics."[106]

However, the success and appeal of these political clubs waned by the 1940s. In 1942, *Obiter Dicta* reported that the clubs "have died natural deaths ... and few tears have been shed at their demise." It had become apparent that involvement in a political club took time away from studying law and offered little in terms of learning rhetorical skills when compared to the model parlia-

---

102 "Two Cabinet Ministers Address Osgoode Tories" *Obiter Dicta* (12 February 1931) at 1 and 4.
103 "Gladstone Club" *Obiter Dicta* (15 November 1934) 2.
104 "Gladstone Liberals Elect New Officers" *Obiter Dicta* (3 April 1928) 4.
105 "Gladstone Club" *Obiter Dicta* (15 October 1934) 2.
106 "Gladstone Liberals Elect New Officers," above note 104 at 4; Paul Dufresne, "Conservative Club" *Obiter Dicta* (15 April 1935) 2; and "Political Clubs" *Obiter Dicta* (21 April 1938) 5. Between 1928 and 1939, women represented approximately 4 percent of the enrollment at Osgoode Hall. See Mélanie Brunet, *Becoming Lawyers: Gender, Legal Education and Professional Identity Formation in Canada*, above note * at 130.

ment or debating.[107] In 1933, one student invited his classmates to re-evaluate their priorities; although public affairs and law were thought to go hand in hand, while they were busy "playing politics" they were not studying law.[108]

Presumably, other activities such as student politics could constitute additional training for public office, but they were not presented as such in the student press. Aspiring lawyers at Laval, Montreal, and Dalhousie were known to dominate this arena, but no direct link was made between elected positions and training for politics.[109] However, even a cursory look at the coverage of student elections at Osgoode Hall shows that women were not seriously considered as political players. Although there came to be women-designated positions in the Osgoode Legal and Literary Society, most were elected by acclamation, either showing a lack of interest among female students or reflecting their small numbers. When three women ran for first Vice-President of the "Legal and Lit" in 1932, *Obiter Dicta* described them as a group of "militant and enthusiastic females" with "plenty of (executive) experience and would look well receiving at the At Home." Meanwhile male candidates had the opportunity to present their individual achievements in their own voice.[110]

What was clear from the language used by professors, visiting lawyer-politicians, and students themselves was that public service and leadership were closely associated and this message was directed exclusively to men. Very rarely were women included in this rhetoric, as the frequent use of the word "men" demonstrates. Women's enrollment in law school was still low, but beyond the numbers, the discourse itself was infused with gendered ideas. Indeed, the type of commitment and service that was expected of these future lawyers was distinctly masculine in its public nature and exercise of power.[111]

---

107 Ralph Standish, "The Great American Game of 'Contacts'" *Obiter Dicta* (26 January 1933) 4; and "Notes and Comments" *Obiter Dicta* (April 1942) 3.
108 Standish, *ibid.* at 4.
109 Law students had a more flexible schedule than other students because many of their professors were also practitioners. As a result, classes were often held at the end of the afternoon, leaving time during the day to engage in extra-curricular activities (Dalhousie University Archives, Faculty of Law, MS-1-13, (G-57)), *Dean: Read, H.E. — Box of Miscellaneous Clippings — Law School, 1952–1961*, "Law School Enrollment Up; First Year Biggest Ever" *Dalhousie Gazette* (19 October 1954) 1; "The Voice of Law Students" *Dalhousie Gazette* (18 November 1952) 2; Sylvio Normand, "Tradition et modernité à la Faculté de droit de l'Université Laval de 1945 à 1965" 33 Les Cahiers de Droit 1 at 165; Nicole Neatby, *Carabins ou activistes*, above note 9 at 27; and Normand, *Le droit comme discipline universitaire*, above note 9 at 122.
110 "Large Field of Candidates Seek Office" *Obiter Dicta* (15 April 1932) 1.
111 For similar observations in the context of modern Britain, see: Matthew McCormack, "Introduction" in Matthew McCormack, ed., *Public Men: Masculinity and Politics in Modern Britain* (Houndmills, Basingstoke, Hampshire: Palgrave Macmillan, 2007) at 2–3.

During this period women were rarely associated with such leadership roles. They were believed to lack the mental and physical strength necessary to withstand the confrontational style of the courtroom, election campaigns, and political office. Associated with the exercise of power, both the legal profession and politics required oratorical prowess, reason, ambition, confidence, assertiveness, aggressiveness, and competitiveness. These traits were admired in men generally but were either thought to be lacking in women or conflicting with characteristics traditionally associated with them.[112]

Although women in Nova Scotia and Ontario gained the federal and provincial vote by the 1920s, it was a development that not everyone readily accepted.[113] Even after women won full political rights in 1929 when they legally qualified as "persons" under the *British North America Act*, their involvement beyond casting a ballot was often frowned upon since many people still believed women should not have a career outside the home or be exposed to the corrupting influence of politics. Therefore, the rough-and-tumble world of politics and public affairs was still deemed the domain of men. Some people thought women were not ready to hold public office because of their lack of experience. Others questioned their abilities to do the job because of a belief that women were mostly driven by their emotions while politics (and legal practice) required reason and logic, qualities "naturally" found in men.[114] Commenting on the only female member of Parliament in the 1930s, a student wrote in the *Dalhousie Gazette*: "Miss MacPhail is most informal and inconsistent — perhaps conforming to the characteristics of her sex — in her politics and decisions."[115] Thus, some men believed that women's involvement in political parties should be limited to "behind-the-scene" support-work, usually at the grassroots level.[116] They recruited volunteers, canvassed door-

---

112 Michael Grossberg, "Institutionalizing Masculinity: The Law as a Masculine Profession" in Mark C. Carnes and Clyde Griffen, eds., *Meanings for Manhood: Construction of Masculinity in Victorian America* (Chicago: University of Chicago Press, 1990) at 133–35, 137, 146, and 150; Matthew McCormack, "Introduction," *ibid.* at 5; and Kit Good, "'Quit Ye Like Men': Platform Manliness and Electioneering, 1895–1939" in Matthew McCormack, ed., *Public Men: Masculinity and Politics in Modern Britain* (Houndmills, Basingstoke, Hampshire: Palgrave Macmillan, 2007) at 144–45.
113 Women in Quebec gained the provincial franchise in 1940.
114 Sylvia B. Bashevkin, *Toeing the Lines: Women and Party Politics in English Canada*, 2d ed. (Toronto: Oxford University Press, 1993) at 12; and Ellen Louks Fairclough, *Saturday's Child: Memoirs of Canada's First Female Cabinet Minister* (Toronto: University of Toronto Press, 1995) at 71 and 80.
115 "Editorial: How, Miss MacPhail" *Dalhousie Gazette* (16 November 1933) 2.
116 Beth Light and Ruth Roach Pierson, eds., *No Easy Road: Women in Canada, 1920s to 1960s* (Toronto: New Hogtown Press, 1990) at 349; Fairclough, *Saturday's Child: Memoirs of Canada's First Female Cabinet Minister*, above note 114 at x and 76; and Joan Sangster,

to-door, did some fundraising, made coffee, and licked envelopes — a sexual division of labour comparable to that found in a society that largely excluded women from the decision-making process.[117] At a time when society was getting used to, and sometimes still rejected, the concept of women as voters, their contribution to the nation was to be made as "partial" citizens by raising the next generation of leaders, leaving them few options in formal politics or the legal profession.[118] Women such as Ottawa mayor Charlotte Whitton and first federal cabinet minister Ellen Fairclough clearly constituted exceptions, but they were examples that ordinary women were neither expected nor encouraged to follow.

* * * * *

PROMPTED TO ENTER THE political arena as public servants and makers of laws, lawyers were believed to be particularly well-trained to guide Canada's destiny. As students, their professors and prominent jurists, often involved in politics themselves, emphasized their duty as members of a noble profession to provide leadership in their community and beyond. Democratic society and good government demanded that able and intelligent men of law contribute their skills and knowledge to the benefit of the nation. Interestingly, most individuals promoting this link between law and politics in the examples cited were Conservatives, perhaps reinforcing their claim to patriotism and distancing themselves from the "feminine" values of reform associated with

---

"The Role of Women in the Early CCF, 1933–1940" in Linda Kealey and Joan Sangster, eds., *Beyond the Vote: Canadian Women and Politics* (Toronto: University of Toronto Press, 1989) at 123.

117 Patricia A. Myers, "'A Noble Effort': The National Federation of Liberal Women of Canada, 1928–1973" in *Beyond the Vote: Canadian Women and Politics*, ibid. at 46–47; Sangster, "The Role of Women in the Early CCF," ibid. at 123; and Dean Beeby, "Women in the Ontario C.C.F., 1940–1950," (1982) 74 Ontario History 4 at 261, 264–65. However, as Sangster suggests: "it is important to remember that this day-to-day support work was essential to the life of the party." Moreover, according to Karen Dubinski, some women found power and purpose in these traditionally feminine activities. Karen Dubinski, "'Who Do You Think Did the Cooking?' Baba in the Classroom" in Margaret Kechnie and Marge Reitsma-Street, eds., *Changing Lives: Women in Northern Ontario* (Toronto: Dundurn Press, 1996) at 194–95. For more on women's involvement in political parties, see Chapter 3: "The Higher the Fewer: Women's Participation in Major Party Organizations" in Bashevkin, *Toeing the Lines: Women and Party Politics in English Canada*, above note 114 at 65–92.

118 On the notion of women as substandard citizens despite the acquisition of the vote, see: Maro Pantelidou Maloutas, *The Gender of Democracy: Citizenship and Gendered Subjectivity* (London: Routledge, 2006) at 74–75 and Paul Ward, *Britishness Since 1870*, above note 53 at 39–40 and 47.

liberalism.[119] Male law students were groomed for political involvement in the classroom and extra-curricular activities. The model parliament, debating, and political clubs were considered especially valuable in mastering parliamentary procedure and public speaking, and establishing contacts with politicians.

Like the legal profession, politics constituted another male-dominated arena, both in numbers and through underlying gender assumptions. The call for lawyers to enter the political world was clearly aimed at men. In addition to the repeated use of "men" in their rhetoric, individuals who promoted this affinity between law and politics assumed desirable candidates possessed specific qualities: independence of means and of mind, reason, physical strength, confidence, and ambition. Women were believed to lack these traits, thus disqualifying them for leadership roles in the legal profession and politics, and reinforcing the link between power and masculinity.

However, by the 1960s, politics as a sideline for future lawyers had lost much of its appeal. When Liberal student Burke Doran invited his Osgoode classmates to be politically active, insisting that "Parliament, too, is a court," his message may have fallen on deaf ears.[120] As a third-year student observed in 1968, a larger part of the "Legal and Lit" budget was being allocated to the hockey team, while political clubs and debates were underfunded.[121] In fact, for this generation of students, politics was no longer the obvious choice for individuals wanting "to shape and manage the affairs of the community."[122] Other avenues, such as Legal Aid clinics, were open to more socially motivated students. For those seeking fame, politics became one occupation among others by which they could enhance their status. Furthermore, the legal profession was undergoing some important changes. With the expansion of the postwar economy and the increased intervention of the state in people's lives, lawyers found better-remunerated and more time-consuming opportunities. The specialized lawyer practising in a large firm or corporate setting progressively displaced the general practitioner working alone or in a small partnership. Under these circumstances, the lawyer did not necessarily have the time or occasion to establish contacts in the community and take on politics as a part-time occupation when public office increasingly demanded the full attention of its candidates.

---

119 For the association of liberals and liberalism with the feminization of American society during the Cold War, see: Cuordileone, *Manhood and American Political Culture in the Cold War*, above note 16.
120 Burke Doran, "Be a Politically Active Student" *Obiter Dicta* (November 1960) 10.
121 Brian G. Armstrong, "The Politics of Apathy" *Obiter Dicta* (January 1968) 1.
122 Cameron Harvey, "Letters to the Editors" *Obiter Dicta* (April 1964) 2.

These changes are visible in lawyers' rate of participation in politics in the twentieth century. For example, from 1920 to the late 1950s, consistently one-third of federal members of Parliament were trained in the law, but this proportion dropped to one-quarter between 1962 and 1984, and since then to an average of 16 percent.[123] Although law is still the most common occupation among politicians, it is no longer considered the only discipline suitable for the training of political elites.[124]

---

123 Based on data from Library of Parliament, Information and Documentation Branch, "Parliamentary Internet: Senators and Members — Occupations of Parliamentarians," online: www.parl.gc.ca (9 February 2004 and 21 September 2007). This trend was also noted in Henrique Urbano, Hubert Reid, and Roland Bélanger, "Les motivations des étudiants de la faculté de droit de l'Université Laval" (Université Laval, Faculté de Droit, May 1972) 38 [unpublished].

124 Normand, *Le droit comme discipline universitaire*, above note 9 at 234.

PART 2

HISTORICAL REFLECTIONS ON THE PRACTICE OF LAW

CHAPTER 5

Stratification, Economic Adversity, and Diversity in an Urban Bar: Halifax, Nova Scotia, 1900–1950

PHILIP GIRARD AND JEFFREY HAYLOCK[*]

INTRODUCTION

MUCH OF THE LITERATURE on the history of the legal profession in Canada falls into one of two categories: studies of a particular provincial bar, or law firm histories, although Wes Pue has explored the ideologies and self-perceptions of the bar at the national level.[1] Studies of urban bars are largely missing from the Canadian literature, and indeed from the literature of other common law countries.[2] Even the term is slightly unfamiliar in the Canadian context, given the dominance of provincial law societies on the professional landscape. Yet there is good reason, especially if one is studying the twen-

---

[*] The authors would like to thank the firm of Borden Ladner Gervais, whose student fellowship program supported the research for this chapter.

[1] W. Wesley Pue, "Common Law Legal Education in Canada's Age of Light, Soap and Water" in DeLloyd J. Guth and W. Wesley Pue, eds., *Canada's Legal Inheritances* (Winnipeg: University of Manitoba, 2001) (in spite of the title, much of the article deals with the goals of the Canadian Bar Association); "In Pursuit of Better Myth: Lawyers' Histories and Histories of Lawyers" (1995) 33 Alta. L. Rev. 730; "Cultural Projects and Structural Transformation in the Canadian Legal Profession" in W. Wesley Pue and David Sugarman, eds., *Lawyers and Vampires: Cultural Histories of Legal Professions* (Oxford: Hart, 2003).

[2] Although focused on a single law firm, G. Blaine Baker's study "Law Practice and Statecraft in Mid-Nineteenth-Century Montreal: The Torrance-Morris Firm, 1848 to 1868" in Carol Wilton, ed., *Beyond the Law: Lawyers and Business in Canada 1830 to 1930* (Toronto: University of Toronto Press for the Osgoode Society, 1990) contains suggestive insights about the role of the Montreal bar as a whole.

tieth-century legal profession, to isolate urban bars as an object of study. It is trite to observe that the large law firm, which emerged in the 1880s and rapidly came to dominate the professional scene, is a phenomenon present only in large cities. There are no large law firms in Medicine Hat, Alberta or Woodstock, New Brunswick. The phenomenal growth in legal work afforded by the presence of large corporations and big government in the larger urban centres, as much or more than their growing population, has attracted lawyers to them for well over a century. This seems so obvious as to be almost devoid of interest, and yet, as Dale Brawn's work on Winnipeg — one of the few serious studies of an urban bar — has shown, there is much to be learned about the growth, governance, self-image, and ideals of the legal profession by taking the bar of a particular city as one's point of departure.[3] As well as helping to illuminate these internal matters, the relationship of urban bars to their hinterland can be used to shed light on urban-rural tensions more generally, and on the growth of cities as nodes of power and innovation in contemporary globalized society.

The goal of this paper is rather more modest and exploratory. We are interested in three challenges posed to the Halifax bar in the first half of the twentieth century: the rapid rise to prominence of several large law firms, which created a new form of professional stratification; the relatively sudden, serious, and ultimately protracted economic decline of the city after the First World War; and, finally, the "diversity challenge" provided by the entry of non-traditional lawyers (women, blacks, and ethno-religious minorities) into the profession. While economic decline was experienced province-wide, large law firms existed only in Halifax and non-traditional lawyers were mostly (although not exclusively) present there.[4] After introducing the city, its economy, and the contours of its bar, we explore the effects and meaning of stratification by analyzing the participation of different legal actors (large firms, traditional two- and three-person firms, and sole practitioners) in legal education, professional governance, and judicial appointments. We then de-

---

3   Dale Brawn, "Dominant Professionals: The Role of Large-Firm Lawyers in Manitoba" in Carol Wilton, ed., *Inside the Law: Canadian Law Firms in Historical Perspective* (Toronto: University of Toronto Press for the Osgoode Society, 1996). There is modest US literature, mostly uncritical and celebratory: Robert B. Bell, *The Philadelphia Lawyer: A History, 1735–1945* (Selinsgrove, PA: Susquehanna University Press, 1992); Jay Brandon, *Law and Liberty: A History of the Legal Profession in San Antonio* (Dallas: San Antonio Bar Association, 1996); James Summerville, *Colleagues on the Cumberland: A History of the Nashville Legal Profession* (Dallas: Taylor, 1996).

4   Sydney had one four-person firm for some years in the 1920s, but it was not maintained at this size.

scribe and analyze the growing diversity of the bar of the interwar years, paying particular attention to the role of those same legal actors in helping or hindering the diversity phenomenon.

HALIFAX: THE URBAN CONTEXT, 1900–1950

HALIFAX WAS A MEDIUM-SIZED city by Canadian standards at the turn of the century, with a population of some 50,968 souls.[5] Manufacturing employed the largest number of people, but the army and navy were also significant employers. British troops withdrew in 1906, but as of 1910 Halifax became the principal base for the Canadian naval service and the "centre of operations and manpower for the regular component of the Canadian army."[6] It was home to the provincial capital and also hosted most of the province's hospital facilities and several institutions of post-secondary education, including the new Nova Scotia Technical College, which opened its doors in 1909. Although the Bank of Nova Scotia moved its headquarters from Halifax to Toronto in 1900, the city was still home to a number of successful banks and trust companies, and the Royal Securities Corporation (RSC). Founded in 1903, RSC became a vehicle for the creation and promotion of all manner of corporate enterprises in Canada, Mexico, and the Caribbean.[7] The city's middle class faced the new century with confidence and optimism, and members of its progressive wing were seriously engaged in the issues of civic and moral reform being debated across North America. This wave of reformism culminated in a 1911 plebiscite that led to the adoption of a "board of control" model of city government, one that promised increased efficiency and better planning in the administration of municipal affairs.[8]

---

5   For this and subsequent years we have used the figure for a larger census division around Halifax-Dartmouth than is usually employed in order to capture the potential client base for lawyers resident in the capital. This larger figure is used when calculating lawyer-population ratios later in the paper. See Table 3, Appendix for the actual figures used.
6   Judith Fingard, Janet Guildford, and David Sutherland, *Halifax: The First 250 Years* (Halifax: Nimbus, 1999) at 121. The sketch of the city's history in this and the subsequent paragraph is largely drawn from this work.
7   Gregory P. Marchildon, "International Corporate Law from a Maritime Base: The Halifax Firm of Harris, Henry, and Cahan" in Carol Wilton, ed., *Beyond the Law: Lawyers and Business in Canada 1830–1930* (Toronto: University of Toronto Press for the Osgoode Society, 1990). Although RSC moved its headquarters to Montreal in fairly short order, it retained an important presence in Halifax.
8   The experiment ended in 1919, however, when a second plebiscite reinstated the traditional form of city government: Henry Roper, "The Halifax Board of Control: the Failure of Municipal Reform, 1906–1919" (1985) 14 Acadiensis 2 at 48.

During the First World War, with former Halifax lawyer Robert Borden serving as prime minister of the country, the city experienced its customary, war-induced prosperity. Unfortunately, the metaphoric economic boom was followed by the largest man-made "boom" in history (prior to 1945) when the French munitions ship *Mont Blanc* exploded in the harbour on 6 December 1917. Some 2000 persons were killed, 9,000 injured, and the industries concentrated in the northern suburb of Richmond were largely destroyed. The explosion proved to be only the most dramatic harbinger of the city's postwar economic decline. With the war's end, a Canada-wide recession hit Halifax particularly hard. During the 1920s the city lost nearly half its manufacturing jobs to corporate mergers that concentrated industrial production in central Canada; the Depression, experienced as a shock in the rest of Canada, was merely another shade of grey in the Maritimes and in Halifax. Nonetheless, the city's population continued to grow at a steady pace, more than doubling between 1921 and 1951, when it reached 138,427, and doubling its share of the provincial population over the half-century, from 10 percent in 1901 to 21.5 percent in 1951.

THE CONTOURS OF THE HALIFAX BAR, 1900–1950

IN A SENSE, THE Halifax bar in 1900 had still not regained, in quantitative terms, the pre-eminence it had enjoyed much earlier in its history. In the eighteenth and early nineteenth centuries, the Halifax bar and the Nova Scotia bar were virtually synonymous, as very few lawyers could be found outside the capital. In the 1820s this began to change, and for the next half-century the bar spread out to virtually every settlement of any size around the province. Halifax's proportion of the provincial bar thus dropped from about half in the 1840s, to 45 percent by 1860, to 36 percent by 1890, and there it would stay until 1940, when it edged up to 40 percent — after that it never looked back.[9] Although Halifax became home to a larger proportion of the provincial bar over the period, the extent to which the city's population was over-represented in its access to lawyers compared to areas outside Halifax actually declined: where Halifax was home to only 11 percent of the province's population but 37 percent of its lawyers in 1900, in 1950 it was home to 21.5 percent of Nova Scotia's population but only 40 percent of its lawyers.

---

9 On the nineteenth-century bar, see Philip Girard, "The Roots of a Professional Renaissance: Lawyers in Nova Scotia, 1850–1910" (1991) 20 Man. L.J. 148; "The Maritime Provinces, 1850–1939: Lawyers and Legal Institutions" (1995) 23 Man. L.J. 380; and *Patriot Jurist: Beamish Murdoch of Halifax* (Ph.D. dissertation, Dalhousie University, 1998).

The bar of the city of Winnipeg, by way of contrast, tended to dominate its province more than its Halifax counterpart. Winnipeg was home to between two-thirds and three-quarters of the provincial bar by 1910, reflecting the population dominance of the Manitoba capital over its hinterland; after 1910, the city never held less than 42 percent of the province's entire population.[10] Over the half-century after 1900 Halifax would never again have as many lawyers as the 118 it had in that year (see Table One, Appendix). Even though the population of the city nearly tripled by 1950, the absolute number of lawyers declined by 1, to 117. The absolute number of lawyers forms a U-shaped curve over the period, with a sharp drop in the first two decades, stability at the bottom of the "U" over the 1920s, then fairly rapid growth in the 1930s, levelling off in the 1940s. The disappearance of more than a quarter of the city's bar in the first two decades of the twentieth century is especially surprising given that the city's economic and population growth were relatively strong over that period. Halifax's population grew by 13 percent in the first decade of the century and by nearly a third in the second. One would expect at least a deceleration in the growth of the bar over the 1910s given the low numbers of new candidates for the bar during the war years, and the loss of some Halifax lawyers on the battlefield. But what we see in the first two decades of the twentieth century is significant shrinkage in absolute numbers, not simply slower growth.

At first glance, it is tempting to explain this dramatic decline as due to the lure of the West. Significant migration of Nova Scotian lawyers westward did occur in the first two decades of the twentieth century. Many young men who might have been recruited to the Halifax bar in the early twentieth century ended up in Vancouver, Winnipeg, Edmonton, and a whole host of small towns in Saskatchewan, from Oxbow to Saltcoats. This phenomenon had begun slowly in the closing years of the nineteenth century but accelerated rapidly in the decade from 1905 to 1914, when at least 92 Nova Scotian lawyers went to the West, then tailed off quickly during the war and immediate postwar years such that, by the 1920s, emigration out West had almost stopped (see Table Two, Appendix). A much smaller out-migration process continued, but with different destinations: Montreal, Ontario, and New York.[11]

A comparison with patterns in other North American centres shows that the decline in numbers in the first two decades of the century, far from being

---

10 Dale Brawn, "Dominant Professionals," above note 3.
11 Numbers and movements of the bar have been derived from *Belcher's Farmer's Almanac* from 1900 until it ceased publication in 1930, *The Canadian Law List* (1900–1950), *The Canadian Almanac* (1900–1950), and the Nova Scotia barristers' rolls held at Nova Scotia Archives and Records Management [NSARM].

unique to Halifax, was being widely experienced. Curtis Cole's work on the Ontario bar has shown growth rates for the first two decades of the twentieth century of -2.5 percent and -0.9 percent, respectively.[12] And a national-level US study of lawyer-population ratios over this period shows exactly the same trend of a peak in the supply of lawyers in 1900, followed by a steady drop down to 1920.[13] Halifax's experience was more dramatic, with a drop from 2.32 lawyers per 1000 population in 1900 to 1.13 in 1920, but was essentially in line with the US trend which saw a drop from 1.5 to 1.1 over the same period (see Table Three, Appendix). Several scholars have suggested that this relative decline in the lawyer population is tied to a decreased resort to litigation and an overall "systemic stabilization" in the late nineteenth century that saw the amount of debt litigation drop substantially.[14] The ongoing decline in the amount of litigation commenced in the Supreme Court and the County Court at Halifax suggests that this factor does indeed have some power to explain the shrinkage evident in the Halifax bar.[15]

It was in the 1920s and 30s that patterns in Halifax diverged most sharply from those elsewhere. By 1920, the slimmed-down Halifax bar reached a degree of stability within its environment. Membership barely changed in the 1920s, then, somewhat surprisingly, jumped by a third in the 1930s, only to plateau again in the 1940s, just before the surge in veterans turning to legal careers would inflate the size of the Halifax bar substantially in the early 1950s. Elsewhere, things developed in the interwar years in a way opposite to that in Halifax: growth in the 1920s and shrinkage in the 1930s, instead of the other way around. The pattern in Halifax did not reflect broader trends

---

12   Curtis Cole, "A Developmental Market: Growth Rates, Competition and Professional Standards in the Ontario Legal Profession, 1881–1936" (1984) 7 Can.-U.S. L.J. 231. Useful overviews of Canadian trends can be found in John P. Nelligan, "Lawyers in Canada: A Half-Century Count" (1950) 28 Can. Bar Rev. 727, and in David Stager and Harry W. Arthurs, *Lawyers in Canada* (Toronto: Statistics Canada and University of Toronto Press, 1990) c. 6.
13   Terence C. Halliday, "Six Score Years and Ten: Demographic Transitions in the American Legal Profession, 1850–1980" (1986) 20 Law & Society Rev. 53.
14   For example, Robert Kagan, "The Routinization of Debt Collection: An Essay on Social Change and Conflict in the Courts" (1984) 18 Law & Society Rev. 323.
15   Philip Girard, "The Supreme Court of Nova Scotia: Confederation to the Twenty-First Century" in Philip Girard, Jim Phillips, and Barry Cahill, eds., *The Supreme Court of Nova Scotia 1754–2004: From Imperial Bastion to Provincial Oracle* (Toronto: University of Toronto Press for the Osgoode Society, 2004) at 157–59. A modest increase in litigation in the Halifax Supreme Court between 1900 and 1925 amounted to a negative growth rate given the population increase over the period, while the slow absolute decline in county court litigation represented a more significant decline when population growth is factored in.

among the number of lawyers called to the provincial bar: coincidentally, exactly the same number of people — 169 — were called in the 1930s as in the 1920s. It is just that few of these new lawyers stayed to practise law in Halifax in the 1920s, whereas substantial numbers of them did so in the 1930s. At the moment we have no easy answer for this; more detailed research on the cohorts of the 1920s and 30s will be required to solve this puzzle.

THE ROLE OF LAW FIRMS IN HALIFAX

AS THE WORK OF Greg Marchildon and Barry Cahill has shown, Halifax lawyers were quick to adopt the law firm form of professional organization in the 1880s and 1890s in order to service the new corporate interests that emerged with Nova Scotia's industrial revolution, and they continued to exploit those opportunities in the twentieth century.[16] Those who trace the emergence of "large" law firms typically use a cutoff of four or five lawyers to denote large firms at this time, and we will use four.[17] We will refer to three types of professional configuration: sole practitioners; "traditional firms," by which we mean two- or three-person firms; and large firms as just defined. By 1900 Halifax was already reasonably well-endowed with large firms, having three four-person firms, one five-person firm, and one seven-person firm. By 1920 there were no longer any four-person firms, but the "big three" had emerged with six lawyers apiece: Henry, Rogers, Harris & Stewart (ancestor of today's Stewart McKelvey); McInnes, Jenks, Lovett & MacDonald (ancestor of today's McInnes Cooper); and Maclean, Paton, Burchell & Ralston (ancestor of today's Burchell Hayman Parish, though the last has been superceded as one of the "big three" by Cox & Palmer). These three firms with their eighteen lawyers alone represented over a fifth (21 percent) of the down-sized Halifax bar. We are also going to include a fourth firm, Pearson, Covert & Rutledge, in our "big-firm" count for at least some purposes, in spite of its being under the four-person cutoff, because of its extensive corporate clientele.

---

16 Gregory P. Marchildon and Barry Cahill, "Corporate Entrepreneurship in Atlantic Canada: The Stewart Law Firm, 1915–1955" in Carol Wilton, *Inside the Law*, above note 3; Barry Cahill, *The Thousandth Man: A Biography of James McGregor Stewart* (Toronto: University of Toronto Press for the Osgoode Society, 2000); Barry Cahill, ed., *Frank Manning Covert: Fifty Years in the Practice of Law* (Montreal and Kingston: McGill-Queen's University Press, 2005).
17 Wayne Hobson, "Symbol of the New Profession: The Emergence of the Large Law Firm, 1870–1915" in Gerard W. Gawalt, *The New High Priests: Lawyers in Post-Civil War America* (Westport, CT: Greenwood Press, 1984).

The biggest shift over this period, however, was the decline in two-person partnerships. Representing 29 percent of the Halifax bar in 1900, their share of the profession fell constantly, reaching only 11 percent by 1950 (see Table Five, Appendix). Brawn found a similar, albeit not quite as substantial, decline in Winnipeg.[18] By 1920 the essential shape of the Halifax bar was set for the next several decades: roughly 50 percent of lawyers were solo practitioners, 20 percent were in large firms, and the other 30 percent were in traditional firms (partnerships of two or three lawyers). The big four proved remarkably resilient over the difficult interwar decades. Two maintained their six-lawyer complement down to 1950, the Pearson firm grew to four in the 1940s, and the Stewart firm grew to ten lawyers. And these four were joined by two new four-person firms that had expanded from smaller entities. Halifax's largest firm usually just missed being in the top ten largest law firms in Canada; in the early 1950s, for example, the Stewart firm had ten lawyers while the smallest of the top ten firms, Aikins MacAulay of Winnipeg, had twelve.[19]

The four large firms continued to service the needs of local companies, such as Eastern Trust, Nova Scotia Steel and Coal, and Nova Scotia Light and Power, both nationally and internationally, but also represented companies with head offices outside the region, such as the Royal Bank of Canada, Famous Players, and the Canadian Pacific Railway. In carrying out this work, lawyers at these firms often became directly involved in the business activities of their clients, whether through serving on their boards of directors or otherwise. It is sometimes suggested that in so doing they internalized the business values of these clients, possibly to the detriment of legal values, and that they in turn sought to redefine the profession in their own image through control of various legal institutions. Brawn suggests that large-firm lawyers dominated the Manitoba Law School, the Manitoba Law Society, and appointments to the judiciary almost to the exclusion of other sections of the Winnipeg bar, with the result that the values of a small elite "became the values of an entire bar."[20] Whatever the truth of this statement for Winnipeg — and we will suggest that, even for the Manitoba capital, it is somewhat overdrawn — such does not appear to have been the case in Halifax for any of these three areas of legal endeavour.

Before looking at the role of large firms in these three fields, however, we wish to critique the model within which this inquiry has usually been con-

---

18 Dale Brawn, "Dominant Professionals," above note 3 at 397.
19 Curtis Cole, *Osler, Hoskin and Harcourt: Portrait of a Partnership* (Toronto: McGraw-Hill, 1995) at 301–2.
20 *Ibid.* at 420.

ducted. Studies such as Brawn's focus on formal mechanisms of control and influence to the exclusion of informal mechanisms and larger cultural patterns. Even if we found large-firm lawyers playing dominant roles in the legal profession's formal institutions, our inquiry would not be complete unless we explored how that authority was experienced, how legitimate it was, whether it inspired resistance, and so on. Likewise, finding a balance of large firm, traditional firm, and sole practitioners in the legal profession's formal institutions does not necessarily mean that a business-driven, corporate-oriented mentality was not highly influential. Such attitudes may be more commonly encountered in large firms, but they are not necessarily absent from other professional configurations. Much depends on the surrounding environment. If business endeavours are constantly lauded and business leaders frequently eulogized in public fora and the media, as they were in the 1920s and 30s, it would be unusual if both aspirant and practising lawyers, whatever their practice type, did not absorb some of this atmosphere.

With that in mind, let us turn to the role of large firms in the institutional legal life of Halifax. Large firms supplied lecturers to Dalhousie Law School in numbers disproportionate to their proportion of the Halifax bar, but they did not exclude sole practitioners or lawyers from two-person firms to nearly the same extent as seems to have occurred at the Manitoba Law School.[21] Apart from the anomalous 1910s, sole practitioners or lawyers from two-person firms always formed between 20 percent and 30 percent of the lecturers at Dalhousie Law School (see Table Six, Appendix). Perhaps more importantly, the deans at Dalhousie were always full-time professors, seldom came from large firms, and sometimes did not come from law practice at all. By contrast, deans at Manitoba were often part-time, usually came from large Winnipeg firms, and often retained their ties to those firms during their deanships.

To be sure, the difference in the timing of the foundation of the two law schools led to two quite different institutions. When Dalhousie Law School was founded by members of the bar in 1883, it was created just before the large law firm became part of the professional scene. Its founders did not belong to large firms, nor did most of its deans. Dean Weldon came directly from academe, and while his successor Dean MacRae came from a Toronto law firm, he had only just entered the practice of law after fifteen years in academe as a student and then a professor at Cornell and Princeton. Dalhousie's third dean, John Read, came from the Halifax firm of Henry, Rogers, Har-

---

21 Ibid. Dale Brawn, *Dominant Professionals*, above note 3, states that lecturers from two-person firms formed only 10 percent of Manitoba Law School lecturers from 1941–59 but does not give figures for the earlier period.

ris & Stewart, as it then was, but he was in many ways the most academic and least practice-oriented of all of Dalhousie's early deans. He had been a Rhodes Scholar, achieved a double-first at Oxford, and ultimately resigned from the deanship to take up a position first in the Department of External Affairs, and later a judgeship on the International Court of Justice. Sidney Smith started teaching at the law school only a year after his own graduation and did only a bit of part-time practice before becoming dean in 1929. And his successor, Vincent Macdonald (dean from 1934–50), was lured back to Dalhousie after a decade spent variously in a large firm in Toronto (he had also practised with the Burchell firm in Halifax in the early 1920s), legal publishing, conducting research for a royal commission, and serving as secretary to the prime minister. Perhaps just as important in shaping the identity of the law school as the background of its deans was the character of its second in command for nearly four decades, Benjamin Russell. Russell practised law in a desultory fashion until his appointment to the bench in 1904, but it was as a legal educator and member of Parliament that he was primarily known to contemporaries.[22]

By the time the Manitoba Law School was founded in 1914, the large law firm was already an established fixture on the Winnipeg legal landscape. The men most associated with its founding, James Aikins, Hugh Robson, and E.K. Williams, were partners in the prestigious Aikins, MacAulay firm, and they continued to be associated with the law school throughout their careers. This large-firm influence had its positive features: Wesley Pue has noted that the Manitoba Law School was at the cutting edge of curricular and pedagogic developments in its early years, in part thanks to the vision of some large-firm lawyers.[23] But the bipartite governance structure put in place in 1914 — a board of trustees appointed half by the university and half by the bar — meant that the Manitoba Law School was not nearly as autonomous from the bar as Dalhousie, which was securely anchored in the university. What the bar could give — a creative push in the 1910s and early 20s — it could also take away. In 1927, for reasons that are still somewhat obscure, the board of trustees decided that a return to the concurrent model of legal education, with half the day spent in a law office and half in lectures, was advisable. And with

---

22 See the entry by Philip Girard on Russell, *Dictionary of Canadian Biography*, vol. XVI (Toronto: University of Toronto Press, forthcoming 2012).

23 W. Wesley Pue, "'The Disquisitions of Learned Judges': Making Manitoba Lawyers, 1885–1931" in G. Blaine Baker and Jim Phillips, eds., *Essays in the History of Canadian Law, vol. VIII, in Honour of R.C.B. Risk* (Toronto: University of Toronto Press for the Osgoode Society, 1999) at 520–36.

that, Manitoba turned away from the mainstream of Canadian legal education until 1965.

As for large-firm dominance in the Nova Scotia Barristers' Society, there were definite tendencies in this direction in the late nineteenth and early twentieth century, exemplified by the long tenures (1896–1903) of corporate lawyer Robert Borden, a member of Halifax's largest and most prestigious law firm, as president of the Society, and Arthur Drysdale as vice-president. But both the Society's governance structure and a certain reaction by the membership to Borden's long presidential tenure permitted a return to a more democratic regime. Only in the 1880s and 90s had the Society made the transition from an old boys' social club to a modern organization exercising delegated legislative powers over admission, discipline, and professional standards.[24] This late start was beneficial in some ways, as the Society was able to begin with a clean slate. There were no benchers as such, life or otherwise. The management of the Society was put in the hands of a council consisting of the president, vice-president, and a secretary-treasurer, plus at least seven other members.[25] It met monthly and carried on most of the Society's business.

It is true that there was no prohibition on council members re-offering, which led to Borden's seven-year presidency, but this in turn inspired some discontent. First, the county members challenged Halifax's ascendancy in the affairs of the Society: the council was doubled from a dozen members to twenty-four in 1904, with each county outside Halifax electing one member, except for Cape Breton County, which had two. This could be done without legislation because the Society's statute required only that there be "at least" seven council members in addition to the table officers and any *ex officio* members.[26] The significance of this expansion was probably mostly symbolic because the monthly meetings of council continued to be attended only by the seven Halifax members as a rule, but the appearance of enhanced accountability seems to have satisfied the non-Halifax members. Then, in 1908 the

---

24 Girard, "The Roots of a Professional Renaissance," above note 9. The Law Society of Upper Canada, by contrast, exercised statutory powers from its foundation in 1797.

25 *Barristers and Solicitors Act*, S.N.S. 1899, c. 27. The secretary and treasurer positions could be combined and usually were. A small number of *ex officio* members also sat on the council. The chief justice was one of these between 1910 and 1929; thereafter, only the attorney general sat *ex officio* until 1946, when the dean of the law school was formally added. The dean seems to have sat on council as one of the elected Halifax members for some decades before that, however.

26 Nova Scotia Barristers' Society (NSBS) minutes, NSARM, microfilm reels 14743-48, minutes of March 1904. Future references will be by date only. In some years Victoria County had no representative because there were no lawyers practising there.

Society sought and received two important amendments to its constituent legislation. One prohibited a president from serving more than two consecutive one-year terms before sitting out two years. The second provided that no more than one member from any firm of solicitors should be eligible for election to any council position. The pattern of serving two one-year terms as president and not re-offering later became regular as clockwork over the next four decades. Contested elections in 1908 and 1909 ushered in a period where large-firm representation on the council almost disappeared. It crept back in but remained in balance throughout the half-century with lawyers practising alone and those in traditional partnerships. Representatives of all these groups regularly achieved the presidency after 1920 and were well-represented on council[27] (see Table Seven, Appendix).

In the 1930s, rural-urban tensions overshadowed big-firm/small-firm issues. In 1930 the possibility of having the annual general meeting in Truro in 1931 was discussed, but the matter was left to the council to decide (which it did, in the negative). Requests from the county bars that annual general meetings should be held throughout the province and that non-Haligonians should be elected as president from time to time were discussed frequently in the later 1930s and early 1940s. In 1939 the enlarged council was finally statutorily recognized: it would comprise seven elected members from Halifax, two from Cape Breton County, and one from each of the remaining sixteen counties. Each year, the two longest-serving representatives from Halifax would have to step down to allow the entrance of fresh blood. In 1946 the interests of county lawyers were further advanced when the Society created a second vice-presidency reserved for a member from outside Halifax. At the same time, the ban on sitting out after holding office for two years was extended from two years to five.[28] And finally, in 1952, an AGM was held outside Halifax for the first time, at the Digby Pines resort on the Bay of Fundy.

Christopher Moore has observed that the early-twentieth-century benchers of the Law Society of Upper Canada tended to be "prominent, wealthy members of establishment law firms and to have something like life tenure once elected to convocation."[29] Brawn goes further, asserting that "a relatively small group of Winnipeg lawyers ... exercised nearly absolute control

---

27 *An Act to amend Chapter 64, Revised Statutes 1900, Entitled "The Barristers' and Solicitors' Act,"* S.N.S. 1908, c. 23.

28 *An Act to Amend and Consolidate Chapter 112 of The Revised Statutes, 1923, "The Barristers' and Solicitors' Act,"* S.N.S. 1939, c. 9; *An Act to Amend Chapter 9 of the Acts of 1939, The Barristers' and Solicitors' Act,* S.N.S. 1946, c. 44.

29 *The Law Society of Upper Canada and Ontario's Lawyers 1797–1997* (Toronto: University of Toronto Press, 1997) at 203.

[until the 1930s] over both the Law Society of Manitoba and the province's system of legal education."[30] Large-firm influence over the provincial law society seems much less marked in the Nova Scotia context, largely as a result of decisions about the governance of the Society taken in the 1880s. The absence of life-benchers and the reforms of the early 1900s meant that it was rather more difficult for a large-firm oligarchy to assert its will over the Society even if it had wanted to do so. After the Borden-Drysdale years, tenures on council tended to be relatively short, in the range of four to six years. This rotation also made it easier for some non-traditional lawyers to find a place on council. Grace Wambolt thus became the first female member of council in 1945, thirty years before a female bencher would be elected to the Law Society of Upper Canada. Vincent Pottier became the first Acadian member of council when elected as the non-Halifax vice-president in 1946, and although no Jewish lawyer made it on to council before 1950, in 1943 council regularly began appointing Jewish lawyers to conduct the annual audit of the Society's books. Black lawyers would have to wait much longer, however, to appear on the council.

Members of large firms did not feature unduly among Nova Scotian appointments to the judiciary either — probably because by the 1920s many large-firm lawyers preferred the combination of wealth, power, status, and intellectual challenge of their current positions to the rather feeble lure of the bench. The path to the bench in Nova Scotia generally lay through political service of some kind, rather than large-firm service.[31] The two might, but need not necessarily, overlap. It was also the case that large-firm lawyers were, in a sense, structurally disadvantaged by being all located in Halifax. Precisely because the link between political patronage and judicial appointment was so strong, appointments had to be spread around the province, and non-Halifax lawyers counted for nearly two-thirds of the provincial bar through most of the period. Of the twenty-four appointees to the Nova Scotia Supreme Court during our period, no fewer than six had held the office of attorney general (five provincial, one federal), and only one of these had been associated with a large firm for any length of time; a further six had been members of Parlia-

---

30   Dale Brawn, "Dominant Professionals," above note 3 at 419.
31   On twentieth-century appointments to the Nova Scotia Supreme Court, see generally Philip Girard, "The Supreme Court from Confederation to the 21st Century" and R. Blake Brown and Susan Jones, "A Collective Biography of the Supreme Court Judiciary of Nova Scotia, 1900–2000" both in Girard, Phillips, and Cahill, *Supreme Court of Nova Scotia 1754–2004*, above note 15; Charles E. Haliburton, *A Biographical History of the Judges of Nova Scotia, 1754–2004: Illustrated and with Some Notes on Nova Scotia Court Houses* (Kentville, NS: Judges of Nova Scotia, 2004).

ment or members of the Legislative Assembly. Only seven, or 29 percent, of these judges had practised with a large firm, and it is important to note that three of these were all appointed by one prime minister: Robert Borden, the only large-firm lawyer to occupy the prime ministerial chair during this period until Louis St-Laurent in 1948. Of his ten appointments, Mackenzie King appointed only three men who came from large firms. It is true that large firms were over-represented among the Halifax appointments, with seven out of twelve such appointments coming from large firms, but the remainder had been associated with small firms.

Number-crunching alone is insufficient to appreciate the unfortunate impact a few large-firm lawyers had on the Nova Scotia judiciary during the interwar years. It was undoubtedly two of Borden's appointments, Robert Harris and Humphrey Mellish, whom J.S. Woodsworth had in mind when he declared in Parliament in 1924 that "corporation influence on the [Supreme Court] was so strong that the court is looked upon by labour as a company department."[32] But not all large-firm lawyers were tarred with the same brush. Tecumseh Sherman Rogers, who had belonged to the same firm as Chief Justice Harris, was regarded by some as the "most honest and fearless" member of the court in the 1920s.[33] While necessarily impressionistic, this evidence suggests that judicial behaviour was assessed based on what judges actually did, not what their background had been.

We suggested earlier that the dominance of large law firms on the Winnipeg scene was perhaps less complete than has been alleged. It is a rather serious claim that large-firm and other lawyers in Winnipeg "did not share a common professional experience," as Brawn states, and one that is rather difficult to credit without hearing a little more from those small-firm lawyers who are supposed to be on the receiving end of the marginalization process initiated by larger firms. Did large and small-firm lawyers in Winnipeg not participate in meetings and rituals by which they affirmed their solidarity as members of a common profession? Admittedly, such rituals often have an element of reinforcing the status quo, even where it contains imbalances of power. But unless there was an epidemic of false consciousness afflicting early-twentieth-century lawyers in Nova Scotia, what are we to make of the constant meetings at which deceased members and judges were honoured, and of the evolving rituals of solidarity that characterized the annual meetings of the Barristers' Society?

---

32 Cited in Philip Girard, *ibid.* at 165.
33 *Ibid.*

Throughout the period, it seems that a special meeting of the Society was called to honour every member from Halifax and every judge who died. There is some evidence that similar meetings of the county bar were held when non-Halifax lawyers passed away. Some of these were undoubtedly better attended than others, but even Ernest F. Doyle, for example, who died in 1935 after a quarter-century of inconspicuous solo law practice in Halifax, received the honour of a special meeting at which it was observed that he applied himself to the practice of his profession in a "quiet, faithful, and unostentatious manner."[34] This tradition, like so many others, began to be disrupted during the war years. At the 1946 annual meeting the small attendance at recent tribute meetings was lamented and members were reminded of their obligation to attend them.[35]

The annual dinner and surrounding activities could also be a focus of group solidarity. Attendance figures for the dinner are available sporadically in the minutes and newspapers from 1930 on, when the tradition of a dinner consequent upon the annual meeting seems to have been inaugurated. The first two attempts were not a roaring success, with only thirty-some members in attendance each year out of a total of 241 across the province. But this seems to have been more a result of the decision to shift the annual meeting to the summer in those years. The 1929 annual meeting had reported a "large attendance" and when the meeting returned to its traditional late winter slot in 1932, attendance bounced back to 62, or some 30 percent of the entire membership, and it continued thereafter at between 60 and 70. Spouses did not attend, and with total large-firm membership standing at under twenty-five lawyers, attendees must have come from all sectors of the bar.

The 1930s and the war years were something of a high-water mark of externally focused sociability. In 1934 the Society invited the Canadian Bar Association to hold its annual meeting in Halifax; the invitation was taken up two years later thanks to James McGregor Stewart, then serving as vice-president of the CBA. He and his wife hosted a garden party for "some 400 delegates and spouses at their Halifax estate ... which made a lasting impression on the guests."[36] When the Society got wind of the plans of the North Carolina Bar Association to pass by Halifax on a convention cruise in 1935, the Council invited the members to stop by for a visit, which some 400 of them did on a sunny August day that year. By the late 1930s the Society was experimenting with other forms of collective sociability. In 1939 it was a bonspiel at the Mayflower Curl-

---

34 NSBS special tribute meeting, 13 Feb. 1935, see above note 26.
35 NSBS annual meeting, 14 May 1946, see above note 26.
36 Barry Cahill, *Thousandth Man*, above note 16 at 65.

ing Club. The next year it was the first annual NSBS golf tournament to be held at the Ashburn Golf Club in Halifax; James McGregor Stewart presented a silver cup to be awarded each year. And during the war years lawyer-servicemen from any jurisdiction who happened to be stationed in Halifax were invited to the Society's annual dinner, which sent attendance soaring.

To close this section, another vignette featuring James McGregor Stewart is suggestive of the professional bonds linking all members of the legal profession. In a 1934 incident recounted in Frank Covert's memoirs, Covert recalled that Stewart had called him in to ask how a particular case was coming. Covert replied that he had

> no worries, that the lawyer on the other side was a police court lawyer. Stewart put his glasses down on the end of his nose, looked over the top of them, and said, "Oh! You don't think much of Police Court lawyers, eh?" He picked up the phone, called H.P. MacKeen, and said "Harry, this young man needs some Police Court work. Give him those Automobile Legal Association cases for a year or two." And MacKeen did. It took some of the conceit out of me and gave me respect for the ability of the police court lawyer.[37]

STRATIFICATION AND DIVERSITY: IS THERE A RELATIONSHIP?

IN 1900, HALIFAX HAD one black lawyer, no women lawyers, no lawyer from any identifiable ethnic minority, and no lawyer who could be identified as other than Catholic or Protestant, though it had a number of lawyers who came from very modest backgrounds in rural and small-town Nova Scotia, and from Halifax itself. By 1950 the city still had only one black lawyer, but it had two women lawyers, one Acadian lawyer (and one Acadian county court judge), and seven Jewish lawyers. There were still noticeable numbers of lawyers who came from modest backgrounds in the city and the countryside but it is likely that their proportion of the Halifax bar was declining.[38] The Halifax bar, like others in Canada, was very slowly becoming more open to what we might call non-traditional lawyers. In fact, these 1950 figures are somewhat misleading: many more "non-traditional" lawyers were present in Halifax at some point during the interwar years than these totals would indicate. An

---

37 Barry Cahill, *Frank Manning Covert*, above note 16 at 41.
38 Mélanie Pascale Brunet, *Becoming Lawyers: Gender, Legal Education and Professional Identity Formation in Canada, 1920–1980* (Ph.D. diss., University of Toronto, 2005) at 85 found that the percentage of the Dalhousie law student body that came from below a middle-class background shrank from 20 percent in the 1920s to 14 percent in the 1930s.

initial cohort of such lawyers entered the profession in the 1920s and 30s but did not sustain itself and was subsequently overwhelmed by a large influx of white Anglo-Celtic men, mostly veterans, into the profession in the late 1940s. The one exception to this trend was the remarkable success of Jewish lawyers, who entered the profession in significant numbers in the 1930s and sustained their presence thereafter. We first describe these trends and then try to analyze them, noting that in this section we take into account the presence of non-traditional lawyers outside Halifax, especially in Yarmouth and Cape Breton, as well as in the capital.

With regard to religion, the under-representation of Catholics at the Halifax bar was quite noticeable in 1900: they formed only 14 percent of the city's lawyers, although comprising 28 percent of the provincial population and 37 percent of the Halifax population. But by 1910 they formed 20 percent of the city's bar and would continue to form between 20 and 25 percent of it up to 1950. The proportion of Catholics in the provincial population was on the rise, to 34 percent provincially and 39 percent in the city by 1951, but while their under-representation at the bar continued, it was not dramatic. It was more noticeable in the large firms, where few Catholics had gained a place by 1950: the McInnes firm had two, the Burchell firm one, and the Stewart firm none out of ten lawyers.[39] The leadership of the Barristers' Society included Catholics from 1914, however, when John J. Power became vice-president. W.J. O'Hearn served as the first Catholic president from 1921–23, and thereafter there were three more Catholic presidents before 1950. The only faith-based convention seems to have been that while the vice-president and the president might both be Protestants, there were never two Catholics holding both top jobs simultaneously.

Another religious group was more conspicuously successful over this period: Jewish lawyers. The first in Halifax appears to have been Harry Webber, originally from Saint John, who was called to the bar in 1918.[40] There was then a lull until the later 1920s, when Charles Rosenblum began practising in Glace Bay. But the 1930s were definitely a golden age for Jewish lawyers with at least thirteen admitted in that decade, of whom six (along with Webber) were still practising in Halifax in 1950, along with one in Yarmouth, and three in Cape Breton (in addition, a few Jewish students had come from Ontario to attend Dalhousie Law School and returned there after being called to the bar

---

39 The Stewart firm was joined briefly by one Roman Catholic lawyer, J.J.A. Powell, in the 1930s.

40 A second Jewish lawyer, Maurice Shulman, had apprenticed for five years for a lawyer in Montreal and was allowed by special resolution to be called to the bar in 1920 after writing an examination, but he appears not to have stayed long in the province.

in Nova Scotia). Jewish lawyers formed 6 percent of the Halifax bar, far above their 1 percent of the city population (and 0.3 percent of the province's population). Most practised on their own or with one partner at most, but several would rise to positions of influence over the next few decades, including Leonard A. Kitz (called in 1939), who would become the first Jewish mayor of Halifax in 1955.

The entry of people of Lebanese-Christian descent into the profession in these years has some similarities to that of the Jews: in both cases first generation immigrants entered the field of commerce and lived frugally so that their children and grandchildren could achieve education. The first, Simon Khattar, was the son of Lebanese immigrants to Cape Breton; he was called to the bar in 1936, developed a thriving sole practice in Sydney, was named a Queen's Counsel in 1955, and created a legal dynasty when his son George joined him in the 1960s. Edward Francis Arab of Halifax, the grandson of Lebanese immigrants, followed Khattar into the bar a year later. After a promising start at legal practice, his career was cut short by his death in battle in the Netherlands in 1944.

Acadian lawyers did not arrive in the capital until the 1940s. Alfred Poirier of West Arichat articled in Halifax and was called to the bar in 1942, while Delmar Amiro of Lower East Pubnico articled with the Burchell firm and stayed in Halifax for much of his career. The three Acadians who qualified before that all practised in the Yarmouth or Digby areas, the Acadian heartland of post-Expulsion Nova Scotia. René Wilfrid Émilien Landry, the first, articled in Halifax while attending law school, and after being called to the bar in 1911 returned to Yarmouth. He then became the principal to Vincent Pottier, who was called to the bar in 1920 and practised there for over twenty-five years, a good part of them with Landry. The genealogy continued with Edward J. Theriault, who articled with Pottier and was called to the bar in 1927. All three men practised together in Yarmouth for a time, but Theriault then moved on to become a Crown prosecutor in Digby. Pottier developed a sterling reputation, serving successively as a member of Parliament, provincial royal commissioner, county court judge, and justice of the Nova Scotia Supreme Court.

Black lawyers were more frequently encountered in Halifax and Sydney in the interwar years than is often assumed. Two black lawyers originally from the Caribbean, J. Eaglan Griffith and Rowland Parkinson Goffe, migrated to Halifax in 1917 and 1920 respectively and spent the rest of their careers in the city.[41]

---

41 Barry Cahill has traced the careers of these early black graduates in "The 'Colored Barrister': The Short Life and Tragic Death of James Robinson Johnston, 1876–1915" (1992) 15 Dal. L.J. 336 at 372–74.

Griffith, originally from the island of Nevis, had come to Halifax by way of New York and McGill. He maintained a sole practice for nearly thirty years, during which time he served as principal to four black West Indian lawyers who had come to Halifax to study law. Goffe, of Jamaican origin, had been called to the bar of Gray's Inn in London and worked there as a lawyer for some years before settling in Halifax. He too maintained a sole practice, for over thirty years. Only one of the next four black West Indian lawyers, however, remained in the province.[42] Frederick Allan Hamilton relocated to Sydney, then home to a sizeable West Indian population. There he flourished, becoming a leader of the Cape Breton bar and achieving a King's Counsel in 1950. Thus, for most of the 1920–50 period there were three black lawyers in the province, all of some seniority and one, in Hamilton's case, of increasing prominence. In addition, the three black West Indian lawyers who left the province, Ethelbert Lionel Cross, B.J. Spencer Pitt, and John James Copland, all articled in Halifax and were called to the Nova Scotia bar. Griffith died in 1944, and Goffe and Hamilton both retired from active practice in 1952, at which time Haligonian George Davis became the second Afro-Nova Scotian lawyer in the province. Following a thirty-year period when there had been three black lawyers of considerable seniority in the province plus a number of black articling students, after 1952 there was only one black lawyer left, and he was a novice. Black lawyers became a novelty in the 1950s in a way they had not been for decades.

The story of female lawyers in Nova Scotia is more puzzling. Some nineteen women were called to the bar in Nova Scotia, most after graduating from the law school, between Frances Fish's admission in 1918 and 1950. But it

---

42   Information on graduates is derived from Christian L. Wiktor, comp., *Dalhousie Law School Register, 1883–1983* (Halifax: Dalhousie Law School, 1983), and from student files held at Dalhousie University Archives; on those called to the bar, from the barristers' rolls held at NSARM. One of the emigrants, E.L. Cross, took up causes involving race relations in Toronto and defended "free thinkers" and atheists in the 1920s: see Susan Lewthwaite's chapter in this volume, and see Constance Backhouse, *Colour-Coded: A Legal History of Racism in Canada, 1900–1950* (Toronto: University of Toronto Press for the Osgoode Society, 1999) at 173–225 for an account of Cross's leadership in getting the provincial authorities to lay charges against members of the Klu Klux Klan (KKK) after an incident in Oakville, Ontario in 1930. B.J. Spencer Pitt also moved to Toronto, where he articled with Cross and was involved in the KKK matter. For many years he organized the Emancipation Day ceremonies marking the end of slavery in the British Empire in 1834. His nephew, Justice Romain Pitt, sits on the Ontario Superior Court. The third emigrant, J.J. Copland, returned to Grenada but continued to encourage aspirant lawyers from the island to attend law school in Canada; one of those who heeded his advice was Julius Isaacs, later chief justice of the Federal Court of Appeal (P. Girard interview with J. Isaacs, 16 November 2000).

seems that Grace Wambolt of Halifax was one of only two women practising law in the entire province at the beginning of 1950, at a time when there were dozens in Ontario.[43] The first three women admitted to the bar, Fish, Emelyn Mackenzie, and Caroline McInnes, all practised law. Fish practised for forty years in Montreal and Newcastle, N.B. where she often represented the poor and underprivileged. Mackenzie was a corporate lawyer in New York, where she became one of the first women members of the New York City Bar Association and was involved in social work and philanthropic activity, while McInnes practised with her father's firm in Halifax until the late 1930s. But after this first flush of activity, down to and including Wambolt's own call to the bar in 1925, what women did with their law degrees becomes more difficult to follow.

Aside from the famous "first trio" and a few women who were only passing through the province,[44] there remain about a dozen women with Nova Scotia roots who were called to the bar up to 1950. Only two aside from Wambolt can be identified with the practice of law, and half have left no trace of professional activity, in Nova Scotia at least. Gertrude Mills (called in 1926) recalled that she "was offered a job immediately by a male lawyer who wanted to encourage women to study law."[45] Instead, she went off to New York, where she was soon joined by Mary Olive Maddin (also called in 1926) and Josephine Dresner (called in 1928). Mills ended up making a career there in legal publishing, but Dresner's fate is unknown. Maddin, who had articled with her father in Sydney, returned home to marriage in 1928, listing her occupation as "stenographer" on the marriage licence. Marjorie Dunsworth (called in 1935) moved to Ottawa where she pursued a career in the federal civil service. May Gladys Anderson of Pictou County articled in New Glasgow and practised there for a dozen years or so after her call to the bar in 1936 but disappeared

---

43 On Wambolt's career, see Jennifer Servinis, "The Exclusiveness of the Legal Profession in Canada and how one Nova Scotian Woman Rose to the Challenge: M. Grace Wambolt Q.C." (unpublished paper, 1998). On women's admission to the bar, see Barry Cahill, "Women at the Bar: Common Law Right or Legislated Privilege? — The Strange Case of Nova Scotia" in Janet Guildford and Suzanne Morton, eds., *Women in Atlantic Canada in the Twentieth Century* (Fredericton: Acadiensis Press, forthcoming 2009).

44 Three women had civil law degrees from McGill, attended Dalhousie Law School for a year, and were then called to the Nova Scotia bar at a time when women could not be admitted to the bar in Quebec. Sadie Lazarovitz (called in 1929) pursued this route as a way of getting admitted to the Ontario bar and it is likely that two other women from Montreal, Florence Seymour Bell (called in 1921) and Elizabeth Neville (called in 1934), did the same.

45 Gertrude Mills "In My Day... A Look Back to Life at Dalhousie Law School in the 1920s" *Hearsay* (Summer 1982) 27.

from view in 1947. Merle Marcella Purtill was also called in 1936 after articling with the Stewart firm but disappeared from professional life thereafter. Maureen O'Mullin Allen articled with the Burchell firm but also disappeared from view after her call in 1941. Ann Eileen Maclean of Port Hawkesbury was called to the bar in 1948 and shortly thereafter became the secretary — a traditionally male position more akin to executive director — of the Barristers' Society, as well as solicitor to the Workmen's Compensation Board.[46] At the very end of our period, Jean Chisholm Macpherson was called to the bar in 1950 and practised thereafter in Antigonish with her husband. She noted proudly on her application for admission that she was "a veteran of World War II." In light of the extreme rarity of female lawyers in Nova Scotia, Grace Wambolt's election to the council of the Barristers' Society in 1945 is even more remarkable. Even if she was one of only two women practising law as of 1950, however, the interwar years show an undeniable female presence at the bar: nearly twenty female articling students over that period, and the presence of two women lawyers in Halifax (Wambolt and McInnes) and one in New Glasgow (Anderson).

How did the Halifax bar respond to these attempts by non-traditional lawyers to enter the profession? We examine this question by looking at patterns in the articling experience of these aspirants.[47] Law school provided valuable credentials and skills, but the real hurdle for entry to the profession was finding an established lawyer with whom one could article. This had always been a problem: Ontario's first black lawyer, Delos Davis, had to get a special act to admit him to the bar because he could not find a principal. Clara Brett Martin had great difficulty finding a principal before the chivalric instincts of a senior Toronto barrister finally came to the rescue. In 1930s Toronto, aspiring Jewish students-at-law usually resolved the problem by articling with co-religionists, often very junior lawyers.[48] The willingness of lawyers from privileged groups to assist those from less privileged groups is an important indicator of the bar's commitment to equality and to access to justice.

---

46 Maclean moved to Calgary and later Hamilton, Ontario, where under her married name, Eileen Maclean Yates, she became an acknowledged expert in municipal law: see obituary in *Hearsay* (Spring 1980) at 27.

47 Bar admission files for lawyers from anywhere in Nova Scotia are filed in the Halifax Supreme Court Records, RG 39C at NSARM. We have supplemented these with information derived from vital statistics records available online: www.novascotiagenealogy.com.

48 Bora Laskin, for example, was obliged to begin his articles with a Jewish fraternity friend who had virtually no practice: Philip Girard, *Bora Laskin: Bringing Law to Life* (Toronto: University of Toronto Press for the Osgoode Society, 2005) at 59–61.

The Nova Scotia experience does not show large firms as unreceptive to the entry of non-traditional lawyers into the profession. Women and members of various minorities articled with large firms during this period. No black lawyer articled with a large firm, but as noted earlier all four black lawyers called to the bar in the 1920s and 30s articled with the same black lawyer, J.E. Griffith. Thus, if this can be construed as discriminatory, then all members of the profession, not just large firms, were responsible. It appears that black lawyers were not made to feel particularly welcome, though we cannot exclude the possibility that they may have preferred to article with a fellow West Indian. Whether the departures of three of these men were motivated by a sense of exclusion, alone or in combination with the perception of better economic opportunities elsewhere, it is not possible to say. But members of the black community could not have failed to note that the one white West Indian who graduated from Dalhousie Law School during this period, Lionel Ryan, was afforded the opportunity of articling at Halifax's largest firm, Henry, Stewart & Smith, in the late 1920s.

The Jewish, Lebanese, and Acadian lawyers demonstrated quite eclectic articling patterns. It was more the exception than the rule that Jewish students articled with Jewish lawyers. Some articled with large firms, some with traditional firms, and some with sole practitioners. Aaron Zive of Halifax articled with the Burchell firm, Nathan Green with Daley, Phinney & Outhit, and Samuel Margolian of Yarmouth with sole practitioner F.W. Bissett of Halifax. Irving Pink of Yarmouth articled there with Acadian lawyer Vincent Pottier. Abraham Sheffman, originally from St. John's, articled with Catholic lawyer Richard Donahoe in Halifax, while in Cape Breton Jewish lawyers always articled with non-Jewish lawyers. Some firms were particularly open to non-traditional lawyers: Pearson Covert and Rutledge in Halifax, for example, welcomed René W.E. Landry, Edward Frances Arab, Michael Greenberg, Leonard Kitz, and George Tamaki as articling students. Acadian Delmar Amiro articled with the Burchell firm, as did Franco-Ontarian Leo Landreville of Sudbury.[49] Aspiring Jewish lawyers seem to have had an easier time getting established in Halifax and, more broadly, in Nova Scotia than in Toronto, where they were markedly ghettoized during these years. The explanation for this difference likely resides in the fact that Toronto's Jewish population constituted, at 7 percent, a much larger proportion of the

---

49 Landreville became a High Court judge in Ontario, the first and to date the only superior court judge whose impeachment was sought under s. 99 of the *Constitution Act, 1867*. See William Kaplan, *Bad Judgment: The Case of Mr. Justice Leo A. Landreville* (Toronto: University of Toronto Press for the Osgoode Society, 1996).

city as a whole than Halifax's small Jewish community. Jewish aspirations to middle-class and professional status could be seen as threatening in Toronto in a way they were not in Nova Scotia.

Female lawyers also had somewhat eclectic articling patterns, although they enjoyed an advantage that most minority lawyers lacked: the possibility of articling with a father or other relative. A number of women articled with large firms with whom they had no obvious family connection, however: Emelyn Mackenzie, Gertrude Mills, and Maureen O'Mullin Allen with the Burchell firm, and Sadie Lazarovitz and Merle Marcella Purtill with the Stewart firm, in addition to Caroline McInnes at her father's firm. Others articled with sole practitioners, and some with traditional firms. A notable feature of the women's articling experience was that virtually all of them worked with King's Counsels, suggesting that senior lawyers felt compelled to set a good example regarding the entry of women into the profession, and that there was no strong ideological objection to their entry. Any interpretation of women's experience with the legal profession seems premature without the testimony of those who "dropped out," but some combination of difficult economic circumstances (possibly resulting in out-migration), lack of enthusiasm by portions of the male bar, and the relative lack of interest by women in traditional private practice must account for the very weak presence of women at the provincial bar.[50]

The Halifax bar was resolutely a white-Anglo-Saxon-Protestant masculine grouping at the beginning of the twentieth century and very largely remained so at mid-century, both in the large firms and at the grassroots level. This uniformity was less evident in legal education, but a somewhat more diverse law student body did not translate in any direct and immediate way into a more diverse bar, except in the case of Jewish students. The larger law firms would not hire blacks or Jews as associates, though some were receptive to academically talented white males from humbler backgrounds, and some had Jewish articling students. Jewish, black, and female graduates showed, however, that it was possible to establish a foothold as a sole practitioner during this period. At a time when roughly half the bar practised as such, it is hard to see this as evidence of marginalization, even though it is not possible thereby to excuse the discrimination practised by large firms. Sole practitioners went on to fill significant positions in subsequent years: Robert Kanigsberg became president of the Barristers' Society, Frederick Bissett a justice of the Supreme Court of Nova Scotia, Nathan Green a provincial magistrate, and so on. Given the prolonged economic decline during these years, and the

---

50 See generally Mary Jane Mossman, *The First Women Lawyers: A Comparative Study of Gender, Law and the Legal Professions* (Hart: Oxford, 2006).

continuing drop in litigation rates, it is particularly surprising that several immigrant black lawyers managed not only to set up shop but also to remain in the province for much or all of their careers.

CONCLUSION

THE DEVELOPMENT OF THE large law firm undoubtedly led to the stratification of the bar, in the sense that the nineteenth-century pattern of a multiplicity of sole practitioners and two-person partnerships was made more complex by the addition of two tiers of medium and large firms. These larger firms congregated in the larger urban areas, with the result that the extensive growth of the legal profession in the nineteenth century was replaced by a more intensive urban growth in the twentieth. This trend was more pronounced in some cities than others — in Winnipeg, say, than in Halifax, where this urban concentration, like the proportion of the city's bar represented by large firms, virtually stalled in the first half of the century before taking off in the second.

Whether this stratification can be equated with a process of marginalization, whereby smaller firms and sole practitioners were seen to be part of an inferior caste and thus largely excluded from the governance of the profession, the halls of legal education, and the judiciary, is more dubious. Certainly the large firms seem both to have weathered the storms of the 1920s and 30s rather well and to have been relatively insulated from the dire economic lot of many smaller firms, but that was largely a function of their different client bases. On the evidence reviewed here, sole practitioners and small firms not only retained their representation in all areas of professional life, but also fought back within the Barristers' Society when they felt their interests were not being served by an emergent dominance of large firms on council, or by the predominance of Halifax in the affairs of the Society.

The relationship of professional stratification to the quest by women and minorities seeking entrance to the profession in the early twentieth century is also somewhat controversial. Existing literature assigns a villainous role to large firms. There is widespread evidence of discrimination by large firms against women and racial and ethno-religious minorities in other jurisdictions during this period, and undoubtedly it existed in Halifax as well. But large firms in Halifax posed no absolute bar to women, nor to lawyers from ethno-religious minorities; where black lawyers were concerned, they behaved no better and no worse than the rest of the profession. The fact remains that this was indeed the period when the barriers to professional entry were overcome, when women lawyers, black lawyers, Jewish lawyers, and other lawyers from minority backgrounds, although not yet Aboriginal lawyers, established themselves in the profession in a way that could not be denied in the future. That this should have happened during Halifax's two most economically adverse decades of the twentieth century, when one might have expected a much more self-interested, blinkered mentality, speaks to a certain sense of public spiritedness and professional *esprit de corps*. Larger structural forces constraining women's lives seem to have had more to do with their limited entry to the practice of law than any actions or omissions by large firms. And if black, Jewish, and other minority lawyers entered the profession mostly as sole practitioners, this need not be equated with marginalization at a time when half the profession practised as such. Some of these pioneering sole practitioners achieved distinction, as has been noted. Others did not enter the limelight but joined the ranks of those who, like Ernest Doyle, served the public and their profession in a "quiet, faithful, and unostentatious manner."

APPENDIX

TABLE ONE: LAWYER NUMBERS

	Halifax	Rest of NS	Total
1900	118	202	320
1910	96	185	281
1920	85	160	245
1930	88	153	241
1940	117	171	288
1950	117	168	285

TABLE TWO: EMIGRATION DESTINATIONS OF NOVA SCOTIA LAWYERS, 1900–24

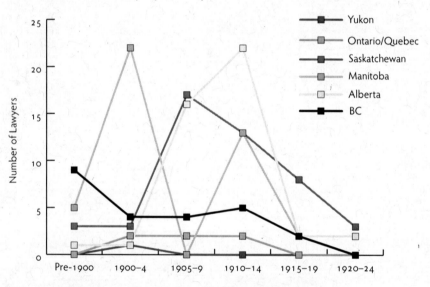

TABLE THREE: LAWYERS PER 1000 POPULATION

	Halifax	Rest of NS	All of NS
1900	2.32	0.49	0.70
1910	1.66	0.43	0.57
1920	1.13	0.36	0.47
1930	1.12	0.35	0.47
1940	1.19	0.36	0.50
1950	0.87	0.33	0.44

TABLE FOUR: CENSUS POPULATION

	Halifax	Rest of NS	All of NS
1901	50,968	409,006	459,974
1911	57,808	434,530	492,338
1921	75,487	448,350	523,837
1931	78,600	434,246	512,846
1941	98,636	479,326	577,962
1951	133,931	508,653	642,584

TABLE FIVE: HALIFAX LAWYERS BY PRACTICE TYPE (%)

	Solo	2-Person	3-Person	Large
1900	48%	29%	3%	20%
1910	66%	19%	6%	9%
1920	54%	14%	11%	21%
1930	46%	21%	11%	22%
1940	61%	16%	0%	23%
1950	49%	11%	14%	26%

TABLE SIX: DALHOUSIE LAW LECTURERS BY PRACTICE TYPE

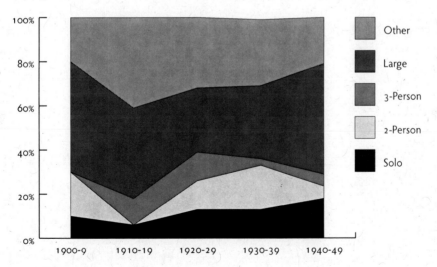

TABLE SEVEN: NSBS OFFICER PRACTICE TYPE (%)

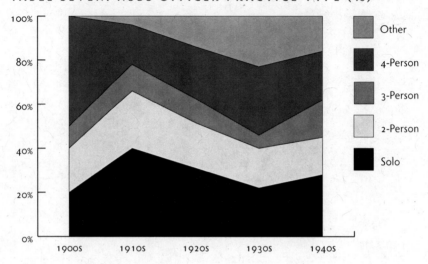

CHAPTER 6

Megafirm: A Chronology for the Large Law Firm in Canada

CHRISTOPHER MOORE

IN RECENT YEARS, CANADIAN judicial biography, a genre once dominated by traditional and celebratory "Lives of the Judges," has been transformed by several very substantial scholarly works that have made significant contributions to Canadian history and legal history.[1] Something similar may be under way with "biographies" of Canadian law firms. Typically little more than a series of celebratory sketches of a firm's partners produced for internal reference only,[2] law firm histories now include at least a few more ambitious studies of

---

1 Ellen Anderson, *Judging Bertha Wilson: Law as Large as Life* (Toronto: University of Toronto Press for the Osgoode Society for Canadian Legal History, 2001); Robert J. Sharpe and Kent Roach, *Brian Dickson: A Judge's Journey* (Toronto: University of Toronto Press for the Osgoode Society for Canadian Legal History, 2003); and Philip Girard, *Bora Laskin: Bringing Law to Life* (Toronto: University of Toronto Press for the Osgoode Society for Canadian Legal History, 2005).
2 Even celebratory partner-biographies can be a fund of precious information about law firm history. Examples include: Gwyneth McGregor, ed., *McCarthy & McCarthy: A History* (Toronto, McCarthy & McCarthy, 1978; unpublished manuscript, copy held by the library of the Law Society of Upper Canada Archives, Toronto, Ontario); Douglas H. Tees, *Chronicles of Ogilvy, Renault 1879–1979* (Montreal: Plow & Watters Print, 1979); Doug Mitchell and Judy Slinn, *The History of McMaster Meighen* (Montreal: McMaster Meighen, 1989); Stanley E. Edwards, *Fraser & Beatty: the First 150 Years* (Toronto: Desktop Publishing Division, Fraser Beatty, 1989); Christine Mullins and Arthur E. Harvey, *Russell & DuMoulin: The First Century, 1889–1989* (Vancouver: Russell & DuMoulin, 1989), and Jack Batten, *A History of Bennett Jones Verchere* (Calgary: Bennett Jones Verchere, privately published, 1997).

law firms, with more in progress.³ Still, the historiography of the large law firm in Canada remains underdeveloped, with even such fundamental matters as the periodization of major events and their causation remaining largely unexplored. This chapter proposes that the historical record shows some notable trends in the size and scope of the large law firm in Canada. The emergence of the large long-lived corporate law firm in Canada occurred roughly between 1860 and 1890 and was followed by a long period of relative stability in the nature of the large law firm. It seems that a second transformative moment of equivalent importance began about 1980 and is still in process.

THE LARGE FIRM IN HISTORY

AS RECENTLY AS 1980, a Canadian law firm needed fewer than one hundred lawyers to rank among the largest in the country, and very few firms had more than a single office in a single city. Today the thousand-lawyer threshold, though not yet reached, may well be a plausible consequence of current trends, and most of the leading Canadian law firms now have international, national, or at least regional networks of offices. This explosion in numbers of lawyers and in geographical reach of the largest firms (a phenomenon not unique to Canada, but paralleled in much of the common law world) has inspired the term "megafirm," which, despite its slightly breathless ring, usefully identifies the new scale of operations of large "branded" law firms. "Megafirm," however, may mislead by emphasizing the sheer size of law firms. Size is probably not the vital factor defining the transformation of large law firms in recent decades, and neither is geographical expansion. It is true that many of the firms under discussion here have been among the largest law firms in their milieu for much of their history, but size and geographical reach are probably less important than changes in organization and ideology that have come about more or less simultaneously. ⁴

---

3   The first substantial Canadian law firm history by a historian was Curtis Cole, *Osler, Hoskin, & Harcourt: Portrait of a Partnership* (Toronto: McGraw-Hill Ryerson, 1995). See also Richard Pound, *Stikeman Elliott: The First Fifty Years* (Montreal: McGill-Queen's University Press, 2002); and Christopher Moore, *McCarthy Tétrault: Building Canada's Premier Law Firm 1855–2005* (Vancouver: Douglas & McIntyre, 2005). Professor Gregory Marchildon and Barry Cahill have in progress a history of the Atlantic Canadian regional firm Sterling McKelvey, and C. Ian Kyer is working on a history of the national firm Faskens.

4   *American Lawyer*'s most recent survey suggests that, although large firms hold a growing share of the legal market, the most profitable law firms have been getting smaller as they focus on an exclusive market for very high-end legal work. Viva Chen, "AmLaw 100: A Look behind the Numbers" *American Lawyer* (30 April 2007), online: www.law.com/jsp/article.jsp?id=1177664676190.

Generally, the quasi-permanent or very long-lived Canadian law firms that are described as "downtown," "elite," or "corporate" focus their attention on a client base drawn from corporations and institutions that engage primarily in large-scale corporate transactions and litigations. The work these clients provide tends to be frequent (if not continuous), complex, sophisticated in the legal issues it raises, and well paid. Canada, like most of the advanced-economy nations of the western world, long ago saw the development of a core group of about six to ten law firms — nicknamed in various countries "the golden circle," "the magic circle," "the seven sisters," and so on — that have secured the largest share of this kind of legal work from the largest corporate and institutional clients in their jurisdictions. These successful corporate law firms are wealthy, prestigious, and advantaged in recruitment by comparison with other law firms, and their pre-eminence often becomes long-term and self-sustaining. These factors are probably more important than sheer size or geographical reach in explaining the power and permanence of the leading firms, though all these phenomena are mutually reinforcing.

ORIGINS OF CORPORATE LAW IN CANADA

THE PERIOD ROUGHLY FROM 1860 to 1890 saw the coming into being of the large, long-lived corporate law firm — slightly earlier in Montreal, slightly later in western Canada — largely as a response to the development in Canada of commercial and industrial capitalism. In the early nineteenth century, most businesses in Canada were still small family enterprises, and they tended to be served by lawyers whose practices also resembled small family businesses. Such practices rarely endured in any identifiable way beyond the individual lawyers. It is difficult today to identify the clients of the earliest Canadian lawyers of prominence (William Warren Baldwin and his son Robert, for instance, in Toronto between 1808 and the 1850s), and it is often difficult to determine what became of their legal practices or even what names the practices were given. Even as they began to have sizeable corporate clients, early law firms often did not see themselves as having a business or fund of "goodwill" that could be sold to successors. Leading practices were sometimes simply wound-up as their practitioners withdrew from practice.[5]

---

5   G. Blaine Baker, "Law Practice and Statecraft in Mid-Nineteenth Century Montreal: the Torrance-Morris Firm, 1848–1868" in Carol Wilton, ed., *Beyond the Law: Lawyers and Business in Canada 1830 to 1930* (Toronto: Osgoode Society and University of Toronto Press, 1990) at 45–91; and "Ordering the Urban Canadian Law Office and Its Entrepreneurial Hinterland, 1825 to 1875" (1998) 48 U.T.L.J. 2 at 175–251.

The emergence of large, long-lived corporate institutions in Canada, however, produced clients with a systemic need for ongoing legal advice, and that change meant that the clientele of a successful lawyer could now become the foundation of an identifiable, ongoing practice more permanent than the work of the individual lawyer or multiple lawyers. As Table One suggests, many law partnerships that acquired a corporate clientele in the mid-nineteenth century quickly took on a coherent identity that continued to exist beyond the name and reputation of the original founders and leaders. Many of these firms have continued to rank among leading Canadian law firms, even into the twenty-first century. "Blake," "McCarthy," "Bennett," "Farris," and other surnames of lawyers from the late nineteenth or early twentieth century are familiar twenty-first-century law-firm brands to many lawyers who would have no knowledge of the individual to whom the surname originally belonged.

TABLE ONE: FOUNDATION DATES FOR SOME LAW FIRMS

In the last 150 years, some once-elite firms have vanished, and a few of today's leading firms are barely 50 years old. Still there has been notable continuity among a pool of firms founded around a period roughly 1860–1890

- Borden Ladner Gervais,* 1823, Montreal
- Fraser Milner Casgrain, 1839, Montreal
- Ogilvy Renault, 1879, Montreal
- McInnes Cooper, 1859, Halifax
- Stewart McKelvey,* 1885, Halifax
- Blakes, 1858, Toronto
- Faskens, 1863, Toronto
- McCarthy Tétrault,* 1877, Toronto
- Osler Hoskin,* 1877, Toronto
- Gowlings, 1887, Ottawa
- Bennett Jones, 1882, Calgary
- Russell DuMoulin, 1889, Vancouver
- Davis & Company, 1892, Vancouver
- Farris Vaughan, 1903, Vancouver

* Earlier or later foundational dates could be suggested for these firms. Arbitrary distinctions must sometimes be made between the older personal form of legal practice and the more permanent law firm that is the subject of this study. The Borden Ladner Gervais firm, for instance, traces its origins back to the opening of practice by William Badgley in Montreal in 1823, though for a generation or so Badgley's practice closely resembled a largely personal and individual law practice. On the other hand, the historians of Stewart McKelvey note 1885 as the year that a merger of two pre-existing Halifax firms created a firm focused on corporate law, and I have accepted their date rather than an earlier one.

The first identifiable moment in the development of a chronology of corporate legal practice, therefore, is the relatively brief period in the mid-nineteenth century that saw temporary and personal law partnerships coalesce into a relatively permanent form. These early corporate law firms provided the emerging Canadian commercial and industrial sector not only with legal services but also with managerial, organizational, and "constitutional" advice. In the nineteenth century, leading corporate lawyers in the major Canadian cities did far more than advocate in court or draft corporate documents. As legal counsellors and often as corporate directors as well, they assisted fledgling business enterprises in creating the corporate structures that the new Canadian railroad companies, manufacturers, retail and wholesale businesses, and financial enterprises required. At the same time, leading lawyers frequently sought election to the colonial or provincial legislatures, where they played notable roles in bringing into being the legislative framework required for large-scale corporate and industrial organizations: drafting and securing passage for laws and regulations in such fields as limited liability (1849 in the United Canadas), incorporation (1850), bankruptcy (1850), banking, shareholding, and corporate finance.

CORPORATE LAW FIRMS WITHOUT CORPORATE STRUCTURES

IN AN ERA LARGELY without management consultants and other specialized professionals, the emerging corporate law firms of the nineteenth century provided their corporate clients not only with litigation and solicitors' services narrowly defined, but also with general business guidance. The classic statement on this relationship may be that of Zebulon Lash of the Blakes firm, one of Toronto's first great commercial law specialists, who reminded his longtime client Sir Joseph Flavelle, a Toronto business pioneer first in industry and then in finance, of the service Flavelle needed from his legal counsel. "You told me it was not a bare legal opinion you wanted, but it was my personal opinion of what it would be right for you to do."[6]

It is striking, however, that even as they were providing crucial organizational advice to their corporate clients, the new corporate lawyers were not applying the same processes to their own law practices. Blaine Baker's stud-

---

6 Lash is quoted in Michael Bliss, *A Canadian Millionaire* (Toronto: Macmillan of Canada, 1978) at 58.

ies of early corporate law firms[7] in Montreal demonstrate two lessons simultaneously: first, the importance of the early corporate lawyers in guiding the development of the business organizations in nineteenth-century Montreal; second, how those lawyers adopted only the most rudimentary organizational structures for their own law firms. Leading business law firms in Canada's nineteenth-century commercial metropolis operated as "loose, informal associations." Usually they had only a handful of partners who sometimes had no written partnership agreements. They got by with rudimentary accounting systems, limited coordination among the lawyers, and unsystematic individual supervision of the work of associate lawyers and law students. Clearly, this lack of organization was not because corporate lawyers were unaware of corporate organizational models; they made their livings by counselling the most sophisticated corporations in the country on these matters. They simply did not want or need such organization in their own law practices. Law firms faced little pressure and little incentive to become highly organized, competitive, profit-maximizing organizations like their clients. They did not need to be organized like banks, manufacturing companies, or railroads, and evidently they did not want to be.

Indeed, there were strong pressures encouraging lawyers not to pursue the same kind of goals towards which they guided their clients. In the nineteenth century and long into the twentieth, the dominant ethos of the legal profession sharply distinguished the professional practice of law from a mere trade or business enterprise. In 1914, Sir James Aikins, founding president of the Canadian Bar Association, senior partner of Winnipeg's leading corporate law practice, and a man who had become very wealthy from the practice of law and the business interests that went with it, declared without irony that the hallmark of the legal profession was its "principled rejection of the profit motive." Lawyers were "officers of the court." They were members of a "learned and honorable profession." Their first allegiance was to the law and to justice, not to competitive business practices or to profit maximization.[8]

---

7   Baker, above note 5, particularly "Ordering the Urban Canadian Law Office and Its Entrepreneurial Hinterland, 1825 to 1875."
8   Studies of the professional ethos among Canadian lawyers include Curtis Johnson Cole, *A Learned and Honorable Body: The Professionalization of the Ontario Bar, 1867–1929* (Ph.D. Thesis, University of Western Ontario, 1987); W. Wesley Pue, "Becoming 'Ethical': Lawyers' Professional Ethics in Early-Twentieth-Century Canada" (1991) 20 Man. L.J. 227–261 (which includes the Aikins quotation); and, more generally, Christopher Moore, *The Law Society of Upper Canada and Ontario's Lawyers 1797–1997* (Toronto: University of Toronto Press, 1997).

There were significant forces inhibiting the adoption of business practices by law firms. By controlling the numbers of articling students they took on, practising lawyers maintained informal but effective limits upon entry to the profession and kept control upon the total number of lawyers competing for the available work. Their law societies, while defending a strict lawyers' monopoly over legal practice, forbade advertising, price competition, and other forms of commercialism by their members. Legal education and socialization strongly reinforced the professional ethos. As long as growth in the profession was controlled and competition among lawyers largely unnecessary, the ideology of a legal profession standing outside and somewhat opposed to the marketplace ideology of its clients continued to influence lawyers, even those in the large corporate law firms whose careers depended on furthering the corporate interests of their clients' businesses. What American scholar Robert L. Nelson has called the ideal of legal practice — "a situation of largely independent professionals selecting their own work"[9] — long remained operative within corporate law firms, even as they guided and assisted their corporate clients towards much more sophisticated forms of business organization. Even at the largest corporate law firms, recruiting remained informal, guided more by social connections than close scrutiny of abilities, and emphasizing collegiality over profitability.

CONTINUITY OF THE NINETEENTH-CENTURY FORM OF THE LARGE LAW FIRM

THIS NINETEENTH-CENTURY MODEL OF operations for corporate law firms was remarkably long-lived. Corporate law firms, even the long-lasting ones, did not grow rapidly in the first two-thirds of the twentieth century. The largest law firm in Canada in 1902 was Beatty & Blackstock of Toronto, an ancestor to today's Fasken law firm, with fifteen lawyers. Fifty years later the largest was Montreal's McMichael, Common (today Ogilvy Renault) with just twenty-four lawyers.[10] Well into the late twentieth century, there was little pressure on elite firms to adopt more businesslike models for their own operations, even as their practices focused more and more on services to businesses. "The old family lawyer ... has become, largely, a thing of the past. The solicitor is more in the world and less in his chambers," declared the prom-

---

9 Robert L. Nelson, *Partners With Power: The Social Transformation of the Large Law Firm* (Berkeley: University of California Press, 1988) at 7.
10 Cole, *Osler, Hoskin, & Harcourt: Portrait of a Partnership*, above note 3 at 294–304, Appendix 2: Largest Canadian Law Firms 1862–1992.

inent Toronto jurist William R. Riddell in 1907, but he quickly continued: "Businessmen as we all are, we should not forget that we are members of a learned and honourable profession."[11] Leading law firms remained casually managed, with limited record-keeping and informal decision making being the norm. Despite the enduring presence of leading firms over many decades, control of corporate law business was not tightly centralized in the hands of a few law firms. In most Canadian cities in this period, the handful of leading corporate practices, with ten or more lawyers, were always surrounded by a great many downtown firms with perhaps half as many lawyers but a rather similar corporate clientele. In 1950 the Dominion Bureau of Statistics still categorized as "large" any Canadian law firm with more than four lawyers.

For most of the twentieth century, a distinguishing feature of the corporate law firm in Canada was closely held leadership by one or a handful of senior lawyers. In New York City, the influential Wall Street law firm Cravath Swaine had developed by 1910 the "up-or-out" system in which newly hired lawyers either were admitted to partnership after about six years or else left the firm's employ. The up-or-out system soon became standard, not only in Wall Street law firms but widely among American corporate law firms (it was adopted at Baker & Botts of Houston, Texas, by the 1920s).[12] In most Canadian corporate law firms, however, there was no equivalent practice for another forty years. Around 1960, when the Toronto firm of Campbell Godfrey & Lewtas (later a component of the national firm Fasken Martineau) adopted the "up-or-out" system, John Godfrey, the *de facto* managing partner, believed it was a significant innovation among Toronto firms. American firms also adopted anti-nepotism and non-discrimination practices much earlier than their Canadian equivalents.[13]

Early corporate law firms in Canada had often been led by a dominant partner with a reputation as a courtroom litigator. D'Alton McCarthy, Edward Blake, and B.B. Osler in Toronto, Eugene Lafleur in Montreal, E.P.

---

11 W.R. Riddell, "Address to the Ontario Bar Association" *Canadian Law Times* (December 1907), reprinted in *The Law Society of Upper Canada Gazette*, Special Issue on Professionalism, 2002, 9–15.

12 Robert T. Swaine, *The Cravath Firm and Its Predecessors 1819–48* (New York: n.p., 1946–48). Kenneth Lipartito and Joseph Pratt, *Baker and Botts in the Development of Modern Houston* (Austin: University of Texas Press, 1991).

13 Only in 1968, with the admission of seven new partners from among its associates, did McCarthy & McCarthy of Toronto move towards a widely held partnership and systematic promotion of associates. Only three lawyers had been admitted to partnership between 1947 and 1967. Some of the new partners of 1968 had been with the firm for more than fifteen years. The situation was broadly similar among other Toronto firms and those in other Canadian cities at the time.

Davis and J.W. Farris in Vancouver, like other founders of leading corporate law firms across Canada, were all prominent litigators, at a time when corporate disputes were frequently settled in court and litigation was an important aspect of corporate practice. As corporations began to settle their dealings in boardrooms more than courtrooms (and perhaps as a consequence), the professional distinction between litigation and solicitor's work grew, and solicitors generally replaced litigators as the senior partners in corporate law firms. Whether barristers or solicitors dominated, however, leadership tended to be closely held far into the twentieth century. The historian of the Osler firm reports that "during the 1950s, Osler, Hoskin, & Harcourt was still a dictatorship" (led at the time by its "proprietor," Harold Mockridge, the nephew of the previous "dictator" and proprietor, H.S. Osler).[14] Beverley Matthews's governance style at McCarthy & McCarthy in the same era led a colleague to characterize him as "a direct descendant of Louis XIV through Lorenzo de Medici."[15] Counterparts or predecessors such as J.S.D. Tory (at Tory & Tory in Toronto), W. Norman Tilley (Tilley Carson of Toronto), R.B. Bennett (at the ancestor firm of Bennett Jones in Calgary), and Albert J. Brown (of the Montreal firm that became Ogilvy Renault) all left reputations as autocratic, even tyrannical, masters of their firms.

There might be a triumvirate or a small ruling bloc in a partnership of ten or twenty lawyers, but, in most firms, authority was closely held and partnership shares very disproportionately allotted to those who held that authority.[16] This dominance of one or a handful of partners flowed from control of relationships with key clients, in an era when firm size closely reflected the size of the firm's key clients. In the era when a "large" Canadian law firm might have ten or fewer lawyers, a single bank, railroad, insurance company, industrial concern, or national retailer was likely to be the foundational pillar of the firm's business. In Toronto, at the start of the twentieth century, Beatty Blackstock, briefly Canada's largest law firm, was virtually the house law firm of the Gooderham distilling and financial empire, and its fortunes waned with those of the Gooderhams (at least until David Fasken took over

---

14   Cole, *Osler, Hoskin, & Harcourt: Portrait of a Partnership*, above note 3 at 116.
15   Moore, *McCarthy Tétrault: Building Canada's Premier Law Firm 1855–2005*, above note 3 at 108.
16   Lore in several law firms recalls a senior partner of earlier times who would briefly join a partners' meeting, called to discuss annual allocation, only to declare: "I'm taking this much; the rest of you can share the other half how you like," and leave. The story, likely apocryphal, suggests the culture that prevailed.

and redirected the firm).[17] Into the 1950s, McCarthy & McCarthy was sometimes considered "Canada Life's legal department." Larger firms usually had a very close and lengthy association with one of the banks.

Because these large clients still entrusted their legal work on the basis of relationships with one or a very few lawyers, the firm-client link tended to be personal and long-lasting. The association of the Blakes firm of Toronto with the Bank of Commerce lasted for generations, as did that of Ogilvy Renault of Montreal with the Royal Bank of Canada.[18] Leighton McCarthy was both head of his Toronto law firm and chairman of Canada Life, a key client, from the 1920s to the 1940s. From the 1920s until the 1960s, Gordon McDougall of Montreal's Lafleur McDougall, and later his protégé William Macklaier, went to Shawinigan Falls annually to settle the annual fee from Shawinigan Water and Power that would be a very large part of the law firm's annual revenues. In Vancouver, Ralph Campney, the dominant partner in Campney, Owen and Murphy, made one trip a year to Toronto and Montreal to sew up his firm's retainers from Eaton's and the Bank of Montreal.[19]

This management system, at once autocratic and unstructured, but closely linked to enduring client relationships, was standard at elite Canadian law firms from the 1860s into the 1970s, and it fits well with the "partners-with-power" interpretation advanced by Robert Nelson to explain why American law firms resisted the bureaucratic structures and management hierarchies that had become standard in corporations and other large organizations.[20] Against the sociological explanations of professional practice advanced by such scholars as Magali Larsen and Eliot Freidson, both of whom stressed

---

17 C. Ian Kyer, "The Transformation of an Establishment Firm: From Beatty Blackstock to Faskens, 1902–1915" in Carol Wilton, ed., *Inside the Law: Canadian Law Firms in Historical Perspective* (Toronto: Osgoode Society and University of Toronto Press, 1996) at 161–206.
18 T.D. Regehr, "Elite Relationships, Partnership Arrangements, and Nepotism at Blakes, a Toronto Law Firm, 1858–1930" in Wilton, ed., *Inside the Law*, ibid. at 207–48. Tees, *Chronicles of Ogilvy, Renault 1879–1979*, above note 2.
19 These examples, all drawn from Moore, *McCarthy Tétrault: Building Canada's Premier Law Firm 1855–2005*, above note 3 at 58, 166, and 220–22, could be duplicated from studies of other law firms.
20 Nelson, *Partners With Power: The Social Transformation of the Large Law Firm*, above note 9. The analysis in another theory of law firm growth, Marc Galanter's *Tournament of Lawyers: The Transformation of the Big Law Firm* (Chicago: University of Chicago Press, 1991) seems to fit large Canadian firms less well, given the relative newness of the up-or-out system that fuels Galanter's "tournament." Even recently, large Canadian law firms have often had a partner/associate ratio close to 1:1, and associates have often been only minimally profitable to their firms. See Moore, *McCarthy Tétrault: Building Canada's Premier Law Firm 1855–2005*, above note 3 at 176 and 331.

internal explanations based on the nature of the profession, Nelson argued that client relations determined how law firms organized themselves.[21] Power within law firms, Nelson proposed, lay not with shareholders or managers, as in a corporate structure, but with those lawyers who controlled the vital relationships with key clients. As a result of this power structure, no matter who might serve as the law firm's managing partner or what the formal structures of the law firm hierarchy might be, lawyers' influence and authority within a firm flowed not from their place in the organization but from control of the client relationship that secured the firm's revenues.[22]

MODERNIZATION

AFTER INCREASING ONLY VERY slowly for most of a century, the numbers of lawyers in large Canadian law firms began to grow much more rapidly soon after the Second World War. The average number of lawyers in the ten largest Canadian law firms had grown from 8 to just 16 between 1902 and 1952, but from 1952 to 1992 the number grew from 16 to 241. In this second period, growth rates in the large firms never lagged below about 70 percent in any decade.[23] The causes of this growth were almost certainly external, driven by legislative requirements on one hand and client needs on the other. In part, the new pace of growth reflected the increased size and continual growth of operations of client corporations, which were now operating on a much larger national or international scale and brought their law firms issues of greater complexity and value than a single dominant lawyer could continue to handle.

In most firms, however, growing size first seems to have come with specialization in response to labour-law and tax-law revisions of the late 1940s that obliged corporate law firms to include labour and tax specialists among the general corporate solicitors and litigators.[24] Slightly later, a more important factor was the increasing complexity of commercial regulation. Reforms

---

21 Magali Larson, *The Rise of Professionalism: A Sociological Analysis* (Berkeley: University of California Press, 1977) and Elliot Freidson, *Profession of Medicine: The Sociology of Applied Knowledge* (New York: Dodd Mead, 1970).
22 Nelson, *Partners With Power: The Social Transformation of the Large Law Firm*, above note 9.
23 Statistics based on Cole, *Osler, Hoskin, & Harcourt: Portrait of a Partnership*, above note 3, Appendix II. Totals: 1951: 16; 1961: 29; 1971: 49; 1981: 91; 1991: 241.
24 See the argument and evidence on this point in Moore, *The Law Society of Upper Canada and Ontario's Lawyers 1797–1997*, above note 8 at 266–67 and *McCarthy Tétrault: Building Canada's Premier Law Firm 1855–2005*, above note 3 at 73–79. Nelson, *Partners With Power: The Social Transformation of the Large Law Firm*, above note 9, also notes

to securities legislation in the 1960s (the benchmark legislation being the *Ontario Securities Act* of 1967) brought in elaborate requirements that for the first time obliged lawyers to take responsibility for "full, true and plain disclosure" in corporate reports and prospectuses. Until then, most corporate-finance projects had not required teams of lawyers. Into the 1970s, very large corporate takeovers were generally conducted by handfuls of lawyers at most, but growing regulatory requirements (and ever more complex legal strategies based on them) steadily increased the numbers of lawyers needed for relatively routine corporate mergers or acquisitions.[25] Even judicial reform projects intended to streamline litigation encouraged a growing reliance on written factums and other forms of "paper-based litigation," which had the side effect of requiring teams of litigators, litigation researchers, and support staff in place of lone advocates.[26] With each increase in the size and complexity of corporate dealings and the legislation covering them, the size of corporate law firms had to keep pace.

Growth in size clearly encouraged some modernization of administrative structures within law firms. Larger administrative and accounting staffs, the introduction of sophisticated technology, recruitment programs targeting law students of talent and ability (and the first tentative steps towards anti-nepotism and anti-discrimination policies), and other changes spread through law firms in the 1960s and 1970s.[27] The old, autocratic style of law firm governance could not survive the rise of larger firms and a greater sharing of responsibility. From about the 1960s, the dominance of one or a handful of senior partners over the large law firms declined, to be replaced either

---

the argument that specialization reinforces professional claims and enables lawyers to resist "proletarianization."

25 I have seen little research to measure this development, but the evidence of a McCarthy Tétrault lawyer, Peter Beattie, on his experience of corporate takeover battles from the 1960s through the 1990s is suggestive. Beattie recalled the Hudson Bay Company's acquisition of Simpsons in 1979 involved only a handful of lawyers on each side. Peter Beattie, oral history interview with Christopher Moore, 8 May 2003 (tape and transcripts in McCarthy Tétrault Archives, Toronto).

26 Mr. Justice Colin Campbell who participated first as a litigation lawyer and later as a judge, on committees to revise litigation procedures, discusses causes of paper-based litigation in an oral history interview with Christopher Moore, 28 April 2003 (tape and transcripts in McCarthy Tétrault Archives, Toronto).

27 The developments are discussed in Cole, *Osler, Hoskin, & Harcourt: Portrait of a Partnership*, above note 3, and Moore, *McCarthy Tétrault: Building Canada's Premier Law Firm 1855–2005*, above note 3. Robert Brown, longtime office manager at Blakes 1948–80, gives an administrator's perspective in Robert Brown, *The House That Blakes Built* (unpublished manuscript, 1980, copy on file at Law Society of Upper Canada Archives).

by consensus-type leaders or elaborate systems of partnership decision making and networks of administrative committees. Soon all of the growing numbers of partners in most large law firms were voting on admission of new partners, allocation of profits among the partners, appointments to executive committees and management committees, and other significant matters of policy or administration.

This rise of partnership-democracy, however, was hardly a decisive movement towards businesslike management of law practices. In rapidly growing law firms, where every partner was newly empowered to vote on all significant firm decisions, capacity for strong central management and leadership actually declined. The law firms were much larger, but their newly diffused and weakened leaderships had limited authority to plan, coordinate, or direct the operations of the law firm. Individual partners were still able to define their own practice areas and develop their own clienteles with a substantial amount of autonomy, so long as they kept the partnership free of outright conflicts and contributed a satisfactory amount of client billings and billable hours. In effect, the number of partners with power in a firm might have increased as the size of law firms increased, but control of client relationships still remained with individual lawyers or groups of individual lawyers, rather than with those identified as the firm's managers.

THE SECOND TRANSFORMATIVE MOMENT 1980-2000

IN 1976, A LONG-RANGE planning committee struck by the Toronto law firm McCarthy & McCarthy to assess the firm's future prospects concluded that the principal strategic objective of the firm should be "to maintain a congenial working atmosphere even at the cost of increased profitability or money incomes."[28] But even in 1976, there were challenges to such affirmations of the traditional ideology of professional practice as something divorced from the world of commerce and competition. As control of education had shifted from the bar to the universities (even in Ontario, where the bar's resistance had been unusually prolonged[29]), the profession's ability to control its own numbers had been eroded. Enrollments in Ontario law schools increased from about 1000 in 1960 to 3700 in 1975, and the growth rate of the profession across Canada rose from about 2 percent annually in 1968 to over 10 percent

---

28 McCarthy Tétrault Archives, Toronto, "Report of the Long Range Planning Committee," October 1977.
29 C. Ian Kyer and Jerome E. Bickenbach, *The Fiercest Debate: Cecil A. Wright, the Benchers, and Legal Education in Ontario 1923-1957* (Toronto: Osgoode Society and University of Toronto Press, 1987).

annually ten years later.[30] The rising number of lawyers in practice eroded lawyers' confidence in being assured a secure practice with a reliable income (though particularly at "Main Street" law practices, rather than among lawyers in large corporate firms). New or ongoing challenges from accountants, management consultants, trust companies, paralegals, and others threatened elements of the old institutional monopoly on practice, and public regulatory regimes and competition laws rapidly eroded the authority of law societies and bar associations to impose fee schedules, prevent price competition, and otherwise maintain the hallmarks of the old non-commercial ideology of the legal profession.

At the same time, client corporations became less accepting of the old lawyer-client relationships in which clients relied on a particular lawyer, his law firm, and its informal billing practices more or less permanently. "Transactional" practice, in which client corporations put much of their legal work out to competitive tender, was replacing the old pattern of long-term lawyer-client relationships based on personal trust. Particularly for mergers and acquisitions, corporate financings, restructurings, and other prime projects, in-house legal departments in major corporations and public institutions began to apply more scrutiny to the work of their legal advisors, to divide their work among several firms, to require law firms to compete for their retainers, and to review and negotiate billing practices and billing rates much more vigorously. As corporate legal departments began to think of outside legal services as just another business service to be secured as efficiently as possible through market forces, law firms would not be able to ignore that pressure.[31]

As law firms and law firm analysts began to adapt to these new circumstances, a view that lawyers, instead of seeing themselves as practising a calling and a craft, should consider themselves competitors in a legal services business began to take hold. This was an international trend, symbolized by the rise of legal magazines like *American Lawyer*, founded in 1979, that treated legal practice as a business that could be planned and managed for maximum competitive advantage much like other businesses. *American Lawyer* became renowned for its AmLaw 100 (and later its Global 100), which ranked law firms, not by traditional measures of firm size or reputation or numbers of

---

30 Moore, *The Law Society of Upper Canada and Ontario's Lawyers 1797–1997*, above note 8 at 306.

31 Precise dating and measurement of this change remain to be established. McCarthy Tétrault lawyers in the early twenty-first century often suggested the trend had greatly strengthened in the previous decade, but almost certainly it had begun earlier among large and sophisticated clients.

leading counsel, but by revenue, as other businesses were judged. Specifically, the measure of the legal services business became profit-per-partner or PPP (sometimes PEP, profit per equity partner, to distinguish those with a true ownership stake in the firm). The quest for PPP did not simply respond to the avarice of partners; in a competitive marketplace, PPP advocates argued, those firms that generated larger profits through better planning and management relative to their competitors would have more capital to invest in all the factors that would provide continued competitive advantage: marketing, professional development, support technology, and particularly the recruitment and retention of the most promising and talented lawyers.

Recalling in 2004 the way that McCarthy & McCarthy began the process of building a national law firm with offices in major business centres across the country, a participant in the process described the thinking of some lawyers in that firm in the 1980s:

> As we could look into the future and see where the practice of law was going, we could see more companies would become national in scope and international in scope. And ... it made sense for us to project ourselves in the marketplace in such a way as to be seen as providing all kinds of services .... This is the right way to organize yourself: to be big, to have lawyers on staff who are specialists in a number of areas and be ... one of what would be a relatively small number of firms capable of handling a complex multi-dimensional transaction. At least that's the market we wanted to be in. And our view was that that market would generate lots of revenue for the firm.[32]

When McCarthy & McCarthy first considered expansion into Calgary in 1979, it was the growth opportunities provided by Alberta's late-1970s energy boom that were emphasized in the partners' discussions. The proposal was framed as a search for competitive advantage: "Without a Calgary connection McCarthy & McCarthy could lose part of its market share and with a connection might well increase its share."[33] In documents such as these, there was no more homage to a "congenial working atmosphere" as the goal of law firm management. An ethos was emerging that took for granted that law firms must identify and adapt to market opportunities and competitive advantages — as other businesses would.

---

32 Blair Cowper-Smith, oral history interview with Christopher Moore, 2 December 2004 (tape and transcripts in McCarthy Tétrault Archives, Toronto).

33 Moore, *McCarthy Tétrault: Building Canada's Premier Law Firm 1855–2005*, above note 3 at 127–28, citing J.C. McCartney memo to Executive Committee, "Business Opportunities in Calgary" (9 October 1979) (unpublished document in J.C. McCartney personal administrative files, McCarthy Tétrault, Toronto).

The first and most noticeable stage in this process of growth as a deliberate exercise in seeking competitive advantage in the legal services business was geographical expansion. Stikeman Elliott of Montreal, founded in 1952 and a relative newcomer to the ranks of large Canadian law firms, had made the first significant step in inter-city expansion by Canadian law firms when it opened an office in Toronto in 1971.[34] A decade later came the series of moves by McCarthy & McCarthy that between 1981 and 1984 took it in rapid succession into Montreal, Calgary, and Vancouver. Attempts by law societies in Alberta and British Columbia to prevent interprovincial mergers delayed the developing trend until the outcome of litigation in 1989 permitted McCarthy & McCarthy and its merger partners to form the national firm called McCarthy Tétrault in 1990. What followed was a general movement by competing firms to consolidate tentative moves towards interprovincial expansion that had begun in the later 1980s. Within ten years, most of Canada's large law firms, previously based almost entirely in a single city, had established themselves in most of the major business centres of the country.[35]

It has been argued that the "number of offices is a proxy for complexity;" that is, that a legal transaction that requires participation by lawyers across several cities or jurisdictions is likely to be a complex and high-value one, relative to purely local matters.[36] The transformational impact of these interprovincial expansions, however, should not be exaggerated. In a perceptive 1993 article, Ronald J. Daniels[37] noted that most of the interprovincial linkages among Canadian firms up to that time were affiliations (that is, little more than agreements among independent firms to cooperate with each other while retaining their separate existence), rather than formal mergers to produce a single revenue-sharing partnership. Daniels argued that such loose affiliations were inherently implausible as economic structures, and he predicted that they might not last. He theorized that they were defensive in nature, catering mostly to client-firms' tendency to assume bigger was better and to law firms' fears of being left behind in the expansion race, but otherwise "bereft of economic value." Indeed, several of the early affiliations among Canadian law firms did break apart later in the 1990s, and several others

---

34 Pound, *Stikeman Elliott: The First Fifty Years*, above note 3, particularly c. 4.
35 Some chronology of these mergers and affiliations is provided in Moore, *McCarthy Tétrault: Building Canada's Premier Law Firm 1855–2005*, above note 3 at 275–76 and 326–27.
36 Michael D. Goldhaber, "Touched by an Angel" *American Lawyer* (October 2007), quoting Linklaters' managing partner Tony Angel.
37 Ronald J. Daniels, "Growing Pains: The Whys and Hows of Law Firm Expansion" (1993) 43:2 U.T.L.J. 147–206.

moved on to become complete mergers.[38] It seems likely that the answer to Daniels's question — "Why do law firms affiliate, despite the theoretical implausibility of affiliations?" — was that in the 1990s few law firms were yet at the stage where their governance structures could tolerate a greater degree of businesslike planning and organization.

TABLE TWO: NATIONAL FIRMS: HOW THEY WERE BUILT AND WHEN[39]

Stikeman Elliott	greenfield	from 1971
McCarthy Tétrault	mergers	from 1982
Fasken Martineau	affiliation	1986
	merger	1999
Goodmans/Phillips Vineberg	affiliation (broken off)	1990s
Oslers/Ogilvy Renault	affiliation (broken off)	1990s
Davies Ward Phillips Vineberg	merger	2000
Gowlings	mergers	from 2000
Borden Ladner Gervais	mergers	2000
Fraser Milner Casgrain	mergers	1998–2002
Osler Hoskin	greenfield	1990s
Blake Cassels	greenfield	late 1990s
Bennett Jones	greenfield	from 2000

- **affiliation**: cooperation among indepenodent firms.
- **merger**: agreement by independent firms to merge into one.
- **greenfield**: expansion of a firm into a new territory through recruitment or transfer of lawyers, without merging or affiliating with existing firms.

FROM GEOGRAPHICAL EXPANSION TO STRUCTURAL CHANGE

FUNDAMENTAL CHANGES IN FIRM governance and business operations inside the large Canadian law firms appear to have followed, rather than led, geographical and numerical expansion. The changes in firm governance that McCarthy Tétrault went through between 1990 and 2003 are both well-

---

38 See Table Two.
39 Sources: drawn largely from Moore, *McCarthy Tétrault: Building Canada's Premier Law Firm 1855–2005*, above note 3 at 275–76 and 326–27, based upon media and periodical reporting.

documented and instructive. Though it marketed itself as a single national firm from 1990 and was in many ways a decade ahead of competitor firms in seeking to build a merged national partnership, McCarthy Tétrault had been obliged, in order to achieve its mergers with independent firms in Montreal and Vancouver in the 1980s, to guarantee substantial autonomy to each of its component parts. Governance of the newly national McCarthy Tétrault firm of the 1990s was based on a federal-style committee structure with equal representation from each of the regional firms. Within McCarthy Tétrault, each region continued to be run in the traditional form by committees of partners with limited managerial authority. In 2001, a senior administrative staff member described McCarthy Tétrault as "four regional silos with a common brand." Even when "Canada's National Law Firm" was the base of McCarthy Tétrault's newly elaborate branding and marketing efforts of the 1990s, senior lawyers freely acknowledged, "We were not really a national firm." In 2004, the head of the firm described his colleagues in the 1990s as "350 lawyers flying in loose formation."[40]

The merger of firms in Montreal, Toronto, Calgary, and Vancouver to form McCarthy Tétrault had not created a unified partnership sharing a single profit pool. In the 1990s, each region within the McCarthy Tétrault partnership received a profit share based on its contribution to firm revenues. Partners within each region then divided the regional share, generally on the traditional partners-with-power model. Theory suggested that national law firms existed to provide seamlessly integrated service to the national operations of large corporations and institutions. Yet the regional offices within this firm, generally acknowledged as the leaders in developing the national law firm in Canada, still effectively practised local law and sometimes competed with each other on national retainers. Partners in each office actually had a financial incentive not to delegate work to another region of their own firm unless absolutely necessary. McCarthy Tétrault was not only subdivided into four largely autonomous units, but within each unit a rather traditional form of governance continued to hold sway. The firm and its competitors, despite their newly national reach and much increased size, still lacked both the means with which to undertake centralized strategic planning and the ability (standard in corporate organizations for a century and more) to use payment as a form of leverage with which to reward firm members who assisted in the achievement of centrally planned goals and objectives. "Partners with power" retained considerable autonomy over client relationships, though with the added complication that, with so many more partners divided among largely

---

40 Moore, *ibid.* at 329*ff.*

autonomous regional practices, every retainer accepted by one partner risked "conflicting out" the firm from other retainers that could well be more valuable or more closely aligned with the firm's interests.

By the 1990s, in other words, the largest law firms in Canada had taken on a new scale of operations without having reformed their organizational structures very much at all. In 2001, Nelson's partners-with-power thesis still fit internal operations at McCarthy Tétrault (and its competitors) well. Despite being "national" for ten years and benefiting from it, McCarthy Tétrault had not made fundamental changes in its management structure. Many of its most valuable deals and clients had become far too big to remain the "property" of individual lawyers, who in any case might leave to join a competitor at any time (given the newly competitive marketplace for individual lawyers' services). As a leading mergers and acquisitions partner at McCarthy Tétrault, very much a partner with power by the old measure, put it: "It's not what we know, it's what the firm knows. When you hire me, you are hiring McCarthys, hiring the promise that I can deliver the whole McCarthy team and all its expertise."[41]

Certainly, this was what the client corporations expected and what the scale of their legal business required, but it remained an open question as to whether traditional forms of firm governance made it possible for Canadian firms to fulfill that promise. Lack of coordination was producing competition and inefficiency within the firm, and the long-dominant partners-with-power culture had begun to threaten the firm's competitive position and its pursuit of maximum profit-per-partner.

FROM PARTNERS-WITH-POWER TO PROFIT-PER-PARTNER

IN THE LATE 1990S, lawyers in the Toronto corporate-commercial practice of McCarthy Tétrault, the part of the firm that was perhaps most exposed to the newly competitive marketplace being imposed on law firms by their preferred clients, began to raise the alarm about the disjuncture between the business of the firm and its business organization. To compete successfully in the newly competitive market for legal services, they argued, a law firm needed to be able to marshal its resources effectively, price the work of its lawyers precisely, and choose which clients and projects the firm should pursue. Such commitments would long have been familiar in business corporations, but they were very daunting goals for traditionally managed law firms where

---

41 Ibid. at 364.

every partner was almost an independent entity, where regional offices were still virtually separate firms, and where firm leaders lacked the tools to design and implement a firm-wide plan of action, or to draw the firm's lawyers into concerted efforts to implement one.[42]

Late in 2001, after extended discussion and consultation, McCarthy Tétrault adopted and began to implement a governance structure intended to bring firm management into line with precepts that were becoming doctrine among law firm consultancies and at the largest and most successful international law firms. To maximize profits, the new theories of law firm management agreed, a law firm needed team practice rather than individual practice, with each team of lawyers (organized by legal specialty or market sector rather than by location) pursuing corporate goals rather than the interests or aspirations of individual partners. The new management theory called for central coordination of the firm's resources and strategic planning about the markets and clients it would pursue. Increasingly, the client's relationship had to be with the firm, not the partner, and law firm managers, rather than individual partners, had to direct the relationship. Briefly stated, McCarthy Tétrault's strategic plan, approved in late 2001 and implemented in the following months, called for the transfer of authority within the firm from a myriad of committees and the partnership at large to a small management team upon which significant authority would be conferred. The firm's partners would now participate in firm management only by electing representatives to a small supervisory board of directors; managing authority would be conferred on a chief executive officer leading an executive management team answerable to him. New management's success would be measured by PPP. A key element in pursuing that goal would be central management control over client relations and over partners' allocations.

From a business perspective, the ability to reward those who best fulfill a firm's goals is a normal management tool. In law firms, however, allocations to partners had traditionally been closely related to a partner's billings and billable hours and had generally been determined by allocations committees elected (or appointed) separately from executive or managing committees. (That is, power as expressed in earnings closely reflected a lawyer's control over relations with firm clients.) Early in the twenty-first century, however, at very large law firms around the world, managerial authority was being assumed by practice groups directed by managers empowered to reward partners for their contributions to firm goals rather than their individual performance or productivity. Authority within the law firms was shifting from

---

42 What follows summarizes a more detailed description in *ibid.*, c. 17.

partners to managers, not because partners particularly liked it, but because in a competitive marketplace for corporate legal services, competitive advantage (as measured by PPP) required it.

The changes at McCarthy Tétrault have been reported publicly, but coverage of other firms in the legal press and the business press suggests that such changes were hardly unique to that firm. The innovations McCarthy Tétrault undertook conformed to the advice given routinely by leading law firm consultancies and advocated in legal business magazines, and in the early twenty-first century they were being adopted in leading megafirms worldwide. As a leading American law firm consultant put it in 2007, the largest American law firm had revenues equivalent to those of the American budget airline JetBlue, but "nobody would propose that pilots run JetBlue."[43] Also in 2007, in a survey of management trends, *American Lawyer* described how the long-established London law firm Linklaters had repositioned itself as one of the world's most profitable law firms by transferring authority decisively from partners to managers and by ruthlessly executing a centrally devised strategic plan. Linklaters' management pruned underperforming departments and partners, much as other profit-maximizing corporate entities did, and focused the firm's efforts on a core of very valuable clients and particularly on their most complex (and most profitable) cross-border transactions. *American Lawyer* quoted a lawyer who left Linklaters to avoid these changes as saying, "By the numbers I made a bad decision. But [by leaving] I can pursue whatever client I want, and no one will stop me." Lawyers who "pursue whatever clients they want," almost perfectly fit Robert Nelson's definition of partners with power in traditionally governed law firms ("a situation of largely independent professionals selecting their own work"). However, that situation no longer described the working ethos of the most profitable and successful large law firms around the world or in Canada. Successful law firms were mastering the twin processes of centralizing decision-making and "institutionalizing the clients."

Among large Canadian law firms, several of the loose associations that typified the 1990s have either collapsed or moved on to formal mergers. Other national firms, including Ogilvy Renault and Stikeman Elliott of Montreal, Blakes and Osler Hoskins of Toronto, and Bennett Jones of Calgary, have avoided the managerial complications of affiliations and negotiated mergers. Their expansions in the late 1990s and early 2000s were achieved through

---

43. Jim Middlemiss, "Doing Business: Beware Hollowing of the Middle" *Law Times* (January 2007) quoting American law firm consultant Bruce MacEwan. The largest Canadian law firms' revenues compare to those of Tim Hortons or Torstar Ltd.

"greenfielding," that is, by opening offices in new markets without seeking mergers with law firms already established there. A few elite corporate law firms — notably Goodmans of Toronto, Farris Vaughan of Vancouver — have been successful and profitable without geographical expansion, confirming that success has more to do with the marketing and management of legal talent than numbers of lawyers or geographic reach. Given the highly competitive market in which the large Canadian law firms now operate, and the international evidence that centrally planned and empowered management provides law firms with substantial competitive advantages over traditionally managed competitors, the movement seems irreversible.

It seems very likely that Canadian megafirms either have or will very soon adopt the new organizational structures or risk losing their clients, their lawyers, and finally their businesses to competitors that have done so. The closing of the Toronto corporate law firm Goodman & Carr in March 2007 may support this hypothesis, for press reports suggested it had many of the traits of a law firm trying to maintain a partners-with-power model in a profits-per-partner world.[44]

CONCLUSION

IN THE PROFITS-PER-PARTNER ETHOS, partners in a law firm may be owners of their firm but they are not its managers, nor even managers of their own practices. In order to achieve the centralized planning and empowered management that the newly competitive market for legal services requires, the traditional situation "of largely independent professionals selecting their own work" is giving way to a situation in which professional practice in a large law firm begins to resemble work elsewhere. Partners in large law firms are well rewarded, their talents and reputations are recognized and praised, and their work can be satisfying, challenging, and important in determining the evolution of the corporate landscape of Canada. But, increasingly, even the most successful partners are part of the law firm organization and subject to its goals and to its directions. In short, lawyers in PPP-oriented megafirms are beginning to resemble employees in other business corporations, in a way they did not during the first century or so of large corporate law firms. This would seem to be the most substantial redefinition of large law firm operations since the large law firm came into being in the later nineteenth century.

---

44 Darryl Lynn-Carlsen, "Culture Unglued: The Demise of Goodman & Carr" *Canadian Lawyer* (July 2007) at 36–41.

The larger consequences of the transition remain to be determined. It is, for instance, an open question of how professional ethics and the professional independence of the lawyer can endure in the PPP legal environment in which law firms become businesses like any other. When a lawyer describes her professional commitment as "I am willing to walk through walls to meet the clients' needs," there is clearly a risk that single-minded focus on client service as the way to maximize law firm profits may erode the conditions under which truly independent legal counsel can be delivered.[45] It may be noted, on the other hand, that the new, competitive, "transactional" law firm, with its larger, more transitory, less permanent clientele, has a wider base of clients and is in some ways actually more independent of individual clients than was the older relationship-based law firm. And even a client-driven market for legal services still has some reasons for valuing professional independence. The sensational case of Arthur Andersen/Enron in 2000–1 (and very recently of the debt-rating agencies that are suspected of failing to provide objective assessment of Asset-Backed Commercial Paper because of their involvement with the firms issuing these debt instruments) suggests that properly functioning markets still require, and will reward, professional independence.

The old ideal of professional autonomy for lawyers, even those in large firms serving large corporate interests, survived so long because it was highly congenial to those who benefited from it, and because the economy of legal services long permitted it. The ideal of the lawyer as an autonomous professional remains powerful. Even among young recruits to the largest firms, the idealization of legal practice as heroic, macho, a kind of single-combat-warrior existence remains surprisingly strong.[46] It is worth noting, however, that such claims are rarely made about other professional organizations. Accountants, bankers, management consultants, and engineers also practise professional skills, submit to licensing bodies, assert professional ethics, work hard, and are well-rewarded for their work. They continue to fit most of the common definitions of professionalism, even though they have worked for a long time in large organizations, as part of teams under supervision, doing assigned work. Other professions, that is, have moved on from heroic

---

45 The phrase is by a partnership candidate quoted by Lincoln Caplan, *Skadden: Power, Money, and the Rise of a Legal Empire* (New York: Farrar, Strauss, and Giroux, 1993) at 273. It is worth noting that the lawyer emphasized the importance of ethical standards in the same sentence.
46 I drew anecdotal evidence on this point in 2007 from the website "Lawbuzz," online: www.lawbuzz.ca and particularly its Big Firm thread, where young associates at large firms frequently expressed alarm at each new sign their firms might "go corporate."

individualism and autonomous partners-with-power practices. It may even be that law firms where highly renowned and senior partners are more like employees than like managers of their own practices will be able to address the perennial law firm crisis of "work-life balance." If the fantasy of lawyers as heroic individuals controlling their own work dies, so too can the cult of the billable hour and the eat-what-you-kill ethos that many lawyers, even in the largest firms, have identified as damaging both to lawyers and to law firms.[47]

It is likely that the period from about 1980 to the present has seen a fundamental, historic change in the nature of legal practice for the elite of lawyers who practise in large corporate law firms. The full dimensions of that transformation, however, remain to be worked out.

---

47 "Work-life balance" may be more than a slogan or aspiration. Large law firms incur significant losses from the departure of talented and experienced associates who leave the megafirms for more congenial working conditions elsewhere. Work-life balance issues became a notable element in McCarthy Tétrault's internal debates about its new governance structure.

PART 3

QUEBEC:
A DISTINCT LEGAL HISTORY

CHAPTER 7

Civil Law, Legal Practitioners, and Everyday Justice in the Decades following the *Quebec Act of 1774*[1]

JEAN-PHILIPPE GARNEAU
(TRANSLATED BY STEVEN WATT, PH.D.)

THE SUBJECT OF LAWYERS who practised in Quebec is a particularly interesting one, especially at the outset of the British regime. Following the *Quebec Act of 1774*, the genesis of the Quebec bar was notably characterized by increasing judicial pluralism and cultural diversity. Authors like Evelyn Kolish and Murray F. Greenwood have done a good job of addressing the problem posed by the administration of French civil law in a British colony with a French Catholic majority.[2] In my own research, I have addressed this question by focusing on active lawyers who, along with judges, were the primary upholders of the colonial legal culture at the turn of the nineteenth century. Indeed, Quebec legal practitioners had to cope with a peculiar mix of two distinct "national" legal traditions (French civil law and English common law). This represented a distinct challenge for British lawyers, who practised in the Quebec civil courts, for they had to refer — at least in part — to French legal traditions.

In this chapter, I present some of the main findings of my current research project on *Canadien* (French-Canadian) and British lawyers who appeared

---

1   (U.K.), 14 Geo. III, c. 83 [*Quebec Act*].
2   Evelyn Kolish, "The Impact of the Change in Legal Metropolis on the Development of Lower Canada's Legal System: Judicial Chaos and Legislative Paralysis in the Civil Law, 1791–1838" (1988) 3 C.J.L.S. 1; Evelyn Kolish, *Nationalismes et conflits de droits: le débat du droit privé au Québec, 1760–1840* (LaSalle, QC: Hurtubise HMH, 1994); Murray F. Greenwood, *Legacies of Fear: Law and Politics in Quebec in the Era of the French Revolution* (Toronto: University of Toronto Press, 1993).

before the civil courts in Quebec City and Montreal during the decades following the *Quebec Act*.[3] In my opinion, such an analysis allows for a better understanding of the relationship between the colonial bar and French civil law that emerged out of a very specific — albeit not unique — context of pluralism after 1774.[4] Civil court dockets demonstrate that despite the system's "bijurality," British attorneys were active court practitioners from the very beginning. In Montreal, although less numerous in the superior jurisdiction of the court of King's Bench, they were pleading more cases than their *Canadien* counterparts at the beginning of the nineteenth century.[5] Court records also suggest that legal practice and rhetoric were highly variable and were not necessarily bound by the rules of either national legal tradition. This chapter begins by briefly describing the legal and professional contexts at the outset of the British regime, before highlighting a few key aspects of the composition and legal practice of the early Quebec bar.

LEGAL AND PROFESSIONAL CONTEXTS AT THE OUTSET OF THE BRITISH REGIME

IN 1774, THE *QUEBEC Act* reintroduced part of the French civil law of the *Ancien Régime* — essentially the Custom of Paris along with a few specific royal ordinances. From that moment forward, the French legal tradition imposed itself, in theory, on all those arguing before the civil courts in Quebec. For

---

[3] I would like to thank the FQRSC for the financial support it has given to this research project. This text is a revised version of the article: "Droit, pluralisme culturel et genèse du barreau québécois: analyse prosopographique de deux générations d'avocats (fin XVIIIe–début XIXe siècles)" in V. Bernaudeat et al. eds., *Les praticiens du droit du Moyen Âge à l'époque contemporaine. Approches prosopographiques* (Rennes: Presses Universitaires de Rennes, 2008) 209..

[4] From this perspective, it is important to note the works of G. Blaine Baker, dealing with the legal culture of English-speaking lawyers: "Law Practice and Statecraft in Mid-Nineteenth-Century Montreal: The Torrance-Morris Firm, 1848 to 1868" in C. Wilton, ed., *Essays in the History of Canadian Law, vol. IV: Beyond the Law: Lawyers and Business in Canada, 1830 to 1930* (Toronto: Butterworths, 1990) at 45–91; "Ordering the Urban Canadian Law Office and Its Entrepreneurial Hinterland, 1825 to 1875" (1998) 48:2 U.T.L.J. 175.

[5] In this paper, the adjectives "British," "anglophone," and "English-speaking" are used interchangeably to describe individuals of British origin or nationality, regardless of whether they were born in the colonies, in Britain, or even in continental Europe. But, in reality, this group is very diverse, as I note further in the discussion. The terms "*Canadien*" and "French-Canadian" are also treated as synonyms, although they refer to a much more narrowly defined historical reality (those individuals living on the territory conquered by the British in 1760, along with their descendants). "Francophone" is used somewhat more broadly, since it sometimes encompasses recent immigrants who spoke French.

obvious cultural reasons, this situation likely favoured French-Canadian legal professionals. But it is also true that some aspects of English law were introduced at the same time or shortly thereafter: such was notably the case in the commercial domain and that of civil liability.[6] Recognizing that Quebec's criminal law was also based on the English common law, the British were favoured in their own way, albeit in different aspects of legal practice. In sum, from 1775 onward, legal practitioners faced the decidedly complex task of familiarizing themselves with the two main Western legal traditions.

It must also be remembered that the profession of lawyer arrived relatively late in Quebec history. In New France, notaries and bailiffs were authorized to represent the population before the courts, but the bar was not officially recognized by the French administration.[7] Under the British regime, the situation of legal professionals was somewhat clarified even if, in the beginning, the same individual could still practise multiple professions. As early as 1764, the new rulers granted lawyers' commissions, first to British lawyers and then to their French-Canadian counterparts. The profession of notary was maintained under the British regime, while the distinction between barrister and solicitor was not established in Quebec (contrary to later developments in Upper Canada).[8] Thus, in practice, the same men were responsible for providing the principal legal services to the population, whether in the courts or in their offices.

It was only in 1785 that the colonial government undertook a restructuring of the legal profession, the main aspects of which would remain in place until the mid-nineteenth century.[9] The roles of notaries and lawyers were henceforth mutually exclusive. A five-year clerkship was required, at the end

---

6   For a more detailed account of specific legal changes that occurred after the 1760 British conquest, see Michel Morin, "Les changements de régimes juridiques consécutifs à la Conquête de 1760" (1997) 57 Revue du Barreau 695.

7   J.A. Dickinson, *Justice et justiciables. La procédure civile à la prévôté de Québec, 1667–1759* (Québec : Presses de l'Université Laval, 1982) at 82–84; J.-P. Garneau, *Justice et règlements des conflits dans la région de Montréal à la fin du régime français* (M.A. Thesis, Université du Québec à Montréal, 1995) at 131.

8   G. Blaine Baker, "Legal Education in Upper Canada 1785–1889: The Law Society as Educator" in D.H. Flaherty, ed., *Essays in the History of Canadian Law,* vol. I (Toronto: University of Toronto Press, 1983) at 49–142. See also Philip Girard, *Patriot Jurist: Beamish Murdoch of Halifax, 1800–1876* (Ph.D. Thesis, Dalhousie University, 1998) at 129.

9   *An Ordinance Concerning Advocates, Attorneys, Solicitors and Notaries, and for the More Easy Collection of His Majesty's Revenues,* 25 Geo. III (30 april 1785), c. 4. Christine Veilleux, *Aux origines du Barreau québécois, 1774–1849* (Sillery, QC: Septentrion, 1997). For a recently published overview of the legal profession in Quebec after 1840, see S. Normand, "La transformation de la profession d'avocat au Québec, 1840–1900" in C. Dolan,

of which the candidate was examined by practising lawyers under the supervision of the lower courts. However, no other selection criteria were established. Clearly, the administrators of the colony were not primarily concerned with creating a social elite, as was attempted in Upper Canada, for example.[10] But in a colonial context where there was no law school,[11] practical training nevertheless assured a certain identity, if not coherence, for the profession.

PORTRAIT OF THE QUEBEC BAR IN 1786 AND 1805

THUS FAR, I HAVE said very little about the genesis of the Quebec bar from the perspective of those lawyers who actually argued before the courts. It remains to be seen how cultural factors like language, geographic origin, or legal training influenced the destiny and the work of these legal professionals. These questions lie at the foundation of my analysis of two groups of legal professionals practising in the districts of Quebec City and Montreal, the first of which encompasses those who were working in 1786 and the second those who were working in 1805.[12]

During the two years covered by the study, a total of forty-seven lawyers were practising in Quebec City and Montreal, twenty-one in 1786 compared to twenty-eight in 1805. Considering the growth of the general population in the colony, the availability of legal services was actually in decline at the beginning of the nineteenth century: there were a little more than 5000 inhabitants for every lawyer in 1786, but more than 7000 in 1805.[13] The ranks of the

---

ed., *Entre Justice et justiciables: les auxiliaires de la justice du Moyen Âge au XXe siècle* (Québec: Presses de l'Université Laval, 2005) at 425–39.

10   G. B. Baker, "Legal Education in Upper Canada 1785–1889," above note 8; Christopher Moore, *The Law Society of Upper Canada and Ontario's Lawyers 1797–1997* (Toronto: University of Toronto Press, 1997).

11   For a brief overview of the early history of legal education in Quebec, see Léon Lortie, "The Early Teaching of Law in French Canada" (1975–76) 2 Dal. L.J. 521. Also see, Sylvio Normand, *Le droit comme discipline universitaire. Une histoire de la Faculté de droit de l'Université Laval* (Québec: Presses de l'Université Laval, 2006).

12   The following sources were examined while constituting these two cohorts: for the year 1786, the case files of the Courts of Common Pleas for the districts of Quebec City and Montreal (BANQ-Qc, TL15 and BANQ-Mtl, TL16); for the year 1805, the case files of the Court of King's Bench for the districts of Quebec City and Montreal (BANQ-Qc, TL18 and BANQ-Mtl, TL19). For multiple reasons, only the superior jurisdiction of these civil courts was taken into account.

13   By comparison, in Nova Scotia, the ratio of lawyers to the general population was 1:3000 in 1820. P. Girard, *Patriot Jurist: Beamish Murdoch of Halifax, 1800–1876*, above note 8 at 132–33.

legal profession appear even more modest when compared to other groups, such as the growing number of justices of the peace.[14] Clearly, the "crisis" of the liberal professions, whose ranks would grow significantly after the 1820s, was yet to be felt within the legal profession.[15]

An analysis of the geographic origins of lawyers gives insight into the rapid evolution of the early bar.[16] While legal practitioners born outside the colony formed a clear majority in 1786, this group was already two times less prominent by 1805, signalling a rather rapid "Canadianization" of the bar.[17] That being said, the origins of immigrants still remained relatively diverse at the beginning of the nineteenth century. Many came from the United States, but the largest numbers were born in Europe, mainly in the British Isles. The impact of this cosmopolitanism was nevertheless mitigated by the presence of "natives," almost all of whom hailed from the cities of Quebec and Montreal.

TABLE ONE: NUMBER OF LAWYERS AND THEIR BIRTHPLACES IN 1786 AND 1805 (QUEBEC CITY AND MONTREAL)

Birthplace	1786		1805	
Quebec / Lower Canada	7	33.3%	18	64.3%
Europe or other colonies	11	52.4%	6	21.4%
Unknown	3	14.3%	4	14.3%
Total	21	100.0%	28	100.0%

This phenomenon can be illustrated using the case of the Community of Quebec City Lawyers, which formed no later than the end of the 1770s. This professional association brought together fewer than a dozen practitioners, among whom immigrants were in the minority. Since seniority partially determined the hierarchy within the bar, newcomers sometimes had to yield their place to indigenous lawyers, who had been practising for a longer period of time. If the

---

14 D. Fyson, *Magistrates, Police and People: Everyday Criminal Justice in Quebec and Lower Canada* (Montréal: McGill-Queen's University Press, 2006) at 57, Table 2.1.
15 F. Ouellet, "Structure des occupations et ethnicité dans les villes de Québec et de Montréal (1819–1844)" in *Éléments d'histoire sociale du Bas-Canada* (Montréal: Hurtubise HMH, 1972) at 182–85; C. Veilleux, *Les gens de justice à Québec, 1760–1867* (Ph. D. Thesis, Université Laval, 1990) at 135–38; R. Gagnon, "Capital culturel et identité sociale: les fonctions sociales du discours sur l'encombrement des professions libérales au XIXe siècle" (1989) 21:2 Sociologie et sociétés 129.
16 See Table One.
17 Although a similar trend was visible in the case of Nova Scotia, the British-born still made up a significant proportion of Upper-Canadian lawyers even after the mid-nineteenth century. P. Girard, *Patriot Jurist: Beamish Murdoch of Halifax, 1800–1876*, above note 8 at 137–38.

lawyers hailing from France, Ireland, and even Prussia appear to have easily accepted the situation, their British counterparts were clearly more resistant, perhaps because they belonged to the same cultural group as the administrators of the colony. Some clearly refused to join the ranks of the emerging Community and even challenged the pre-eminence of the older members of the bar (who were *Canadiens*). It was likely this antagonism that doomed the Community, since no trace of it remained after 1786. When it rose from the ashes at the beginning of the nineteenth century, collaboration among its members, whose origins remained diverse, no longer seemed to be a problem. This was likely because of the relative "Canadianization" of the legal workforce.[18]

If diversity of origins diminished over time, linguistic duality remained a defining characteristic of the Lower-Canadian bar for a much longer period.[19] It is true that anglophones were less numerous in 1805, dropping from a little more than 50 percent to less than 35 percent of the total. However, their presence in court remained just as important as that of francophones, and sometimes more so. Considering the British ascendancy in the administration of justice, it becomes clear that the English language actually played a key role in the application, and perhaps even the definition, of French law in Quebec.

In any case, these findings suggest that the French legal tradition did not significantly hinder newcomers to the early Quebec bar who were less familiar with the French language or with French civil law.

TABLE TWO: WRITTEN LANGUAGE USED BY LAWYERS IN 1786 AND 1805 (QUEBEC CITY AND MONTREAL)[20]

Language	1786	1805
English	11	10
French	10	18
Total	21	28

---

18   For more details, see M. Nantel, "La communauté des avocats" (1945) 10 Les Cahiers des Dix 263; J.-P. Garneau, "Une culture de l'amalgame au prétoire: les avocats de Québec et l'élaboration d'un langage juridique commun (tournant des XVIIIe et XIXe siècles)" (2007) 88:1 Canadian Historical Review 113 at 129–33. See also G. Blaine Baker, "Public Frivolity and Patrician Confidence: Lower Canada's Brothers-in-Law, 1827–1833" in *Mélanges offerts par ses collègues de McGill à Paul-André Crépeau* (Cowansville, QC: Yvon Blais, 1997) at 43–73.

19   See Table Two.

20   It should be mentioned that two lawyers were actually of German origin: Charles Thomas, active in 1786, wrote his legal proceedings in English. In 1805, George Vanfelson, who was married to a French-Canadian woman, had definitively adopted the French language in his daily legal practice.

At first glance, the Quebec bar was mainly drawn from the liberal or merchant *petite bourgeoisie*.[21] However, it is interesting to note that there were relatively few legal professionals whose fathers had practised the same profession (three or four at most). That being said, many of the lawyers who came from abroad had clearly come to the colony with the aim of seeking their fortune. In fact, the legal profession was sometimes seen as the last resort of those hoping to avoid slipping down the social ladder, at least in the eighteenth century. Thus, Alexandre Dumas, a protestant from a relatively wealthy family of French merchants, obtained a lawyer's commission following the failure of his business, a development that nevertheless provoked an outcry from the bar.[22]

TABLE THREE: SOCIAL ORIGINS OF LAWYERS IN 1786 AND 1805 (QUEBEC CITY AND MONTREAL)[23]

Father's Occupation	1786	1805	Total*	%
Seigneurs, Civil and Military Officers, Clergy (Anglican minister)	4	2	6	12.8%
Professionals	3	7	9	19.1%
Merchants	3	9	11	23.4%
Tradesmen	1	4	5	10.6%
Unknown	10	6	16	34.0%
Total	21	28	47	100.0%

* Since two lawyers (the son of a professional and the son of a merchant) were practising in both 1786 and 1805, they have been counted only once in this column.

Moreover, the number of families involved in small business was quite significant, especially in 1805. If the liberal professions were also well-represented overall, lawyers whose fathers were legal professionals were, all things considered, relatively rare.[24] For example, in 1805, only five of twenty-eight legal professionals fell into this category and they were all drawn from the same three families, one of which was *Canadien* (the Panets), and two of

---

21　See Table Three.
22　D. Roberts, "Alexandre Dumas" in Library and Archives Canada, *Dictionary of Canadian Biography Online*, vol. 5, online: www.biographi.ca/EN/ShowBio.asp?BioId=36503&query=alexandre%20AND%20dumas.
23　The father's occupation has been used as the indicator of social origins in preparing this table. For the 1786 cohort, the social origins of many legal practitioners remain unknown because they had only recently immigrated to the colony.
24　These data agree with those of C. Veilleux, *Les gens de justice à Québec, 1760–1867* (Ph. D. Thesis, Université Laval, 1990) at 172–75.

which were American Loyalists (the Sewell brothers and the Ogdens). Thus, even if the phenomenon could be observed among both francophones and anglophones, the legal profession was clearly not the stronghold of great dynasties of legal professionals. Furthermore, the sons of artisans or tradesmen were able, without much difficulty, to join the ranks of this small legal elite.

The level of education was in most cases limited to studies at a classical college, and in exceptional cases at a university. In 1805, this was the case with fifteen of twenty-eight lawyers. Some of the immigrants had attended English Inns of Court and had been called to the English bar, like James Monk.[25] James Kerr, a Scot, had even practised in England for a certain period, following the judges of Westminster as they journeyed through the English countryside.[26] Among the Canadian-born, only Benjamin Beaubien, the son of a rural merchant, had left the country to complete his legal education (in Philadelphia).[27] But for the majority, legal knowledge was acquired through clerkships, sometimes with a lawyer from the other linguistic group. A more detailed study of this process remains to be completed, especially with regard to the professional and intellectual lineages of legal professionals. But it is nevertheless clear that clerks frequently worked in more than one legal practice and that, at least for a few months, 25–30 percent of them trained with a member of the other linguistic group.[28] Finally, there was a transfusion of youth in the candidates for the bar (passing from thirty to twenty-four years old on average), another aspect of the important change the bar was undergoing during the period.

LEGAL ACTIVITIES AND THE LAWYERS' CLIENTELE

ON THE WHOLE, THE study of cases shows that British lawyers were just as active as their Canadian-born counterparts. Even when they were fewer in number, as in 1805, anglophone lawyers initiated cases more frequently before the civil courts in both Montreal and Quebec City. In Montreal, the

---

25 J.H. Lambert, "James Monk" in Library and Archives Canada, *Dictionary of Canadian Biography Online*, vol. 6, online: www.biographi.ca/EN/ShowBio.asp?BioId=37156&query=james%20AND%20monk.
26 P. M. Chiasson, "James Kerr" in *ibid,*, vol. 7 online: www.biographi.ca/EN/ShowBio.asp?BioId=37598&query=james%20AND%20kerr.
27 Library and Archives Canada, "James Peale (1749–1831)," online: http://epe.lac-bac.gc.ca/100/206/301/lac-bac/real_stories-ef/www.lac-bac.gc.ca/miniatures/05150127_e.html.
28 C. Veilleux, *Les gens de justice à Québec, 1760–1867*, above note 24 at 209–11. See also G. Blaine Baker, "Ordering the Urban Canadian Law Office and Its Entrepreneurial Hinterland, 1825 to 1875" (1998) 48:2 U.T.L.J. 175.

three most active British prosecutors in 1805 initiated more proceedings than the French Canadians who practised during that year.[29] The services of anglophones were primarily retained by litigants drawn from the same linguistic group. But some 30 percent of British litigators' clientele of was made up of French Canadians. By contrast, less than 20 percent of British litigants retained the services of French-Canadian lawyers. There were nevertheless cases where French Canadians, like Benjamin Beaubien, dedicated most of their legal practice to British clients.

TABLE FOUR: ETHNICITY OF LAWYERS' CLIENTS IN 1805 MONTREAL[30]

	Clients				
	Anglophone	Francophone	Mixed	Unknown	Total
Viger, D.B.	7	37	0	2	46
Bédard, J.	3	36	0	4	43
Panet, Narcisse	6	40	0	0	46
Lacroix, J.D.	7	40	0	0	47
Beaubien, B.	17	7	1	5	30
Bender, F.-X.	3	5	0	0	8
Francophone practitioners	**43**	**165**	**1**	**11**	**220**
Reid, J.	78	57	0	7	142
Ross, D.	59	41	1	13	114
Sewell, S.	82	16	3	5	106
Ogden, D.	24	0	0	0	24
Anglophone practitioners	**243**	**114**	**4**	**25**	**386**

In Montreal, in 1805, British lawyers represented farmers just as often as their French-Canadian colleagues, which meant that they frequently had to

---

29 See Table Four.
30 This table was created using the case files of the Court of King's Bench for 1805 See "Dossiers de la Cour du banc du roi du district de Montréal, 1795–1850," Montreal case file (BANQ-Mtl, TL19, S4, SS1); note that these historical sources are discussed more generally above at note 12. In some cases, it was still not possible to identify individual lawyers either because the information was not included in the sources or because the litigants were not represented by a lawyer (this was frequently the case for defendants, who often chose not to appear in court and did not always hire a lawyer).

deal in French civil law.[31] Likewise, the commercial regulations of English law do not seem to have discouraged French-Canadian lawyers since the latter acted on behalf of merchants fairly regularly.[32]

TABLE FIVE: SOCIAL AND OCCUPATIONAL DISTRIBUTION OF PLAINTIFFS ACCORDING TO THE ETHNICITY OF THEIR LAWYER (MONTREAL, 1805)

	Anglophone practitioners		Francophone practitioners	
Seigneurs, Civil and Military Officers, Clergy (Anglican minister)	28	10.0%	6	3.7%
Professionals	6	2.1%	7	4.3%
Merchants	132	47.0%	58	35.8%
Tradesmen	40	14.2%	25	15.4%
Farmers	58	20.6%	32	19.8%
Other	0	0.0%	3	1.9%
Unknown	17	6.0%	31	19.1%
Total	281	100.0%	162	100.0%

Thus, at the beginning of the nineteenth century, the mixing of French laws and the common law does not seem to have had a significant impact on the prosperity of lawyers from either cultural group. Despite their cultural affinity with French law, French Canadians do not appear to have used this advantage to dominate the market for legal services. Many factors explain this situation. First, trials for debt largely dominated judicial activity, a field where the differences between French and English law were not necessarily relevant to settling the matter at hand. Meanwhile, British litigants represented at least half of the users of the courts under study. And British litigants showed a clear preference for retaining the services of a British lawyer. Finally, many British lawyers were fairly quick to familiarize themselves with the finer points of French law. In fact, it would seem that the most skilled among them even began to master it.[33]

---

31 See Table Five.
32 However, it is somewhat difficult to draw definitive conclusions from these data given the higher number of unknowns among francophone practitioners' clients.
33 For example, take the case of Jonathan Sewell, a well-known figure to historians of Lower Canada. F. Murray Greenwood, "Jonathan Sewell," *Dictionary of Canadian Biography Online* (2000), online: www.biographi.ca.

With regard to French-Canadian lawyers, some of them mainly practised in the lower levels of civil jurisdiction, where their anglophone counterparts seem to have been less prevalent. Several French Canadians also ran in legislative elections. Of the fourteen legal professionals elected to the Assembly after 1792, eleven were French Canadian. Yet the French-Canadian lawyers who most regularly attended legislative sessions were not necessarily those with the largest clienteles. In fact, the opposite would appear to be true.

CONCLUSION

AT THE CLOSE OF this brief sketch, a clear conclusion emerges: at the turn of the nineteenth century, access to the colonial bar was not exclusively reserved for one ethnic group. It is true that without the *Quebec Act*, it is far less likely that French Canadians would have played such an important role in the administration of civil justice. But many other factors besides cultural affinity with French law impacted on the division of labour within the courts. In fact, in everyday judicial practice, French civil law was rarely invoked by lawyers. In the lower courts, legal arguments do not seem to have been expressed in the formal language of academic law. When the authority of positive law was invoked, it was most often in the context of recent colonial legislation, usually of a procedural nature. Otherwise, it was expressed in vague forms such as "the law of the land."[34] To find examples of a higher level of legal culture, it would no doubt be necessary to examine the files of the provincial appeals court or the legal commentaries published by contemporary lawyers. Nevertheless, the cultural diversity of legal practitioners remains an important characteristic of beginnings of legal practice in the province of Quebec. The different cultural backgrounds and linguistic duality that were present in the courts helped shape a practical and original knowledge in terms of law and justice.

---

34 Jean-Philippe Garneau, "'Une masquerade de Jurisprudence Françoise'? Droit civil et pratique judiciaire dans la province de Québec à la fin du XVIIIe siècle" in Benoît Garnot, éd., *Normes juridiques et pratiques judiciaires du Moyen Âge à l'époque contemporaine* (Dijon: Presses universitaires de Dijon, 2007) at 431–40.

CHAPTER 8

The Legal Profession and Penal Justice in Quebec City, 1856–1965: From Modernity to Anti-Modernity[1]

DONALD FYSON

INTRODUCTION

THE STATE'S USE OF the criminal justice system[2] to regulate rapidly expanding and industrializing urban societies in the nineteenth and twentieth centuries has long been and continues to be an object of great historiographical interest. Insofar as Quebec is concerned, however, the field is relatively new and there are still very significant gaps in our basic understanding of state regulation in Quebec cities. Thus, we know an increasing amount about social regulation in the metropolis of Montreal, in the nineteenth and early twentieth centuries.[3] However, with a few exceptions, we know little about the

---

1 An earlier version of this paper, with less emphasis on the legal profession and the judicial establishment, will be published in the proceedings of a colloquium held in Cordoba, Spain: "Criminal Justice in a Provincial Town" in *Modernidad, Ciudadanía, Desviaciones y Desigualdades* (Córdoba: Servicios de Publicaciones Universidad de Córdoba, 2009) (forthcoming).
2 I use the terms "criminal justice system" and "penal justice system" interchangeably here to refer to the entire range of state institutions designed to regulate explicitly criminalized behaviour, from police, through the courts, to prisons. For a more lengthy discussion, see Donald Fyson, *Magistrates, Police, and People: Everyday Criminal Justice in Quebec and Lower Canada, 1764–1837* (Toronto: Osgoode Society for Canadian Legal History by University of Toronto Press, 2006) at 19–20.
3 For example, the work of the members of the *Centre d'histoire des régulations sociales* (CHRS) in Montreal, online: www.unites.uqam.ca/chrs. Among others, Jean-Marie Fecteau, *La liberté du pauvre: sur la régulation du crime et de la pauvreté au XIXe siècle québécois* (Montréal: VLB, 2004) and Jean-Marie Fecteau *et al.*, "Emergence et évolu-

transformation of penal justice elsewhere in Quebec in the period before the Quiet Revolution. This chapter presents some preliminary reflections drawn from a research project underway on the penal justice system in Quebec City from the mid-nineteenth to the mid-twentieth century.

Though Quebec City was the second largest urban area in Quebec and experienced the same processes of industrialization, urban expansion, and poverty as Montreal and other major Canadian urban centers, it followed a quite different trajectory. A city of comparable size to Montreal in the 1850s, it grew much more slowly than its rival, rising from about 55,000 inhabitants in 1860 to about 160,000 in 1950, when Montreal had reached almost ten times that size. Economically, its influence also waned: in the 1850s, it was a major international port, but this declined from the 1870s onwards, and by the twentieth century Quebec City was no more than a regional service centre, though also the provincial capital. Partly as a result, and alone among major Canadian cities, Quebec City also became significantly less ethnically diverse. In 1850, the francophone population was only just in the majority, with the remainder mainly Irish and English. But by the 1950s, francophones accounted for almost 95 percent of the population, the result of an exodus of anglophones (largely in the last quarter of the nineteenth century) and very little compensatory immigration. This was in contrast to the persistently bicultural and increasingly cosmopolitan nature of Montreal. In short, while Montreal became a metropolis, Quebec City increasingly became a provincial town. Penal justice in this provincial capital also became increasingly provincial: closed-in on itself, kept out of the public eye, and, in general, resistant to modernity. And, as we will see, the judges, lawyers, court officials, and police who constituted the system's human face followed this trend as well.

SCANDAL, MODERNITY, AND RESISTANCE TO CHANGE

LET US BEGIN WITH a couple of notorious affairs that bracket the period and give some flavour of the underside of criminal justice in the city and of the city's prevailing legal culture. In the mid-1850s, the criminal justice establishment in Quebec City was the subject of a series of complaints. In 1853, the city was the scene of a riot by Catholics against the visit of a radically anti-Catholic Italian preacher, Alessandro Gavazzi (a former Catholic priest who had

---

tion historique de l'enfermement à Montréal, 1836–1913" (1992) 46:2 Revue d'histoire de l'Amérique française 263.

renounced the Church and embraced Protestantism).[4] A government investigation into the riot suggested that the city's police force, composed mainly of Irish Catholics, had essentially stood by and allowed the riot to take place, with some witnesses suggesting the police may even have actively supported the rioters. The report of the investigating commissioners also suggested that the city's chief criminal justice officer, the police magistrate John Maguire, also an Irish Catholic, had done little to lead his men in suppressing the riot.[5] In the years following, there were further repeated complaints against Maguire's actions as a police magistrate. Among others, he was accused of acting high-handedly towards other magistrates and judicial officials, and also of protecting agents, called "crimps," who illegally lured indentured sailors away from their ships. The result was a further inquiry in 1857, this time by the colony's Legislative Assembly, which rebuked Maguire but stopped short of recommending his removal.[6] In the end, he remained police magistrate in Quebec City for another decade, and was then made a Superior Court judge.

Jumping forwards over a century, in the late 1950s, the Quebec City press began a campaign against what they denounced as corrupt practices in Quebec City's municipal court. Among others, they accused municipal officials of running a system whereby people with the right connections who were accused of minor offences, notably traffic infractions but also including driving under the influence, could pay off court officials, municipal councillors, and even a judge and have their charges disappear, or at least be reduced. In 1965, a provincial royal commission of inquiry into the affair, the Commission Sylvestre, suggested that in the period of 1958–1963 alone, tens of thousands of cases had been dealt with in this manner, and those responsible included one of the two municipal court judges, Rodolphe De Blois (the other judge, Émile

---

4 On the Gavazzi riots in Quebec City, the only treatment of any depth remains Robert Sylvain, *Clerc, garibaldien, prédicant des deux mondes: Alessandro Gavazzi (1809–1889)* (Québec: Centre pédagogique, 1962) at 2:344–83; see also, on the equivalent riots in Montreal, Elinor Kyte Senior, *British Regulars in Montreal: An Imperial Garrison, 1832–1854* (Montreal: McGill-Queen's University Press, 1981) at 109–33; Vincent Breton, *L'émeute Gavazzi: pouvoir et conflit religieux au Québec au milieu du 19e siècle* (M.A. Thesis, Université du Québec à Montréal, 2004); and Daniel Horner, *A Barbarism of the Worst Kind: Negotiating Gender and Public Space in the Aftermath of Montreal's Gavazzi Riot* (M.A. Thesis, Queen's University, 2004).
5 Canada, *Report of the Commissioners Appointed to Inquire into the Conduct of the Police Authorities on the Occasion of the Riot at Chalmers' Church on the 6th of June, 1853 and to Inquire into the State of the Police Force of the Said City* (Quebec: Rollo Campbell, 1854).
6 Province of Canada, Legislative Assembly, *Journals of the Legislative Assembly of the Province of Canada* (Quebec/Toronto: Rollo Campbell), for 1854–1855: Appendix BBB; for 1856: Appendix 52; for 1857: 73, 568–69, and Appendices 27 and 37.

Morin, was apparently blithely unaware of, if not deliberately blind towards, the actions of his colleague), along with the court clerks, a dozen municipal councillors, and perhaps even the local crown prosecutors. Charges were laid against eighteen people, but after very long and tortuous legal proceedings, including endless and largely dilatory procedural moves by the defendants' counsel and a fortuitous fire that destroyed tens of thousands of potentially incriminating court records, nothing came of it. De Blois had retired in 1962, effectively putting an end to the practices complained of, and most of the charges were dismissed, in part on the basis of insufficient evidence; the last municipal councillor to face charges died in 1970, before his trial was over.[7]

These two affairs are interesting because of what they can tell us about the relationship between the modernization of criminal justice in Quebec City and the transformation of its legal profession. One of the great debates in Quebec historiography concerns the degree of modernization, whether economic, social, cultural, or institutional, of Quebec society in the period before the so-called Quiet Revolution of the 1960s, and the role played therein by the province's elites. For some, modernization began in earnest in the mid-nineteenth century, roughly in line with most Western societies, with dynamic elites, both francophone and anglophone, driving the process. For others, the process did not really get underway until the 1960s, with Quebec before the 1960s stuck in a resolutely premodern mould, largely due to the backward values of its francophone elites.[8] One aspect of this debate concerns the modernization of the state, seen by some as occurring from the 1840s onwards, or even before, with the growth of a modern, bureaucratic state, while for others, the Quebec state remained significantly undeveloped and resistant to modernization until the great reforms launched in the early 1960s.[9]

---

7   Jean-Paul Brodeur, *La délinquance de l'ordre: recherches sur les commissions d'enquête* (LaSalle, QC: Hurtubise HMH, 1984) at 220–37; Charles-Auguste Sylvestre, *Rapport de la Commission d'enquête sur l'administration de la justice à la Cour municipale de Québec* (Québec: La Commission, 1965).

8   The literature is extensive; for an overview of some of the themes, see Jacques Rouillard, "La Révolution tranquille: rupture ou tournant?" (1998) 32:4 Journal of Canadian Studies 23 or Gérard Bouchard, "Une nation, deux cultures. Continuités et ruptures dans la pensée québécoise traditionnelle (1840–1960)" in Gerard Bouchard, *La construction d'une culture: Le Québec et l'Amérique française* (Sainte-Foy, QC: Presses de l'Université Laval, 1993) at 3–47.

9   Despite a fairly substantial historiography, there is as yet no overview of the modernization debate with regards to the state, but among others, see Donald Fyson, *Magistrates, Police, and People*, above note 2; Jean-Marie Fecteau, *La liberté du pauvre*, above note 3; Allan Greer and Ian Radforth, eds., *Colonial Leviathan: State Formation in Nineteenth-Century Canada* (Toronto: University of Toronto Press, 1992); James Iain Gow, *Histoire de l'administration publique québécoise, 1867–1970* (Montréal: Presses de l'Université

The 1850s complaints against Maguire do indeed reflect the struggle within the city's judicial establishment around putting in place a modern, bureaucratic, utilitarian-type of judicial administration. Maguire felt that he, as the city's only professional criminal magistrate, appointed by the central administration, should control the entire everyday criminal justice system in the city, including the police. This conflicted with an older system, with its roots in the *Ancien Régime*, which was based on unpaid, amateur justices of the peace, generally appointed from among the elites, who felt it to be their paternalist duty and right to dispense justice. But this conflict also revealed the deep splits within Quebec City's legal establishment. Much of the evidence against Maguire was provided by other prominent members of the judiciary and bar, including Robert Henry Russell, the chief of police; Robert Symes, an active justice of the peace; Charles Secretan, Jr., a rising local lawyer; and the Grand Jury that convened after the Gavazzi riots, headed by Thomas Carey, the publisher of the conservative *Quebec Mercury*. Maguire's desire for centralized control also clashed with the views of court clerks and other officials for whom the criminal justice system was a series of interdependent fiefdoms and who resisted the imposition of bureaucratic control and accountability.

In the end, Maguire's vision partly won out, though not perhaps in the way he would have liked. In 1856, even before the final inquiry into Maguire's conduct, the central administration, at the behest of the Quebec City Council, had passed a law adding another local court — the Recorder's court. Beginning its sittings in early 1857, it was held by a professional magistrate who operated in parallel with the police magistrate. The government thus resolutely moved toward professionalizing the magistracy, taking everyday justice largely out of the hands of unpaid justices of the peace. In 1858, the city's police force was also reorganized to make it more accountable. But these reforms also introduced a significant degree of municipal control: the Recorder's Court was paid for by the city, though the recorder himself was appointed by the central administration, and the police force created in 1858 was partly under the control of municipal authorities.[10] In professionalizing

---

de Montréal, 1986); Michèle Dagenais and Denise Baillargeon, eds., *État: De nouvelles perspectives en histoire canadienne* (1997) 17:1-2 Cahiers d'histoire, special issue.

10   Antonio Drolet, *La Ville de Québec: histoire municipale. Volume III: de l'incorporation à la Confédération (1833–1867)* (Québec, QC: Société historique de Québec, 1967); Martin Dufresne, *La justice pénale et la définition du crime à Québec, 1830–1860* (Ph.D. Thesis, University of Ottawa, 1997) and "De la police de la cité à la police de la ville: la nouvelle police à Québec dans la première moitié du 19e siècle" in Pedro Fraile, ed., *Modelar para gobernar: el control de la población y el territorio en Europa y Canadá: una*

everyday criminal justice while at the same time partially delegating it to municipal authorities, the government was following a model adopted in many other North American cities and bringing justice in Quebec City up to what was then the modern standard.[11] This definitively marked the death of an older system based on volunteer lay-magistrates and a semi-professional constabulary and gives significant weight to those who see the mid-nineteenth century as a period of rapid modernization of the state.[12]

At the same time, however, the municipalization of justice, and thus its localization, opened the door to the sort of practices that led to the Quebec City Municipal Court scandal of the late 1950s and early 1960s. The scandal, indeed, revealed that values quite other than modernism reigned in the city's legal culture. In this direct descendant of the Recorder's Court that was established in the 1850s, instead of the triumph of modernism, we find the persistence of attitudes and practices that were profoundly anti-modern. Despite being professional and highly bureaucratized, the judicial bureaucracy was evidently not impartially at the service of the population, nor fully accountable, but, rather, at the service of largely elite interest groups and parallel power structures. The testimony of the witnesses before the Commission Sylvestre described a whole range of petty corrupt practices and low-level exchanges of favours between citizens who received tickets and the judges and aldermen who took care of the problem for them, in defiance of what should have been the established bureaucratic procedures. This is more in line with the view of Quebec institutions before 1960 and Quebec francophone elites as being profoundly resistant to change and modernization. And indeed, the practices of the municipal court represented a systematic end-run around the rules, apparently condoned by and participated in not only by a significant part of Quebec's judicial establishment, but also by a significant segment of the city's population. A century after the "modernization" of criminal justice

---

perspectiva histórica (Barcelona: Publicacions Universitat de Barcelona, 2001) at 125–35; Michael McCulloch, "Most Assuredly Perpetual Motion: Police and Policing in Quebec City, 1838–58" (1990) 19:1 Urban History Review 100; Jean-François Leclerc, "La Sûreté du Québec des origines à nos jours: quelques repères historiques" (1989) 22:2 Criminologie 110; Gérald Gagnon, *Histoire du Service de police de la ville de Québec* (Sainte-Foy, QC: Publications du Québec, 1998). Between 1858 and 1885, the authorities experimented with varying degrees of mixed municipal and central control of the police force, and between 1870 and 1877 the municipal police was even replaced by a provincial force, but the experiment was short-lived and from 1889, the police force was definitively municipal.

11 Greg Marquis, "The Contours of Canadian Urban Justice, 1830–1875" (1987) 15:3 Urban History Review 269.

12 On the older system, see Donald Fyson, *Magistrates, Police, and People*, above note 2.

in the city, the system evidently retained a decidedly premodern flavour, not much different from what one might find under the *Ancien Régime*.

This balance between modernization and resistance to change was one important characteristic of local criminal justice in Quebec City from the mid-nineteenth to the mid-twentieth century. This paper briefly explores three aspects of this. The first is the historical and historiographical perception of Quebec City as a *"gros village"* in terms of criminal justice, in other words, an oversized village where not much happened and where what did happen was kept within the village, out of sight from outsiders. The second is the evident lag in the modernization of criminal justice in Quebec City over the century. And the last is a possible explanation: the domestication of the legal profession in Quebec City in what became an increasingly provincial capital city.

THE *"GROS VILLAGE"*

THE EXAMINATION OF THE two affairs with which this paper began are noteworthy not only for their content, but also because in the period they bracket, they are almost the only times that the operation of criminal justice in Quebec City caught the public's eye in any significant way. There were occasional high-profile moments, such as the suppression of the anti-conscription riots in 1918, and a few notorious cases dealt with at least in part in Quebec City, such as the Aurore Gagnon affair or the murder trial of Wilbur Coffin, but over the century, there appears to have been only one other large-scale public scandal concerning the city's criminal justice system. In the early 1920s, the province's attorney general and premier, Louis-Alexandre Taschereau, was accused of having used his influence to engineer a cover-up for those who had raped and murdered a young Quebec City girl, Blanche Garneau, possibly because they were the relations of fellow politicians.[13] However, the accusations focused more on Taschereau and the Liberal Party than on the Quebec City judicial establishment, and while an investigation delved into the operations of the police and crown prosecutors in the capital, it exonerated everyone involved.[14] The public issue remained largely a political one, with little critical discussion of criminal justice in the capital. This mutism was in contrast to Montreal, which had a long string of highly public and critical inquiries into both the police and the courts from the late nineteenth century forward.[15]

---

13   Réal Bertrand, *Qui a tué Blanche Garneau?* (Montréal: Les Quinze, 1983).
14   Bibliothèque et Archives nationales de Québec (BAnQ-Q), E110, Fonds Commission royale d'enquête sur l'administration de la justice dans l'affaire Blanche Garneau.
15   Jean-Paul Brodeur, *La délinquance de l'ordre* (LaSalle, QC: Hurtubise HMH, 1984).

Keeping crime in Quebec City out of the limelight was how Quebec City's residents liked it. As a journalist declared in 1910, "Au grand désespoir des reporters, au grand plaisir des policiers et au contentement général des citoyens, les vols et les crimes sont rares à Québec."[16] Or again, to cite one writer describing Quebec City in the early 1930s, "Modern Quebec is not a criminal city, as anyone can see by watching its life, attending the courts, or examining statistics."[17] An examination of the coverage of criminal justice in Quebec City newspapers in the first three decades of the twentieth century does indeed suggest that, while crimes in Quebec City were reported, the most striking coverage was generally given to sensational crimes that happened elsewhere, notably in Montreal, but also further afield. Not all was placid in Quebec City, and there were occasional complaints about immorality or the problems of juvenile delinquency, but these remained relatively tame. Further, when the criminal justice system in Quebec City was commented on, it was generally to praise the police, judicial officials, and judges for their good work, not to criticize them for their shortcomings.[18] The desire to preserve the peaceable image of the city has extended even to recent times: one historian who tried to investigate the Blanche Garneau incident in the early 1980s was met with a wall of resistance and silence to his inquiries.[19]

This view of Quebec City's relative calm is also echoed in the historiography. Consider the recent official history of Quebec City's police force. Commenting on the only judicial inquiry into the police, which in the late 1940s essentially exonerated the city's morality squad of charges of protecting brothels from prosecution, the author declares quite baldly "rien de grave ne s'était produit si l'on compare l'enquête Morin à celle qui toucha tout le corps de police de Montréal à la même époque.... Le Service de police de Québec resta dans son ensemble fiable et honnête, si ce n'est de quelques indisciplinés vite ramenés à l'ordre."[20] In sum, in terms of criminal justice, Quebec City

---

16   "To the great despair of reporters, to the great pleasure of policemen and the general contentment of the citizens, thefts and crimes are rare in Quebec City." *Le Soleil* (12 January 1910) 10.
17   William Wood, ed., *The Storied Province of Quebec: Past and Present*, vol. I (Toronto: Dominion, 1931) at 228.
18   This is based on a preliminary examination of *Le Soleil* and the *Morning Chronicle*.
19   Réal Bertrand, *Qui a tué Blanche Garneau?*, above note 13 at 7–13.
20   "Nothing serious had happened if we compare the Morin inquiry to that that concerned the entire Montreal police force at the same time.... The Quebec City Police service remained on the whole trustworthy and honest, apart from a few undisciplined members quickly brought back into line." Gérald Gagnon, *Histoire du Service de police de la ville de Québec*, above note 10 at 160–61.

very much plays the role of the *"gros village"* beside its dangerous metropolitan neighbour, Montreal.

And yet, there was still quite a lot of crime and criminal justice going on in the capital. If overall conviction statistics are used as an indicator, there was certainly less criminal prosecution in Quebec City than in Montreal. From the 1870s to the 1920s, the number of convictions in the judicial district of Quebec, which included the capital, was consistently lower than in that of Montreal, which had a rate between one and a half and three times higher than the Quebec district; from the 1930s to the mid-1950s, the rate in the Montreal district was between five and eight times higher. At the same time, however, the Quebec district's rate was still far higher than that of all of the other districts in the province apart from Montreal. Similarly, from the mid-1880s to the 1920s, the rate of homicide charges in the district of Quebec appears to have been lower than that in the district of Montreal, but not remarkably so: based on some very preliminary data, the Montreal rates were perhaps one and a half to two times those of the Quebec district. Quebec City certainly was a "criminal city," far more so than the true villages; it was just not as criminal as Montreal.

CRIMINAL JUSTICE AS AN ANTI-MODERN PHENOMENON

THE PERSISTENCE OF CRIME in Quebec City, however, did not lead to any real questioning of the structures and operation of the criminal justice system. After its initial modernization in the early to mid-nineteenth century, the system remained profoundly recalcitrant to further change through to the 1960s, lagging further and further behind Montreal in terms of the modernization of both structures and practices. For example, after the courts and police in Quebec City underwent substantial bureaucratization in the middle of the nineteenth century, the system remained little-changed in the century that followed. Quebec City had no separate juvenile court until 1940, three decades after Montreal. And there were apparently no female police officers in Quebec City until the 1980s, while in Montreal they were initially hired in the early twentieth century.[21] Further, magistrates and police in Quebec City participated less in the culture of public information and statistics that

---

21 Jean Trépanier, "Protéger pour prévenir la délinquance: l'émergence de la Loi sur les jeunes délinquants de 1908 et de sa mise en application à Montréal" in Renée Joyal, ed., *L'évolution de la protection de l'enfance au Québec* (Québec: Presses de l'Université du Québec, 2000) at 72–85; Tamara Myers, *Caught: Montreal's Modern Girls and the Law, 1869–1945* (Toronto: University of Toronto Press, 2006).

was increasingly characteristic of the modern state. Thus, in Montreal, from the 1860s to the First World War, both the municipal court and the police published detailed annual reports of their activity. In contrast, the municipal court in Quebec City apparently never published any annual activity reports, and the Quebec City police force stopped publishing its annual report in the mid-1860s; though on occasion both did provide overall statistics to the city's newspapers.[22] The structures of punishment also changed slowly, if at all. Quebec City's first penitentiary-style prison was built in the mid-1860s (thirty years after Montreal's) and remained in use until the 1960s, while Montreal's was replaced in the early twentieth century. Likewise, Montreal's first women's prison opened in 1876; but in Quebec City, not until 1931.[23]

The pattern of the offences for which people were charged in Quebec City also suggests a good deal of bureaucratic and judicial conservatism. One striking example from the nineteenth century is riot prosecutions. In theory, riot prosecutions were the state's most majestic response to the collective violence that gripped cities in nineteenth-century Canada, including Quebec City and Montreal. After a riot or violent strike had been put down by police or military intervention, what could be more awe-inspiring than the full-scale state trial of rioters, followed by suitable punishments? A close study of riot prosecutions in Quebec City, however, reveals something quite different. For a variety of reasons, including the vagaries of the trial process and the attitudes of urban elites, such trials were essentially a complete dud as a means of establishing state authority: notably, the overall conviction rate for city riots was something like 5 percent. In Montreal, formal riot prosecutions were fairly rapidly abandoned by the 1850s, in favour of the use of a variety of more summary measures that were far more effective ways of making examples of rioters. But in Quebec City, authorities persisted in launching elaborate riot prosecutions right through to the early 1880s, when riots themselves most likely declined and disappeared in the city.[24]

---

22 In this respect, the institutions in Quebec City were similar to those at the provincial level: the first annual report published by the Ministry of Justice and its predecessors was in 1967, though statistics on the activity of the different courts were published between 1860 and 1929.

23 Jean-Marie Fecteau, Marie-Josée Tremblay, and Jean Trépanier, "La prison de Montréal de 1865 à 1913: évolution en longue période d'une population pénale" (1993) 34:1 Cahiers de droit 27; Pierre Landreville and Ghislaine Julien, "Les origines de la prison de Bordeaux" (1976) 9:1-2 Criminologie 5; Martin Mimeault, La prison des Plaines d'Abraham (Sillery, QC: Septentrion, 2007).

24 Donald Fyson, "The Trials and Tribulations of Riot Prosecutions: Collective Violence, State Authority and Criminal Justice in Quebec, 1841–1892" in Susan Binnie and Barry

Similarly, the overall pattern of offences in Quebec City remained in a nineteenth-century mould well into the twentieth century. That is, the domination of public order and regulatory offences, such as vagrancy and disorderly conduct, that were the focus of those who sought to regulate the urban "dangerous classes" in the nineteenth century remained prevalent in Quebec City but declined in large urban areas such as Montreal in the twentieth century, replaced largely by traffic offences.[25] Despite the fact that Quebec City fully participated in the automobile boom, traffic offences did not become a significant part of criminal justice there until the 1950s; and then, as we have seen, they were subject to systematic fixing.

Criminal justice in the capital was thus hardly characterized by the notions of "progress" so dear to liberal modernity. There were a few exceptions to this: for example, from the mid-1860s to the early twentieth century, Quebec City's municipal council formally regulated brothel prostitution (though still considering it illegal), adopting a practice that Montreal would use only very briefly.[26] But, in general, criminal justice in Quebec City remained profoundly resistant to change, and far more so than in Montreal.

THE DOMESTICATION OF THE JUDICIAL ESTABLISHMENT

MUCH OF THIS RESISTANCE to change can of course be attributed to broader socio-economic factors, notably the relative stagnation of Quebec City from the 1870s to the 1940s. But a more specific factor was what might be called the domestication of the judicial establishment in the city. This can be seen both in its changing ethnic character, which became more and more francophone, and in its centring on Quebec City itself.

In the middle of the nineteenth century, the judicial establishment in Quebec City reflected the intense inter-ethnic relations, especially between francophones and anglophones (the latter being essentially a mix of Irish, English, and Scots), that characterized its society. Police and judicial officers

---

Wright, eds., *Canadian State Trials*, vol. III (Toronto: Osgoode Society/University of Toronto Press, 2009) (forthcoming).

25   Donald Fyson, "The Judicial Prosecution of Crime in the Longue Durée: Quebec 1712–1965" in Jean-Marie Fecteau and Janice Harvey, eds., *La régulation sociale entre l'acteur et l'institution : pour une problématique historique de l'interaction* (Québec: Presses de l'Université du Québec, 2005) at 85–119.

26   Patrick Allen, "Prostituées de rue et maisons de débauche au Québec : la répression de la prostitution par le système de justice étatique, 1880–1905" (M A Thesis, Université Laval, 2007).

were both anglophone and francophone, with perhaps a slight domination by anglophones, but criminal justice operated largely in English, with official documents and court registers generally in English, given that the target population was more anglophone than francophone. Symbolically, the seal of the Recorder's Court was in English only.

But the gradual loss of ethnic diversity in Quebec City's population, and the provincialization of the town's economy and society, was also reflected in the criminal justice system. Its magistracy, judicial bureaucracy, and bar became increasingly dominated not just by francophones, but by people who came from the Quebec City region itself. As the table below shows, in the 1870s and 1880s, when francophones made up between two-thirds and three-quarters of the city's inhabitants, anglophones still occupied almost half of the most important positions in the everyday penal judicial hierarchy, such as magistrates and court clerks; most came from elsewhere. Among the francophones as well, there were several who were born elsewhere in the province. But by the 1920s, almost all of the principal officers were francophones, and almost all were from Quebec City or its immediate hinterland. They were drawn from Quebec City's small legal elite, often closely tied to local political clans. Quebec City's local magistrates, for example, included not only several former local members of the provincial or federal parliament or city council, but also relatives of local politicians, such as Eugène Desrivières, assistant recorder and then recorder from 1912 to 1945, who was the nephew of premier Louis-Alexandre Taschereau.

TABLE ONE: ETHNICITY OF PRINCIPAL PENAL OFFICERS IN QUEBEC CITY, 1860–1960

Judicial Office	1860	1870	1880	1890	1900	1910	1920	1930	1940	1950	1960
Judges of the Sessions of the Peace	A	F	F	F	F	F	F	FA	F	F	F
Recorders/Municipal Court judges	F	F	F	F	F	F	F	F	F	F	F
Crown prosecutors	A	A	FA	FA	FA	FA	FA	FA	F	F	F
Chief of the municipal police	F	F	F	F	A	F	F	F	F	F	F
Head of the Sûreté (in Quebec City)	–	FA	F	F	F	F	F	F	F	F	F
Clerk of the Crown	F	A	A	A	F	F	F	F	F	F	F
Clerk of the Peace	F	F	A	F	F	F	F	F	F	F	F

Judicial Office	1860	1870	1880	1890	1900	1910	1920	1930	1940	1950	1960
Recorder's/Municipal Court clerk	A	A	A	A	A	A	F	F	F	F	F
Coroners	F	F	F	F	F	F	F	F	F	F	F
Sheriff	A	A	A	FA	F	F	F	F	F	F	F
High Constable	F	F	F	A	A	A	A	A	A	F	F
Gaoler/Prison governor	A	A	A	A	F	F	F	F	F	F	F

"F" represents francophones, "A" represents anglophones of various origins. Queen's/King's Bench and Superior Court judges not included. Based largely on Quebec public accounts, along with a variety of complementary sources such as directories.

The bar also became increasingly provincialized. In the late eighteenth and early nineteenth century, the bar in Quebec City was very mixed, anglophone and francophone, and as a result developed what Jean-Philippe Garneau has termed a *"culture de l'amalgame"* — an intercultural mixing of French and British influences.[27] As Christine Veilleux has shown, however, the nineteenth century, and especially its second half, saw a process of localization of the bar: between 1850 and 1867, just under half of those admitted to the Quebec City bar were born in the city itself, and another third in rural Quebec, largely the areas around Quebec City.[28] If we look at lawyers who actually practised in Quebec, from Confederation through to the mid-1930s, we find this same trend further solidified. Through that period, about half of practising lawyers had been born in Quebec City itself; a little under half came from what we might call (and is still today) Quebec City's natural hinterland, namely smaller towns or rural areas in the eastern half of Quebec, from east of Trois-Rivières to the Gaspé; and less than 5 percent came from anywhere else. Further, an increasingly dominant proportion of these lawyers (perhaps three-quarters in the last third of the nineteenth century and close to 90 percent in the first decades of the twentieth) were francophones.[29] This pattern

---

27 Jean-Philippe Garneau, "Une culture de l'amalgame au prétoire: les avocats de Québec et l'élaboration d'un langage juridique commun au tournant des XVIIIe et XIXe siècles" (2007) 88:1 Canadian Historical Review 113.
28 Christine Veilleux, "Les gens de justice à Québec, 1760–1867" (Ph.D. Thesis, Université Laval, 1990) at 146.
29 This is based on an initial 20 percent sample of the biographies in Pierre-Georges Roy, *Les avocats de la région de Québec* (Lévis, QC: Le Quotidien, 1936). The results remain preliminary, and do not allow for distinguishing lawyers who engaged in criminal practice from those who did not.

continued through to the 1950s, with 90 percent or more of practising lawyers in Quebec City in 1960 identified as francophone. Further, since throughout the period most Quebec City lawyers had been educated at Laval University, the potential for unity in training and thought, and thus judicial conservatism, was evident. This was especially the case since, as Sylvio Normand and Mélanie Brunet have shown, the law faculty at Laval, through to the 1950s, was indeed a very conservative institution, with faculty and students firmly attached to traditionalist visions of society, and also very inbred, essentially recruiting its faculty from among its own graduates.[30]

Finally, the decline in cultural diversity also extended to the police. In the late 1860s, the police force was about half anglophone and half francophone; by the late 1890s, it was about two-thirds francophone; and by the 1920s and 1930s, very largely francophone.[31] Further, by the early twentieth century, the police force in Quebec City was markedly older than that in Montreal: in 1921, according to the census, a third of police in the capital were fifty years or older, whereas in Montreal, the number was less than 20 percent. Though further study is needed, this once again gives the image of a police force increasingly uniform, and increasingly set in its ways.

To this must be added the fact that the population targeted by the criminal justice system became increasingly francophone, and the system increasingly targeted people from Quebec City and its surrounding area. In the 1870s, francophones made up about half of defendants brought before the police magistrate or recorder, and about 40 percent of those in the Quebec prison, with a very significant Irish presence among the others; by the first two decades of the twentieth century, francophones accounted for 75 to 80 percent of arrestees and prisoners. In the 1850s, a significant proportion of people brought before the system were outsiders, such as sailors or soldiers; by the 1920s, "strangers" continued to make up perhaps a third of those accused of crimes, but instead of being people from overseas, almost all of these came from the surrounding countryside. The end result was that criminal justice by the 1920s and 1930s had become essentially an affair *entre nous*, concerning the city's native population and that of the surrounding hinterland. And this despite the fact that newspaper coverage in the first decades of the twentieth

---

30   Sylvio Normand, *Le droit comme discipline universitaire: une histoire de la Faculté de droit de l'Université Laval* (Québec: Presses de l'Université Laval, 2005); Mélanie Brunet, "Becoming Lawyers: Gender, Legal Education and Professional Identity Formation in Canada, 1920–1980" (Ph.D. Thesis, University of Toronto, 2005) at 175–264.
31   On this, see Louis Turcotte, "Les conflits entre policiers et citoyens à Québec, 1870–1900" (M.A. Thesis, Université Laval, 2007).

century often made a point of underscoring the otherness of those accused of crimes who were not of francophone descent or came from elsewhere.

My working hypothesis is that this domestication of criminal justice was a potent cause of conservatism and indeed anti-modernism, as a closed and self-perpetuating judicial elite was less amenable to criticism and change. The inquiry into Blanche Garneau's murder in the 1920s came up against a systematic wall of obfuscation from local officials, which continued for decades afterwards. The Morin Inquiry into the police in the late 1940s was headed by the same municipal court judge who in the late 1950s was apparently unaware that his colleague and clerks were systematically subverting the course of justice. The destruction of a large swath of the judicial archives in the early 1960s was perhaps the logical conclusion of this sort of internal cohesion, though the affair remains obscure; perhaps it really was just a fortuitous accident! Without the ethnic and other cleavages that continued to characterize criminal justice in Montreal, there was less opportunity for public criticism, at least until the late 1950s.

This does not mean that the criminal justice establishment in Quebec City was entirely devoid of people who might have held more progressive views, even in the first half of the twentieth century. For example, in 1919, Charles Langelier, a former Liberal cabinet member under Honoré Mercier who was Quebec City's Chief Judge of the Sessions between 1910 and 1920, made the astonishingly progressive proposal (for the time and place) that prostitution in the city be both legalized and regulated, going entirely against the grain of a city dominated by conservative Catholic values.[32] Or again, in the early 1940s, one of Quebec City's crown prosecutors was none other than Jean Lesage, future leader of the provincial government that instituted the Quiet Revolution.[33] But while it is also possible to identify a few other such examples, they remained very much the minority and also seem to have had little permanent impact. Hence, Langelier's proposals were not put into practice, and he died a year later. The judges on the bench immediately after his tenure, Arthur Lachance and Philippe-Auguste Choquette, demonstrated considerable moral conservatism and hostility to modernity. Among others, in 1924, when

---

32 Charles Langelier, *La prostitution: ses dangers, son remède: lettre ouverte à son Honneur le maire et à MM. les échevins de la cité de Québec* and *La prostitution: ses dangers, son remède: deuxième lettre ouverte à son Honneur le maire et à MM. les échevins de la cité de Québec* (Québec: Imprimerie nationale, 1919); Andrée Désilets, "Charles Langelier" *Dictionary of Canadian Biography Online*, vol. 14, online: www.biographi.ca/EN/ShowBio.asp?BioId=41630.

33 Dale C. Thomson, *Jean Lesage and the Quiet Revolution* (Toronto: Macmillan, 1984) at 41–42.

a Quebec City cinema projected "Flaming Youth," an iconic Jazz Age film that featured that most modern of female characters, the flapper, the judges convicted the owner of indecency, even though the film had been passed by the strict provincial board of censors.[34] As for Lesage's appointment in 1939 by the new provincial Liberal government, it seems to have been more of a political reward than anything else. More work remains to be done before coming to any firm conclusion regarding these and other potential progressives in the provincial capital, but their long-term impact on the nature of the criminal justice system in Quebec City appears to have been minimal.

CONCLUSION

THE ISSUES RAISED IN this chapter are only tentative beginnings of a reflection on criminal justice and the legal profession in Quebec City. In particular, the judicial culture of the legal profession certainly needs further exploration and definition. But we can nevertheless make some preliminary observations. At the beginning of the period, the legal professionals involved in penal justice were a mix of francophones and anglophones and of people trained in Quebec City and elsewhere. But through the century that followed, as Quebec City itself became more inward-looking and more homogenous, so too did the criminal justice system. Its members were increasingly recruited from the city itself or its immediate hinterland and reflected the increasing lack of diversity among local elites. This inward vision, and the professional solidarity that came from a shared background and uniform legal culture, made possible scandals such as the cover-up of the murder of Blanche Garneau in the early 1920s or the systematic fixing of municipal courts that was brought to light in the late 1950s and early 1960s. The link between the *gros village* mentality and anti-modern judicial practices was clearly expressed by Gonzague Champoux, one of the assistant clerks of the municipal court, in his testimony before the Commission Sylvestre. In explaining how the system worked, he stated that "... un système de tolérance s'exerçait à l'endroit d'amis ou de parents, soit des échevins ou des employés." Perfectly banal patronage and low-level corruption as one might find anywhere. But Champoux went much further in his definition of friends: "On considérait toujours

---

34 Full coverage of the trial is given in the *Morning Chronicle* and *Le Soleil* in January 1924; the case files are in BAnQ-Q TP12,S1,SS1,SSS1 #s 187420–187423 and 224363–224372. In the end, Lachance, J. only imposed a nominal fine, judging that, though the film was certainly indecent (whatever the board of censors had decided), the cinema owner had acted in good faith. On the board of censors, see Pierre Hébert et al., eds., *Dictionnaire de la censure au Québec: littérature et cinéma* (Saint-Laurent, QC: Fides, 2006) at 576–81.

la Ville de Québec comme composée de membres d'une même famille; la plupart des gens se connaissaient. Alors, au fond, ce sont tous des amis, les Québecois."[35] Between family, between friends, what need of a modern criminal justice system? With little taste for innovation and, indeed, a distinctly anti-modern stance, the provincial capital's legal professionals ensured that, in the twentieth century, penal justice in Quebec City lagged far behind that of the province's metropolis, Montreal.

---

35 "A system of toleration existed with regards to friends or family, either of aldermen or of employees.... We always considered Quebec City as made up of members of the same family; most people knew each other. Fundamentally, all Quebec City residents are friends." Sylvestre, *Rapport de la Commission d'enquête*, above note 7 at 145–46.

PART 4

THE RULE OF LAW, IMPEACHMENT, AND BUREAUCRATIC REGULATION

CHAPTER 9

The Court and the Legal Profession: Loyalist Lawyers and the Nova Scotia Supreme Court in the 1780s

JIM PHILLIPS

IT IS NOT UNUSUAL in our age for lawyers to criticize judges, although such critiques are generally restricted to private conversations. Our history, in contrast, reveals a number of instances in which attacks on the judiciary by members of the legal profession have been public in nature and unrestrained in content. None are more remarkable than the campaign against two judges of the Nova Scotia Supreme Court (NSSC) by a small coterie of Loyalist lawyers in the 1780s and early 1790s. The lawyers went after the bench in the Legislative Assembly and the press, accusing them of both incompetence and partiality. They were successful in persuading the assembly first to demand an inquiry into the judges' conduct, and later to pass articles of impeachment against them, although ultimately the attempt to remove them from the bench failed.

This chapter provides a brief account of these events.[1] But its particular focus, given the theme of this volume, is the response of the judges to the lawyers' critiques, especially their use of the power available to them to determine who could practise law in the NSSC. In being granted the power to regulate

---

1   For fuller accounts see: Barry Cahill and Jim Phillips, "Origins to Confederation" in Philip Girard, Jim Phillips, and Barry Cahill, eds., *The Supreme Court of Nova Scotia, 1754–2004: From Imperial Bastion to Provincial Oracle* (Toronto: Osgoode Society for Canadian Legal History by the University of Toronto Press, 2004); and J. Phillips, "The Impeachment of the Judges of the Nova Scotia Supreme Court, 1790" (2006, unpublished) and J.B. Cahill, "The Judges Affair: A Nova Scotia *Cause Célèbre*" (1988, unpublished). I am working on a monograph-length account of the events described here.

itself in the 1797 *Law Society Act*, the bar of Upper Canada was unique among North American jurisdictions. Although the English bar was self-governing, the dominant model of professional regulation (admission, discipline, etc.) in the empire was for judges to supervise the profession.[2] Nova Scotia was no exception. From the founding of Halifax, the high courts — General (from 1754 the Supreme) Court, Chancery, and Governor's Council, which doubled as the Court of Appeal — determined who was to be admitted to practise before them and disciplined members of the bar. Not until 1811 was the absolute authority of the judges diminished in any way, and that was only via a statute that prescribed the period of apprenticeship at five years. The statute specifically retained the judges' power otherwise to decide who could practise, requiring them "to examine and enquire, by such ways and means as they shall think proper, touching his fitness and capacity to act as an Attorney."[3] Not until 1872 did the Nova Scotia bar become self-regulating.[4]

In responding to the attacks upon them in the 1780s, the judges used their full arsenal against their lawyer-critics. The judges found them in contempt of court, and then employed their authority to regulate the profession to disbar the lawyers from practice and threatened other lawyers who might have assisted the judges' critics with a similar disbarment. The virulence of the judges' response was not simply the result of the personal attacks on them. Their actions were also motivated by politics. When they attacked the bench, the Loyalist lawyers and their (mainly Loyalist) allies in the assembly were attacking, more generally, the old Tory elite that ran the colony, and the latter interpreted it that way as well. Moreover, the judges and their supporters on the Governor's Council characterized any criticism of an established institution like the NSSC or its judges as not simply dissent, but as tantamount to disloyalty.

The principals in this story were four men — lawyers Jonathan Sterns and William Taylor, and NSSC judges Isaac Deschamps and James Brenton. Sterns and Taylor were two of a coterie of elite American lawyers who came to Halifax

---

2   Christopher Moore, *The Law Society of Upper Canada and Ontario's Lawyers, 1791–1997* (Toronto: University of Toronto Press, 1997) at 15.
3   *Regulation of Attornies, Solicitors and Proctors Act*, Statutes of Nova Scotia, 1811, c. 3, s. 5. See generally Barry Cahill, "The Origin and Evolution of the Attorney and Solicitor in the Legal Profession of Nova Scotia" (1991) 14 Dalhousie Law Journal 277.
4   *Statutes of Nova Scotia*, 1872, c. 19. The context for this change is examined in Philip Girard, "The Roots of a Professional Renaissance: Lawyers in Nova Scotia, 1850–1910" in Dale Gibson and Wesley Pue, eds., *Glimpses of Canadian Legal History* (Winnipeg: University of Manitoba Legal Research Institute, 1991).

with the Loyalist migration of the mid-1780s.[5] These men competed with the small local bar, and with each other, for the limited legal work available. Taylor was not very successful, but Sterns, a Harvard graduate who was described in 1783 as the best lawyer in the city, was. He built up an extensive practice in both the NSSC and in Vice-Admiralty.[6] By the mid-1780s, he and other Loyalist lawyers were beginning to criticize two of the NSSC judges for both their partiality to certain lawyers and litigants and their level of competence.

Although the NSSC in the 1780s nominally had three judges, a chief justice and two assistant (puisne) judges, for most of the later 1780s, there was no chief justice on the ground.[7] Chief Justice Bryan Finucane died in August 1785, and his replacement, Jeremy Pemberton, did not arrive until 1788. Pemberton sat for just one term (Michaelmas 1788) and then left the colony. His replacement, Thomas Strange, did not arrive until mid-1790. In the absence of a chief justice, the NSSC was staffed by just the two assistants. The senior assistant judge, and thus the acting chief justice, was Deschamps, a non-lawyer. Probably originally Swiss, he had arrived in Halifax in the fall of 1749, a few months after its founding. A reasonably successful merchant in the early 1750s, he acquired substantial land grants in Windsor and in the new townships of Falmouth, Newport, and Horton. During the 1760s he carried out a large number of official commissions and held many minor offices, through which he built up excellent connections with the Halifax elite, and these subsequently secured his appointment to the NSSC in 1770. He served in the assembly from 1759, the year after its founding, until 1783, representing in turn Annapolis County, Falmouth Township, and Newport Township. In 1783 he became a member of the Governor's Council of Twelve, and consequently vacated his assembly seat. Reflecting this period's rather different view of the separation of powers than our modern one, therefore, he was a Member of the House of Assembly (MHA) and then a councillor for all his years on the bench. He did have some judicial experience on appointment, even if no legal training. From 1761 he sat as a judge of the Inferior Court of Common Pleas

---

5 The best account of the Loyalist migration and settlement in Nova Scotia is by Neil MacKinnon, *This Unfriendly Soil: The Loyalist Experience in Nova Scotia, 1783–1791* (Kingston: McGill-Queen's University Press, 1986).
6 For Sterns, see *A Directory of the Members of the Legislative Assembly of Nova Scotia, 1758–1958* (Halifax: Public Archives of Nova Scotia, 1958) at 332; Halifax, Nova Scotia Archives and Records Management [NSARM], Supreme Court Records (Halifax, RG 39, Series J, vols. 7–11); Edward Winslow to Ward Chipman (7 July 1783) in W.O. Raymond, ed., *Winslow Papers 1776–1826* (Saint John: New Brunswick Historical Society, 1901) at 97.
7 The brief summary of the history of the Court and its judges given here is from Cahill and Phillips, "Origins to Confederation," above note 1.

(ICCP), the lower Civil Court for King's County, and was its first justice. In fact he served on two ICCPs — in 1768 he was sent to Saint John's Island (known as P.E.I. since 1798) as Chief Justice of the ICCP there. He was also an active Justice of the Peace and at least twice before his appointment to the bench had been on special commissions of oyer and terminer and general gaol delivery.[8]

The other assistant judge was James Brenton, a lawyer but a man with relatively little judicial experience when complaints began to be made about the judges. A native of Newport, Rhode Island, and from an elite family in that colony, Brenton clerked in Boston for James Otis, Jr. After qualifying, he emigrated to Nova Scotia circa 1760, probably because of a useful family connection: his sister Mary was the wife of Joseph Gerrish, naval storekeeper and a member of the council. He practised law in Halifax and won election to the assembly, serving as MHA for Onslow Township (1765–70) and for Halifax County (1776–85). He was solicitor general from 1768–74 and 1776–77, and from 1779 until his appointment to the bench in 1781 served as attorney general.[9]

These two judges came under increasing attack by members of the bar, especially but not exclusively Sterns, from circa 1785, and by 1787 matters were approaching a crisis point.[10] The lawyers' complaints were of various kinds — the judges did not fully understand either the rules of procedure or the substantive law, they favoured certain parties,[11] and they tried to force juries to deliver verdicts in line with the bench's view of a case. A sense of the atmosphere in court can be obtained from the judges' later description of the September 1787 session on circuit at Annapolis:

---

8   For these see Council Minutes for 1762, NSARM, (Halifax, RG 1, vol. 188 at 293) and Council Minutes for 1767, NSARM (Halifax, RG 1, vol. 189 at 84). For Deschamps see G.M. Tratt, "Isaac Deschamps," vol. 5, *Dictionary of Canadian Biography Online*, online: www.biographi.ca/EN/ShowBio.asp?BioId=36488&query=Isaac%20AND%20Deschamps.

9   For Brenton see A.C. Dunlop, "James Brenton," vol. 5, *Dictionary of Canadian Biography Online*, online: www.biographi.ca/EN/ShowBio.asp?BioId=36409&query=james%20AND%20brenton.

10 See generally Jim Phillips, "The Impeachment of the Judges of the Nova Scotia Supreme Court, 1790," above note 1. The allegations are also contained in two contemporary pamphlets: *Collection of the Publications Relating to the Impeachment of the Judges of His Majesty's Supreme Court of the Province of Nova Scotia* (Halifax, 1788) [*Collection of Publications Relating to the Impeachment of Judges*], and *The Reply of Messrs Sterns and Taylor to the Answers Given by the Judges of the Supreme Court of Nova Scotia to the Facts by Them Related, When Aummoned before the House of Assembly of that Province* (London, 1789) [*The Reply of Messrs Sterns and Taylor*].

11 Sterns later asserted that the judges "judged Men, nor Causes": Letter to Blowers (19 March 1788) in *Collection of the Publications Relating to the Impeachment of Judges*, ibid.

the Conduct and behaviour of Mr. Sterns during this term towards the Court had been so glaringly indecent in address and language that they were frequently tempted to proceed to measures of severity with him, that the Order and Dignity of the Court might be preserved.... [T]he stile and manner of his controverting the Opinion of the Chief Justice was so rude and disrespectful, that the Chief Justice was under the necessity of ordering him to set down and be silent. The bold attacks this practitioner had repeatedly made upon the Authority of the Court would have justified us, in the Eyes of an astonished Public, if we had suspended him from all further practice.[12]

By 1787 the dissatisfaction among the bar with the judges had spread to non-lawyer assemblymen, and in November of that year Major Thomas Millidge, the Loyalist member for Digby Township and a former surveyor-general of New Jersey, moved that "dissatisfactions having prevailed ... relative to the Administration of Justice in the Supreme Court," there should be a committee of the whole house to investigate the facts. His motion was unanimously approved,[13] and Millidge's opening contribution to the debate was to state that "the conduct of the [judges] ... had, in many instances, been highly improper," that "a number of his Constituents" had complained to him, and that "in conversation with many of the bar they had repeatedly declared they conceived the Justices incompetent to fill the bench." The committee took oral evidence from Sterns, in which he cited eleven cases to support his assertion that the judges "did not appear to have justice always in view" and "were not competent for the administration of Justice."[14] Taylor provided a written statement that cited half a dozen cases and corroborated Sterns, concluding with his opinion "that the Judges of the Supreme Court are both incompetent and partial, and altogether unequal to the administration of Justice."[15]

The assembly forwarded an address to Lieutenant Governor Sir John Parr and the Council, based on Sterns's testimony, asking him to "institute an Enquiry into [the judges'] Conduct, in such a Manner, that a fair and impartial Investigation may take place, that the Public be fully convinced of their Innocence or Criminality, and that they themselves may be satisfied in what they have an undoubted right to expect, a Trial by their Peers."[16] Parr

---

12   *The Reply of Messrs Sterns and Taylor*, above note 10 at 9.
13   *Assembly Journals* (28 November 1787) at 24.
14   Transcript of Sterns's Oral Testimony, Halifax, NSARM (Assembly Papers, RG 1, vol. 302, No. 17). Other quotations in this paragraph are from the same source, unless otherwise specified.
15   Taylor's Statement, NSARM, (Assembly Papers, RG 1, vol. 302, No. 37)
16   *Assembly Journals* (1 December 1787) at 27.

asked for and received a response from the judges; it flatly denied all the allegations and called them "the bare Opinions and Assertions of two dissatisfied Practitioners."[17] Two months later the Governor's Council unanimously rejected the allegations, calling them "groundless and Scandalous" and also asserting that the judges "by their answers" had "fully acquitted themselves of all imputation of mal-Conduct in office." The Governor's Council also published extracts from its proceedings in the *Halifax Gazette*, "to prevent as far as can now be done the Mischievous tendency of the Accusation & in vindication of the Character of the Justices."[18]

For Parr, the episode was but one more example of the havoc that Loyalist demands were wreaking on his administration. He had long had trouble with the Loyalists, finding himself constantly beset by their complaints about land-granting and provisions, and he worried (rightly) that the Loyalists wanted political power and administrative offices.[19] As he acidly observed with reference to the Legislative Assembly's demand for an inquiry into the judges, "it is not an easy matter to manage and satisfy an expecting Loyalist, their present want is every office in government."[20] The Loyalists achieved substantial representation in the assembly in the election of 1785, returning thirteen of the thirty-nine members. They were in a minority but were able to exercise an influence disproportionate to their numbers, in part because they were able to coalesce with an existing group of "opposition" members, the "hinterland" assemblymen who had a tradition of being at odds with those beholden to the Halifax establishment. As Beck argues, the influence of men used to powerful assemblies increased the constitutional awareness of many existing members and encouraged the assembly to demand more power in the colony.[21] But to Parr and the Tories on his council, including the judges, the Loyalists' belief in strong legislatures, a product of the political culture of their homelands, was dangerous. "[W]hatever Loyalty these Lawyers may have brought with them from the States," he told London, "is so strong tinctured with Republican Spirit, that if they meet with any encouragement it may be attended with dangerous consequence to this Province. One of them

---

17 The judges' response appears in *The Reply of Messrs Sterns and Taylor*, above note 10, the quotation is at 4.
18 Council Minutes (28 February 1788), NSARM (RG 1, vol. 213 at 139–40).
19 See generally Neil McKinnon, *This Unfriendly Soil*, above note 5.
20 Parr to Evan Nepean (18 April 1788), NSARM (Colonial Office Series 217, vol. 60, at 177).
21 J.M. Beck, *The Politics of Nova Scotia: Volume 1, 1710–1896* (Tantallon, NS: Four East, 1985) at 46.

[Sterns] aims at being the Wilkes of Nova Scotia."[22] This attitude was responsible for the council's dismissal of the assembly's concerns in so perfunctory a fashion and it also shaped the judges' dealings with their critics.

Sterns and Taylor responded to the council's decision in the newspapers, publishing a series of documents and articles, some responding to Plain Truth, (Attorney General and future Chief Justice Sampson Salter Blowers) who defended the judges. March 1788 saw, in the words of one contemporary, a "press war" over the issue.[23] Sterns and Taylor did not use intemperate language about the judges, they reserved that for Blowers and, to a lesser extent, the council for its handling of the assembly's petition. And most of the ink was spilled over the question of whether they had fomented the agitation or whether it was a more general concern of assemblymen. But the lawyers did publish in the *Halifax Journal* the substance of their testimony before the Legislative Assembly, and in doing so publicized their critiques of the judges.

The judges' response to the newspaper articles came as soon as Easter term opened in April 1788. On April 1st the first order of business was, as usual, the charge to the Grand Jury.[24] Nothing was said in the charge about the attacks on the judges, but after it was concluded Sterns and Taylor, present in court and with substantial caseloads, were called forward and asked about the recent press publications. When they admitted authorship, Justice Deschamps ordered the prothonotary to have their names stricken from the barristers' rolls for contempt. They asked to be heard in their own defence, but this was denied.

In finding the men guilty of contempt, Justice Deschamps argued that to criticize the judges was to attack the institution of the court itself. He stated:

> The gross and violent Scandal contained in the public Papers printed by *John Howe* on the 6, 12, 20, and 27th March, under the Signature of *Jonathan Sterns* and *William Taylor*, are too atrocious to pass unnoticed; and sorry we are to observe, that the Lenity, Indulgence and Moderation hitherto extended by the Court towards you as Practitioners, instead of exciting in you a decent and respectfull Submission to their Authority, has by an un-

---

22 Parr to Nepean (8 March 1788), NSARM (Colonial Office Series 217, vol. 60 at 173).
23 The phrase is councillor John Halliburton's: see Halliburton to Nepean (20 April 1788), NSARM (Colonial Office Series 217, vol. 60 at 288). The various press entries are in *Collection of the Publications*.
24 The proceedings of that day were reported at length in the *Halifax Gazette* on April 8th, and the account here is taken from that source. It includes Deschamps's speech finding the two guilty of contempt. For another brief account see Halliburton to Nepean (20 April 1788), NSARM (Colonial Office Series 217, vol. 60 at 288).

accountable Depravity of the human Heart, only encouraged you to resume Opposition to their Power, and to attempt, by one of the boldest Attacks that ever was made — publickly to asperse the Characters of the Judges of this Court, which in its Tendency aims at the Subversion of the Constitution of the Court itself — these wicked Efforts, fruitless and ineffectual as they have proved, are yet so criminal in their Nature as to call loudly for legal Censure and Condemnation, lest, if they should be permitted to pass with impunity, the Court might seem to merit that Contempt and Disregard, which you have so daringly endeavoured to involve them in.[25]

Justice Deschamps cited just two authorities to support his view that what the lawyers had done was contempt. One was Blackstone, who among various other things described contempt as including "speaking or writing contemptuously of the Court, or Judges acting in their Judicial capacity,"[26] even if out of court. The other was the 1786 English case of Walter, a printer, who had published an attack on Lord Loughborough, Chief Justice of Common Pleas. Perhaps ironically, given that one of the lawyers' complaints was that the judges did not know the law very well, after the contempt finding the lawyers consulted the law officers of the Crown about the scope of contempt, who in turn argued that Sterns and Taylor had been contemptuous.[27]

That opinion is not available, but by contemporary English understandings the law officers may not have been entirely correct. There was some precedent for the NSSC judges' action, although it was only in the early eighteenth century that contempt had been widened to include what the lawyers had done. Prior to that attacks on judges made out of court by persons not party to a case were not seen as covered by the law of contempt, although in some instances the government prosecuted for seditious libel.[28] But in the 1720s there was a series of cases in which judges summarily punished general criticisms of the courts as contempt, the offence being named "scandalizing the court." Those cases arose because the use of seditious libel in clearly political prosecutions came under attack, an attack made more effective by the rapid growth of the periodical press, and because some prosecutions foundered with the unwillingness of grand juries to indict, or trial juries to con-

---

25 *Halifax Gazette* (8 April 1788).
26 William Blackstone, *Commentaries on the Laws of England*, Facsimile of first, 1765–69 edition (Chicago: University of Chicago Press, 1979), Book 4 at 282.
27 Halliburton to Nepean (20 April 1788) NSARM (CO 217, vol. 60 at 288).
28 This discussion of the English law is based on D. Hay, "Contempt by Scandalizing the Court: A Political History of the First Hundred Years" (1987) 25 Osgoode Hall L.J. 431. The quotations in this and the subsequent paragraph are at 439 and 475, respectively.

vict. As Hay notes, "[t]he undoubted advantages of attachments for contempt over all other forms of proceeding were the elimination of those unpredictable juries ... and the speed with which the court could proceed." Certainly Deschamps would have been grateful for both, given the context of a heated press war over the judges. Any kind of jury proceeding would have run a considerable risk of the lawyers not being convicted, and a delay might have allowed them to rally support. Indeed, as noted, Sterns and Taylor were not even given the opportunity to argue in their own defence — the admission of authorship was enough to convict.

Not only was the offence of contempt by scandalizing the court a relatively recent innovation, it was also a very controversial one in England. Although Blackstone approved of it in the passage cited by Justice Deschamps, including it among his list of the ways contempt could occur, it fell into desuetude for some thirty years, until revived in the 1760s to deal with the bitter party controversies that marked the early years of the reign of George III. Publisher William Almon was cited for contempt in 1765 for his criticisms of Lord Mansfield's handling of the government's prosecutions for libel of John Wilkes, and other prosecutions followed, notably that of publisher William Bingley in 1770. Yet these proceedings were also heavily criticized as an unconstitutional undermining of English liberties, and again the power to punish the contempt of scandalizing the court fell into disfavour. Hay suggests that there was no eighteenth-century case of this type after 1770, and that "the contempt power of scandalizing the court was thus very nearly stillborn." As noted, Deschamps cited a 1786 case, but this was a libel prosecution. Although he did not use the term "scandalizing the court," referring only to contempt, this is surely what Sterns and Taylor were guilty of. Thus this was a device used in the colony at a time when it was considered of dubious legality in the mother country.

Finding Sterns and Taylor guilty of contempt was one thing; choosing the punishment was another. As Deschamps noted, the court had "many weapons of Punishment" available to it: "Indictment, Fines, Imprisonment and Severe Damages," but it chose none of these, perhaps because it was concerned not to make martyrs of the two lawyers who had, judging from the Assembly proceedings of the previous year, considerable public support. Instead, Deschamps invoked the court's power to regulate the bar:

> as Servants of the Court you are answerable to your Masters; as Officers here, you are amenable to your Superiors the Judges. Your good Behaviour was the Condition of your Admission, and the Tenure by which you hold your Offices. And as you have been so obstinately blind to that Respect and

Reverance, which is due to the Court, in which you have hitherto been permitted to move and act, we hold it our indispensable Duty, to consider you as unworthy of any further Favor or Support, and consequently we order you to be struck off the Roll of Attorneys as an Example, that the Law and Justice of the Land requires at our Hands.[29]

Thus the judges chose to hit their critics in the pocketbook, leaving them free to criticize the court but unable to practise their profession.

Two days later, on April 3rd, because the press attacks had included the Governor's Council for its handling of the Assembly's complaint, Sterns and Taylor were also barred from practising before that body, which meant that they could not handle appeals or Chancery cases, because the Lieutenant Governor was Chancellor.[30] After an unsuccessful attempt to rally popular support for their cause in the colony, Sterns and Taylor left for England. Their parting gesture was an open letter to "the Freeholders and other Inhabitants of the Province" in which they reiterated their determination to get the judges removed.[31] But their principal mission was to be reinstated to the bar.

The judges were not finished with the refractory lawyers. Before leaving for London, Sterns sought to maintain his practice. The day after he had been disbarred, he sent an advertisement to the *Halifax Gazette*, assuring "his numerous Friends who have entrusted their Causes to his Management" that "notwithstanding the Event of Yesterday" their cases "shall be duly attended to by a Gentleman of Probity and Abilities, who will act in his Behalf." In short, "the Business of his Profession will be carried on as usual at his Office, by a Gentleman duly authorized to act as an Attorney."[32] He chose Daniel Wood, a leading pre-Loyalist member of the bar. He told Wood that he had a "great deal of business" pending in the NSSC and offered him the use of his office, including his two clerks. Wood would pay Sterns £300 per year, and presumably take all the fees for himself.[33] It seems that Wood did appear in court on behalf of at least one of Sterns's clients; Sterns was present, presumably in the public gallery, and spoke to Wood before being roughly spoken to by Justice Brenton. The judges then used an intermediary, Mr. Holmes (presumably Loyalist merchant Benjamin Mulberry Holmes, a supporter of Sterns), to tell Wood that they "would not permit any practitioner that was concerned with you [Sterns] to carry on business." Wood was worried enough

---

29 See above note 25.
30 Council Minutes (3 April 1788) NSARM (RG 1, vol. 213 at 142–43).
31 *Halifax Journal* (24 April 1788).
32 *Halifax Gazette* (8 April 1788).
33 Sterns to Daniel Wood (10 April 1788) NSARM (CO 217, vol. 60 at 325).

to call on Deschamps, who informed him that "nothing should be suffered to [be] done that appeared before them, either in your [Sterns's] handwriting, or in the hand of your clerks, or anything that came from your office." While Wood had not foreseen any difficulty with the arrangement and was keen to accept Sterns's offer, he declined it, worried that the vengeful judges "may dismiss me unheard in the same manner they have you."[34] Thus the judges were able to use their power to regulate who could practise in the courts to bully Wood into submission.

Sterns and Taylor's attempts to be reinstated at the bar in London were not successful. In the opinion of the law officers of the Crown in London, this could only be achieved by an apology and petition to the NSSC and the Governor's Council.[35] Taylor, whose career in Halifax was less successful than Sterns's, gave up the ghost. He got married in London to the daughter of fellow New Jersey Loyalist, Major Philip Van Cortland of Halifax, and eventually returned to New Jersey, where he died in 1806. But Sterns returned, late in 1789, determined to discredit the judges and resume his practice at the bar. He proved able to revive the judges' question, helped by two cases in 1789 in which the judges' conduct had provoked widespread criticism. When the Legislative Assembly met in early 1790, it conducted its own full-blown investigation, eventually passing seven articles of impeachment that incorporated accusations of improper behaviour in eleven cases and also accused the judges of lying in their response to the Governor's Council in 1787. The assembly also passed an address to the King, asking him "to institute such a Court here for the trial of those Judges as may be competent to that purpose."[36] The attempt to impeach the judges ultimately went nowhere. Secretary of State Grenville flatly refused to create any sort of court in the colony to try the judges, and the matter was instead referred to the Committee of the Privy Council for Trade and Plantations. The committee exonerated the judges while admitting they had made some procedural errors in a few cases.

In the interim Sterns sought reinstatement at the bar once a new chief justice, Thomas Strange, arrived in mid-1790. Strange's detailed account of the proceedings between him and Sterns reveals, again, the links drawn by

---

34 Wood to Sterns (19 April 1788) NSARM (CO 217, vol. 60, at 327).
35 See Sir Archibald MacDonald's opinion, NSARM (Brenton Halliburton Papers, Manuscript Group 1, vol. 334, No. 1).
36 See *The Humble Petition of the House of Representatives of the Province of Nova Scotia ... to the King's Most Excellent Majesty; together with the Articles of Impeachment ....* (London, 1790). The quotation is at 4.

colonial judges between the NSSC and the political authority of the crown.[37] Sterns and Strange had some discussions about the language to be used in the former's petition to the court for reinstatement, but that matter was easily enough resolved. The real sticking point was Strange's insistence that Sterns had to apologize to the Governor's Council before the court would hear his petition. At first Sterns refused to do so. He considered himself to have been treated badly by Lieutenant Governor Parr and his council, arguing that they had acted for political reasons, and that he and all other citizens had the right to criticize the colonial administration. Chief Justice Strange was not interested in talk of constitutional liberties; he wanted Sterns to retract his criticism of the politicians as well as the judges and saw the former as "indispensable." Indeed, he was prepared to use his own position of strength — he could prevent Sterns from practising his profession — to achieve that: "as the Court had him now within its power, it would be a breach of its duty to the Government not to stipulate for a proper confession to it."[38] Sterns railed against the demand, "sometimes with tears, sometimes with vehemence," but in the end he had no choice but to apologize to both bodies.

The travails of Jonathan Sterns and William Taylor show the extent to which, in the *Ancien Régime* of colonial government, courts were seen as intimately tied to political authorities and very much part of the power structure. When the Loyalists sought to advance their interests within Nova Scotian society and politics, they were resisted by many in the pre-revolutionary establishment who branded them as ungrateful, refractory, and, at worst, disloyal — an irony that highlights the fact that many Loyalists wanted to retain both their allegiance to the crown and their own, more democratic and independent, traditions of colonial governance. For Sterns and Taylor the entrenched establishment's response to Loyalist concerns was made doubly effective by the power that the NSSC judges had to decide who could practise before them. When the court disbarred them for contempt, it not only indicated that it regarded any criticism of the judiciary as contemptuous, but it was also able to reinforce that finding by cutting off their ability to make a living.

---

37 For this proceeding, see Thomas Strange to Nepean (21 Aug. 1790) NSARM (CO 217, vol. 62 at 274–83).
38 *Ibid.*

CHAPTER 10

"Guardians of Liberty": R.M.W. Chitty and the Wartime Idea of Constitutional Rights

ERIC M. ADAMS[*]

AS WAS IMMEDIATELY APPARENT to Law Society of Upper Canada Treasurer D'Alton Lally McCarthy, the gathering storms of war in Europe meant dramatic changes for Canada's legal profession. Ottawa would need lawyers to serve, not just as soldiers, but in the various branches of the rapidly expanding wartime state. Writing to Ernest Lapointe, minister of justice, in the early days of September 1939, McCarthy offered his assistance in finding members fit for the task.[1] Undoubtedly, the government's needs were great. Using the virtually unlimited constitutional jurisdiction afforded by the *War Measures Act*,[2] the federal government created dozens of new boards, tribunals, commissions, and corporations to control production, consumption, prices, profits, rents, wages, and salaries in the Canadian economy. "[I]n the twinkling of a pen," Robert Bothwell and William Kilbourn explain, Canada passed "from a free enterprise system regulated by ten jealously competing sovereignties to a centrally directed economy regulated by the government's

---

[*]   This paper is drawn from a chapter in my S.J.D. dissertation, *The Idea of Constitutional Rights and the Re-making of Canadian Constitution Law* (University of Toronto, Faculty of Law, in progress as of 2008). I thank Susan Lewthwaite, Robert Leckey, Sarah Krotz, and Ashley Reid for their assistance in the preparation of this version.
1   Letter from McCarthy to Lapointe (6 September 1939) in Christopher Moore, *The Law Society of Upper Canada and Ontario's Lawyers 1797–1997* (Toronto: University of Toronto Press, 1997) at 222–23.
2   R.S.C. 1927, c. 206.

perception of the needs of the war."[3] While over a thousand lawyers and law students put their legal careers on hold to serve overseas, the bulk of the profession remained at home participating in, litigating against, or strenuously opposing the changing nature of Canadian wartime government.

True to McCarthy's prediction, lawyers abounded in Canada's bureaucratizing wartime state. Henry Borden neglected his lucrative practice in Toronto to serve as counsel and key advisor to the Department of Munitions and Supply and its minister, the "absolute monarch of Canadian war production," Clarence Decatur Howe.[4] Donald Gordon, the charismatic and domineering chair of the Wartime Prices and Trade Board (WPTB),[5] similarly recognized the need for lawyers. In organizing the WPTB, he demanded "a list of a dozen lawyers across the country, lawyers who don't give a damn about the law, just want to get things done."[6] With the issuance of general wage and price controls late in 1941, the WPTB hired hundreds of lawyers to investigate compliance, deter black markets, and, on occasion, prosecute offenders.[7] From Ottawa, lawyers like Robert Fowler and Harry Anger set board policy and oversaw the issuance of thousands of price regulations, while leading members of the bar staffed regional offices to enforce them. On the road to their judicial careers, Wishart Spence and John Arnup took leaves from their law firms to prosecute price and rental infractions in Toronto. Toiling long hours, six days a week, enforcing thousands of ever-changing regulations, the lawyers of the WPTB, Arnup fondly remembered, "created a little fraternity of [its] own. We became blood brothers."[8] It was not just the front lines, Arnup

3   Robert Bothwell and William Kilbourn, *C.D. Howe: A Biography* (Toronto: McClelland & Stewart, 1979) at 134–35.
4   M.H. Hennessy, "The Industrial Front: The Scale and Scope of Canadian Industrial Mobolization during the Second World War" in B. Horn, ed., *Forging a Nation: Perspectives on the Canadian Military Experience* (St. Catherine's, ON: Vanwell, 2002) at 141. The government passed legislation creating the Department of Munitions and Supply a week before the war but did not activate the department and appoint Howe until April 1940: *The Department of Munitions and Supply Act*, S.C. 1939 (2d Sess.), c. 3, as amended. See also Jeff Keshen, "Growth, Opportunity, Strain" in *Saints, Sinners, and Soldiers: Canada's Second World War* (Vancouver: UBC Press, 2004).
5   PC 2516 (3 September 1939), *Proclamations and Orders in Council* (Ottawa: King's Printer, 1940) at 40.
6   Joseph Schull, *The Great Scot: A Biography of Donald Gordon* (Montreal: McGill-Queen's University Press, 1979) at 56.
7   See Jeff Keshen, "One for All or All for One: Government Controls, Black Marketing, and the Limits of Patriotism, 1939–1947" (1994–95) 29 J. of Cdn. Stud. 111. See also G.D. Sanagan, "The Road to Tomorrow: Canada's Wartime Controls" (1942–43) 12 Fortnightly L.J. 217.
8   Osgoode Society Interview with John Arnup (4 November 1982), Toronto, Archives Ontario, C81 at 136 [Arnup Interview]. The expertise John Arnup developed during his

implied, forging bonds in service to country, but legal work on the home front as well.

Toronto lawyer and editor of the *Fortnightly Law Journal*, Robert Michael Willes Chitty, greeted the WPTB and its mandate with less enthusiasm. In bimonthly columns throughout the war, Chitty railed repeatedly against all aspects of what he called "bureaucratic dictatorship"[9] but reserved his greatest scorn for the WPTB's "price fixing and rent restriction,"[10] along with other centralized efforts to control "the economic life of the country."[11] At first, Chitty attacked the "new batch of boards and commissions" on federalist principles, arguing that the federal government lacked the constitutional authority to extend its reach into the domain of provincial jurisdiction over property and civil rights.[12] Drawing on deeper constitutional principles, he also charged the government with "filching ... civil liberties of every kind" and "shatter[ing]" democratic principles.[13] As *amicus curiae*, D.L. McCarthy and J.J. Robinette raised similar constitutional arguments — albeit in more delicate fashion — in the mid-war reference testing the constitutional validity of the government's wartime regulations.[14] In concurring judgments, the Supreme Court upheld the regulations and put the constitutional validity of the *War Measures Act* and all of its attendant regulations beyond doubt.[15] In print, an indignant Chitty blasted the Court for "rubber stamp[ing] ... the

---

time at the WPTB served him well after the war. See John Arnup, "Recent Cases on Rental Regulations" (1947) 25 Can. Bar Rev. 625 and "More Cases on Rental Regulations" (1948) 26 Can. Bar Rev. 1057.

9 R.M.W. Chitty, "*Inter Alia*: Political Bureaucratic Inroads on Freedom" (1942–43) 12 Fortnightly L.J. 34 at 34.

10 R.M.W. Chitty, "War Measures: Constitutional Aspect" (1941–42) 11 Fortnightly L.J. 198 at 199 ["Constitutional Aspect"].

11 Ibid.

12 Ibid. Chitty ignored the Privy Council's clear ruling to the contrary in *Fort Frances Pulp and Power Company v. Manitoba Free Press Co.* (1923), A.C. 695 at 704 [*Fort Frances*].

13 "Constitutional Aspect," *ibid*.

14 *Reference as to the Validity of the Regulations in Relation to Chemicals*, [1943] S.C.R. 1 [*Chemicals Reference*]. Although the particular regulations in question dealt narrowly with chemicals and certain delegated orders of the chemicals controller, the government took pains to stress that the "methods of control" under view were "identical to that adopted in other fields in connection with the conduct of the war." In other words, what was at stake was the entire administrative edifice of the wartime state.

15 Evidencing less comfort with the "sweeping and drastic" delegation of legislative authority from Parliament to Executive, Davis J. nonetheless reached the same conclusion in reasoning that a "safety valve" existed: Parliament could amend or repeal the *War Measures Act* if it so chose: *ibid*. at 26–27.

government's bureaucratic designs on the liberty of the individual."[16] Federalism and rhetorical appeals to British-inspired civil liberties, Chitty realized, would not be enough. What Canada needed, he now believed, was American-style constitutional rights.

The politics surrounding patriation of the *Constitution Act, 1982*[17] with its *Canadian Charter of Rights and Freedoms*[18] has tended to overshadow the early days of Canada's rights revolution. We have largely viewed our modern rights history as a combination of politics on the one hand — Pierre Trudeau's efforts to blunt Quebec nationalism — and idealism on the other — the values of individual liberty and human dignity inspired by the *Universal Declaration of Human Rights*.[19] Our constitutional history is richer and more complicated. Michael Chitty's wartime fight for constitutional rights reveals one strand in this larger story and highlights the ever-present role of lawyers and legal thought in Canada's history of constitutional change. In some ways, Chitty's appeal for constitutional rights trod venerable soil. By invoking the image of lawyers as the guardians of liberty, he drew on the classic late-Victorian tenets of rule of law constitutionalism,[20] while also borrowing from Lord Hewart's tirades against the "new despotism" of the expanding administrative state.[21] In these respects, Chitty proceeded from the British legal thought that largely defined the Canadian legal imagination and to which he had obvious and deep connection. But Chitty's wartime turn to *entrenched* constitutional rights also presaged the increasing influence of American ideas in Canadian legal thought. Yet in seeking constitutional rights to protect the traditional ideals of the limited state — in effect, to bring *Lochner*-era constitutionalism to Canada — Chitty called for rights at a moment when the concept itself was in transition. In this way, Chitty's contribution to the dawning "age of human rights"[22] is an ironic one. In the end, he took part in a revolution not entirely of his intention.

---

16 R.M.W. Chitty, "*Inter Alia*: The Responsibility of Parliament for the Orders of the Dictators'" (1942–43) 12 Fortnightly L.J. 177 at 178.
17 *Constitution Act, 1982*, being Schedule B to the *Canada Act 1982* (U.K.), 1982, c. 11.
18 *Canadian Charter of Rights and Freedoms*, Part I of the *Constitution Act, 1982*, being Schedule B to the *Canada Act 1982* (U.K.), 1982, c. 11.
19 GA Res. 217(III), UN GAOR, 3d Sess., Supp. No. 13, UN Doc. A/810 (1948).
20 Classically stated, of course, in A.V. Dicey, *Introduction to the Study of the Law of the Constitution*, 9th ed. (London: Macmillan, 1945).
21 G. Hewart, *The New Despotism* (London: Ernest Benn, 1929).
22 George Egerton, "Entering the Age of Human Rights: Religion, Politics, and Canadian Liberalism, 1945–1950" (2004) 85 Canadian Historical Review 451.

ROBERT MICHAEL WILLES CHITTY

BOTH FOLLOWING AND EVADING family tradition, Michael Chitty left England as a young man to pursue his legal career in Canada. Born in 1893, the youngest child of Sir Thomas Willes Chitty and Emily Eliza Newbolt, family custom demanded that Michael defer to the career wishes of his eldest brother.[23] Given the six generations of lawyers preceding him, it must not have been terribly surprising when Michael's brother Thomas Henry Willes Chitty chose law.[24] Clearly, law was in the family blood. Michael and Henry's great-great-grandfather, Joseph Chitty, had authored the renowned treatise on contracts still widely in use in the early twentieth century, as it is today.[25] His father, "recognised as one of the greatest common law lawyers of the day," achieved modest fame as editor-in-chief of the first edition of *Halsbury's Laws of England* and senior master and King's Remembrancer.[26] The Chitty tradition, it seemed, was not just one of law, but specifically of the practitioner-scholar; the legal writer. It was to this Victorian ideal that Michael Chitty forever aspired.

But if Chitty was to find a career in law, he would have to find it somewhere other than England. When he returned home from Marlborough College, Thomas Henry had already been called to the bar. Good lawyers that they were, the Chittys found a loophole in their family custom. It was determined that practising law in the colonies would not offend the unwritten rule of fraternal hierarchy. So, with family connections charting the course, Michael Chitty crossed the Atlantic in 1912 to begin his articles of clerkship with Toronto lawyer Ernest Edward Arthur Duvernet. Within two years, the First

---

23 Familial details are found in John Honsberger, "Robert Michael Willes Chitty, Q.C." (1994) 28 L.S.U.C. Gazette 79 at 82 ["Chitty, Q.C."], and the Special Memoriam Issue (1971) 19 Chitty's L.J. 37. The Chitty genealogy is also usefully, if unofficially, traced online: www.thepeerage.com/p22381.htm#i223806. See also the memoirs of Michael's nephew, Thomas Hinde in *Sir Henry and Sons: A Memoir* (London: Macmillan, 1980) at 21 [*Sir Henry*].
24 Sadly, Chitty's son indicated that his father had "always wanted to be a soldier. But for one hundred years Chittys had been lawyers and his preference was scarcely considered." After sustaining serious injury in the First World War — a fellow soldier accidentally shot him in the chest — Henry Chitty gave up the practice of law and spent the rest of his mostly unhappy life as a schoolmaster: *Sir Henry, ibid.* at 7.
25 Joseph Chitty, *A Practical Treatise on the Law of Contracts Not under Seal, and upon the Usual Defences to Action Thereon* (London: S. Sweet, 1826), now in its 29th edition as *Chitty on Contracts* (London: Sweet & Maxwell, 2004).
26 Ernest Jelf, "Sir Thomas Willes Chitty, Bart., K.C." (1929) 15 Transactions of the Grotius Society v at v. A cursory Internet search suggests the family tradition continues. Evidence suggests that Robert A. Chitty, a lawyer in the State Attorney's Office of Florida, is Michael Chitty's grandson.

World War returned him to Europe. In 1914 Chitty sailed back to England with the Toronto Regiment, 3rd Battalion, along with his fraternity brother, erstwhile study partner, and future Chief Justice of the Supreme Court of Canada, John Cartwright.[27] A shell blast sustained at Givenchy, France, seriously wounded Chitty's leg, and, by circuitous route and circumstance, he finished the war in Texas training American pilots.[28] At war's end, he returned to Osgoode Hall to complete his articling and joined Cartwright and many other young veterans at the call to the Ontario bar on 20 May 1920.[29] The eclectic legal career of Michael Chitty had begun.

When that career ended some fifty years later, Chitty had left an indelible mark on the field of Canadian legal letters. He is best remembered today for lending his name to two journals — *Chitty's Law Journal* and its successor, *Chitty's Law Journal and Family Law Review*. His career in legal writing began in earnest in 1923 when he joined the staff of the Canada Law Book Company as assistant editor of the *Dominion Law Reports*. Over the next several decades, Chitty served variously as assistant editor of the *Ontario Law Reports*, editor of *Canadian Criminal Cases*, and writer and editor of numerous practice guides, an abridgement of Canadian criminal cases, and several texts on topics ranging from chattel mortgages to motor vehicle liability.[30] In 1931, he began his true labour of love: editing and writing for the *Fortnightly Law Journal (FLJ)* — a compendium of bench and bar news, case comments, and short articles directed at the Ontario bar. In addition to all that, Chitty practised civil litigation in an assortment of small firms before eventually working under his own shingle. Still, one is left with the distinct impression that he devoted his principal energies to his legal writing.

That writing — especially his opinionated and provocative editorializing in the *FLJ* — earned him a certain prominence among his peers. By 1941, his colleagues had elected him bencher, a position from which he led the attack

---

27 See John Cartwright's contribution to the Chitty Memoriam Issue (1971) 19 Chitty's L.J. 37 at 46. On Cartwright generally, see W. Kenneth Campbell, "The Right Honourable John Cartwright" (1978) 12 L.S.U.C. Gazette 326.

28 "Chitty, Q.C.," above note 23 at 84–85. See also the wartime tales of "Uncle Mike" in *Sir Henry*, above note 23 at 10–11.

29 "Chitty, Q.C.," *ibid.* at 86.

30 See, for example, Robert Michael Willes Chitty: *A Digest of Canadian Case Law: 1920–1925* (Toronto: Canada Law Book, 1926); *Chattel Mortgages and Bills of Sale* (Toronto: Canada Law Book, 1927) (as editor); *Bicknell & Seager's Division Court Manual* (Toronto: Canada Law Book, 1928) (as editor); *Ontario Annual Practice* (Toronto: Canada Law Book, 1941–); *The Ontario Statute Citator* (Toronto: Canadian Law List, 1948); and *The Law of Motor Vehicle Liability Insurance in the Common Law Provinces of Canada* (Toronto: Canada Law Book, 1948).

against Caesar Wright's efforts to wrench legal education from the hands of the profession.[31] In an ultimately losing cause, Chitty argued strenuously throughout the 1940s that legal education should remain "vocational training" on the British model.[32] Although Chitty agreed that law was a "learned profession,"[33] he believed that the learning in question should take place in the workaday world of legal practice. Surely the method of legal education that had produced the leading lights of the British bar would be good enough for Canada. As a friend recalled, Chitty proceeded from an "unspoken assumption of English superiority in manners, ethics, ability, politics, and judicial wisdom."[34] Presumably legal training could be added to that list. But aside from his conservative disposition, his fierce attachment to practical legal training owed much to his faith in the scholarly nature of legal practice. If his family history had demonstrated anything, it was that lawyers had much to contribute to the understanding of the common law. From the editor's chair of the *FLJ*, Chitty sought not only to clarify but also to shape the law. In that capacity he fought his battles for legal education and launched his assault against the wartime administrative state. "His editorials might not have passed the editorial board of the *Harvard Law Review*," John Arnup conceded, "but his readers were never in any doubt as to what he meant."[35]

CHITTY AND THE CANADIAN BAR ASSOCIATION

FROM THE OUTSET, CHITTY aimed to convince his fellow lawyers of his causes, not only in print but also in person. To that end, he was an active member of the Canadian Bar Association (CBA) throughout the war. Officially formed (after a false start in 1896) in 1915 and incorporated by an Act of Parliament in 1921,[36] the CBA had ebbed and flowed in influence during its existence, but it entered the war years nonetheless firm in its commitment to "defend the constitutional principles whose history, [and] whose meaning [we] know better than the layman."[37] Certainly, Chitty stood on guard. At the 27 January 1940

---

31 See C. Ian Kyer and Jerome E. Bickenbach, *The Fiercest Debate: Cecil A. Wright, the Benchers, and Legal Education in Ontario 1923–1957* (Toronto: University of Toronto Press for the Osgoode Society, 1987) at 139.
32 *Ibid.* at 187–88.
33 R.M.W. Chitty, "*Inter Alia*: The Annual Dinner of the School of Law of the University of Toronto" (1942) 11 Fortnightly L.J. 242.
34 R.L. Cartwright, "Mike Chitty as I Knew Him" (1971) 19 Chitty's L.J. 37 at 40.
35 Special Memoriam Issue, above note 23 at 43.
36 An Act to Incorporate the Canadian Bar Association, S.C. 1921, c 79
37 D.L. McCarthy, "The Canadian Bar Association" (1941) 19 Can. Bar Rev. 525 at 531.

meeting of the CBA's Ontario section, he and his fellow lawyers noted with distress the state's "insidious encroachments on the simple fundamental rights of the individual," worrying further that "rights necessarily suspended in wartime may be lost for good."[38] Observing that "this country is now engaged in a war to preserve the rights of the individual," Chitty and his CBA colleagues vowed to fight their own war against the "menace of bureaucracy."[39]

In Ottawa, the changing face of wartime government had just begun to take shape. The week before declaring war, the government invoked the *War Measures Act (WMA)*, authorizing the executive to "do and authorize such acts and things" as deemed "necessary or advisable for the security, defence, peace, order and welfare of Canada."[40] Immediately turning to address issues of domestic security, the federal government issued a series of executive orders known collectively as the *Defence of Canada Regulations (DOCR)*.[41] The regulations authorized the executive to intern enemy aliens, censor speech, outlaw groups, and arrest and detain individuals without charge or trial.[42] At their most restrictive, the *DOCR* outlawed virtually all forms of anti-war dissent. In

---

38 "Midwinter Meeting, Ontario Section Canadian Bar Association" (1939–40) 9 Fortnightly L.J. 215 at 215 ["Midwinter Meeting"].
39 *Ibid.*
40 R.S.C. 1927, c. 206. The Privy Council had previously upheld the Act's broad transfer of power and wide scope for executive discretion, noting that times of war afforded the executive "considerable freedom" to determine the appropriate measures required: *Fort Frances*, above note 12 at 705. See also *Re Grey*, [1918] 57 S.C.R. 150 at 166, Fitzpatrick, C.J.: "It seems to me obvious that parliament intended, as the language used implies, to clothe the executive with the widest powers in time of danger. Taken literally, [section 3] contains unlimited powers." For a history of the Act see F.M. Greenwood, "The Drafting and Passage of the *War Measures Act* in 1914 and 1927: Object Lessons in the Need for Vigilance" in W. Wesley Pue and B. Wright, eds., *Canadian Perspectives on Law & Society: Issues in Legal History* (Ottawa: Carleton University Press, 1988) at 291.
41 PC 2483 (3 September 1939), *Proclamations and Orders in Council* (Ottawa: King's Printer, 1940) at 27. The regulations themselves were published separately as Canada, *Defence of Canada Regulations* (Ottawa: King's Printer, 1939). The *DOCR* were amended throughout the war and additional consolidations were published in 1940, 1941, and 1942.
42 See generally, Ramsay Cook, "Canadian Freedom in Wartime" in W.H. Heick and R. Graham, eds., *His Own Man: Essays in Honour of Arthur Reginald Marsden Lower* (Montreal: McGill-Queen's University Press, 1974) at 37. Based largely on the Defence of Canada Order of the First World War, the *DOCR* had been prepared by the Committee on Emergency Legislation the previous year and approved by Cabinet, King later admitted, "almost unread and unconsidered." Nor did Parliament examine them in the special sessions of Parliament preceding Canada's declaration of war on 10 September 1939. See Committee on Emergency Legislation, *First Report* (Ottawa: King's Printer, 1939). King's quote is from L-R. Betcherman, *Ernest Lapointe: Mackenzie King's Great Quebec Lieutenant* (Toronto: University of Toronto Press, 2002) at 276. See generally

addition, regulation 21 enabled the minister of justice to order the preventative detention of any person deemed a threat to "public safety or the safety of the State."[43] In the first months of the war, the government used the regulations to imprison Canadian fascists,[44] silence pacifists and war critics, and monitor "enemy aliens" living in Canada.[45] By the summer of 1940, the government amended the regulations to declare the Communist Party of Canada and the Jehovah's Witnesses illegal organizations, on the rationale that both groups had opposed Canada's participation in the war.[46] By war's end, the government had jailed over two thousand individuals under the *DOCR*, fined many thousands of others, banned hundreds of newspapers and periodicals, and seized and destroyed thousands of books and other publications.[47]

The few *DOCR* cases that found their way into the courts reveal a judiciary largely unsympathetic with the civil liberties claims of the accused. As a majority of the Manitoba Court of Appeal explained, "In war ... parliament may take from the Courts their judicial discretion and substitute it for the autocracy of bureaucrats."[48] "At this grave moment in our struggle, not only for the democratic way of life but for our very existence," Ontario's Supreme Court observed, "it may be imperative that our ancient liberties will be placed in pawn for victory."[49] "War," the judges approvingly quoted, "could

---

D. Robinson, "Planning for the 'Most Serious Contingency': Alien Internment, Arbitrary Detention, and the Canadian State 1938–39" (1993) 28 Journal of Cdn. Stud. 8.

43 The regulations explicitly disentitled detainees the right of *habeas corpus* and the right of judicial appeal. Instead, detentions under regulation 21 could be appealed to an advisory committee appointed by the government. For a history of similar British provisions, see A.W.B. Simpson, *In the Highest Degree Odious: Detentions without Trial in Wartime Britain* (Oxford: Clarendon Press, 1992).

44 See M. Robin, *Shades of Right: Nativist and Fascist Politics in Canada, 1920–1940* (Toronto: University of Toronto Press, 1991).

45 See R. Whitacker and G.S. Kealey, "A War on Ethnicity? The RCMP and Internment" in F. Iacovetta, R. Perin, and A. Principe, *Enemies Within: Italian and Other Internees in Canada and Abroad* (Toronto: University of Toronto Press, 2000).

46 For the Communist Party ban see: PC 2363, 8 June 1940 in Canada, *Proclamations and Orders in Council*, vol. 2 (Ottawa: King's Printer, 1940) at 108 and R. Whitaker, "Official Repression of Communism During World War II" (1986) 17 Labour/Le Travail 135. For the ban on the Jehovah's Witnesses see PC 2943, 4 July 1940 in Canada, *Proclamations and Orders in Council*, vol. 2 (Ottawa: King's Printer, 1940); *House of Commons Debates* (4 July 1940) at 1319 (Hon. Ernest Lapointe); and W. Kaplan, *State and Salvation: The Jehovah's Witnesses and Their Fight for Civil Rights* (Toronto: University of Toronto Press, 1989).

47 Ross Lambertson, *Repression and Resistance: Canadian Human Rights Activists, 1930–1960* (Toronto: University of Toronto Press, 2005) at 69.

48 *Yasny v. Lapointe* (1940), 74 C.C.C. 29 at 30 (Man. C.A.).

49 *Ex parte Sullivan* (1941), 75 C.C.C. 70 at 77 (Ont. S.C.).

not be carried on according to the principles of *Magna Carta*."⁵⁰ Yet for all of the obvious legal implications of the *DOCR*, Chitty and the CBA, indeed the legal profession more broadly, paid them relatively little heed.⁵¹

Chitty's concerns in 1940 about the state's "insidious encroachments on the simple fundamental rights of the individual" had nothing to do with the *DOCR* and everything to do with pre-war legislation (mostly tax statutes) that created administrative bodies possessing adjudicative functions.⁵² Wary of the general trend towards administrative government, the CBA characterized such measures as an attack on "the personal liberties and property rights of the subject."⁵³ As the war progressed, tax regimes proved to be the least of Chitty's worries. With the WPTB's implementation of widespread wage and price controls in December 1941, Chitty's worst fears were realized: the "octopus arms of bureaucracy"⁵⁴ had taken control of the Canadian economy. Thereafter, the WPTB and its regulations remained his predominant concern. He did express unease about the *DOCR's* curtailment of judicial review, advocating that those "guilty of subversive activities" should be tried in open court,⁵⁵ but elsewhere he praised the government's campaign against domestic communists and fascists and called for the hanging "of these ringleaders of treason and sedition."⁵⁶ In a similar vein, he characterized the pacifist musings of an Alberta schoolteacher as "heinous" and reproved the magistrates

---

50 Ibid. at 75, quoting *Ronnfeldt v. Phillips* (1918), 35 T.L.R. 46 (C.A.).
51 The sharpest criticism of the *DOCR* emerged from the Co-operative Commonwealth Federation, civil liberties groups, and the leftist and liberal press: see *House of Commons Debates* (27 February 1941) at 1069–1071 (Hon. M.J. Coldwell), (3 March 1941) at 1186–1191 (Hon. T.C. Douglas); B.K. Sandwell, "Defence of Liberty" *Saturday Night* (10 February 1940) 12; A.R.M. Lower, "Wartime Democracy in Canada" (1940) 102 *The New Republic* 505; F.A. Brewin, "Civil Liberties in Canada During Wartime" (1940–42) 1 Bill of Rights Rev. 112; G.M.A. Grube, "Freedom and the War" (1939) 19 Can. Forum; "Civil Liberties in War Time" (1940) 20 Can. Forum 106; and "Those Defence Regulations" (1940) 20 Can. Forum 304. But see James Francis, "The *War Measures Act*: A Summary of the Cases Reported" (1941) 19 Can. Bar Rev. 453 for a brief and largely uncritical treatment of the few reported cases.
52 The lawyers specifically cited the *Power Commission Act*, R.S.O. 1937, c. 62; the *Securities Act*, R.S.O. 1937, c. 265; the *Succession Duty Act*, R.S.O. 1937, c. 26; the *Income War Tax Act*, R.S.C. 1927, c. 97, as am. by S.C. 1939 (First Session) c. 6 and S.C. 1940 c. 34; and the *Income Tax Act*, R.S.O. 1937, c. 25.
53 "Midwinter Meeting," above note 38.
54 R.M.W. Chitty, "*Inter Alia*: Discussion of the Functions of War-time Emergency Boards" (1941–42) 11 Fortnightly L.J. 209 at 209 ["Emergency Boards"].
55 R.M.W. Chitty, "Sacrifice of Liberty in Aid of War Effort" (1940–41) 10 Fortnightly L.J. 129 at 130.
56 R.M.W. Chitty, "Canadian Fascists: Another Penalty for Sedition" (1940–41) 10 Fortnightly L.J. 33 at 33.

"altogether too lenient... view of the accused's... subversiveness."[57] His writing exhibited no concern for the DOCR's curtailment of freedom of speech, association, and religion. Similarly, in all of Chitty's wartime editorials, he never mentioned Japanese Canadians except to briefly argue that the right of "due trial" should not apply to "alien enemies."[58] In theory, the government's mass expulsion, dispossession, and detention of the Japanese Canadians living in British Columbia should have provided Chitty with the most egregious example of wartime property rights abuses.[59] The omission does not distinguish Chitty from his professional peers, or indeed much of the country at large, but it is telling nonetheless.

As wartime economic controls increased, so did the hyperbole of Chitty's attacks. He mostly abandoned the more technical constitutional argument that the *WMA* and its attendant economic regulations offended the constitutional division of powers[60] and focused instead on rhetorical broadsides. He frequently highlighted the irony that "while fighting men toil towards victory and defeat of dictatorships on the battle fronts of the world, our politicians at home have assured the victory of dictatorship at home."[61] Indeed, the dictatorial nature of Canadian administrative government became a common theme in Chitty's writing. He described the Canadian government with references to "would-be-Hitlerism,"[62] "incipient totalitarianism,"[63] "puppet tyrants,"[64] and

---

57 "Recent Canadian Cases" (1940–41) 10 Fortnightly L.J. 148 at 148, specifically the comment on *R. v. Coffin*, [1940] W.W.W. 592 (Alta. Pol. Co.). See also comments on *R. v. Bronny* (1940), 74 C.C.C. 154 in "Recent Canadian Cases" (1940–41) 10 Fortnightly L.J. 164, and *Saporito v. The King* (1941), 76 C.C.C. 158 (B.C.S.C.) in "Recent Canadian Cases" (1941–42) 11 Fortnightly L.J. 36.
58 R.M.W. Chitty, "*Inter Alia*: The Apparent Objects of Internment without Trial" (1940–41) 10 Fortnightly L.J. 130.
59 The literature on the experience of Japanese Canadians during the war is large. For a recent treatment see Patricia E. Roy, *The Triumph of Citizenship: The Japanese and Chinese in Canada, 1941–67* (Vancouver: UBC Press, 2007).
60 "Constitutional Aspect," above note 10.
61 R.M.W. Chitty, "*Inter Alia*: Totalitarian Government by Controllers' Orders" (1942–43) 12 Fortnightly L.J. 146 at 146 ["Totalitarian Government"]. See similar comments at "*Inter Alia*: The Shortcomings of the Profession as the Guardian of Liberty" (1942–43) 12 Fortnightly L.J. 81 at 82, and "*Inter Alia*: Prospects at Home: The Reference to the Supreme Court" (1942–43) 12 Fortnightly L.J. 161 at 161.
62 R.M.W. Chitty, "*Inter Alia*: Legislative Fight to Dominate the Courts" (1939–40) 9 Fortnightly L.J. 65 at 65.
63 "Totalitarian Government," above note 61.
64 R.M.W. Chitty, "*Inter Alia*: The Latest Proof of Dictatorship at Home" (1942–43) 12 Fortnightly L.J. 177 at 177.

Nazism.[65] Blaming lawyers for their complacency and indolence in allowing the administrative state to entrench itself,[66] Chitty cajoled his colleagues to reclaim their historic role as "the guardians of liberty under the rule of law" and "the chosen champions of civil rights."[67] Although Chitty liked to claim that he stood "entirely alone in calling attention to these various obvious dangers of bureaucracy,"[68] he had found an attentive, if less strident, audience at the CBA.

In 1941, the CBA established a Special Committee on Civil Liberties "to deal with the question of the restrictions on civil liberties in the light of the long-standing function of our legal profession as the guardian of liberty under the rule of law."[69] Ottawa lawyer, Gustave Monette, chaired the main committee, and Chitty served as chair of both the Ontario subsection and the parallel Committee on Legislation Affecting Civil Liberties.[70] The inspiration for the Special Committee on Civil Liberties stemmed not only from Chitty's prodding, but also from the CBA's close relations with the American Bar Association (ABA). The numerous ties between the associations multiplied and tightened during the war. Tradition offered both CBA and ABA presidents honourary status in the other's association, and executive members often attended each other's meetings. With the cancellation of the CBA's 1942 annual meeting (on the "suggestion" of the government's controller of transport), the entire council of CBA executives traveled to Detroit to participate in the ABA's annual meeting.[71] Among the aspects of the ABA specifically catching the attention of CBA President D.L. McCarthy (in yet another appearance in this chapter), was its Committee on the Bill of Rights. When the CBA struck its own Special Committee on Civil Liberties in 1941, members explicitly en-

---

65 R.M.W. Chitty, "*Inter Alia*: Political War of Attrition on the Courts" (1941–42) 11 Fortnightly L.J. 98 at 98.
66 "Emergency Boards," above note 54.
67 R.M.W. Chitty, "*Inter Alia*: The Shortcomings of the Profession as the Guardian of Liberty," above note 61.
68 R.M.W. Chitty, "*Inter Alia*: Freedom of the Press and Government Advertising" (1942–43) 12 Fortnightly L.J. 274 at 274.
69 "Report of Section on Administration of Civil Justice" in *Minutes of Proceedings of the Twenty-Fifth Annual Meeting of the Canadian Bar Association* (Ottawa: National Printers, 1942) 222 at 224.
70 See "Annual Meeting" in *Minutes of Proceedings of the Twenty-Sixth Annual Meeting of the Canadian Bar Association* (Ottawa: National Printers, 1943) 15 at 53, and "Report of Committee on Legislation Affecting Civil Liberties" in *Minutes of Proceedings of the Twenty-Seventh Annual Meeting of the Canadian Bar Association* (Ottawa: National Printers, 1945) 211.
71 The Editor, "War and the Legal Profession" (1942) 20 Can. Bar Rev. 616 at 616 ["War"].

visioned its "work and scope" to mirror its ABA counterpart.[72] If the CBA's Special Committee on Civil Liberties revealed American influences in its inception, so too did it carry the imprint of Chitty and his concerns about the administrative state.

"THE WISDOM OF THE PAST": A CANADIAN CONSTITUTIONAL BILL OF RIGHTS

THE MOST NOTABLE WARTIME product of the CBA's Special Committee on Civil Liberties was the report it issued at the CBA's 1944 annual meeting and subsequently published in the *Canadian Bar Review*.[73] Most strikingly, the report called for the Canadian entrenchment of an American-style constitutional bill of rights, the first time the CBA had gone on record in support of such a transformative initiative.[74] But the document is also a study in tensions and contradictions — undoubtedly the product of its several authors and uncertain blending of British and American constitutional principles. Throughout lurks Chitty and his effort to define constitutional rights as the domain of righteous lawyers, limited government, and *laissez-faire* economics.

As a preliminary matter, the report struck a note of deference. Under the heading "Principle and Extent of Control Not Opposed," the report stressed that

> this Association ought not to do anything that might appear to antagonize, or even directly criticize the principle of full control, during the war, of the citizen, his liberty, property and activities, to the extent that the Government deem necessary for the safety of the nation.[75]

But elsewhere, warnings of creeping "dictatorship," "autocracy," and "despotism" signal Chitty's substantive and stylistic influence and belie the notion of

---

72 G.H. Aikins, "War and the Legal Profession" (1942) 20 Can. Bar Rev. 621 at 625. For the ABA's Committee on the Bill of Rights see "Activities of Bar Association Committees: The American Bar Association's Committee on the Bill of Rights" (1940–41) 1 Bill of Rights Rev. 63.

73 "Report of Committee on Civil Liberties" in *Minutes of Proceedings of the Twenty-Seventh Annual Meeting of the Canadian Bar Association* (Ottawa: National Printers, 1945) 184, reprinted at "Report of Committee on Civil Liberties" (1944) 22 Can. Bar Rev. 598 ["Report"] cited to Canadian Bar Review.

74 Previously, calls for entrenched constitutional rights in Canada had emanated from leftist circles concerned about state repression of communist and other radical voices. See Eric M. Adams, "Canada's 'Newer Constitutional Law' and the Idea of Constitutional Rights" (2006) 51 McGill L.J. 435.

75 "Report," above note 73 at 600–1.

outright support.⁷⁶ Distilled, the report assumed that civil liberties entailed the right of individuals to traditional common law legal processes: lawmaking by legislatures and adjudication by courts. In making this case, the report championed the "separation of the legislative, administrative and judicial powers," and highlighted as its principal concern, "judicial jurisdiction being assigned to the executive or their special boards and administrative officers."⁷⁷ By his own estimation, Chitty's views had won the day. He later claimed with satisfaction that

> the seed which .... I have in large measure helped to cultivate, has taken root and this Association is now becoming fully alive to the fact that it must play its part in eliminating these abuses of power by bureaucrats [and] autocrats.⁷⁸

In other words, Chitty's wartime crusade had become an official position of the CBA.

In broadest terms, the report pledged support for governmental administrative control during the war in exchange for the dismantling of its administrative capacities when peace had been restored. "Once hostilities have ceased and an armistice has been signed," the report served notice, "the nation had better suffer some inconveniences, and restore liberty."⁷⁹ Restoring liberty, from the report's perspective, entailed a return of the strict separation of powers. By casting the issue of civil liberties largely as one of legal process, the report, much like Chitty's other wartime writing, avoided grappling with the substantive issues raised by the government's selective curtailment of civil liberties. The report never discussed the DOCR's limits on political and religious expression or association, or the government's treatment of Japanese Canadians. The result was a civil liberties report replete with references to rights, liberties, and freedoms but notably silent on the harshest civil liberties restrictions of the war.

Worried that the administrative state might prove obdurate, the CBA went further than Chitty ever had in proposing constitutional remedies. Invoking "the wisdom of the past," the report listed seven "essential constitutional landmarks and principles."⁸⁰ The first three touchstones were unsurprising.

---

76 Ibid. at 603–4.
77 Ibid. at 602.
78 "Report of Committee on Legislation Affecting Civil Liberties" in *Minutes of Proceedings of the Twenty-Seventh Annual Meeting of the Canadian Bar Association* (Ottawa: National Printers, 1945) 211 at 212.
79 "Report," above note 73 at 601.
80 Ibid. at 616.

In citing *The Magna Carta*, *The Petition of Right* (1628), and *The Bill of Rights* (1689), the report laid claim to uncontroversial features of British — and by extension, Canadian — constitutional law. The report had made clear earlier that Canadians remained British subjects, protected by the "Rule of Law... the guarantee of all essential liberties."[81]

But Britain was no longer the only constitutional lodestar in the sky. For its final four landmarks, the report turned to the United States' Bill of Rights, specifically the First, Fourth, Fifth, and Sixth Amendments.[82] "We wonder if... Canada," the authors concluded, "had not better follow the American procedure, and incorporate these rights and liberties of the subject in our own Constitution, for greater guarantee that our democrats will not forget Democracy."[83] The report downplayed the significance of blending American and British constitutional traditions, emphasizing their inherent similarities. Dicey himself had recognized that American institutions "are in their spirit little else than a gigantic development of the ideas which lie at the basis of the political and legal institutions of England."[84] Still, the adoption of judicially enforced constitutional rights promised to fundamentally a foundational element of British and Canadian constitutional law: the supremacy of Parliament. For all of the report's attention to the democratic credentials of legislation, its concluding call for entrenched constitutional rights suggests at least a modicum of suspicion, not only of the growing power of the executive, but of legislatures as well. The rising popularity of the Co-operative Commonwealth Federation (CCF) likely lingered uncomfortably in the minds of some members of the CBA.[85] Detecting a leftward drift in Canadian pol-

---

81 *Ibid.* at 602.
82 *Ibid.* at 616, 617. The First Amendment concerns the separation of church and state and entrenches freedom of speech, press, and assembly. The Fourth Amendment provides the right "of the people to be secure in their persons, houses, papers, and effects, against unreasonable searches and seizures." The Fifth Amendment protects against self-incrimination and states that no person may "be deprived of life, liberty or property, without due process of law." The Sixth Amendment entrenches the right to "a speedy and public trial... and to have the assistance of counsel for his defence." US Const. amend. I, IV, V, VI.
83 "Report," *ibid.*
84 A.V. Dicey, *Introduction to the Study of the Law of the Constitution*, 9th ed. (London: Macmillan, 1945) at 139. See also David Schneiderman, "A.V. Dicey, Lord Watson, and the Law of the Canadian Constitution in the Late Nineteenth Century" (1998) 16 Law and His. Rev. 495 at 503–6.
85 The war years saw the CCF peak in popularity. Polling the support of nearly 30 percent of Canadians in 1943, the CCF was, for a brief period, the most popular political party in the country. In 1943 the Ontario CCF was elected as the Official Opposition, and the following year the Saskatchewan CCF formed the first socialist government in North

itics, if not law, the report recognized that unwritten constitutional principles would fail to constrain legislative intentions to extend administrative government and increase economic intervention. Protecting the property rights of the future required more robust constitutional models.

This call for constitutional rights placed the CBA's Special Committee on Civil Liberties on the leading edge of a wartime movement to give renewed purpose to the idea of constitutional rights and freedoms. From the outset, the language of rights and freedoms framed Allied participation in the war. Mackenize King told Canadians that this was a "fight for freedom,"[86] while Franklin Roosevelt captured his nation's attention expressing the necessity of the freedoms of expression and religion, and from want and fear.[87] Churchill and Roosevelt's *Atlantic Charter* further declared freedom as one of the guiding principles of the postwar world.[88] In CBA meetings, in the pages of law reviews, and in after-dinner speeches, Canadian lawyers routinely turned to the idea of constitutional rights and liberties to frame the wartime crisis, to differentiate themselves from the rights-denying enemy, and to emphasize the importance of law and the legal profession in times of war and in peace. The pressing wartime "question for the lawyer," Caesar Wright stated with his usual perspicacity,

> is how to best reconcile the demand for maximum unfettered governmental interference with human liberties, which is called for in the name of efficiency, with the minimum interference with the individual, which is called for in the name of human dignity, or man's fight for liberty under the law.[89]

Canada's lawyers may have leaned in different directions on that question, but the position of Chitty and the CBA Committee on Civil Liberties was clear. Liberty under the law demanded a limited state constrained by the "Rule of Law" — a law that needed to be bolstered by the presence of entrenched constitutional, property, and due process rights.

America. See Walter Young, *Anatomy of a Party: The National CCF 1932–1961* (Toronto: University of Toronto Press, 1969) at 320.

86 Mackenzie King, *Canada and the Fight for Freedom* (Toronto: MacMillan, 1944).

87 See Cass R. Sunstein, *The Second Bill of Rights: FDR's Unfinished Revolution and Why We Need it More than Ever* (New York: Basic Books, 2004).

88 *Atlantic Charter*: 14 August 1941, 55 Stat. 1603, 204 L.N.T.S. 381. For a perceptive take on the constitutional implications of the Charter see V. Evan Gray, "The New Legitimacy of Government" (1942) 20 Can. Bar Rev. 682.

89 "War," above note 71 at 617.

CONCLUSIONS

THE ALLURE OF CONSTITUTIONAL rights in the eyes of the CBA proved to be short-lived. Although Chitty continued to push the association to take stronger positions on the need to protect "property rights,"[90] the CBA became increasingly concerned about the postwar drift towards "so-called economic and social rights."[91] With the CCF and John Diefenbaker joining the chorus calling for a Canadian bill of constitutional rights[92] — including equality rights — and with the United Nations moving towards the passage of the *Universal Declaration of Human Rights*, the CBA backed away from its support for international and domestic bills of rights.[93] In the decade after the war, as the concept of human rights and fundamental freedoms replaced what lawyers had once called civil liberties, as equality rights came to suggest not only limits on the state but duties the state owed citizens, as the voices of marginalized groups and citizens increasingly demanded the right not to be discriminated against, Canada's lawyers lost some of their self-appointed monopoly in defining the meaning of constitutional rights and freedoms. In that changing landscape of Canadian constitutional culture, some of the profession's certainties about the meaning of constitutional liberty gave way.

Michael Chitty, for his part, continued to fight his wartime battles confident in the prudence of his views. In 1950 he represented the Canadian Federation of Property Owners Association in a constitutional challenge to the final

---

90 *The 1946 Year Book of the Canadian Bar Association and the Minutes of Proceedings of the Twenty-Eighth Annual Meeting* (Ottawa: National Printers, 1947) at 148.
91 "Report of Committee on Legal Problems on International Organization for the Maintenance of Peace" in *The 1949 Year Book of the Canadian Bar Association and the Minutes of Proceedings of the Thirty-First Annual Meeting* (Ottawa: National Printers, 1949) 191 at 195.
92 See Canada, Parliament, Special Joint Committee on Human Rights and Fundamental Freedoms, *Minutes of Proceedings and Evidence* (Ottawa: King's Printer, 1947); Canada, Parliament, Special Joint Committee of the Senate and House of Commons on Human Rights and Fundamental Freedoms, *Minutes of Proceedings and Evidence* (Ottawa: King's Printer, 1948).
93 The CBA's position against the UDHR was shared and influenced by the ABA. See "Report of the Committee on Legal Problems" in *The 1948 Year Book of the Canadian Bar Association and the Minutes of Proceedings of the Thirtieth Annual Meeting* (Ottawa: National Printers, 1949) 141 at 142–43. On the ABA's position see Frank E. Holman, "An 'International Bill of Rights': Proposals Have Dangerous Implications for U.S." (1948) 34 Am. Bar Ass. J. 984, 1078 at 1080. On the collaboration between the ABA and CBA see "Declaration on Human Rights: Canadian, American Bars Ask Delay of Action" (1948) 34 Am. Bar Ass. J. 881. For the CBA's role in influencing Canada's ambivalent position on the UDHR see William Schabas, "Canada and the Adoption of the Universal Declaration of Human Rights" (1998) 43 McGill L.J. 403 at 439.

vestiges of the Wartime Leasehold Regulations.[94] He lost. Disappointment followed in 1957, when the Law Society of Upper Canada agreed to accept the accreditations of university-based law schools. Nonetheless, Chitty remained a prominent — if increasingly eccentric — figure of the Ontario bar: writing, litigating, provoking, lawyering. He was, John Arnup fondly remembered, "truly a person identified by the word 'a character'."[95] That Chitty may appear to us now to be fighting against history is, of course, only a product of passing time. His crusades are no less important for their failure. Indeed, his call for entrenched constitutional rights reveals much about the role of lawyers in the transition to a constitutional law dominated by concerns about the protection of individual rights. R.C.B. Risk and R.C. Vipond have written that "in Canada there was no *Lochner*, much less a *Lochner* era,"[96] but there was a moment in Canadian constitutional history when lawyers yearned for one. That backdrop provides the necessary context for John Willis's efforts to defend the administrative state against the "King Canutes of the legal profession,"[97] not to mention his antipathy for rights talk and lawyers.[98] Above all, in Chitty's call for entrenched constitutional rights — its hostility to certain forms of state power and its overlooked repressions, its regard for the past and its eagerness for change, its British rhetoric and its appeal to American constitutional ideals — we capture a glimpse of both the legal world that was, and glimmers of the new one just coming into view.

---

94 *Reference as to the Validity of the Wartime Leasehold Regulations*, [1950] S.C.R. 124.
95 Arnup Interview, above note 8 at 315.
96 R.C.B. Risk and R.C. Vipond, "Rights Talk in Canada in the Late Nineteenth Century: 'The Good Sense and Right Feeling of the People'" in R.C.B. Risk, *A History of Canadian Legal Thought: Collected Essays* (Toronto: Osgoode Society for Canadian Legal History, 2006) 94 at 95.
97 Willis to Editor Canadian Bar Review, 7 December 1942, "The Law of Our Today" (1943) 21 Can. Bar Rev. 51 at 54.
98 See J. Willis, "What I Like and What I Don't Like about Lawyers: A Convocation Address" (1969) 76 Queen's Quarterly 1. See generally "Administrative Law Today: Culture, Ideas, Institutions, Processes, Values: Essays in Honour of John Willis" (2005) 55 U.T.L.J. 311.

PART 5

RACE ISSUES: DIVERSIFYING THE BAR AND ITS LEGAL STRATEGIES

CHAPTER 11

Ethelbert Lionel Cross: Toronto's First Black Lawyer

SUSAN LEWTHWAITE*

ETHELBERT LIONEL CROSS WAS the fourth known black lawyer called to the bar in Ontario and the first to establish a law practice in Toronto.[1] Until

---

* I am grateful to Mike Sulek for research assistance and to the Law Foundation of Ontario for providing funding for the larger project of which the research in this paper represents one small part. Several people provided comments on an earlier draft of this paper, and I thank each of them: Elise Brunet, Katherine Corrick, Jim Phillips, and Sophia Sperdakos. I also thank Barry Cahill of Nova Scotia Archives and Records Management, and Kathryn Harvey of Dalhousie University Archives for providing information and copies of documents from the time Cross spent in Nova Scotia. I am particularly grateful to Kathryn Harvey for providing a copy of Cross's graduation photograph from Dalhousie Law School, the only photograph of good quality of Cross that I have been able to locate.

1 The first black lawyer in Ontario is now believed to be Robert Sutherland, who was called to the bar in 1855 and who is the subject of a paper in this volume. On Sutherland, see also Ian Malcolm, "Robert Sutherland: The First Black Lawyer in Canada?" *The Law Society of Upper Canada Gazette* 26, no. 2 (2 June 1992) 183–86; Christopher Moore, "Walkerton — not about the water!" *Law Times* (19 June 2000) 9. For years it was thought that Delos Rogest Davis, who was called in 1886, was the first black lawyer in Ontario; see Lance C. Talbot, "History of Blacks in the Law Society of Upper Canada" *The Law Society of Upper Canada Gazette* 24, no. 1 (March 1990) 65–70 [Talbot]; Julias Isaac, "Delos Rogest Davis, K.C." *The Law Society of Upper Canada Gazette* 24, no. 4 (December 1990) 293–301; Owen Thomas, "Delos Rogest Davis" *Dictionary of Canadian Biography*, vol. XIV (Toronto: University of Toronto Press, 1998) at 274–75. For a summary of what was known about early black Ontario lawyers in the late twentieth century, see Talbot, *ibid.*, Christopher Moore, *The Law Society of Upper Canada and Ontario's Lawyers, 1797–1997* (Toronto: University of Toronto Press, 1997) at

recently, nothing was written about him, and he appears to have been forgotten. However, in a pioneering article on black lawyers in Ontario, Lance Talbot notes Cross's call to the bar and states that his "career was short-lived when, in 1937, after encountering professional difficulties, he left the practice of law."[2] Still more recently, Constance Backhouse has presented a far richer portrait of Cross as a spokesman for the black, Jewish, and trade union communities in events that took place following Ku Klux Klan (KKK) activities in Oakville, Ontario in 1930.[3] In this instance, Cross successfully pressured the Attorney General of Ontario to prosecute the local KKK leaders, one of whom was convicted and sentenced to a term in jail, to considerable public outcry in some circles.

This study seeks, through newspaper and other contemporary accounts, to flesh out the life and career of Lionel Cross and demonstrates that Cross was an "outsider" in the Toronto legal profession not only because of his race, but also because of his immigrant status and his views on religion and other issues. Cross neither kept a low profile, nor did he attempt to join the rank of the city's elite. Cross remained an "outsider," and from that position consistently held virtually all of the entrenched local authorities — the police, the judiciary, the criminal law, and the church — to account. His is a fascinating story that shows an outsider's attempts to uphold the principles of British justice as he saw them in interwar Toronto.

177–79; and Constance Backhouse, *Colour-Coded: A Legal History of Racism in Canada, 1900–1950* (Toronto: University of Toronto Press and the Osgoode Society, 1999) at 177, 18n and 20n [Backhouse]. Robert Sutherland practised principally in Walkerton, while Delos Davis and his son, Frederick Homer Alphonso Davis, the third black lawyer called in Ontario (in 1900), practised in Amherstburg. The uncertainty about the race of early members of the bar is not unique to Ontario or indeed to Canada. As Walter J. Leonard wrote, "No one ... is exactly certain who the first black lawyer in America was, or the exact number and nature of those who followed him until the 1940s.": "The Development of the Black Bar" (1973) 407 Annals of the American Academy of Political and Social Science 135.

2   Talbot, *ibid.* at 66. The official record of Cross's legal career as represented by information of a public nature in the Law Society of Upper Canada's records is very sparse. Those records show that Cross was called to the bar in Nova Scotia on 12 December 1923, after which he moved to Ontario, where he enrolled with the Law Society, articled with E.F. Singer, and was called to the bar on 20 March 1924. He practised in Toronto until 1937, when he was disbarred.

3   Backhouse, above note 1 at c. 6; "History Will Judge," Speech at the London, Ontario call to the bar, 30 September 2002. I will not repeat here all the details of this interesting case, which Backhouse covers thoroughly in her book.

Ethelbert Lionel Cross was born on 29 October 1890 in San Fernando, Trinidad, the son of Eloise and François Cross.[4] His only sibling was a sister nine years his junior. He attended Naparima College in Trinidad, a secondary school founded by Presbyterian missionaries from Nova Scotia in 1900, modeled loosely on the Pictou Academy.[5] Judging from the writing skills and wide-ranging interests evident in Cross's later life, it appears that the education Naparima College provided him was of high quality and that Cross must have been an eager pupil. At the school, Cross learned to play cricket and later said that "his enthusiasm for the game is as much a manifestation of the ardent love he has for it as a tribute to the institution of his student days."[6]

In 1910, at the age of twenty, Cross left the West Indies and moved to New York, where he began a journalistic career principally with the *New York News*. While he was in New York in 1912, his father died, leaving Cross the sole supporter of his mother and sister back in Trinidad. After his father's death, he sent his mother $30 a month. Cross relocated to Halifax in 1915, where he got a job as editor of *The Atlantic Advocate*, a newspaper that served Nova Scotia's black community.[7]

---

4   The biographical sketch of Cross's life before he became a lawyer in the first few paragraphs is, unless otherwise noted, derived from an interview that formed part of the newspaper coverage of the arrest of Ernest Victor Sterry, an event discussed more fully below, in "Learned to be Atheist at his Mother's Knee" *Toronto Daily Star* (12 January 1927) 34, and documents in Cross's First World War military service file in, Cross, Ethelbert Lionel Regimental No. 931405, Ottawa, Library and Archives Canada (RG 150, Accession 1992–1993/166, Box 2165-11). I am grateful to Library and Archives Canada staff for providing photocopies of the contents of this file. Some newspaper reports from 1930 report Cross's birthplace as England, which appears to be incorrect; in, for example, "Klansmen's Names Demanded of Price by Negro Barrister" *Globe* (17 March 1930) 13–14, Cross is described as "a negro barrister of British birth." Perhaps these reports intended to identify Cross as a British citizen.
5   "With the Cricketers" *Toronto Daily Star* (20 February 1929) 7 ["With the Cricketers"]. Naparima College, or "Naps," as it is referred to by those intimately acquainted with it, continues to educate young Indo-Trinidadians and counts among its graduates past prime ministers of Trinidad and Tobago. Information on the College was found online: www.naparimacollege.edu.tt and www.naparima.org in August 2007.
6   "With the Cricketers," *ibid*.
7   Cross was editor of this publication by June 1916 and until January 1917, but I have been unable to pinpoint the exact date when he took on this position. Few issues of *The Atlantic Advocate* appear to have survived, and none outside of Nova Scotia. On the publication, see Philip L. Hartling, "'Devoted to the Interests of Colored People': *The Atlantic Advocate*, Nova Scotia's First Black Magazine" (January 1992) Halifax, Nova Scotia Archives and Records Management Pamphlet, (V/F v. 371 #25) [Hartling]; Barry Cahill, "The 'Colored Barrister': The Short Life and Tragic Death of James Robinson Johnston, 1876–1915" (1992) 15 Dal. L.J. 371–72 [Cahill]. I am grateful to Barry Cahill of NSARM for sending me a copy of the Hartling piece.

Cross was in Halifax when the First World War erupted, and he enlisted for military service on 2 January 1917, at age twenty-six, joining the Second Construction Battalion, which primarily consisted of "Negroes."[8] On his attestation papers, Cross reported that he was unmarried and had no children. He listed his religion as Roman Catholic and his occupation as "journalist." Cross and the other members of his battalion sailed out of Halifax on 28 March 1917 on the *S.S. Southland*, "crossing the Atlantic during one of the worst weeks of unrestricted submarine warfare."[9] They landed at Liverpool, England on April 7th, and proceeded to France on May 17th. Shortly after arriving in England, Cross was promoted to sergeant. The Second Construction Battalion was attached to the Canadian Forestry Corps, and the military service of most of its members consisted of logging and milling near the Franco-Swiss border to provide desperately needed lumber for the war effort.[10] Cross served nineteen months in France and then six months in England before his discharge in June 1919. He sailed back to Halifax on the *S.S. Aquitania*. Upon discharge, Cross was reported in good health, 5'8-1/2" tall, and weighing 172 pounds — he had gained 5 pounds since the time of his enlistment. His discharge certificate refers to him as "colored," the only indication of his race that appears in his military service file: his enlistment papers describe his complexion as "dark." One of the addresses Cross listed on his discharge papers was that of Dr. C.C. Ligoure, a medical doctor originally from the same home town in Trinidad as Cross, with whom Cross might have lived for a short time after his enlistment or from whose Halifax home Cross's mail was forwarded to him.[11]

Lionel Cross was almost twenty-nine years old when he returned to Halifax after the war. Why he did not resume his journalistic career we do not

---

8   Military officials did not permit blacks to enlist in the war's early days. For restrictions on black enlistment and the formation of the Second Construction Battalion, see Calvin W. Ruck, *The Black Battalion 1916–1920: Canada's Best Kept Military Secret* (Halifax: Nimbus, 1987) at 6–13 [Ruck]; Robin Winks, *The Blacks in Canada: A History*, 2d ed. (Montreal and Kingston: McGill-Queen's University Press, 1997) at 313–18 [Winks].
9   Winks, *ibid.* at 318; see also Ruck, *ibid.* at 20. According to Ruck, before leaving for overseas duty, the battalion held a street parade in Dartmouth led by its own brass band; *ibid.* at 19.
10 Winks, *ibid.* at 318; C.W. Bird and Lt. J.B. Davies, *The Canadian Forestry Corps: Its Inception, Development and Achievements* (London: HM Stationery Office, 1919); Ruck, *ibid.* at 20. Some battalion members were eventually assigned to line units and participated in trench combat.
11 Discharge papers from military service file; information on Dr. Ligoure from Hartling, above note 7 at 4.

know,[12] but he enrolled in the law program at Dalhousie University. He articled with John Eaglen Griffith, a black lawyer in Halifax,[13] and, having passed all his final year examinations, was called to the bar of Nova Scotia on 12 December 1923.[14] Cross was one of seven West Indians who graduated from Dalhousie Law School between 1900 and 1931, most of whom articled with Griffith, and all of whom subsequently left the province.[15]

After Cross's call to the Nova Scotia bar he appears to have returned to Trinidad briefly[16] but then moved to Toronto, where he enrolled at Osgoode Hall Law School. He articled with Ephraim Frederick Singer, a Toronto-based Jewish lawyer,[17] and was called to the bar in Ontario on 20 March 1924, the fourth known black lawyer to have been called in the province and the first

---

12 Journalistic opportunities must have been hard to come by in a city still reeling from the devastation wrought by the 1917 Halifax Explosion. The newspaper of which Cross had been editor before he went overseas, *The Atlantic Advocate*, appears to have ceased publication in 1917, probably a casualty of the explosion; in any case, it did not long survive Cross's departure. Another possibility is that Cross had lost faith in journalism. As P. Fussell notes, "A lifelong suspicion of the press was the one lasting result of the ordinary man's experience of the war": *The Great War and Modern Memory* (London: Oxford University Press, 1975) at 316 [Fussell].

13 Griffith followed a similar path as Cross did after him, having been born in Nevis in the British West Indies, he emigrated to the United States and later to Canada. Griffith was educated at New York University, where he obtained an LL.B. degree, and at McGill University, from which he graduated with a B.C.L. Griffith arrived in Halifax in late 1916 and was admitted to the bar of Nova Scotia four months later. He practised in Halifax until his death in 1944. Cahill, above note 7 at 372–74.

14 In his final-year examinations, Cross got a Class I in Domestic Relations, Class II in Equity, Conflicts, and Practical Statutes, and Pass in Evidence, Constitutional Law, Mortgages, and Procedure. I thank Kathryn Harvey of Dalhousie University Archives for providing Cross's examination results.

15 Barry Cahill identifies seven West Indian graduates of Dalhousie Law School in this period and assumes they were all black: Cahill, above note 7 at 374. According to Philip Girard, new research identifies one of them, Lionel Ryan, born in St. Kitts, as white and of Irish Catholic descent; e-mail from Philip Girard to the author, 9 November 2007.

16 The Dalhousie student newspaper printed the following notice in November 1923: "Lionel Cross of the '23 Class has returned to his home in the British West Indies where he will practice": *Dalhousie Gazette* (7 November 1923) 3. I am grateful to Kathryn Harvey of the Dalhousie University Archives for taking the trouble to find and send me this useful reference.

17 It was not unusual for black law students to article with Jewish lawyers. For the difficulties early black students faced in finding articling principals, see Constance Backhouse, "Gender and Race in the Construction of 'Legal Professionalism': Historical Perspectives" (Paper presented to the Chief Justice of Ontario's Advisory Committee on Professionalism, First Colloquium, October 2003) at 6–7; Backhouse, above note 1 at 177, 20n; and for a general discussion of the difficulties black lawyers faced, see Talbot, above note 1 at 66–68.

since 1900.[18] He set up a law office at 131-1/2 Queen Street West, which must have been roughly across Queen Street from Osgoode Hall, establishing the first black law practice in the city.[19] Shortly afterwards, he made his first appearance at the Toronto Police Court, an event covered by the *Toronto Daily Star*. In a brief column in the Police Court news, the *Star* reported: "There was something of a mild sensation in court to-day, when E. Lionel Cross, LL.B., Toronto's solitary colored advocate, appeared . . . ." According to the *Star* reporter, Cross "exhibited all the assurance of a seasoned habitue [sic] of court precincts."[20] In many instances when newspaper articles mentioned or quoted Cross, they included a reference to his race. In early years the uniqueness of his position was noted as above,[21] and in some later instances he was referred to in more complimentary terms such as "a cultured colored barrister," "a colored gentleman," and "noted negro lawyer."[22]

As Toronto's sole "colored advocate" for five years,[23] and one of two for the remainder of his career, Cross was something of a local personality. He built up his law practice, which the *Toronto Daily Star* described as "wide." Reportedly the majority of his clients were "white folk rather than the people of his own color."[24] What is possible to reconstruct about his legal career from newspaper reports is far from complete. However, we do know that Cross appeared at every level of court from the Toronto Police Court to the Court of Appeal at Osgoode Hall. Of the six known trials in which he represented people accused of criminal offences, we know the outcome of five, and Cross

---

18 Talbot, *ibid.*, notes at 66, "Between 1900 and 1923 no Blacks were called to the Bar in Ontario."
19 The street address of Osgoode Hall is 130 Queen Street West. Cross remained at that Queen Street address until 1930, when he moved to the Yonge Street Arcade, where his office was located from 1930–34, and then to 33 Adelaide Street West, where he remained until his disbarment in 1937. *Canada Law Lists*, 1925–36 (Toronto: Canada Law List, 1937). Cross is not listed in the 1937 Law List.
20 "Like Seasoned Habitue [sic]" *Toronto Daily Star* (3 April 1924) 3.
21 Similarly, he was referred to as "Toronto's sole colored legal practitioner" in "Fraud Charge Delayed" *Toronto Daily Star* (15 October 1925) 4.
22 "Arrest Atheist Editor/Charge of Publishing a Blasphemous Libel" *Toronto Daily Star* (11 January 1927) 1; "Blasphemy Charged against Editor of '*Christian Inquirer*'" *Toronto Daily Star* (11 January 1927) 18; "Blasphemous Libel Is Charged against Editor of Pamphlet" *Globe* (11 January 1927) 9; "Colored Citizens Are Represented in Many Professions and Trades" *Toronto Daily Star* (15 March 1930) 12.
23 Cross was joined by Bertrand Joseph Spencer Pitt, who appears to have been the only Ontario lawyer to have articled with Lionel Cross, in 1928. Pitt was originally from Grenada. On Spencer Pitt, see Talbot, above note 1 at 67–68; Backhouse, above note 1 at 177, 20n; S. Taylor, "B.J. Spencer Pitt: A Forgotten Icon" *Share* (21 February 2002) 9. Talbot notes that the bulk of Pitt's clients were Canadians of Polish origin: at 67.
24 "Learned to be Atheist at his Mother's Knee," above note 4.

did not win any of them. His apparent lack of success in the courtroom does not necessarily reflect poorly on his abilities as a lawyer, however. Cross attracted the kinds of clients not likely to appear sympathetic to juries or police magistrates and whose situations may have made successful defence cases difficult. Most of them were probably immigrants, if their names are any indication, and on the margins of contemporary Toronto society. In April 1924, his first appearance in a Toronto courtroom, Cross appeared as defence counsel for a man named Petrio Bolsu on an unspecified charge. He later represented John Kogonock on a charge of reckless driving, and Martti Laine, a Finn, on a charge of wounding. Only one of his clients that we know about was "colored," Charles Winn, convicted of assault at the Toronto Police Court in late December 1932.[25]

In the last three cases, evidence suggested guilt and despite his best efforts on behalf of his clients, Cross was unable to save them from conviction. John Kogonock had been sitting dazed at the wheel of his car at a railway crossing at King and John Streets at 4:20 in the morning, "Micawber-like, waiting for something to turn up," when a policeman happened upon him and arrested him. At the Police Court trial, Cross tried to argue that the conduct of the accused had not endangered anyone: "it was a quiet hour of the morning" and only the milkmen on their rounds were on the streets. The police officer had reported that the man had been drinking. "What do these drinking motorists care about people on the streets?" asked Magistrate Browne, and sentenced Kogonock to pay $25 and costs and to serve seven days in jail.[26] At the criminal Assizes trial of Martti Laine, accused of stabbing fellow Finn William Keskinen in the face with a knife, scarring him for life according to newspaper headlines, Cross repeatedly tried to get the victim to admit that he could not positively identify his attacker. However, Keskinen stalwartly insisted, through an interpreter, that Laine, whom he knew, was the man who had stabbed him, and the jury convicted Laine.[27] The complainant who had charged Charles Winn with assault testified at the Police Court trial that "He

---

25 Newspaper coverage of these trials is from *Toronto Daily Star*: On Petrio Bolsu, see "Like Seasoned Habitue [sic]," above note 20 at 3; on John Kogonock, under the subheading "Hour before the Dawn," see "Men's Police Court: Question by Accused Delays Proceedings" (26 December 1930) 2; on Martti Laine, under the subheading "Slashed Cheek," see "Men's Police Court: Youth Admits Theft/Goes to Reformatory" (17 April 1931) 2 and "Stabbed in Cheek/Has Scar for Life" (29 April 1931) 1; and on Charles Winn, see "Men's Police Court: Some 50 Celebrants Sorry and Penitent" (27 December 1932) 2.

26 "Men's Police Court: Question by Accused Delays Proceedings," *ibid*.

27 "Men's Police Court: Youth Admits Theft/Goes To Reformatory," under subheading "Slashed Cheek" and "Stabbed in Cheek/Has Scar for Life," both above note 25.

sprawled into my car and there was liquor on his breath." Cross, apparently trying to cajole the complainant into dropping the charge, declared: "It was the spirit of the occasion," and asked the complainant: "Aren't you willing to forgive?" But appealing to the good nature of the complainant did not work; "he didn't feel in the forgiving mood." The magistrate asked: "'What was the spirit of the occasion? Gin?' 'No, jackass whiskey,'" replied Cross, and the magistrate fined Winn $5 or five days;[28] so much for the success of humour in the courtroom.

Cross's law practice included civil matters as well as criminal. He represented the members of the First Baptist Church in seeking an injunction to restrain the trustees and clerk of the church "from interfering with the pastor of the church in his duties."[29] Most of this kind of work has not left much trace in published sources such as the newspapers from which most of this research into Cross's practice was drawn.

Much of what we are able to find out about Cross's legal career in such sources arises from his involvement with an organization called the Rationalist Society, a "free-thought" group of secularists, atheists, and agnostics formed in 1925 and active until about the mid-1930s.[30] The officers of the Rationalist Society were white, working-class Torontonians, yet they retained Cross as legal counsel for their organization, a relationship that was maintained for the thirteen-year period during which Cross practised law in the city.[31] Cross's representation of the rationalists led him to act as defence

---

28 "Mens Police Court: Some 50 Celebrants Sorry and Penitent," above note 25. The offence may have taken place on Christmas Day, the "occasion" to which Cross referred.
29 "Ask No Interference with Church Pastor" *Toronto Daily Star* (3 September 1932) 29.
30 There had been predecessor free-thought organizations in the city from about the time of Confederation, but the older organizations appear to have disappeared before the First World War. The publication of *Secular Thought*, founded in the 1880s as the principal organ of free-thought news and discussion in Canada, ceased publication around 1911. See R. Cook, *The Regenerators: Social Criticism in Late Victorian English Canada* (Toronto: University of Toronto Press, 1985) at c. 4, for a discussion of the earlier organizations. After a hiatus of close to fifteen years, the Rationalist Society of Canada formed in 1925, and incorporated the following year. I have not been able to trace any relationship between the Rationalist Society and its predecessors, but as Cook notes, at 52: "The threads of free thought activities are difficult to pull together, for much of the documentation has disappeared."
31 The two leading figures in the Rationalist Society of Canada were William Henry Styles and Bertram Elijah Leavens. We know they were white because their photographs appeared in the newspaper: "Rationalist Society Officers" *Toronto Daily Star* (20 January 1927) 17. The incorporation papers for the society list Styles's occupation as rigger and Leavens's as cabinet maker. Rationalist Society letterhead named Cross as the organization's counsel from 1926 to 1938. The organization's documents are in the file

counsel at two criminal trials that took place in 1927, one for theft and the other for blasphemous libel. Such clients as the rationalists, who challenged the moral authority of religion and the legitimacy of police authority, were not likely to be heard sympathetically by devout and conformist judges or jury members, and the prosecution won both cases, verdicts that were upheld upon appeal. Cross also represented the Rationalist Society in 1932 when it sought an injunction against the Toronto police to restrain them from interfering in rationalist public meetings.[32]

Cross appears to have supported the rationalist cause philosophically, in addition to acting as the society's legal counsel. On at least two occasions, Cross was the featured speaker at Rationalist Society Sunday night meetings, once speaking on capital punishment and on another occasion, intriguingly, on "The Female of the Species and Satan."[33] When one of the rationalists put together a newsletter called *The Christian Inquirer*,[34] Cross, whose law office was in the same building from which the *Inquirer* was published, was one of the few advertisers.[35] Cross had identified his religion as Roman Catholic on his attestation papers when he enlisted for military service in the First World War, an affiliation he appears to have shed by the mid-1920s. Perhaps his experience overseas during the war had turned him against religion.[36]

Ministry of Government Services, Companies and Personal Property Security Branch, Toronto, "Rationalist Society of Canada," C. 26135.

32 "Asks Court to Enjoin Police Interference" *Toronto Daily Star* (29 August 1932) 1; "Halt Street Meet Case" *Toronto Daily Star* (24 October 1932) 2.

33 Notices of Rationalist Society Sunday-night meetings appeared regularly in the Saturday *Toronto Daily Star*. The notices of the meetings at which Cross was to speak appeared on 7 January 1928 at 22 and 9 February 1929 at 11. The meetings took place on the day following the appearance of the notices: on Sunday, 8 January 1928 (females and Satan) and 10 February 1929 (capital punishment). Unfortunately, the newspapers did not cover those meetings, so exactly what Cross said is not known.

34 "A Pithy, Popular Presentation of Profound Problems Perplexing the Public," The *Evening Telegram* reprinted parts of the first issue under the heading "Paper on which Charge is Based" (11 January 1927) 18.

35 "Blasphemous Libel is Charged against Editor of Pamphlet," above note 22. When the police broke up a rationalist street meeting in August 1929, an eyewitness reported that "a colored man" had been speaking critically about Chief of Police Draper just before the police moved in. It could have been Lionel Cross, who was an outspoken critic of the city's police. "Police Disperse Two Street Meetings" *Toronto Daily Star* (19 August 1929) 6.

36 As one historian of the British rationalist movement has noted, "Many men either became unbelievers or met unbelievers during their military service": B. Cooke, *The Blasphemy Depot: A Hundred Years of the Rationalist Press Association* (Oldham: Rationalist Press, 2003) at 77. Perhaps Cross, like Wilfred Owen, the First World War poet, became

The publication of the first edition of *The Christian Inquirer* in January 1927 led to its editor's arrest by Toronto Morality Police on a charge of blasphemous libel, possibly the only occasion upon which such a charge was levied in English Canadian legal history.[37] The editor, Ernest Victor Sterry, and his Rationalist Society supporters immediately retained Cross to defend Sterry on this charge. Cross remained Sterry's lawyer throughout the ensuing trial and appeal. Ironically, it was left to those outside the local elite to articulate the principles of freedom of speech that ought to be, they argued, the basis of civic life.

When Sterry appeared in court to find out whether he would have to face trial for blasphemous libel, both he and Cross appeared stunned when crown officials brought forward an additional charge against him — one of theft.[38] That complaint, which had apparently been made more than two years before,[39] had been brought forward by Joseph Ying, who accused Sterry of having stolen $200 from him. Ying alleged that he had given Sterry a deposit of that amount to arrange for a laundry licence. That licence had never materialized, and Sterry never paid Ying the money back. Sterry's trial on the theft charge took place at the Toronto Police Court on 1 February 1927 before Magistrate Browne. The main argument of Cross's defence was that Sterry had merely acted as the middleman in the transaction and that he had been an employee of a man named John Pearson, who had taken the money and disappeared.[40] The fact that Sterry had signed a paper that documented the arrangement with Ying showed that his intention had not been theft,

---

disillusioned at the "inability of the civilian world — especially the church — to understand what was going on": Fussell, above note 12 at 289.

37   The exact nature of the case is explored in detail below. Although the Sterry case appears to be the only blasphemous libel case in English Canadian history, there were several instances of such cases in Quebec; Marika Tamm, "Blasphemy Trials in Quebec, 1900–1935" University of Toronto, May 1992 [unpublished paper]. I thank the author for permission to use the information contained in her paper and Jim Phillips for bringing the paper to my attention.

38   The headline in the *Evening Telegram* reads as follows: "Remand on Blasphemy Charge/Sterry Also Accused of Theft" and the subheading "Chinaman's Allegation Comes as Surprise to Editor of '*Christian Inquirer*'" (11 January 1927) 1. According to this account, "the latter charge [of theft] appeared to have come as a surprise to the accused editor and kept his colored counsel, E.L. Cross, and himself wagging their heads for a long time."

39   The charge had been laid originally in August 1924: "Arrest Atheist Editor/Charge of Publishing a Blasphemous Libel," above note 22 at 1.

40   This trial was reported in the local newspapers as part of their regular coverage of Police Court news: "Sterry is Sentenced to Four Months' Term" *Toronto Daily Star* (1 February 1927) 31; "Editor Sterry is Jailed" *Evening Telegram* (1 February 1927) 14.

argued Cross. The defence also questioned the motives of the police who had not acted on Ying's complaint for some time; as Cross said: "Sterry has been around town for three years and not until the charge of blasphemous libel [was] brought against him does the theft charge appear against him." Sterry himself testified that he was "well-known" in the city: "I spoke on the streets and at Queen's Park," he was reported in the *Star* as having said on the stand.[41] In other words, if the police had wished to arrest him they had plenty of opportunities to do so before, and they had not, until the blasphemous libel charge had been laid against him.

Police Magistrate Browne dismissed the defence arguments and said he did not believe Sterry's account of the transaction. His judgment may have been based on the insistence of Joseph Ying and his friend John Sing, who appeared as a witness, that they had never met or seen this Mr. Pearson and knew nothing of him, whereas Sterry testified that the four of them[42] were together on the occasion when Sterry had signed the agreement.[43] Pearson was described in both the *Star* and the *Telegram* as a man so big as to have been unforgettable. Sterry was convicted and sentenced to four months' determinate and for an indeterminate period not to exceed six months. According to the *Telegram*, "the sentence appeared to come as a big surprise to the accused and also to his counsel, Lionel Cross, colored barrister, who fought the charge every inch of the way."[44]

Sterry appealed the theft conviction, and the appeal represents one of two known occasions when Lionel Cross appeared at the superior courts at Osgoode Hall, in this case at the Supreme Court of Ontario.[45] In both instances, Cross's demeanour before the superior court judges was not as deferential as the judges expected. Cross tried to link his arguments to larger philosophical issues, for which the judges had no patience. Cross based the appeal of Sterry's conviction for theft in part on the admissibility of the evidence of Joseph Ying: "'I objected at the trial,' said Mr. Cross, 'to the Chinaman swearing on the bible, believing that his conscience was not bound as he was not a

---

41 "Sterry is Sentenced to Four Months' Term," *ibid*.
42 Sterry, Ying, Sing, and Pearson.
43 Cross stated in court: "The Chinaman must have met Pearson" in "Sterry is Sentenced to Four Months' Term," above note 40.
44 "Editor Sterry is Jailed," above note 40.
45 Although Cross appeared on behalf of Sterry at the appeal, he did not file the appeal documents himself. Isadore Levinter did so: "Sterry Appeal Likely to be Heard To-morrow" *Evening Telegram* (3 February 1927) 1; "Sterry Theft Appeal Entered at Osgoode" *Toronto Daily Star* (9 February 1927) 1.

Christian.'"[46] Justice Orde said there was no appeal on that ground, and the lawyer representing the Crown at the appeal, Francis Patrick Brennan, objected: "My honorable friend should not say they are not Christians without proof." Chief Justice Latchford urged Cross to "pass up that point" or "pass from that."[47]

Cross moved along to his next point, arguing that there had been no offence of theft. There was some discussion with the judges over the issue of colour of right[48] and about the agreement Sterry had signed with Ying. Chief Justice Latchford admonished Cross for touching on questions of fact: "There is no appeal to this court on questions of fact," he said, and urged Sterry to: "[c]ome to the point." Cross contended that Sterry might be the object of a civil suit, but not a criminal action because there had been no intention of theft. "But how will you get around the fact that the [C]riminal [C]ode says it is a crime?" asked Judge Latchford. Cross replied: "I argue that this case does not come within the province of the section of the Code." Mr. Justice Middleton "remarked that Mr. Cross seemed to be arguing on the law as it existed 100 years ago," and Chief Justice Latchford said that the wording of the law had changed "to meet conditions in which men steal money now," the old wording of steal, take, and carry away having been removed. "Your lordships seem to be en bloc against me," said Cross.[49] "The law is against you," replied the Chief Justice; "the facts established by the evidence in this case show that a crime has been committed under the law." Cross's final argument was that the sentence appeared rather severe. "But you have not leave to appeal the sentence," replied Mr. Justice Orde. Mr Justice Middleton said that the sentence did not seem severe to him, "four months definite only." With that, the appeal was dismissed.

---

46 "Sterry Loses Appeal from Theft Verdict" *Toronto Daily Star* (11 February 1927) 19. This is an interesting argument, given that Sterry "affirmed" but would not swear on a Bible before giving evidence at his blasphemous libel trial. According to the *Toronto Daily Star*, when Sterry took the stand: "He affirmed, not taking the oath, saying that he belonged to no religious denomination": "Why He Doesn't Believe in 'The God of the Jews'" *Toronto Daily Star* (15 March 1927) 3.

47 "Sterry Appeal is Dismissed" *Evening Telegram* (11 February 1927) 3; "Sterry Loses Appeal from Theft Verdict," *ibid*. This account of the appeal is based on these two newspaper reports.

48 Colour of right "generally, although not exclusively, refers to a situation where there is an assertion of a proprietary or possessory right to the thing which is the subject-matter of the alleged theft.... The term... is also used to denote an honest belief in a state of facts which, if it actually existed would at law justify or excuse the action done...." *The Dictionary of Canadian Law*, 2d ed. (Toronto: Carswell, 1995) at 203.

49 That remark of Cross's appears in identical wording in both the *Toronto Daily Star* and the *Globe*.

It was the Sterry blasphemy trial, however, that made Lionel Cross a local celebrity.[50] Toronto Morality Police officers arrested Ernest Victor Sterry in the late afternoon of January 10th, after Inspector David McKinney had read and taken exception to the contents of the first issue of *The Christian Inquirer*, "a new effort in Toronto's literary field" that purported to be "[d]ifferent from anything obtainable in Canada today."[51] "It was so different," wrote the *Globe*, "that it has landed Sterry in the police net."[52] In the *Inquirer*, Sterry wrote, in part:

> It is blasphemy of the worst description to call any pretended history a Divine Revelation, which sets forth God as a being who delights in the murder of those creatures he has brought into existence. Read your Bible, if you have not done it before, and you will find in it hundreds of passages relating to the Divine Being, which any moral and honest man would be ashamed to have appended to his character.[53]

The police charged Sterry with blasphemous libel under section 198 of the *Criminal Code*.[54] "Whether any particular published matter is a blasphemous libel or not is not a question of law," the Code said, "[p]roviding that no one is guilty of blasphemous libel for expressing in good faith and in

---

50 The discussion of the Sterry trial in this paper focuses on Cross's role as defence counsel. Much more could be said about the case, about which I am writing another paper.
51 "Blasphemous Libel is Charged against Editor of Pamphlet," above note 22.
52 *Ibid.*
53 The *Inquirer* went on:

> The God of the Bible is depicted as one who walked in the Garden of Eden, talked with a woman, cursed a snake, sewed skins together for clothes, preferred the savoury smell of roast cutlets to the odors of boiled cabbage, who sat in a burning bush or popped out from behind the rocks, this irate Old Party who thunders imprecations from the mountain or mutters and grouches in the tabernacle, and whom Moses finds so hard to tame, who in his paroxysms of rage has massacred hundreds of thousands of his own Chosen People, and would often have slaughtered the whole lot if cunning old Moses hadn't kept reminding him of "What will the Egyptians say about it?" This touchy Jehovah whom the deluded superstitionists claim to be the Creator of the whole universe, makes one feel utter contempt for the preachers and unfeigned pity for the mental state of those who can retain a serious countenance as they peruse the stories of His peculiar whims, freaks and fancies, and His frenzied megalomaniac boastings.

> I have been unable to track down a surviving copy of *The Christian Inquirer* in any library or archives. There is no copy in the indictment file at the Archives of Ontario. Excerpts were published *verbatim* in the newspapers and copied into the indictment. This transcription is from "Paper on which Charge is Based," above note 34, into which parts of the text of the *Inquirer* were copied.

54 R.S.C. 1906, c. 146.

decent language, or attempting to establish by arguments used in good faith and conveyed in decent language any opinion whatever upon any religious subject."[55] The case was very unusual, "practically unique in British legal annals," according to the *Globe*. Assistant Crown Attorney Edward J. Murphy, who represented the Crown at the trial, said: "This is almost the only one in a century."[56] "It is the most unusual charge ever tried in a Canadian court," said the *Telegram*, "and has but one precedent in the past 100 years in the British Empire."[57] Cross recognized the unique nature of this case: "There have been two cases under this charge in England, and so far as I am aware there have been only two," he told a reporter for the *Telegram*. "Mr. Sterry is an atheist, and the case is one to decide whether he has contravened the [C]riminal [C]ode by expressing his opinion on the Christian religion."[58]

Cross was the principal defence counsel in this case from the time of Sterry's arrest[59] through the appeal of his Sessions Court conviction. One other lawyer was also involved: Nathan Waldo assisted Cross at the trial.[60] The case rapidly became a *cause célèbre* not only in Toronto, but even outside Canada, and it got a lot of attention in the press.[61] The American Rational-

---

55 J. Crankshaw, J.E. Crankshaw, and A. Chevalier, *Crankshaw's Criminal Code of Canada*, 5th ed. (Toronto: Carswell, 1924) s. 198.
56 "Blasphemous Libel is Charged against Editor of Pamphlet," above note 22.
57 "Will Prosecute the Second Blasphemy Case in Over 100 Years" *Evening Telegram* (11 January 1927) 18.
58 "Remand on Blasphemy Charge/Sterry also Accused of Theft," above note 38. The cases referred to involved publications by free-thought organizations in England, whose example Sterry may have intentionally followed. The literature on blasphemy prosecutions in England is vast; recent surveys include: Joss Marsh, *Word Crimes: Blasphemy, Culture, and Literature in Nineteenth-Century England* (Chicago: University of Chicago Press, 1998); David Nash, *Blasphemy in Modern Britain, 1789 to the Present* (Aldershot: Ashgate, 1999).
59 Cross accompanied Sterry to the police station when he was arrested; "Blasphemous Libel is Charged against Editor of Pamphlet," above note 22.
60 Waldo was Jewish and the son of a rabbi. In 1928, Toronto police issued a warrant for Waldo's arrest on a charge of attempting to influence a juryman in the trial of Waldo's brother-in-law, Dr. Benjamin Cohen, for performing an illegal operation, most likely an abortion. After he learned that Toronto police were looking for him, Waldo fled the city, possibly crossing the border into the US When Dr. Cohen took the stand on the charge of conspiracy arising from the alleged attempt to influence the juryman, the Crown Attorney asked him: "Where's Waldo?" to which Dr. Cohen responded that he did not know. It was this charge of conspiracy that led to Waldo's disbarment: "No Further Arrests in the Jury Scandal" *Toronto Daily Star* (1 June 1928) 1; "Decision is Reserved on Appeal for Bail" *Toronto Daily Star* (30 June 1928) 3; "Dr. Cohen Committed on Conspiracy Count" *Toronto Daily Star* (14 September 1928) 2; "Struck Off Roll" *Toronto Daily Star* (21 February 1929) 40.
61 According to an editorial, "The Sterry Case," that appeared in the *Toronto Daily Star* (30 March 1927) 6, "all over the world, it seems, literary persons are discussing [it]."

ist Association, the Chicago and Detroit chapters of which were particularly strong, sent moral support and funds to help with the defence.[62] For a time, a rumour circulated that the great American lawyer Clarence Darrow would come to Toronto to help defend Sterry.[63] Cross may even have corresponded with Darrow about it.[64] Some members of the executive of the Toronto Rationalist Association told newspaper reporters that if Darrow were to come, he would have to act as junior to Lionel Cross,[65] that suggestion showing the extent to which local Rationalists desired to stir things up. To insist that one of the most famous lawyers on the continent, a white American, should defer to the local lawyer, a "colored" Torontonian, represented a reversal of the usual order of things that contemporaries must have noted and that some must have found shockingly presumptuous. After such rumours had circulated for a couple of months, Cross let it be known that "Darrow would be unable to attend the proceedings on account of illness."[66]

There was never any doubt that Sterry was responsible for the contents of the *Christian Inquirer*, as he freely admitted that he had published the paper and delivered about 500 copies of it himself at various locations around the city, including City Hall and Queen's Park.[67] So the legal issue involved in the trial focused on whether or not the language could be regarded as "decent."

The Sterry trial was mentioned in *Time* on three occasions, "Atheist" (24 January 1927); "Blasphemy" (7 February 1927); and "Jehovah, Jupiter, Baal" (28 March 1927). An article in the *Toronto Daily Star*, "Handling of Sterry Case is Criticized in U.S. Press/Too Much Dignity Given It" (2 April 1927) 19, quoing the following American newspapers, provides an indication of the extensive coverage the case was given outside Canada: *Louisville Times, Peoria Transcript, Rock Island Argus, Fort Worth Record-Telegram, Indianapolis News, New Orleans Item, Brooklyn Daily Eagle,* and *Omaha World-Herald.*

62 "Defence Fund for Sterry Being Launched in U.S.A." *Evening Telegram* (13 January 1927) 1.
63 "Would Send Darrow to Aid Blasphemy Case" *Evening Telegram* (12 January 1927) 6; "Says Darrow's Help Promised to Sterry" *Toronto Daily Star* (14 January 1927) 8; "Sterry Will Be Defended by Darrow" *Evening Telegram* (14 January 1927) 1. The Sterry case took place only two years after the famous Scopes "monkey trial," in which Clarence Darrow had unsuccessfully represented Tennessee schoolteacher John Scopes. Scopes had been fired for teaching evolution to students in his science class. This case pitted evolutionists against creationists and although the latter won, Darrow had succeeded in making the creationists appear sufficiently inconsistent and irrational that many awarded Darrow the moral if not the actual victory in the trial. Darrow himself was a lifelong agnostic.
64 Newspaper reports show that Cross was in contact with other representatives of the American rationalist movement. For example, in "Sterry Will Be Defended by Darrow," *ibid.*, Cross told a reporter: "I have had word from our friends in New York," who had told him that Darrow would come.
65 "May Ask for Darrow But Only a Junior" *Toronto Daily Star* (24 January 1927) 3; "Sterry Will Be Defended By Darrow," above note 63.
66 "Darrow Not Coming" *Toronto Daily Star* (12 March 1927) 3.
67 "Why He Doesn't Believe in 'The God of the Jews,'" above note 46.

The *Star* summarized the issue: "What is blasphemous libel? How far can anyone go in criticism of the Christian religion before he or she has committed a blasphemous libel and is therefore liable to prosecution under Section 198 of the *Criminal Code*?"[68] "It is the choice of language that is involved in Mr. Sterry's case," wrote the *Telegram*,

> it is not whether his education is inferior to that of other apostles who couch their arguments in decent language. There is the more important fact that vulgar or profane language can transform a legitimate philosophical argument into a blasphemous libel. Vulgar or profane language can make a statement which in itself is not vulgar or profane, a vulgar or profane statement.[69]

From early on, it became clear that Cross would face an uphill battle defending Sterry. Police Magistrate Browne, committing Sterry for trial, declared that the Crown had to establish:

> that the statements contained in the publication are blasphemous and I believe that they are blasphemous, inasmuch as it is a most indecent and offensive attack on Christianity and the scriptures, couched in the most scurrilous and opprobrious language. I find it was the defendant's intention to asperse and vilify Almighty God in composing and publishing these scandalous, impious, blasphemous and profane libels of God.[70]

This statement pretty much sums up the view of the police and the Crown, a view with which the judges involved in the appeal did not disagree. Sterry was committed for trial, Cross entered a plea of not guilty, the Crown asked for a remand for one week, and Sterry was released on $1,000 bail.[71] The trial was postponed a couple of times, and it finally began on 14 March 1927, with Sterry appearing before Judge Coatsworth and a sessions jury. The courtroom was filled long before the proceedings began, demonstrating the fever pitch of public interest in the case.[72]

---

68 "Arrest Atheist Editor/Charge of Publishing a Blasphemous Libel," above note 22.
69 "Blasphemy Charged against Editor of '*Christian Inquirer*,'" above note 22.
70 "References to Deity Called Blasphemous/Sterry Is Committed" *Toronto Daily Star* (25 January 1927) 1.
71 Aaron Newton, a Yorkshireman, "who says he has been an atheist since he was a boy," provided bail. Newton said that reading Fox's "Book of Martyrs" had "set him 'against religion,' though his grandfather was a clergyman." "Remand On Blasphemy Charge/Sterry Also Accused of Theft" *Evening Telegram* (11 January 1927) 1. Newton was not an office holder in the Rationalist Society of Canada at this time.
72 "Sterry Puts Up Fight Disputing Allegation of Blasphemous Libel" *Toronto Daily Star* (14 March 1927) 19. By the time this trial began, Sterry was in jail, having been convicted of theft.

From the outset, Cross expressed the view that this was an important case, stating that a "tremendous issue was at stake."[73] Cross consistently explained to newspaper reporters that he had chosen to take on Sterry's blasphemy case because of his "appreciation of the freedom of thought." On the day following Sterry's arrest, Cross told a *Star* reporter

> that the case at issue was one which dealt with the fundamentals of liberty itself. "I am a colored man," he said, "but I can truthfully say that I prefer the slavery of the body to the slavery of the mind and, if I had to make a choice, I would go back to the slavery of the body."[74]

Cross's belief in freedom of thought and speech was one of the main tenets throughout his defence of Sterry: "any one was free today to criticize the Bible or any other book."[75] That argument remained one of the main principles in the defence case throughout the trial and the appeal.

Cross and the other rationalists deeply resented insinuations that they were foreign agitators. During the days following Sterry's arrest, some newspapers, particularly the *Evening Telegram*, emphasized the link between the Canadian rationalists and the American body of the same name in a series of articles.[76] Cross reacted with some hostility to insinuations that he was American and "denied with considerable warmth that he came originally from the United States. 'I was born in the British West Indies, saw war service overseas, and am now pleased to call myself a Canadian,'" he asserted.[77] Others branded the rationalists and Sterry as Communists, an allegation Sterry "wished to correct." He denied being Communist himself, and explained:

> The Rationalist Society is not interested in political affairs as a body.... There may be one or two who have some leaning in that direction, but the larger element are either Conservative or Liberal in their politics.... So far as Communism is concerned we have always held that rationalist thought should take up all our efforts.[78]

---

73 "Sterry Committed with Renewed Bail" *Globe* (26 January 1927) 10. The same comment is reported in "References to Deity Called Blasphemous/Sterry is Committed," above note 71. The *Star* quotation continued: "If the Godhead has a sense of humor, He might laugh at the things we say about religion."
74 "Learned to be Atheist at His Mother's Knee," above note 4.
75 "Expect Sterry Case to Go to Jury Today" *Globe* (15 March 1927) 14.
76 "Would Send Darrow to Aid Blasphemy Case," above note 63; "Defence Fund for Sterry Being Launched in U.S.A.," above note 62; "U.S. Is Controlling Centre of Toronto's Rationalism" *Evening Telegram* (13 January 1927) (page number unreadable).
77 "Says Aid Offer Meant Betrayal of Client" *Toronto Daily Star* (15 January 1927) 15.
78 "Says Darrow's Help Promised to Sterry" *Toronto Daily Star* (14 January 1927) 8.

When the trial opened on March 14th, Cross objected to the reading of the indictment before the jury, arguing that "the wording would prejudice the case of his client."[79] Cross objected to the indictment on a number of points.[80] Crown Attorney Murphy said that the wording of the indictment conformed to section 852 of the *Criminal Code* and so "no credence" should be given to Cross's objections. When Cross tried to insist that the jury be sent from the courtroom when the indictment was read, Judge Coatsworth said: "But the indictment must be read. You can't swear the jury unless they hear the indictment."[81] The indictment was duly read, and Cross entered the plea of not guilty. The jurors were then selected; according to the *Star*, thirteen were "stood aside" by the Crown and four challenged by the defence.[82] The jury was then sent away while Cross presented his objections to the indictment, which the judge dismissed, and ordered the jury called back in.

The trial lasted less than two days, beginning March 14th and ending before noon the following day. Unsurprisingly, the trial focused on the language of *The Christian Inquirer*. The arresting officer, David McKinney, was the principal witness during the first day of proceedings. At one point Nathan Waldo, assisting Cross in the defence, asked permission to distribute copies of *The Christian Inquirer* to the jury so it could look at them while Inspector McKinney was being cross-examined. "We don't want to spoil the jury's appetite for dinner by perusing these," said the Crown, to which Cross objected.[83] The defence counsel argued that "the charge involved alleged blasphemy against the Christian religion," and if it was an attack on the Jewish God, there was no crime.[84] This line of thought caused the pious Inspector McKinney to remark that he did not know that there was more than one God. Nathan Waldo asked if he had heard of Jupiter and Zeus, and whether he believed in the Trinity.[85]

---

79 "Sterry Puts Up Fight Disputing Allegation of Blasphemous Libel," above note 72.
80 "First, the language ... of the indictment is archaic and obsolete; second, the accusation and description is very much to the prejudice of the accused; third, we must be limited to the four corners of the section of the code, under which we are charged, there is no similar description of the offence in the code; fourth, we are not being tried under English decisions; fifth, the indictment should be amended striking out objectionable matter; sixth, the code does not define what is blasphemous libel and the Crown has no right in the indictment positively to describe it. It is a question of fact for the jury." "Didn't Intend Libel of God, Says Cross" *Evening Telegram* (14 March 1927) 1 and 26; "Sterry Puts up Fight Disputing Allegation of Blasphemous Libel," *ibid*. These two accounts are almost identical.
81 "Didn't Intend Libel of God, Says Cross," *ibid*.
82 "Sterry Puts Up Fight Disputing Allegation of Blasphemous Libel," above note 72.
83 "Didn't Intend Libel of God, Says Cross," above note 80 at 1.
84 "Sterry Puts Up Fight Disputing Allegation of Blasphemous Libel," above note 72.
85 "Didn't Intend Libel of God, Says Cross," above note 80 at 1.

Mr. Murphy objected. The defence asked Inspector McKinney if he would be prepared to lay charges with regard to other books "being circulated in Toronto by well known authors" that contained similar statements. Mr. Murphy again objected: "That has nothing to do with this case. Surely the inspector does not have to crawl all over the bookshelves."[86]

The other principal witness at the trial was Sterry himself, who took the stand in his own defence. Sterry claimed his objective was "to liberalize the public opinion." The churches in Toronto were always doing that, he said, and "he thought that he was sufficiently learned to voice his thoughts." Sterry claimed to be a "hylo idealist," the term coming from the Greek word for "matter." He expounded at length on the subjects he had studied that made him qualified to voice an opinion on religious issues. Sterry said that he "was doing this in good faith ... and firmly believed everything that he had printed." Cross said: "This man says that he does not believe in God. If so he did not commit blasphemy. What Sterry has written is no different than recognized ministers have said." Murphy countered: "My learned friend is trying to prove that two wrongs make a right ... he thinks because a half dozen people think like Sterry that it is the proper thing." Cross tried to read excerpts from Sir George Fraser and other prominent experts on the question of blasphemy, but was cut off. "I will go to others higher than this court. Perhaps your [H]onor will be a little more charitable to me then," Cross stated, which was "vehemently objected to by the [C]rown." Sterry, not doing his case any favour, launched into an "excited harangue" about his beliefs, and the judge ordered him not to make a speech. Sterry said he wanted to disillusion the jurors in regard to certain Biblical passages, "trying to show the crudity, absurdity and blasphemy of this Bible." Sterry made a remark about "'hard-shelled Baptists,' who still believed all that was in the Bible," and Cross interrupted, warning him: "Don't mention any particular creed, please."[87]

The defence and prosecution cases wrapped up the following day, March 15th. "Cross emphasized 'freedom of speech' in his remarks to the jury and pleaded that Sterry had published *The Christian Inquirer* for the purpose of giving to the world the result of long and careful study. Any man had the right to express a personal opinion." The defence wondered: "Why did the police have to defend the Christian religion?"[88] In his address to the jury, Crown Attorney Edward J. Murphy said:

---

86 "Sterry Puts Up Fight Disputing Allegations of Blasphemous Libel," above note 72.
87 The quotations from this paragraph are all from "Why He Doesn't Believe in 'The God of the Jews,'" above note 46.
88 *Ibid.*

> Were the [C]rown to tolerate and permit such a wicked and profane libel of God to go unnoticed it would deal a death blow to the state as a Christian state.... [A] man who in a place of public resort applies opprobrious epithets to names held in reverence by all Christians, ought in my opinion to be severely punished not for differing from us in opinion, but for permitting a nuisance which gives us pain and disgust.[89]

Murphy concluded:

> He is no more entitled to outrage our feelings by obtruding his impiety on us and to say he is exercising his right of discussion than [he is] to ... run up and down the street naked and to say he is exercising his right of locomotion. He has a right of discussion, no doubt ... but he must use all his rights so as not to infringe the rights of others.[90]

Judge Coatsworth made a charge to the jury in which he emphasized the importance of the Christian religion and the Bible to Canadian law and society, leaving no doubt about the "official" view of the link between the Christian religion and the state.[91] It took the jury less than half an hour to convict Sterry.[92] Sterry appeared for sentencing on March 16th. Cross asked for a suspended sentence: "In view of the fact that a conviction has been found ... I think the law has been sufficiently vindicated ... I think the ends of justice might be fairly met by suspended sentence and an undertaking not to publish any more such statements. I recommend that to your [H]onor," said Cross. According to the *Star*, Cross spoke "in tones slightly nervous and strained," the only time his courtroom demeanour was described in such terms. Judge Coatsworth thought "the offence is too serious to pass by without some punishment." He sentenced Sterry to sixty days, to run consecutively to the sentence he was currently serving for theft. He also recommended an order for Sterry's deportation.[93]

---

89 "Find Sterry Guilty of Blasphemous Libel" *Toronto Daily Star* (15 March 1927) 1.
90 *Ibid*.
91 *Ibid*. One of the subheadlines of this story reads: "An Impressive Charge to the Jury was Delivered by Judge Coatsworth."
92 All the newspapers consistently report that the jury deliberated for twenty-five minutes. "Find Sterry Guilty of Blasphemous Libel," above note 89; "Verdict of Guilty Returned by Jury in Blasphemy Case" *Globe* (16 March 1927) 11.
93 "Sixty Days to Editor/Deportation to Follow/Sentence upon Sterry" *Toronto Daily Star* (16 March 1927) 1. This newspaper account noted that such an outcome was unusual; under Canadian law, a person was not liable to deportation if he or she had resided in the country for more than five years, and Sterry had lived here for sixteen. Other newspaper reports that mention the possibility that Sterry might be deported are "May Deport Sterry" *Toronto Daily Star* (16 March 1927) 9; "To Deport Sterry" *Toronto Daily*

Cross filed notice of appeal in the middle of April. The appeal was based on several criticisms of the police and the Sessions Court judge: that the conviction was contrary to law and evidence and against the weight of evidence; that the evidence did not disclose any criminal offence; that the indictment was defective; that the trial judge wrongfully excluded certain defence evidence; and that the trial judge wrongfully misdirected the jury as to the law and the evidence "and included in his address material that prejudiced the minds of the jury against the accused."[94] The appeal was thus based on several arguments that had been presented at Sterry's original trial, along with a few new points. Cross argued that the Crown's view that Sterry's publication was offensive to devout Torontonians was never substantiated at the trial because no witnesses had been called to testify to that effect other than the arresting police officer. Cross also argued that the judge's charge to the jury was prejudicial to his client.

As had been the case at the appeal of Sterry's theft conviction, at this appeal Cross was less deferential towards the judges than they were accustomed to, and he tried to raise philosophical issues, to which the judges responded with impatience. The appeal was heard on 4 May 1927 and, despite the lengthy list of grounds upon which the appeal was based, it was dismissed in less than an hour. Cross "was told in no uncertain terms that the language used by Sterry was an offence against the Christian religion. Chief Justice Latchford said he could not understand how any jury could have found otherwise," a sentiment to which his four colleagues concurred.

Cross tried to argue that "[b]lasphemy laws are a heritage of the past, born of intolerance."[95] Chief Justice Latchford retorted: "A history of blasphemy may be of interest to you. It is not of interest to the court. Let us get down to the facts."[96] There was some discussion about the meaning of the word "decent" as applied to language, and Cross said that "[l]anguage used should not indict any man," and referred to George Bernard Shaw and H.G. Wells. "You don't happen to have looked up the definition of the word 'decent' in the

---

Star (16 March 1927) 24; "Deportation of Sterry Being Sought by Police" Globe (16 March 1927) 11; "To Do 60 Days in Jail and to be Deported, Sentence on Sterry" Globe (17 March 1927) 13. For the use of deportation as a tool to rid the country of "undesirable" immigrants in the early twentieth century, see Barbara Roberts, Whence they Came: Deportation from Canada, 1900–1935 (Ottawa: University of Ottawa Press, 1988).

94 Grounds for the appeal are listed in "Ask Leave to Appeal Sentence on Sterry" Toronto Daily Star (13 April 1927) 12.

95 "Blasphemous Libel Appeal Is Dismissed" Evening Telegram (4 May 1927) 1.

96 The appeal was reported in "Sterry Conviction Upheld/Court Considers Language an Insult to Christianity" Toronto Daily Star (4 May 1927) 2; "Blasphemous Libel Appeal is Dismissed," ibid.; "Appeal by E.V. Sterry is Dismissed by Court" Globe (5 May 1927) 15.

English dictionary?" asked Mr. Justice Riddell. "'Decent' means 'seemly.' You seem to have the wrong conception of the meaning of the word." The judges expressed impatience at Cross's attempt to bring authors other than Sterry into the discussion. When Cross "pointed out that learned authors had used terms similar to those for which Sterry had been found guilty," Chief Justice Latchford replied: "What if they did? .... We are not concerned with that. We are concerned with Sterry." Mr. Justice Riddell "said he was firmly convinced that Sterry's language was indecent in the eyes of Christians." Cross "contended that such a law should not exist in the present age." Mr. Justice Orde "stressed that Canada was 'a country which had been based on religion.'" Chief Justice Latchford lost patience when Cross tried to argue that point, and said: "I must ask you to come to the point," adding that unless counsel did so his lordship would refuse to listen. Cross said that Sterry had not been given a chance, to which Justice Riddell replied: "What chance does he want? Does he want us to say that that language was decent?" The appeal court judges considered Judge Coatsworth's charge to the jury quite proper, and the appeal was dismissed.[97]

The Sterry trials had taken up four months of Lionel Cross's time. One wonders how much he was paid for his efforts. Sterry himself would not have had the money and neither would the executive of the Rationalist Association of Canada, all of whom were working-class men and women. Funds for the Sterry defence were solicited at Rationalist Society public meetings, but we have no way of knowing how much money those efforts raised.[98] Some newspaper articles suggested that American and British Rationalist Associations had sent money towards a defence fund but, again, whether they did and how much that might have amounted to, and how much Cross might actually have pocketed for his services, is unknown. Cross continued working on the case, trying to win Sterry early release from prison. Cross visited Sterry at the Ontario Reformatory at Guelph one weekend in September and told the *Star*, "it looks now as though he will probably have to serve the full term. I do not anticipate that he will be out until probably early in November. So far the parole board has taken no action about his release though I have made representations in his behalf."[99] Sterry was eventually released from

---

97   Unless otherwise noted, the quotations in this paragraph are from "Sterry Conviction Upheld/Court Considers Language an Insult to Christianity," *ibid.*
98   For example, a notice, "The Sterry Blasphemy Appeal," appeared in the *Toronto Daily Star* (21 March 1927) 35, and again on (23 March 1927) 24. The subheading read: "Freedom of Speech and the Liberty of the Press are in Peril!"
99   "Cross Sees Sterry in the Reformatory" *Toronto Daily Star* (28 September 1927) 3.

the reformatory and remained in the city, despite the efforts of the Toronto police to have him deported. Sterry set himself up as an art dealer,[100] and although he remained involved in the rationalist cause, he kept a relatively low profile after his release from jail.[101]

Apart from his legal career, Cross is also of interest as an eloquent writer who expressed views on several subjects that might be regarded as ahead of their time. Between 1926 and 1930, he wrote at least ten letters to the editor that were published in the *Toronto Daily Star*. The content of some of these letters is worth examining in some detail because they appear to be the only surviving documents that Cross wrote himself.[102] Three themes run through these letters. Foremost is Cross's commitment to freedom of thought, speech, and assembly, and his criticism of the Toronto police for perceived violations of those deeply held principles. Second is skepticism about organized religion. Frequently these two threads are related, as much of what Cross says about freedom and about the police arose from his view that the Toronto police targeted groups of Torontonians unfairly, such as the rationalists, whose beliefs did not coincide with those of the majority of the city's population. A third subject on which Cross wrote and spoke was race relations.

Cross's views on religion might be inferred from his support of the rationalists and some of his own writings. He appears to have thought of religion as a backward way of thinking that ill-prepared people for life in the modern world. In response to an article that appeared in the *Toronto Daily Star* in late

---

100 Toronto City Directories for 1929 and 1933–38 list Sterry's occupation as fine art and stamp dealer. Advertisements for Sterry's shop appeared in the *Toronto Daily Star* on 24 November 1933 at 36 and 19 February 1938 at 32.

101 Sterry chaired a Rationalist Society meeting in October 1928, which broke out in an uproar. On that occasion, Joseph McCabe, "England's leading exponent of evolution," spoke at Margaret Eaton Hall: "McCabe Meeting Ends in Disorder" *Globe* (15 October 1928) 14. McCabe had been a Catholic priest known as Father Anthony before his "conversion" to free-thought, and was a leading free-thought speaker in Britain, North America, and the Antipodes. A brief account of McCabe's career can be found in F.J. Gould, *The Pioneers of Johnson's Court: A History of the Rationalist Press Association from 1899 Onwards*, rev. ed. (London: Watts & Co., 1935) at 18–20. For a full biography, see Bill Cooke, *A Rebel to the Last Breath: Joseph McCabe and Rationalism* (Amherst, NY: Prometheus Press, 2001). Sterry also spoke at a Rationalist Society meeting in October 1932, on "My Objections to the Christian Scheme of Salvation," notice in *Toronto Daily Star* (8 October 1932) 24.

102 I have been unable to locate papers of Cross or records relating to his legal practice in any archival repository. Nor have I been able to locate records of the Rationalist Society apart from the organization's incorporation file, Ministry of Government Services, Companies and Personal Property Security Branch, Toronto, "Rationalist Society of Canada," C. 26135.

January 1926, in which the writer quoted US President Calvin Coolidge and a "well-known psychologist" who recommended religion as a cure for crime, Lionel Cross wrote a lengthy letter to the editor. "Too often is the baseless assertion made as to the relationship between crime and religion," he wrote. "I shall let Havelock Ellis, the great English criminologist, answer that question. He says: 'It seems extremely rare to find intelligently irreligious men in prison.'" Cross continued:

> is it not time that we got away from that barbaric idea about the depravity of man and his fallen nature? Man is not naturally depraved, nor is his nature fallen. He is gradually but steadfastly progressing upwards in the arts and civilization and these are accomplishments to his honor and not to his shame .... I feel sure ... that if half the effort devoted to religion were given to the promulgation and teaching of the social sciences and the real things concerning man's nature most of the ills which now afflict us would vanish.[103]

Similarly, Cross argued for the relaxation of laws that restricted various activities on the Sabbath: "The times do change, and we with them," he wrote.

> [S]ome day Toronto (and; for that matter, all Canada) will fall in line with other countries ... which have realized that Sunday is a creation of man, and not man a creation of Sunday; thus disproving, as countries having the open Sunday have done, that a nation that does not make a fetish of the Sabbath still prospers, and is no worse off thereby, despite the jeremiads of its puritans.[104]

Police suppression of Rationalist Society meetings brought scathing criticism from Cross. "I have been trying to reconcile our ideas of British liberty with the attitude of the police in breaking up the meetings on the street of those with unconventional ideas, while religious gatherings are undisturbed," he wrote in a letter to the editor of the *Star*.[105]

> What can be the reason for this form of persecution? I got it straight from the lips of a police inspector in charge of the division where these speakers hold forth. This officer did not deny the right of speech to these persons, but

---

103 "Crime and its Causes" *Toronto Daily Star* (2 February 1926) 6. In the letter, Cross disputed the contention that the crime rate, particularly among young people, was increasing, quoting statistics from a *New York Times* editorial of 28 December 1925.
104 "Toronto's Sabbath" *Toronto Daily Star* (15 September 1928) 6.
105 "Rationalists' Meetings" *Toronto Daily Star* (3 August 1929) 4. This letter is quoted here in full because it represents an important theme in Cross's writings, that of freedom of speech, which Cross consistently articulated throughout his entire legal career.

informed me that their views were objectionable to many people and to the police, and that was sufficient reason for dispersing them; furthermore, the police were under no obligation to protect any speakers on the street but religious ones.

The meetings of the Rationalist Society, whose counsel I am, are well conducted; the crowds are model, and the attendants do everything to cooperate with the police in seeing that the sidewalks are kept clear. These people try to obey the law.

I have appealed to the police commissioners and the chief of police to remedy this condition of things as doing an injustice to a body of citizens whose only fault is that their views are unorthodox. But this appeal has been to no purpose. Is it not possible to arouse an enlightened public sentiment to correct this?[106]

Cross consistently opposed attempts by the police to extend their powers in the interwar years. In response to anti-communist hysteria, the "Red Scare" of the 1920s, the municipal government contemplated the introduction of a bylaw that would require all persons wishing to speak on the streets to secure a permit from the Chief of Police. An editorial in the *Toronto Daily Star* opposed this measure, which would in effect make the Police Chief the "censor of opinions for the city." Cross wrote a letter of support to the *Star*, declaring the editorial "a gem" that "should reflect the considered opinion of every reader. A reactionary spirit is now stalking," said Cross, "and what cannot be done directly it is being endeavored to do indirectly."[107]

In addition to criticizing the police, Cross took on some members of the clergy who were well-ensconced among the ranks of the city elite. Cross attended St. Alban's Cathedral to hear the Rev. F.C. Ward-Whate respond to the "atheists of Toronto" and reported back to a rationalist gathering that the Reverend had said if he were the attorney general, he would have put the rationalists in jail and then had them all deported, and would "have a disinfecting squad visit the office of *The Christian Inquirer*." A copy of Cross's letter to Rev. Ward-Whate was published in the *Star*, in which Cross said:

> on behalf of the Rationalist Society and *The Christian Inquirer*, whose counsel I am, I take up the gauntlet thrown down by you, and I am authorized by these two organizations to invite you to leave the security of your coward's

---

106 *Ibid.*
107 "No Civic Censor Wanted" *Toronto Daily Star* (19 September 1929) 6; "Reactionism Abroad" *Toronto Daily Star* (27 September 1929) 6.

castle — the pulpit — and engage with me in public debate on the merits of this question.

When he received no response to this challenge, Cross threatened, on behalf of the Rationalist Society and *The Christian Inquirer,* to sue for slander.[108]

Despite his tough words, Cross abhorred brutality, including that practised by the judicial and educational systems. "Can we ever 'reach men's hearts through their skins'?" he pondered. "Retributive measures on the subject of crime is a good theme for magistrates, crown attorneys and the clergy to expatiate upon; but retribution is an evil." He urged fuller scientific investigation into the causes of the evils that led men to commit crimes.[109] Similarly, he supported "the new state of things which humanize the attitude of the school towards the child," writing a scathing response to a critic of the new system:

> Such views are antiquated and pernicious, and need to be repudiated.... If your correspondent could appreciate the mischief that has been done to the child mind out of sheer ignorance to sympathize with its workings, rather than tanning the youngers' hides, he would be inclined to feel that in most cases the process should be reversed.[110]

Lionel Cross was not afraid to take on the white establishment for its racist views, as Constance Backhouse has shown.[111] Cross's comments on race issues show his courage, fearlessness, and deeply held views on principles of justice, as well as an eloquent turn of phrase. In early June 1926, representatives of the Ku Klux Klan visited Toronto as part of a campaign to boost membership north of the border, "to bring about the biggest Protestant revival the world has known."[112] On June 2nd, one of them, "an emissary of this world-saving body," went to Lionel Cross's Queen Street office and tried to convince him to "enlist the members of my race to lend a helping hand in the redemption

---

108 "Bible is Ridiculed by Rationalists" *Toronto Daily Star* (17 January 1927) 7; "Calls Upon Pastor for Public Debate" *Toronto Daily Star* (19 January 1927) 20; "He Threatens to Sue on St. Alban's Sermon" *Toronto Daily Star* (21 January 1927) 4.
109 "Crime and its Causes," above note 103. It is not difficult to see why one of Cross's lectures to a Rationalist Society meeting was on the subject of capital punishment, to which Cross was most likely opposed.
110 "Punishing Children" *Toronto Daily Star* (10 July 1929) 4. Cross went on to say that the "best opinion on pedagogies" on the issue of gender of teachers was that "[t]here should be an equal number of teachers of both sexes in the schools. The adult hand of both is equally necessary to mould the adolescent mind and give it true balance and perspective."
111 Backhouse, above note 1, c. 6.
112 "Canada Doesn't Need It" *Toronto Daily Star* (2 June 1926) 6.

of this sorely stressed world ..." in return for which Cross would be given half the membership fee per "each Kleagle cub I had taken into the fold," at the time the not inconsiderable sum of $5.[113] "One marvels at the superb and unabashed nerve of some of the genus *homo*," wrote Cross in a letter to the *Toronto Daily Star*. Describing the views of his interviewer as "iridescent tosh," Cross said that once his visitor had finished presenting his case, Cross "flayed this movement most unmercifully.... I am convinced," he went on,

> that this scheme stands unmasked as having the same motives as those self-appointed saviors in the United States whose activities have left a train of bloodshed and crime in their wake. Under the cloak of patriotic sentiment they have been able to enfold their dupes in their meshes, gulling them by appealing to their baser passions and arousing all the ignoble fires of prejudice both religious and racial.
>
> And all this in the name of Christianity! Verily, the Christian has been dubbed the most intolerant of all religionists.
>
> My answer ... is that if Canada needs the Ku Klux Klan or any other organization of its ilk, then I, for one, am sorry for Canada.[114]

Constance Backhouse has written in depth about an incident that occurred in Oakville in early 1930, in which local representatives of the KKK interfered in a relationship between a white woman and an allegedly black man.[115] Backhouse describes how Cross mobilized the black, Jewish, and trade union communities to pressure the attorney general to lay charges against one of the main perpetrators, which he did, and the man, a chiroprac-

---

113 The membership fee was $10 per head, of which Cross was to be given $5, according to the arrangement his visitor proposed. By this time the KKK had broadened its targets to include Jews, Roman Catholics, and immigrants, as well as blacks, to become a nativist organization anxious to preserve "American values." Although the KKK had broad support in parts of the United States, such support was on the wane by 1926 and dwindled rapidly after that. The KKK made inroads into some Canadian communities, particularly in Saskatchewan, but it did not gain a lot of popular support in most of Ontario; in fact, many Ontarians viewed Klan activities with concern. For summaries of KKK activities in Canada, see Winks, above note 8 at 320–25; Backhouse, above note 1 at 181–93. For more detail, see Julian Sher, *White Hoods: Canada's Ku Klux Klan* (Vancouver: New Star Books, 1983); Martin Robin, *Shades of Right: Nativist and Fascist Politics in Canada, 1920–1940* (Toronto: University of Toronto Press, 1992); William Peter Baergen, *The Ku Klux Klan in Central Alberta* (Red Deer: Central Alberta Historical Society, 2000); Allan Bartley, "A Public Nuisance: The Ku Klux Klan in Ontario, 1923–1927" (1995) 30 Journal of Canadian Studies 3 at 156. Bartley argues that the robust culture of the Orange Order prevented the KKK's infiltration into Ontario.
114 "Canada Doesn't Need It," above note 112.
115 Backouse, *ibid.*, c. 6. The man later claimed to be not black, but part Aboriginal.

tor named Dr. Phillips, was convicted — a conviction that stood on appeal. It is worth quoting here some of what Cross said, in this case at a public meeting "largely composed of white people." As Cross had argued in the Sterry case, he related the specific issue in this instance to a more general one of rights: "This is not a question of intermarriage, but of constitutional rights. It is a question of whether we are to allow this secret order to exist, whether the law is to be obeyed . . . ."[116] Cross continued: "It is absurd, and is treason to the state that a body of men, perhaps 2,000 should say to 8,000,000 Canadians: 'We shall enforce the laws; you can't.'" He went on:

> Most of you as white people, may have peculiar ideas of the negro. You are not to blame. Must he be considered a man or should he be considered an indefinable, something ranging between a man and a beast?
>
> There were great negro civilizations in Africa decades ago, explorers have discovered. . . . The present dominance of the white race did not always exist. One Roman has said that the ugliest and stupidest of the early slaves were the Anglo-Saxons.
>
> So long as we have these hooded bands we have a form of slavery . . . . We are not entirely free here. Certain theatres and hotels exclude colored people. I look to labor as being the institution above all others — certainly not the church — as the solution of this terrible situation wherein the minority must suffer.[117]

At another public meeting at which a number of people spoke out against the activities of the KKK, Cross said:

> Once we were brutes and chattels, but we are gradually winning respect and a place in the world . . . . I am not concerned with the supremacy of any one race. If it were possible for the negro race to become so, I would do anything to defeat that end. I am interested in the welfare of all races. I plead for equal opportunity and tolerance that would make us "brothers all for a' that."[118]

Cross claimed that the Klan issued threats against him when he would not stop making comments about them — an accusation Klan members hotly denied. Despite the potential dangers to his safety, Cross consistently argued

---

116 "Says Law Not Vindicated in Oakville Klan Episode" *Toronto Daily Star* (17 March 1930) 15.
117 *Ibid.*
118 "Has No Negro Blood, Klan Victim Declares" *Toronto Daily Star* (5 March 1930) 1–2. The reference to "brothers all for a' that" is to a poem by the Scottish poet Robert Burns, "For A' That."

that the Klan's behaviour was outside the law and ought not to be tolerated, a view that many Torontonians of all races and religions shared.

About a year and a half after the Oakville KKK incident, Cross was called upon to comment on a policy that the University of Western Ontario enacted that would ban "colored" students not born in Canada from enrollment. This measure was intended to limit the number of black students entering the university's medical school, purportedly "for clinical reasons." As the university's executive secretary, Colonel Walter James Brown, explained, "white patients in hospitals repeatedly objected to their being examined by negro students, so that we found this step necessary to maintain our standards of learning."[119] When the *Toronto Daily Star* reporter asked Cross for his views on the university's policy, Cross clarified that the real objection was to the examination of white women by black medical students, and went on: "It is regrettable that such narrow prejudice should be shown and that a colored man should be asked to qualify himself in order to command the respect of his white brothers. And when he attempts to do so that every difficulty should be placed in his path so as to keep him down."[120] Throughout his career in Toronto, then, Cross spoke out on race relations issues and stood up to white authorities who expressed racist views or attempted to implement or enforce racist policies.

In addition to being known for his legal career and his social activism in interwar Toronto, Cross was a celebrated sports figure in the city, a noted cricketer who played for several Toronto clubs. Before emigrating, he had played "big cricket" in the West Indies, "the youngest player representing the southern part of the island on an eleven that opposed a formidable array of international cricketers...." He remained involved in the sport after leaving the West Indies, first in New York, then in Halifax and Montreal before moving to Toronto, and he had been chosen to represent Ontario in interprovincial games "on more than one occasion." E.S. Jackson, author of the regular *Toronto Daily Star* column at the time, "With the Cricketers," acknowledged Cross's abilities as a player — "the man of many centuries" would be the nickname Jackson would call him — and his authority on the sometimes arcane rules of that sport: "Perhaps there are few men in Toronto more thoroughly conversant with the rules of cricket than Mr. Cross...." Jackson considered

---

119 This account is from "Western Draws Color Line Except for Canadian-Born" *Toronto Daily Star* (13 August 1931) 1–2. The *Star* took care to solicit the views of representatives of the black community, including "colored Toronto barrister" Lionel Cross, as well as university officials.

120 *Ibid.*

Cross an ambassador for cricket: "It is men like E. Lionel Cross who are helping to make cricket more popular in Canada."[121]

Lionel Cross's legal career and his life in Toronto came to an end when he was disbarred in January 1937, having practised law in Toronto for almost thirteen years. According to the notice published in the *Globe*'s "Osgoode Hall News," he was disbarred for "conduct unbecoming a barrister and solicitor in that he appropriated to his own use funds belonging to a client."[122] Constance Backhouse, noting that several subsequent black members of the Ontario bar shared the same fate as Cross, has speculated that members of the legal community used the concept of professionalism to exclude outsiders.[123] As was mentioned early in this paper, Cross tended to have clients on the margins of society, principally immigrants. He spent a lot of time and energy working on behalf of the Rationalist Society, and one wonders how they could have paid him for a fraction of the time he devoted to their cause. He must have struggled even harder than usual to maintain his law practice during the Depression.[124] Cross appears to have been such a strongly and consistently principled man that it is hard to accept that he would have intentionally deceived and stolen from clients. He would have been painfully aware that as one of only two black lawyers in the city at the time, his behaviour would set an example. During his legal career, Cross had been deferential to no authority except to the concepts of liberty and justice. Cross had been a thorn in the side of Toronto authorities for years, lecturing the police and the public about the concept of British liberty, arguing that the laws were antiquated and should be changed, questioning the legitimacy of the authority of the Christian religion as the basis for civic society, skewering institutions for racist views and policies, and challenging the views of Ontario judges and the law in the Sterry trials and appeals. With Cross's disbarment, that thorn was

---

121 "With the Cricketers" *Toronto Daily Star* (23 October 1928) 11 and (20 February 1929) 7.
122 "At Osgoode Hall" *Globe* (25 January 1937) 7. Law Society member files and records of disciplinary proceedings before February 1986 are closed to researchers, so the precise nature of the charge against him is never likely to be known.
123 Backhouse, "Gender and Race in the Construction of 'Legal Professionalism': Historical Perspectives," above note 17.
124 Lance Talbot speculates that the Depression must have lain behind the difficulties that led to Cross's disbarment. Talbot also points out that the most lucrative types of legal practice, such as corporate litigation and real estate, would have been largely closed to black lawyers in Cross's time. The types of law that would have been open to him would have been criminal and small-scale civil causes, neither of which would have generated much income for lawyers. The evidence found in researching this paper bears out Talbot's view, above note 1.

extracted.[125] The fact of Cross's disbarment should not be ignored, but neither should his career be forgotten because it ended badly.[126] On the contrary; it should be celebrated. Cross's courage at representing unorthodox and unpopular views so doggedly throughout his thirteen-year practice in Toronto is remarkable, and the fact that he was Toronto's first black lawyer makes his achievements even more noteworthy.

---

125 I have tried without success to find out what happened to Lionel Cross after his disbarment. He appears to have left Toronto and never to have returned, for which one could hardly blame him. City directories show him listed for the last time in 1936, after which he disappears permanently. I wondered whether he might have returned to Trinidad and tried contacting the Law Society, Bar Association, National Archives and Library but got no response to my queries. Perhaps Cross went elsewhere, to make a fresh start in a new place where no one knew his history.

126 Writing about the first black lawyer in Halifax, James Robinson Johnston, Barry Cahill speculates that the manner of Robinson's death — he had been murdered by his brother-in-law — had come to overshadow his life and career and he had largely been forgotten until recently. Cahill, above note 7. Cross's case is similar. The cloud of his disbarment seems to have hung over his reputation, so that although he had been a well known figure in Toronto for about a decade from the mid-1920s to the mid-1930s, he too had largely been forgotten.

CHAPTER 12

If Your Life Is a Leaf: Arthur Eugene O'Meara's Campaign for Aboriginal Justice

HAMAR FOSTER

> Of course he was right. History shows that.... But the present offered no such comfort to a man on the way down, who could not ask the future to support him.
>
> <div align="right">Marilyn Bowering, <i>To All Appearances a Lady</i>[1]</div>

THE LAWYER WHO DEVOTES himself to an idea is a figure with a long history in the legal profession. The idea may be the relief of poverty, religious dissent, civil liberties — almost anything, really, that involves financial sacrifice and the overcoming of entrenched opposition.[2] Whatever it is, one quality that distinguishes this sort of lawyer from the more traditional kind is that, although both advocate for clients and both require adversarial skills, the former also advocates a cause. And lawyers who do this, whose careers become the tireless pursuit of a cause, can pay a high price for their dedication. This is so whether or not they transgress, or are seen as transgressing, against the canons of legal ethics or the standards of professional responsibility.

"Cause lawyering" is perhaps less well-defined than it was a century ago or even a generation ago, because it is now much more common for lawyers to work only one side of the street. By this I mean that many lawyers only prosecute or defend, work for capital or labour, or for governments or First

---

[1] M. Bowering, *To All Appearances a Lady* (Toronto: Penguin Canada, 2007) at 30.
[2] See, for example, Raymond Challinor, *A Radical Lawyer in Victorian England: W.P. Roberts and the Struggle for Workers' Rights* (London: I.B. Tauris & Co., 1990).

Nations. Being a "hired gun," which is a loaded concept if ever there was one, is out of fashion. This sort of lawyer may or may not be a "cause lawyer" — an admittedly contestable concept — but often is not. Someone like Edward Greenspan, for example, may confine his practice largely to criminal defence cases and may genuinely and legitimately believe in the importance of such work; but like the well-paid securities lawyer who specializes in initial public offerings, he does not advocate a cause in the sense that I intend, primarily because no real financial sacrifice is involved.

However, I do not wish to engage in a debate about who is and who is not a "cause lawyer." Not surprisingly, there is a literature on this (there is a literature on almost everything these days) and I refer the interested reader to it.[3] But I will take a working definition from this literature that seems to me to fit my subject rather well. On this view a cause lawyer is one who "works out of the professional mainstream, at financial if not personal cost, engaging in moral activism for marginalized clients."[4] Arthur Eugene O'Meara was such a lawyer.

Born in small-town Ontario in 1861, he came from a family of Anglican priests. His father was, for a time, a missionary to the Ojibwa in the part of what is now Ontario where the Robinson Treaties[5] were negotiated in the early 1850s. Frederick Augustus O'Meara translated religious writings, including the New Testament and the Book of Common Prayer, into Ojibwa. A "strong evangelical, firm in his opinions," the senior O'Meara was zealous and had "the true missionary spirit." But he was thought by some to lack judgment.[6]

All of Arthur's four brothers also became priests and one of them, Thomas, became principal of Wycliffe College in Toronto.[7] Arthur bucked this

---

3   See, for example, the collections of essays edited by Austin Sarat and Stuart Sheingold, beginning with *Cause Lawyering: Political Commitments and Professional Responsibilities* (New York: Oxford University Press, 1998) and including *Cause Lawyering and the State in a Global Era* (New York: Oxford University Press, 2001); *Something to Believe In: Politics, Professionalism, and Cause Lawyering* (Stanford: Stanford University Press, 2004); and *The Worlds Cause Lawyers Make: Structure and Agency in Legal Practice* (Stanford: Stanford University Press, 2005).

4   Paul E. Parker, reviewing *Cause Lawyering: Political Commitments and Professional Responsibilities,* above note 3, in (1998) 8:6 Law & Pol. Book Rev. at 283–86.

5   An account of these treaties by the Hon. William B. Robinson may be found in Alexander Morris, *The Treaties of Canada with the Indians of Manitoba and the North-West Territories Including the Negotiations on which They Were based* (Toronto: Belfords, Clarke & Co., 1880; Fifth House reprint, 1991) at 16–21.

6   Entry on Fredrick Augustus O'Meara by Thomas R. Millman in the *Dictionary of Canadian Biography,* vol. XI (Toronto: University of Toronto Press, 1982).

7   And is also one of the very few contemporary family sources on Arthur O'Meara: see below note 41.

trend. He studied law, was called to the bar, and practised in Toronto and in St. Thomas, Ontario, from 1886 to 1906. A year after his call he married Marion Katie Greene who was, appropriately, a clergyman's daughter. They had two children: Kathleen in 1892 and Robert — known in the family as "Robin" — in 1897. In the course of his career O'Meara represented the Lord's Day Alliance before the Judicial Committee of the Privy Council in a case that appears in Canadian constitutional law texts to this day.[8] Mysteriously, he was also a member of the firm of Macdonald, Marsh, and O'Meara for at least a year. I say "mysteriously" because the Macdonald in this firm was Sir John A. Macdonald, prime minister of Canada.[9]

After twenty years at the bar Arthur seems to have had what today might be called a midlife crisis. In any event, he experienced a belated attraction for the family vocation. In this frame of mind he engaged in a number of lengthy discussions in 1906 with family friend Isaac Stringer, Bishop of Selkirk, who had come to Toronto to try to secure more missionaries for his new diocese. The result was Arthur's decision to uproot his wife and children and leave both Ontario and the legal profession to become a missionary to the miners of the Yukon.

The family appears to have lived there for at least two years, and Arthur not only annoyed the locals by complaining about their morals — notably the failure of white men to marry their female Aboriginal partners — but also by campaigning for a residential school and a treaty for the Aboriginal peoples of the north. By then he had clearly discovered in himself his father's evangelical fervour, or perhaps found a new focus for it. This may be gleaned from an article he wrote in 1907, describing the missionary work he had done on a trip to Teslin Lake. Contact with Aboriginal people had obviously moved and inspired him, and the article provides a glimpse not only of his religious zeal but also of a certain tendency towards self-righteousness that would get him into trouble, both then and later on. "When," he asked his readers, "shall we of the Church of England in Canada awake fully to the fact that ... our main duty is, not merely to carry on a school here and there for the benefit of a few Indian children, but to send the good news of eternal salvation through Christ to 'every creature' of the Indian people now practically in heathen

---

8   *Attorney General for Ontario v. Hamilton Street Railway*, [1903] AC 524 (J.C.P.C.), one of the first cases in which a very broad interpretation of Ottawa's criminal law power was advanced.
9   See the published law lists for 1890–91: H.R. Hardy, ed., *The Canadian Law List, 1890* (Toronto: Imrie & Graham, 1890); H.R. Hardy, ed., *The Canadian Law List, 1891* (Toronto: Copp, Clark Co., 1891). I am indebted to Susan Lewthwaite for hunting down this reference for me.

darkness as dense as could be found in China."[10] The reference to China is to a contemporary debate in the Church over the future of Indian missions in Canada, and to the fact that many felt that the money raised by organizations such as the Church Missionary Society would be better spent on missions to Asia and Africa. O'Meara disagreed.

When he saw that treaties were not about to happen — with the waning of the gold rush the mining population had declined sharply, thereby removing much of the pressure on Aboriginal peoples — Arthur moved the family to British Columbia, where boom times and development were having the opposite effect. He then completed his return to his origins by being ordained an Anglican priest and threw himself into the campaign to resolve "the B.C. Indian Land Question" that was just getting underway.[11] By 1908, for example, there had been trouble in Nisga'a and Gitxsan territory over homesteading, and farther south the Salish tribes had sent delegations to England and to Rome to seek redress for their land claims. Indeed, in that year a large delegation of various tribal leaders descended on Ottawa and obtained an audience with Prime Minister Laurier, who according to newspaper reports told the chiefs that the land question "would be settled as soon as possible, and their rights protected."[12]

Notwithstanding the prominence of many Aboriginal people in these and earlier protests, the provincial government had maintained for decades that the Indians would be quite content — and the land question would go away — were it not for mischief-making missionaries. This refrain was about to change. Soon lawyers would replace the clergy as the outside "agitators" that both Ottawa and Victoria tended to see behind all the demands. Because Arthur O'Meara had the misfortune to be both a lawyer and a missionary, he therefore enjoyed a status that appears to have made him doubly obnoxious to the government. He was in this respect a truly transitional figure.

For the twenty years following 1908, O'Meara was indefatigable. He helped to found the Conference of the Friends of the Indians of British Col-

---

10   Rev. A.E. O'Meara, "Work in Far Away Yukon" *The New Era* (December 1907) 423 at 425–26 (copy kindly supplied by Ms. Mary Haig-Brown).

11   Until then he had been only a deacon. Bishop Stringer subsequently regretted having ordained him, although they appear to have remained friends.

12   See Robert Galois, "The Indian Rights Association, Native Protest Activity and the 'Land' Question in British Columbia, 1903–1916" (1992) 8 Native Studies Review 1 at 8 and 8n. Galois adds that, when it returned, the delegation was met by "several hundred Indians" and that there was a procession and "impromptu celebration" at the reserve in North Vancouver. See also Neil J. Sterritt *et al.*, *Tribal Boundaries in the Nass Watershed* (Vancouver: UBC Press, 1998) at 99 and 139.

umbia, an organization modeled on nineteenth-century developments in the US, and he not only attended Friends meetings in that country but also maintained contact with the Aborigines Protection Society in England. He was active on other fronts, as well. Most significantly, although it is not clear that he was a member of the bar after he left Ontario, he was a sort of unofficial counsel to the Nisga'a by 1910 and — not without a considerable amount of maneuvering and in-fighting — counsel for the Allied Indian Tribes of British Columbia from 1916 to 1928.[13] He filed both the Cowichan Petition of 1909, which was a critical event in the history of the land question, and the much better known Nisga'a Petition of 1913.[14]

Because of the events set in motion by the Cowichan Petition, in the spring of 1911 O'Meara came as close as anyone ever had come to obliging the government to submit the question of unextinguished Aboriginal title in British Columbia to the courts. Or, for that matter, closer than anyone *would* come until the Supreme Court of Canada's decision in the *Calder* case in 1973.[15] Dominion order in council 1081 in May of 1911 proclaimed the Laurier government's intention to force British Columbia into court to defend its claim that provincial land was unencumbered by Aboriginal title.[16] It also included a

---

13 The Allied Tribes was an organization formed in 1916 that was intended to replace and merge earlier groupings such as the Indian Rights Association and the Interior Tribes of British Columbia. On the "Friends of the Indians" phenomenon in the US, see Francis Paul Prucha, ed., *Americanizing the American Indians: Writings by the "Friends of the Indian," 1880–1900* (Lincoln: University of Nebraska Press, 1978) (reprint of 1973 Harvard University Press edition).

14 On the Cowichan Petition see Hamar Foster and Benjamin L. Berger, "From Humble Petitions to Legal Demands: The Cowichan Petition of 1909 and the British Columbia Indian Land Question," which includes a copy of the petition as an appendix. It is in Hamar Foster, Benjamin L. Berger, and A.R. Buck, eds., *The Grand Experiment: Law and Legal Culture in British Settler Societies* (Vancouver: UBC Press, 2008) at 240–67. The Nisga'a Petition is now available as an appendix to Hamar Foster, Heather Raven, and Jeremy Webber, eds., *Let Right Be Done: Aboriginal Title, the Calder Case and the Future of Indigenous Rights* (Vancouver: UBC Press, 2007) [*Let Right Be Done*].

15 *Calder v. Attorney General of British Columbia* may be found, *inter alia*, at (1973), 34 DLR (3d) 145 (S.C.C.) [*Calder*]. The legal obstacles to litigating the land question, chief among which was the sovereign immunity of the crown from suit, are discussed in Hamar Foster, "We Are Not O'Meara's Children: Law, Lawyers and the First Campaign for Aboriginal Title in British Columbia, 1908–1928" in *Let Right Be Done*, ibid. ["We Are Not O'Meara's Children"].

16 This particular strategy was devised by T.R.E. McInnes, the lawyer retained by the Dominion government in 1909 to advise it on whether unextinguished Aboriginal title existed in BC. He concluded that it did and recommended that Ottawa sue selected homesteaders in the Skeena to oblige the province to defend the crown grants it had issued to them. See Hamar Foster, "A Romance of the Lost: The Role of Tom MacIn-

memorandum by O'Meara making the case for such action, a memorandum described by the order in council as "substantially correct."[17]

But the idea of a lawsuit was doomed when the Liberal government of Prime Minister Wilfrid Laurier made free trade with the United States a prominent issue in the 1911 Dominion election and, for this and other reasons, lost the election to Robert Borden. With Conservative administrations now installed in both Ottawa and Victoria, talk of forcing British Columbia into court quickly came to an end. Instead, the two governments entered into an agreement in 1912 to establish a royal commission to deal with the simmering dispute between them over the number, size, and proprietary status of the province's Indian reserves.[18] The main condition of this agreement — to which of course no Aboriginal peoples were party — was that the matter of Aboriginal title would be taken off the table. It also provided that the various bands would have to consent, as required by the *Indian Act*,[19] to any reduction in their reserved lands. The first condition was faithfully observed; the second, notwithstanding that it was formally included in the agreement, was soon reversed by statute. And when the royal commission's report came down, the implementing legislation put forward in the 1920s stated that, as amended, the report constituted a final adjustment of all matters pertaining to Indian lands in the province. Although told by officials that this referred only to Indian reserves and not the larger question of Indian title, O'Meara and the Aboriginal groups he represented were not prepared to rely on bureaucratic assurances alone. They therefore opposed the agreement and soldiered on.[20]

I have discussed the details of the years of trying to get the land question into court elsewhere.[21] Suffice it to say that the main features of the campaign

---

nes in the History of the British Columbia Indian Land Question" in G.B. Baker and J. Phillips, eds., *Essays in the History of Canadian Law, vol. VIII* (Toronto: Osgoode Society for Canadian Legal History, 1999) at 171–212.

17 See PC 1081 (1 May 1911).

18 The McKenna-McBride Agreement of 1912, which led to the creation of the commission known informally by the same name. Its substantial, four volume report was completed in 1916 but did not become public until several years later: see Canada, *Report of the Royal Commission on Indian Affairs for the Province of British Columbia* (Victoria: Acme Press, 1916). The agreement, made on 24 September 1912, is reproduced at pp. 10–11 of the report.

19 R.S.C. 1906, c. 81, ss. 48–49.

20 See the transcript of the meetings held in Victoria, BC, in August of 1923 between senior Indian Department officials and the executive committee of the Allied Tribes, Vancouver, BC Archives (MS-0997).

21 See "We Are Not O'Meara's Children," above note 15. As the title suggests, other lawyers also involved themselves in the campaign, notably J.M.M. Clark, K.C., of

after 1911 include the filing of the Nisga'a Petition with the British Privy Council; an unacceptable compromise proposal by the Dominion government in 1914; and a couple of occasions after that when it looked as though some sort of resolution would be possible. In fact there were times, notably in 1916 and the early 1920s, when the land question received a considerable amount of press and some government representatives seem to have thought that treaties in British Columbia were possible.[22] But I think that, in retrospect, the high watermark of the campaign was in 1911, when the Laurier government appeared to have committed itself to forcing British Columbia into court.

After making a concerted effort to persuade the Borden government to do more, O'Meara and the Nisga'a expressed their opposition to the McKenna-McBride Agreement by petitioning the Privy Council in London in 1913. His state by then can be gleaned from a telegram he sent to a lawyer who was active in the Friends of the Indians at that time. After confirming that he had filed the petition, O'Meara reported that he was starting to collapse under the strain and had been "constrained by medical advice to take a short rest."[23] Thereafter he appears to have lived a life of hotel rooms, underfunded travel, and unremitting labour in an increasingly hopeless cause. The carnage of the First World War ensured that the British government would not intervene in the land question if Ottawa did not want it to — and it did not. Equally problematic, the ratification of the McKenna-McBride Report by both the province and the Dominion by 1924 meant that both governments now had what they wanted.[24] This was clear when the Allied Tribes finally secured a hearing before a joint parliamentary

---

Toronto, with whom O'Meara first worked, then replaced. See also E. Palmer Patterson II, "Arthur E. O'Meara, Friend of the Indians" (1968) 58 Pacific Northwest Quarterly 90 and the more sympathetic treatment by Mary Haig-Brown, "Arthur Eugene O'Meara: Servant, Advocate, Seeker of Justice" in Celia Haig-Brown and David A. Nock, eds., *With Good Intentions: Euro-Canadian & Aboriginal Relations in Colonial Canada* (Vancouver: UBC Press, 2006) at 258 ["Servant, Advocate, Seeker of Justice"].

22 W.E. Ditchburn, Indian superintendent for British Columbia, outlined a procedure for making treaties to Deputy Superintendent General of Indian Affairs Duncan Campbell Scott in November of 1922 and told one of his Indian agents in March of 1923 that a settlement was expected that year: Ditchburn to Scott, 28 Nov. 1922 and Ditchburn to the Indian agent at New Westminster, 2 March 1923, Ottawa, Library and Archives Canada, (RG 10, Series c-II-3, Vol. 11047, File 33/General, pt. 6).

23 Telegram from O'Meara to F.C. Wade (June 1913), Vancouver City Archives (KC, 21, Wade family fonds, Add. MSS. 44 at 502-D-5 file 9, record ID 60386).

24 Although the two governments continued to wrangle about implementing the report until 1938, BC got the lands that were cut off the reserves pursuant to the report, plus an assurance that it had no more obligations in the matter. Ottawa gained full control of the remaining reserves free of provincial interference. Simply put, any leverage previously enjoyed by the Allied Tribes up to that point was gone.

committee in 1927. The government of BC Premier John Oliver refused to attend, and the members of the committee almost voted to terminate the process after hearing the first submission by Deputy Superintendent General of Indian Affairs Duncan Campbell Scott.[25] That the committee concluded there was no merit to the claim of Aboriginal title in BC is therefore hardly a surprise.

By the spring of 1928 the Indian Department was compiling a dossier on O'Meara with a view to laying charges under a recent amendment to the *Indian Act* that made it an offence to raise funds for advocating Aboriginal claims against the government without permission.[26] The authorities were frustrated by the difficulties they were encountering in building a case but were nonetheless determined to do so. Informants were consulted, reports were filed, and Scott kept a close watch over the whole process.[27] O'Meara, however, outsmarted them: he died suddenly of heart failure in April, before any charges could be laid.[28]

The last twenty years of his life, which I have so sparingly outlined above, were dedicated to one end: a recognition of Aboriginal rights in BC that would finance the transformation of the Aboriginals of the province into economically self-sufficient Christian citizens. He was, in short, a lawyer with a cause. In my view at least three questions, all of which might be asked of any such lawyer, arise. The first: was O'Meara any good as a lawyer? Or was he as incompetent as some of his opponents in government portrayed him to be, a sort of Irish-Canadian Don Quixote, tilting ineffectively at windmills? Second, where might his passion for this cause have come from? And third, what did it cost him, financially and emotionally?

O'MEARA AS LAWYER AND ADVOCATE

O'MEARA WAS A GOOD lawyer — of that I have no doubt. Nearly every letter and document he authored that contained legal advice or a legal opinion that

---

25 See Canada, *Special Committees of the Senate and House of Commons Meeting in Joint Session to Inquire into the Claims of the Allied Indian Tribes of British Columbia, as Set Forth in their Petition Submitted to Parliament in June 1926: Proceedings, Report and the Evidence* (Ottawa: 1927) [*Special Committee Report, 1927*]. Scott so impressed some committee members that, given BC's non-appearance, they saw little point in proceeding. Cooler heads — that is to say, heads more sensitive to the optics of the situation — prevailed.

26 S.C. 1926–27, c. 32, s.6. Originally s. 149A of the *Indian Act*, above note 19, it became s. 141 in the 1927 consolidation and was dropped from the Act in 1951.

27 See correspondence between Scott and his informants and officials in the early months of 1928 at Ottawa, Library and Archives Canada (RG 10, Vol. 3823, File 59, 335-5).

28 The *Victoria Times* noted his death on 3 April 1928, stating that "for twenty years he had been working in the interests of the British Columbia Indians."

I have read reveals considerable competence. On everything from Aboriginal title to rights to the foreshore of Indian reserves, the accusation that his advice was unsound is, simply, untrue. One example must suffice. When the Allied Tribes appeared before the 1927 special parliamentary committee, O'Meara relied upon the decision of the Judicial Committee of the Privy Council in the *St. Catherine's Milling* case to support their argument that, until Aboriginal title is extinguished by treaty, it forms a burden on the underlying title of the Crown, a burden that is acknowledged by section 109 of the *British North America Act*.[29] This is not only the accepted interpretation of the *St. Catherine's Milling* case today; it was also a reasonable interpretation in 1927.[30] However, because the decision referred to "lands reserved for the Indians," the committee members were having none of it. The decision, in their view, was about *Indian Act* reserves and had nothing to do with pre-existing Aboriginal title. One member of the committee even accused O'Meara of misleading his clients. But of course O'Meara was right. As he told this particular M.P., everyone who had studied the case knew that it concerned traditional territory, not a statutory reserve. "They know nothing of the kind," was the response.[31] This was typical of the treatment O'Meara tended to receive during the last decade of the campaign.

Part of the reason was the negative climate of the day with respect to Aboriginal rights, and part of it is that, by the mid-1920s, O'Meara's skills were failing. He was no longer a good advocate, and there is a difference between a good lawyer and a good advocate — although some are blessed with being both. One way to appreciate this difference might be to compare O'Meara to John Mortimer's "Old Bailey hack," the inimitable Horace Rumpole. Rumpole's knowledge of the law appears to have been confined to the reasonable doubt principle and the forensic significance of blood stains; but he could cross-examine the stripes off a police sergeant's arm with one hand tied behind his back.[32] He was, first and foremost, an advocate: someone skilled in persuasion.

---

29 Now the *Constitution Act, 1867* (U.K.), 30 & 31 Victoria, c. 3. See *St. Catherine's Milling & Lumber Co. v. R.* (1888), 14 App. Cas. 46 (J.C.P.C.) [*St. Catherine's Milling*].
30 Although in 1927 the applicability of the argument to British Columbia might depend upon whether the *Royal Proclamation of 1763*, R.S.C., 1985, Appendix II, No. 1. applied in the province. But O'Meara was not alone in thinking that it did. Télésphore Fournier, the Dominion minister of justice in 1875, assumed that it did, and so did lawyers J.M.M. Clark, K.C., counsel for the Indian Rights Association, and F.C. Wade, K.C., of the Friends of the Indians.
31 *Special Committee Report, 1927*, above note 25 at 215–17.
32 See, for example, John Mortimer, "Rumpole and the Last Resort" in *Rumpole and the Golden Thread* (New York: Penguin, 1983) at 245. In this episode Rumpole fakes his own

O'Meara, by contrast, knew the law but, at least towards the end, not how to persuade. His legal arguments were sound and form the basis of the law of Aboriginal title today. But his zeal for the cause led him to annoy almost everyone and to inundate them with so much material that government officials, who were lukewarm about Aboriginal title to begin with soon stopped listening. In particular, O'Meara's great failing as an advocate was an addiction to lengthy quotations. In the various extant transcripts of the many meetings that he and the Allied Tribes had with government ministers and officials throughout this period, the sighs are almost audible as he promises to be brief and then drones on for pages. On the other hand, he must have felt he had to do this: his listeners simply weren't getting it. When one is rolling stones uphill in a good cause, one tends, understandably, to make maximum use of the material at hand.

Of course, even if O'Meara had been a better advocate he may have done no better. The people he represented were short of resources and struggling to overcome ancient and deeply felt tribal animosities; and when he met with provincial and Dominion politicians or appeared before commissions, he was usually playing to very unsympathetic audiences. These are some of the factors that probably led J.M.M. Clark, K.C., the lawyer that O'Meara originally worked with and then replaced, to recommend that the terms proposed by Ottawa in 1914 as conditions of referring the title question to the courts be accepted.[33] These terms, which many people saw as inadequate even then, look like a pittance today. O'Meara recommended against acceptance and, as a result, was appointed to represent the Allied Tribes as well as the Nisga'a. So Clark departed, no deal was made and Aboriginal title in British Columbia remains a live issue today. That alone was a signal contribution.

Although he never gave up the fight, O'Meara's skills suffered after years of unrewarded labour, constant travel, and often savage public criticism. Nor did this criticism end with his death. As late as 1967, one of the few writers who had noticed him described O'Meara as an "Indian lover" who "fastened his meager mind" on the Aboriginal title claim. He was, according to this

---

death to flush out a solicitor who owes him money. When this fellow approaches Hilda, Rumpole's "widow," hoping to avoid full payment, he tries to flatter by telling her that Rumpole was a fine lawyer. "A fine lawyer?" she replies, confused. "He never told me." "And of course, a most persuasive advocate," adds the solicitor. "Oh, yes," says Hilda, "he told me *that*." There is a difference.

33 The terms proposed by Ottawa included acceptance of the McKenna-McBride Commission report, sight unseen; agreement that if the courts found unextinguished title it would be extinguished on the same financial terms as the numbered treaties; and that Ottawa, not the tribes, would decide who their lawyer would be.

view, "neither a good missionary nor a good lawyer."[34] It would be another forty years before a genuinely sympathetic assessment appeared in print.[35]

"PSYCHOLOGIZING" THE MAN

I CLEARLY CANNOT KNOW why O'Meara deferred becoming a priest to pursue a legal career, nor why the BC Indian land question came to dominate the last two decades of his life. But there is one interesting bit of evidence that might be a small part of the explanation. When his father, who was no less determined a person, was a missionary to the Ojibwa, a lawyer and entrepreneur by the name of Allan Macdonnell took up the cause of Indian and Métis title in the region around Sault Ste. Marie.[36] Macdonnell, as O'Meara would do more than half a century later, represented Aboriginal groups in negotiating with the government and tried unsuccessfully to have their title decided by the courts. He also clashed with O'Meara's missionary father, who was more inclined than Macdonnell to acquiesce to government plans for the Indians. This all happened before Arthur was born, but the more one delves into Macdonnell's career, the more it seems a model for Arthur's — if only because it provided a way for Arthur to choose a different path from his father and his uniformly clerical brothers and to opt for the law when he left school, rather than the priesthood.

There is a further, intriguing parallel with Macdonnell that cannot explain O'Meara's career but that says a great deal about how governments tended to respond to lawyers with a cause. In 1853 the Province of Canada passed *An Act to Make Better Provision for the Administration of Justice in the Unorganized Tracts of Country in Upper Canada*.[37] Section 9 provided that "any person

---

34   John Morley, *Roar of the Breakers* (Toronto: Ryerson Press, 1967) at 105–6 [*Roar of the Breakers*].
35   See Mary Haig-Brown, "Servant, Advocate, Seeker of Justice," above note 21. Ms. Haig-Brown and I discovered each other through O'Meara's sole lineal descendant, Mrs. Gail Gatehouse of Victoria, BC, when Ms. Haig-Brown was researching her essay and I was researching "We Are Not O'Meara's Children," above note 15. We exchanged drafts and research notes.
36   See Alan Knight and Janet E. Chute, "A Visionary on the Edge: Allan Macdonnell and the Championing of Native Resource Rights" in Haig-Brown and Nock, eds., *With Good Intentions*, above note 21 at 87–105 [Knight and Chute]. See also the material on the elder O'Meara and Macdonnell in Janet E. Chute, *The Legacy of Shingwaukonse: A Century of Native Leadership* (Toronto: University of Toronto Press, 1998).
37   16 Vict., c. 176. Years later a version of s. 9 was included in the *Indian Act* and then the *Criminal Code*, R.S.C. 1985, c. C-46, when the latter was enacted in 1892. It was not dropped from the *Criminal Code* until 1954.

inciting Indians or half-breeds frequenting or residing in such tracts of country ... to the disturbance of the public peace ... shall be guilty of a felony," punishable by no more than five and no less than two years' imprisonment. George Brown of the Toronto *Globe* alerted Macdonnell by sending him a copy of the bill, and Macdonnell, with good reason, wrote back that it might be more accurate if the law were renamed "an Act to procure the conviction of Allan Macdonnell."[38]

Seventy-four years later, when parliament made it an offence for lawyers to pursue Aboriginal claims against government without government consent, the minister of the interior made it clear that O'Meara was one of the targets.[39] So in BC, section 141 of the *Indian Act* might well be described as an act to procure the conviction of Arthur Eugene O'Meara. As Scott made clear shortly before O'Meara died, if his department received reliable evidence that O'Meara was "collecting money from Indians for the further prosecution of the Aboriginal claim we will take steps to prosecute him."[40]

WHAT IT ALL COST

UNJUSTLY AND PUBLICLY ACCUSED of both incompetence and fleecing the Indians, O'Meara pressed on until his death. He did not give up, not even after the parliamentary committee referred to above dismissed the claims of the Allied Tribes in 1927 and parliament effectively rendered his life's work illegal by enacting section 141. Worse still, it appears that his obsession also may have cost him the love and respect of his family. His brothers and sister worried about him, and about the effect of what he was doing on his wife and children. He borrowed money from Thomas to finance the campaign for title and found it difficult to pay it back. Thomas in particular fretted about the stress Arthur appeared to be under and inquired rather plaintively on at least two occasions about when the Indians would "pony up," presumably so he could get his loan back. Arthur appeared to be living on very little, which meant that his family was too, and everyone was very concerned.[41]

---

38 Quoted in Knight and Chute, above note 36 at 98.
39 *Debates of the House of Commons*, vol. 175 (15 Feb. 1927) at 324–25.
40 D.C. Scott to W.E. Ditchburn, 3 Feb. 1928, Ottawa, Library and National Archives Canada (RG 10, Vol. 3823, file 59, 335-5).
41 The only significant batch of family letters I have found is in the O'Meara Papers at Wycliffe College in Toronto, where Thomas O'Meara was principal. For some reason the correspondence files for the period 1916–18, unlike the others, contain family letters as well as college business, and I am grateful to Tom Power of the Wycliffe College Archives for facilitating my access to this source. The quoted reference is in a letter from

But there are only a few letters and I have been able to locate only two photographs. One, taken at Whitehorse in 1907, shows Arthur and his fellow clergy at the First Synod of the Diocese of Yukon. The other was taken in England during O'Meara's attempt during the First World War to persuade the British government to intervene in the BC Indian land question. While there he visited his son, Robin, who was in the army. In the photograph, Robin is in uniform and his father stands stiffly, with one hand, Napoleon-style, in his suit jacket. Although Robin was liable to be dispatched to the killing fields across the Channel any day, the two men do not touch. There is a distinct, empty space between them. Mrs. Gail Gatehouse, who is Arthur's only grandchild and Robin's only child, advises that her father never spoke of her grandfather, not ever.[42] "When you are not feeling holy," Leonard Cohen has written, "your loneliness tells you you've sinned."[43]

Arthur O'Meara, flawed like the rest of us as he was, devoted the last twenty years of his life to a worthy cause. A sense of how it must have felt may be gleaned from a speech he made long before the bitter defeats of the 1920s, at a time when the campaign for title was only about two years old and when success seemed only months away. It was at the Aberdeen School in Vancouver, on an evening in April of 1910. After being introduced by his friend and fellow member of the Friends of the Indians, F.C. Wade, K.C., he laid out the case for "The Indians' Title to the Lands of B.C." His audience turned out even though there was a horse show competing for their attention, not to mention a meeting at City Hall about the new site for the University of British Columbia.[44] I will not reproduce very much of that speech here, although it is a competent and persuasive outline of the history of the land question to 1910 and the law that would ultimately be brought to bear in resolving it.[45] But

---

Thomas to Arthur (29 December 1916), Toronto, Wycliffe College Archives (11 (2P) O'Meara, 1916–1918 Correspondence, A -W.).

42 This photograph was kindly provided to me by Mrs. Catherine Tuck of Charlottetown, P.E.I., Mrs. Gatehouse's second cousin.
43 From Leonard Cohen, *The Sisters of Mercy*, ©1967 Sony Music Entertainment (Canada) Inc.
44 What follows in the next paragraph is from "Rev. A.E. O'Meara's Lecture on the Indians' Title to the Land of B.C.," delivered at the Aberdeen School, Vancouver, 22 April, 1910 at 8:15 p.m., BC Archives (MS-0421). When I first examined this manuscript in the early 1990s it was complete. That is no longer the case: the first page and probably the last three or four pages are now missing. I have therefore relied on the notes I took on then for the missing material.
45 It also reflects the arguments that O'Meara and Clark (see above note 21) put in the Cowichan Petition the year before and in a document Clark prepared for submission to the Dominion government: see "Statement of Facts and Claims on Behalf of the Indians of British Columbia," BC Archives (NWp 970.5 C593s).

I will quote a few excerpts from a passage towards the end of the speech that provide a glimpse of the man and his cause.

The continuing uncertainty about land injured everyone, he said, Indian and non-Indian alike. He maintained that the Indians in particular faced a future that promised "a wave of settlement" and railway construction, and "they do not know what it contains for them. Their very tribal existence seems to be threatened & they do not see what we are going to give them instead of it. And because they look out into the future with uncertainty they are dissatisfied — gravely dissatisfied." What was needed, he suggested, was a settlement that was final, just, and reflected a compromise between the opposing views. He then described what he saw as the essence of the Indian position: "God made us and our forefathers as well as He made the white people and their forefathers. He made these great valleys, these mountains, these rivers. He stocked the mountains and forests with game and the rivers with fish, and he gave all this to our forefathers." O'Meara concluded by stating that "Justice ... is one of the laws of the great Creator of the universe, and I am convinced that the just settlement of this problem will ... bring the greatest advantage to all the interests of the province." A motion of thanks received unanimous approval, and the mover noted that what they had just heard was news to a great many of them. It also seemed rather reasonable.

Yet this is the view that British Columbia repeatedly rejected and that, by 1927, Ottawa also abandoned, notwithstanding its special responsibility for Canada's Aboriginal peoples. Indeed, only two months after this speech the Victoria *Daily Colonist* warned its readers, no doubt referring to the likes of O'Meara and the Friends of the Indians, that because Indians could not be expected "to appreciate the fundamental principles of the laws of the white race ... their acquiescence in the application of those principles to them is likely to be rendered needlessly difficult by unwise advisors." What were those principles? Two days earlier the editors had elaborated upon one of them. When the British Crown acquired sovereignty over British Columbia by settling it, they wrote, this "extinguished *ipso facto* every right or claim that may have been held or enjoyed by present occupation or immemorial possession by any other sovereign people, or tribe. This is no new principle. It is as old as history itself."[46] They of course cited no authority for this ancient "principle." They did not need to. That is an advantage that editors, unlike lawyers and courts, enjoy even today.

When he died, Arthur left his widow nothing but two life insurance policies, thus putting the lie to the charge that he had become rich on the backs

---

46 Victoria *Daily Colonist* (23 and 25 June 1910).

of the Nisga'a and other tribes.⁴⁷ Just as disheartening, Peter Kelly, who had been the chairman of the Allied Tribes, reflected years later that they might have done better without him.⁴⁸ Although O'Meara did not live to hear that heart-breaking assessment, he died knowing he had failed. Vindication would be posthumous, and anonymous. And although his legal arguments are there to be seen in Canadian caselaw today, almost no one has heard of him. Yet such lawyers= are very much a part of the history of the profession.

Comparisons are tempting, but odious. An obvious one is with Bruce Clark, the Canadian lawyer who so vigorously advocated Aboriginal rights from the mid-1970s to the late 1990s.⁴⁹ Like O'Meara, he was a "cause lawyer." Like O'Meara, he was a good lawyer but, in traditional terms, a bad advocate.⁵⁰ Like O'Meara, he sacrificed financial security and family time to the cause. And, like O'Meara, he ended his career unburdened by success and out of favour even with many of those on whose behalf he had advocated.

Unlike, Clark, however, O'Meara never really got to test his mettle in an Aboriginal title case; nor, apart from the possibility that he may have been soliciting funds in violation of section 141 of the *Indian Act* immediately before his death, did he engage in extra-legal activities or attack the legitimacy of the judicial system he so very much wanted to have adjudicate his clients' claim. Nor was he disbarred, as Clark was — although this may be an unfair point of comparison because it is not clear that O'Meara was a member of the bar during his years as counsel for the Nisga'a and the Allied Tribes. But

---

47 See the BC Archives, Probate Records (GR 2205) and Genn Collection (Add. M.S.S. 1950, Box 141, File 2).
48 *Roar of the Breakers*, above note 34 at 116, and confirmed by the late Reg Kelly, one of Peter's sons, in an interview with me in 1995.
49 Not to be confused with J.M.M. Clark, K.C., counsel for the Indian Rights Association in BC until 1916.
50 The quality of his legal analysis is most evident in *Native Liberty, Crown Sovereignty — The Existing Aboriginal Right of Self-Government in Canada* (Montreal: McGill-Queen's University Press, 1990). *Indian Title in Canada* (Toronto: Carswell, 1987), on the other hand, is less effective, mainly because it is really a sustained attack on the trial judge in *Attorney-General for Ontario v. Bear Island Foundation; Potts. v. Attorney-General for Ontario* (1984), 49 O.R. (2d) 353. I have not read his most recent book, and his success record in court is not good. On Clark generally see the starkly contrasting views of Paul McKay in *The Ottawa Citizen* for 4 April 1999 and Tony Hall in "Ethnic Cleansing and Genocide in North America and Kosovo: The Disbarring of Dr. Bruce Clark by the Law Society of Upper Canada in the Context of the Evolving Jurisprudence of Crimes against Humanity," online: http://209.85.173.104/ search?q=cache:DRwvHE2tu8IJ:www.thepeoplespaths.net/articles/EthnicCleansing990411.htm+Paul+McKay%22+%26+%22Tony+Hall%22 I %26 I %22Bruce+Clark.%2 2+%26+%22ethnic+cleansing%22&hl=en&ct=clnk&cd=1&gl=ca.

it is difficult to imagine Arthur O'Meara at the barricades at Gustafsen Lake, or attempting to arrest Canadian judges for treason and complicity in genocide.[51] Perhaps this is simply because the times were different. Still, like his clients — and like their descendants, who brought the *Calder* case to court forty years after his death — O'Meara did not lose his faith in the promise of "British justice," even though, in many respects, he had ample reason to do so.[52] After all, section 35 of the *Constitution Act, 1982*,[53] which recognizes and affirms existing Aboriginal rights and title, and cases such as *Calder*, *Delgamuukw*, and *Haida*, were the legislative and judicial achievements of Bruce Clark's day, not O'Meara's.[54] In short, O'Meara, unlike Bruce Clark, stuck with the system, more or less.

If I am right about this, perhaps a better comparison might be with Methodist missionary and amateur archeologist James Mellon Menzies, the subject of a recent profile in *The Globe and Mail*.[55] Like O'Meara, Menzies was born in a small Ontario town, albeit a generation later. He became a missionary to China, thus contributing to the trend towards foreign missions that O'Meara opposed. But, like O'Meara, he did ground-breaking work there that, until recently, was ignored because he was seen as a "running dog of the imperialists" or a "foreign devil." Yet those who knew him saw him as someone who respected ancient Chinese culture and who ensured that his archaeological finds were not spirited away to foreign museums. They also

---

51   Donn Downey, "Unrepentant Native Rights Lawyer to Receive Law Society Reprimand: Report Questions Bruce Clark's Tactics in Pursuing Justice for Clients" *Globe and Mail* (29 June 1996) A3. A disclosure is necessary here, however. I may not be an objective commentator on this issue because, although Dr. Clark has cited some of my work and we engaged in a brief correspondence in the 1990s, I declined to join his cause. Subsequently, and notwithstanding that I have never been a member of the NDP, some of his supporters included me in a list — a long list — of "NDP mafias in Academia ... and other members of the 'Indian Industry'" who tried to "assassinate the truth" during the stand-off at Gustafsen Lake, see online: http://209.85.173.104/search?q=cache:EY18 nblL4pEJ:sisis.nativeweb.org/clark/feb2097.html+%22Indian+industry%22+%26+%2 2Hamar+Foster%22+%26+%22mafia%22&hl=en&ct=clnk&cd=1&gl=ca.

52   Striking film exists of Frank Calder addressing an annual Nisga'a Convention in the 1960s that was debating whether to launch a title lawsuit. In it he stresses that "British justice," and not the Nisga'a, was on trial. In conversations with him Frank also told me that he saw himself as carrying on the tradition of his father, Arthur Calder, and O'Meara.

53   Being Schedule B to the *Canada Act 1982* (U.K.), 1982, c. 11.

54   See *Calder*, above note 15, and accompanying text; *Delgamuukw v. British Columbia*, [1997] 3 S.C.R. 1010; and *Haida Nation v. British Columbia*, [2004] 3 S.C.R. 511. Frank Calder regularly invoked the idea of British justice when advocating for Aboriginal title in the 1960s.

55   Geoffrey York, "New Respect for 'Old Bones'" *Globe and Mail* (19 January 2007) F4–F5.

testify to his being ignored in China for ideological reasons and ignored in Canada because of his increasingly unfashionable status as a missionary.

This comparison may be too charitable to O'Meara, who was an ardent supporter of residential schools. Nonetheless, like Menzies he saw Christianity as naturally indigenous, rather than foreign, and felt called to combine his religion with justice for Aboriginal people. And, like Menzies, he died largely unrecognized by both his countrymen and by the people to whom he devoted his life's energies. Perhaps the fact that Menzies and his contribution are now beginning to be noticed means that O'Meara's will be too. We shall see.

In the same song I referred to earlier, Leonard Cohen wrote that "if your life is a leaf that the seasons tear off and condemn," the Sisters of Mercy "will bind you with love as graceful and green as a stem."[56] When Arthur O'Meara's heart stopped suddenly on 2 April 1928, I think he must have felt very much like Cohen's leaf. One can only hope that his Christian faith provided him, at the end, with the grace that was denied him — and that he denied himself — during his life.

---

56   *The Sisters of Mercy*, above note 43.

PART 6

GENDER ISSUES: THE IMPACT OF WOMEN ON THE PROFESSION

CHAPTER 13

"Into the Rough of Things": Women Lawyers in British Columbia, 1912–1930

DOROTHY E. CHUNN AND JOAN BROCKMAN*

RESEARCHERS AND ACADEMICS HAVE focused considerable attention on the first women admitted to the legal profession in Canada and other western countries.[1] While the "firsts" are extremely important, the women who followed these trailblazers into law during the early twentieth century have received little notice.[2] This paper, which is based on an oral history project about the thirty-nine women who began legal studies (twenty-four of whom were admitted to the bar) in British Columbia between 1912 and 1930, is an attempt

---

* We are grateful to the Law Foundation of British Columbia for funding this research, in part. Thanks also to Bernice Chong and Denise Evans for research assistance and to Constance Backhouse and Wesley Pue for bringing this volume to fruition. Finally, we want to extend a special thank you to the many people who made the study possible through their participation in interviews and in other ways.

1 See, for example, Constance Backhouse, "'To open the way for others of my sex': Clara Brett Martin's Career as Canada's First Woman Lawyer" (1985) 1 C.J.W.L. 1; Lois Yorke, "Mabel Penery French (1881–1955): A Life Re-Created" (1993) 42 U.N.B.L.J. 3; Gilles Gallichan, *Les Québécoises et le barreau: L'histoire d'une difficile conquête 1914–1941* (Sillery, QC: Septentrion, 1999). For an ambitious exception, see Mary Jane Mossman, *The First Women Lawyers: A Comparative Study of Gender, Law and the Legal Professions* (Oxford: Hart, 2006) [*The First Women Lawyers*].

2 For Canadian follow-up studies, see Mary Kinnear, "That There Woman Lawyer: Women Lawyers in Manitoba 1915–1970" (1992) 5 C.J.W.L. 2; Cecilia Morgan, "'An Embarrassingly and Severely Masculine Atmosphere': Women, Gender and the Legal Profession at Osgoode Hall, 1920s–1960s" (1996) 11 C.J.L.S. 19 ["An Embarrassingly and Severely Masculine Atmosphere"]; Sandra Petersson, "Ruby Clements and Early Women of the Alberta Bar" (1997) 9:2 C.J.W.L. 365.

245

to address the imbalance. The BC story began with Mabel French who in 1912 became the first woman to enter the legal profession in that province, thereby replicating her earlier "victory" in New Brunswick. As we and others have previously documented, French's admission to the bar was the outcome of a protracted struggle with the Law Society of British Columbia that established the legal precedent for other (white) women to enter the profession.[3] Subsequent to the French decision, thirty-eight women began legal studies and/or gained entry into the legal profession in the province over the next two decades (see Appendices A and B). In this paper, we look at the twenty-four women who were called to the bar and practised for at least a short time, with particular emphasis on eight who were still working lawyers into the 1960s and 1970s.[4]

We preface our analysis with a brief note on our methodological approach to the oral history component of the study. We then discuss the similarities and differences among the twenty-three women who followed French with respect to getting in, staying in, and moving up in the legal profession. What were their motivations and paths of entry and their experiences of articling, studying, and finding employment? Why did they stay in or leave the profession? To what extent did their career trajectories resemble or differ from those of male lawyers? In the final section, we assess the impact of women's entry into the legal profession in British Columbia. What difference did the implementation of formal equality and equal opportunity make for women who were admitted to law during the early twentieth century? We conclude that overall, while these pioneer women lawyers hardly transformed the legal profession, their presence did entrench and justify the political decision that gave them entry to it.

A METHODOLOGICAL NOTE

THE STUDY DATA CONSIST of archival documentation, including the Law Society of British Columbia records, media reports, and interviews. Unfortu-

---

[3] Joan Brockman, "Exclusionary Tactics: The History of Women and Visible Minorities in the Legal Profession in British Columbia" in Hamar Foster and John McLaren, eds., *Essays in the History of Canadian Law: British Columbia and the Yukon* (Toronto: Osgoode Society for Canadian Legal History, 1995) at 508 ["Exclusionary Tactics"]; W. Wesley Pue, *Law School: The Story of Legal Education in British Columbia* (Vancouver: UBC Faculty of Law, 1995) [*Law School*]; Dawna Tong, "A History of Exclusion: The Treatment of Racial and Ethnic Minorities by the Law Society of British Columbia in Admissions to the Legal Profession" (1998) 56:2 The Advocate 197; Joan Brockman and Dorothy E. Chunn, "'A New Order of Things': Women's Entry into the Legal Profession in British Columbia" (2002) 60:3 The Advocate 185 ["A New Order of Things"].

[4] We have included two women, Florence Katherine Frost and Viola McCrossan (DeBeck), who began their legal studies before 1930 but were not called until later.

nately, when we began our research in 1995, all of the women lawyers under study were either deceased or unable to participate in an interview. We were thus reliant on interviews with family members, friends, and colleagues to try to flesh out our archival and media data. To locate interviewees, we asked all of the major and local newspapers in the Victoria and Lower Mainland areas to publish a letter describing the project and inviting individuals with information about any of the pioneer women lawyers to contact us. Interviews took place between 1995 and 1998. Each researcher conducted short telephone interviews with informants and both researchers were present for the semi-structured, in-person interviews that were conducted during that time. Most of the interviewees consented to be publicly identified in any papers and publications that come out of the project. Except for instances where the identity of the interviewee is directly relevant to the discussion, however, we have maintained anonymity, providing only the date of the interview.

ENTERING THE LEGAL PROFESSION AFTER FRENCH

ONCE MABEL PENERY FRENCH successfully challenged the Law Society's exclusion of women from the legal profession in British Columbia, those who followed her over the next two decades were able to find articles and begin legal studies. Although we cannot assume that the end of the legal prohibition made it easier for every woman who wished to pursue legal studies after 1912 to do so,[5] our examination of motivation, paths of entry, and experiences of articling and studying suggests that some of the doors were opened for white, middle-, and upper-class women and that "getting in" was less of a concern for them. At the same time, the fact that many of these women articled at a limited number of firms may be an indication that they were not welcomed by some of the men in other firms or by the legal profession in general.[6]

The women who followed French took up legal studies for a variety of reasons. Some had a conscious, articulated love of law or a desire to use law for

---

5 We only know the number of women who were accepted and, of those accepted, the number who completed their legal studies. We do not know the number of women who applied and were not accepted for articling positions between 1912 and 1930.

6 Even in the early 1950s some male lawyers refused to hire women. Professor Pue gives the example of Ian Shaw's statement to Mary Southin, "Well, Miss Southin, I have to tell you we've never had a woman student here and I don't think after talking to my partners we are about to start,": *Law School*, above note 3 at 234–35. Such discrimination was still quite pronounced into the 1970s; see Lynn Smith, Marylee Stephenson, and Gina Quijano, "The Legal Profession and Women: Finding Articles in British Columbia" (1973) 8:1 U.B.C. L. Rev. 137.

positive ends. Janet Gilley (called 1924) loved debating in high school and began her bachelor's program at UBC with the idea of becoming a lawyer when she completed her undergraduate degree. For reasons unknown, she "laid aside her ambition" for a short time, but six months after graduation when pondering her future, she asked herself: "Why not do what I want to do and become a lawyer?"[7] Ann Sutherland (called 1920) was strongly motivated "to do things to help people ... that were the underdog," a goal that "might have brought her into either law or social work."[8] For Kathryn Bradshaw (Reade) (called 1922) it was her parents' friends who "made her feel ... that she was capable of doing anything she wanted to do" that led her into law.[9]

Many of the women in our study did not initially have lawyering in mind as a career option, however. They came into law for other reasons. One was financial. Leonie Lalonde (called 1919) wanted to become a doctor, but her parents could not afford to send her to eastern Canada to study and her more affluent uncles were only willing to finance her education if she studied law. As she later recalled, "[t]hey were both averse to women doctors and they certainly didn't help me."[10] Another motivation for more connected and/or affluent women to pursue legal studies was encouragement from fathers, uncles, and family friends who were lawyers. Mabel Morris (Miller) (called 1927) did not intend to become a lawyer. She wanted to pursue a music career and was offered a full scholarship to the Juilliard School of Music. Because she felt her family needed her in Vancouver, however, she turned down the scholarship and her lawyer father got her a job in a law office. As a result, Morris "saw perhaps that this would be something that she could do, that she would find interesting."[11]

Similarly, Jean Kennedy Whiteside (Drew) (called 1924) grew up surrounded by relatives and family friends who were lawyers and she worked in her father's office.[12] When she decided to study law, he proffered the following

---

7   Dorothy G. Bell, "Vancouver and Westminster Women in the Profession of Law" *Vancouver Province* (1 February 1925) 5 [Bell]. See also Joan Brockman and Dorothy E. Chunn, "'Imagine That! A Lady Going to an Office': Janet Kathleen Gilley" in Constance Backhouse and Jonathan Swainger, eds., *People and Place: Historical Influences on Legal Culture* (Vancouver: UBC Press, 2003) at 153 ["Imagine That!"].
8   Interview #3 by Joan Brockman and Dorothy E. Chunn (4 December 1995).
9   Interview #4 by Brockman and Chunn (17 August 1996) [Interview #4].
10 Interview of Mrs. Leonie Anderson conducted by Mrs. Maryla Waters (February 1979) Tape 1-1 at 8 [Anderson interview]. Interview conducted as part of the Aural History Programme, B.C. Legal History Collection Project, University of Victoria, Faculty of Law; Interview #6 conducted by Brockman and Chunn (16 August 1996) [Interview #6]; *Law School*, above note 3 at 230.
11 Interview #4, above note 9.
12 Telephone interview of Jean Kennedy Whiteside conducted by Brockman (18 June 1998).

advice: "If you are determined to become a lawyer, don't learn to type [or] ... you will be used as a secretary."[13] For Eveleen Seaton (called 1923), who was working in a law office during the First World War, the idea of studying law came as a surprise suggestion from her employer. He urged her to take up legal studies "because if the war keeps on you and I will be the only ones left in the office!"[14]

With respect to entry, the Law Society of British Columbia recognized two main paths to legal qualification during the early twentieth century. The first was to complete a baccalaureate degree and article for three years. The second and more common route into law for both women and men was to article for five years. After 1914, all articling candidates were expected to attend lectures at either the Vancouver Law School (1914–1943) or the Victoria Law School (1914–1923), albeit only at the latter was attendance compulsory and strictly monitored.[15] Of the women in our study with a bachelor's degree, some obtained a B.A. from a university in another Canadian province (Edith Paterson, Ann Sutherland) and the rest graduated from the University of British Columbia after it opened in September 1915 (Kathryn Reade Bradshaw, Janet Gilley, Jean Whiteside).[16] Finding articles was accomplished in three, often overlapping, ways: family connections; women-friendly law firms; and previous employment as a legal secretary or clerk in a law firm or legal department.

Several of the women in our study found articles through family connections. Kathryn Bradshaw articled in her father's office in Victoria and practised there before she was called.[17] Mabel Morris (Miller) began articles with her father, Charles Morris, as principal at the age of seventeen.[18] Women with no relatives who were lawyers living in British Columbia were often able to turn to family friends and acquaintances. Such was the case with Leonie Lalonde, for example; her mother contacted a lawyer she knew who accepted Leonie as an articling student.[19]

Certain law firms were also receptive to women seeking articles. Russell and DuMoulin set a historic and symbolic precedent when Joe Russell agreed to act as principal for Mabel Penery French. The firm engaged five

---

13 Interview #15 conducted by Brockman and Chunn (17 June 1998) [Interview #15].
14 Bell, above note 7.
15 *Law School*, above note 3 at 44–60.
16 The University of British Columbia opened in temporary facilities, moving to its present location after the First World War. See Jean Barman, *The West Beyond the West: A History of British Columbia* (Toronto: University of Toronto Press, 1991) at 193.
17 Interview #7 conducted by Brockman and Chunn (17 August 1996) [Interview #7].
18 Interview #4, above note 9 (16 August 1996).
19 Anderson interview, Tape 1-1, above note 10 at 10.

more women, including Hilda Cartwright (called 1921), before the death of Joe's brother, Finley Russell, in 1939.[20] Similarly, Arthur Whiteside, first cousin to Jean Kennedy Whiteside (Drew) was principal to four other women who began their legal studies before 1930: Gladys Kitchen, Winnifred McKay, Saddie Brown, and Florence Katherine Frost. Janet Gilley articled at another Whiteside firm, (Whiteside, Edmonds and Whiteside) with Henry Lovekin Edmonds as her principal. Leonie Lalonde, the first woman to complete all her legal training in British Columbia (called 1919), articled at a firm in which Bob Smith, son of the feminist Member of the Legislative Assembly, Mary-Ellen Smith, was a partner.[21]

The five-year articling option was a path into the legal profession for many of the women who qualified in the early twentieth century. Quite often these women came into law after first working as a clerk or secretary in a law firm or legal department and then completing articles in the same firm or department. Even women from affluent/connected families that could well have afforded to send them to university chose this path. For instance, Viola DeBeck who came from one of the most prominent families in the province was a secretary to George McCrossan, the corporation counsel, city of Vancouver, and began articles with him as her principal in 1920.[22]

Significantly, however, the option of qualifying without first having to obtain a university degree made it possible for less connected/affluent women to study law. Several women in our study were "working girls" (Mackie, Ringland, Gordon, Seaton) in law firms or legal departments before they decided to apply for articles, sometimes at the suggestion of firm lawyers or others. Mildred Gordon worked in a law office when she was in high school.[23] Her father owned a small business and was a reeve of South Vancouver before it joined Vancouver so the family "definitely had some standing in that community,"[24] but they were not rich and Mildred "had to get out and go to work."[25] Fortunately, the future Mr. Justice David A. MacDonald, who was then a lawyer in the firm, "recognized that she had exceptional brains and ability" and encouraged Mildred to take up law, acting as her principal until he was appointed to the British Columbia Supreme Court.[26]

---

20 *Law School*, above note 3 at 230.
21 Anderson interview, Tape 1-1, above note 10 at 15.
22 "Nos Disparus: Viola McCrossan" (1980) 38 The Advocate 517.
23 Interview #1 conducted by Brockman and Chunn (9 July 1995) [Interview #1]; Interview #2 conducted by Brockman and Chunn (10 July 1995) [Interview #2].
24 Interview #12 conducted by Brockman and Chunn (6 January 1998) [Interview #12].
25 Letter to Brockman and Chunn (14 April 1994); Interview #2, above note 23.
26 Interview #1, above note 23.

The first and second Victoria women to be called came from even more modest middle-class families and also began as clerk/stenographers. Muriel Ringland (Bland) (called 1919) lived with her mother who owned a fancy dress goods store in the city for a time. In 1910 she began working as a stenographer at city hall where F.A. McDiarmid was city solicitor. She continued as his secretary when he went into private practice in 1913 (McDiarmid and McKay) and began articles with him as her principal in 1914 (McDiarmid and Gaban). Similarly, Dorothy Mackie's father started out trying to homestead in Saskatchewan and then moved the family to Victoria where he either managed or possibly had a partnership in a furniture store.[27] She began as a clerk in the legal department of BC Electric, articled there, and became a corporation lawyer.[28]

EXPERIENCES OF ARTICLING AND STUDYING

WE WERE UNABLE TO obtain detailed accounts about the articling experiences of the women in our study, but the little information we have supports the conclusion of others that articling was like a system of "indentured labour" during the early twentieth century in British Columbia.[29] Both women and men endured long hours, low pay, and considerable expense. Of the women in our study, for instance, Leonie Lalonde worked eight hours per day, six days per week, and attended law classes in the evenings. She earned $25 a month as an articling student, but each of her qualifying examinations cost $50 to write. If she had not lived at home and been able to pay for her exams in installments, she would likely not have completed her articles.[30]

While most articling students were exploited, women were subject to sexism as well during their articles and legal education. When Mildred Gordon worked at the Vancouver firm of Bourne and Des Brisay, for instance, the male lawyers completely overloaded her because she was "so thorough"; they used to skip off to Scott's Café and "leave her hours and hours of work."[31] The same informant also asserted that officially Mildred Gordon was second in her graduating law class, but her brothers had told the informant that Mildred was top of her law school class and not given credit for it; "they had to have a man that would be the top . . . it's just pure discrimination."[32]

---

27 Interview #13 conducted by Brockman and Chunn (21 May 1998) [Interview #13].
28 "Nine New Lawyers Called to the Bar" *Daily Colonist* (26 January 1925).
29 *Law School*, above note 3 at 1.
30 Anderson interview, Tape 1-1, above note 10 at 17.
31 Interview #2, above note 23.
32 *Ibid*.

Many of the women who ultimately made it through articles and legal education were probably successful in part because of direct or indirect support from other women. Leonie Lalonde often studied with Bessie Cruickshank and Gladys Kitchen (from New Brunswick)[33] and "always admired Edith Paterson" (called 1916) as a role model.[34] The three women in our study from New Westminster — Jean Whiteside, Janet Gilley, and Sarah ("Pat") Rennie — were lifelong friends and Jean and Janet frequently travelled to Vancouver together to attend law lectures.[35] Likewise, Mildred Gordon and Mabel Morris, who were both called in 1927, had been close friends since elementary school where they vied for the highest grade and they remained friends through their legal studies and over the years.[36]

STAYING IN THE LEGAL PROFESSION AFTER FRENCH

AS GETTING INTO LAW became easier for some women after French, obstacles to staying in the legal profession became the issue. Clearly, there was a high attrition rate among the women called between 1912 and 1930 in British Columbia. Although twenty-four of the thirty-nine women in our study (62 percent) were called to the bar, only eight (20.5 percent) ended up practising for any length of time. Moreover, most of the women who did practise law for longer periods still experienced career interruptions. The reasons for leaving the legal profession permanently or temporarily were ideological and structural. Entrenched ideas about the sex-specific roles of men and women were reflected in a masculinist organization of legal education and practice that seriously disadvantaged women, but which women did not overtly challenge for the most part.

Leaving Law

FOR SOME OF THE women who practised for an abbreviated period, leaving law for good after marriage represented adherence to normative femininity and masculinity.[37] They subscribed to the key assumptions embedded in the

---

33 Anderson interview, Tape 1-1, above note 10 at 30.
34 *Ibid*.
35 "Imagine That!" above note 7 at 158.
36 Interview #4, above note 9 and Interview #10 conducted by Brockman and Chunn (12 July 1997) [Interview #10].
37 In the case of Florence Frost who began articles in 1924, illness delayed her call until 1938 and death ended her fledgling legal career in 1945.

ideology of the traditional nuclear family that women's primary responsibility is the "private" domestic realm of caregiving and housework and that married women, especially those with young children, should not work outside the home. Leonie Lalonde practised law for a mere three years before she married and implemented her philosophy of "husbands come first."[38] As she explained retrospectively, "I wanted to have children so I knew that I was quite sure I wouldn't be doing both, being a good wife and mother and practising. It is more than the average woman could do, really. And I was average."[39] Likewise, Kathryn Bradshaw was called in 1922 and ceased practising after her marriage in 1925, but, according to her daughter, she did not feel that "she was giving up anything when she got married.... [S]he was very much in love with my father and it was a very exciting wonderful thing."[40]

Ironically, both of these women had to generate income later in life and neither returned to law. Widowed in 1953 at the age of 58, Lalonde was not prepared to do the work that would have been required to update her legal knowledge after being out of the legal profession for almost thirty years. Instead, she took in boarders and did other temporary, caregiving work to supplement her survivor's benefits.[41] Similarly, Bradshaw found herself divorced with two children to support in the late 1930s, but she was not qualified to practise law in the United States where she was living and had to remain because of custody arrangements with her ex-husband. Things were "very difficult financially" and she took on typing and boarders until she carved out a new career for herself as a college registrar in California.[42]

In some cases, women who accepted hegemonic ideas about gender roles may still have given up legal practice somewhat reluctantly in response to social pressure related to the expectation that married women stayed at home. Jean Whiteside left law after she married in 1925, only a year after being called, and although she had no children, never returned to practice. As one interviewee put it, "Oh, that's the way it was. You got married, you stopped working."[43] Informally, however, Whiteside continued to give legal advice to people and to help people with estates and wills for the rest of her life.[44] Similarly, Dorothy Mackie, who articled and then worked in the legal department of the BC Electric corporation for four years after being called,

---

38   Interview #6, above note 10.
39   Anderson interview, above note 10, Tape 1-2 at 46.
40   Interview #7, above note 17.
41   Interview #6, above note 10.
42   Interview #7, above note 17.
43   Interview #15, above note 13.
44   Ibid.

"was expected to [and did] resign her position upon her marriage" to Leslie Harmsworth in 1929,[45] but she returned to paid employment as a secretary later in life.[46]

Unlike Whiteside, other women in our study (for example, Paterson, Rennie) who married, but did not have children, continued to practise law after marriage. When asked in 1923 whether she would "renounce your career or cupid," Edith Paterson (called 1916) said she would renounce neither. Twenty-one years later, at the age of 52, she married her law partner of twenty-one years and continued practising.[47]

Moving in and out of Law

PERHAPS PREDICTABLY, THE WOMEN in our study who practised law for any length of time were unmarried (Cartwright, Gilley, Sutherland), married but childless (Paterson, Rennie), or women who left practice and returned to lawyering out of necessity after being widowed or divorced (Gordon, McCrossan, Morris). The legal work that they did usually conformed to gender ideologies with respect to the type of practice and accommodated family responsibilities, including deference to a husband's career and caregiving to children and elders. Virtually all of them had at least one career interruption that took them out of law for a time.

With respect to practice, the women lawyers in our study seem to have experienced more difficulty than did their male counterparts in finding a position in a legal firm. They may have worked at the firm with which they articled for a time after being called, but they tended to end up either as sole practitioners with restricted practices that sometimes made it hard to eke out a living, or they worked with husbands and other relatives. One of the challenges for women lawyers was to convince potential clients that they were as competent as any man. Janet Gilley who was a sole practitioner in New Westminster from 1924 until she retired at the end of 1972, deliberately used only her initials and last name, "J.K. Gilley," in the sign on the door of her office when she began practising in 1925. A journalist, writing about "Vancouver and New Westminster Women in the 'Profession of Law,'" thought there was "nothing unusual" about the sign on the office door until she walked in:

---

45 Letter to Brockman and Chunn, undated.
46 Interview #13, above note 27.
47 "Exclusionary Tactics," above note 3 at 529; Ann Paige, "Base Charge Is Refuted: Professional Women Not Misfits Says Ann" *Vancouver Daily World* (20 May 1923).

> Then both office and sign assume remarkably astonishing connections for they serve, not the masculine master of law that one involuntarily visualizes before entering, but a tall, slight girl with eyes almost black as the straight-bobbed hair — eyes that are wide and studiously quiet with a hint of fun in the corners — eyes that miss nothing in their glance.[48]

Mildred Gordon was probably one of the most successful sole practitioners among the women in our study, both financially and professionally.[49] She practised in Courtenay, BC from 1949 until she sold her practice in the 1970s. Although inundated with work, she could not find anyone she considered suitable to partner with. As one of our interviewees put it, all the possibilities were "either incompetent, mean, or crooked!"[50] Consequently, Mildred worked under unrelenting pressure for her entire career and she had no time even to take on articling students who might have been of assistance.[51]

Competent legal secretaries helped some women maintain a solo practice, however. Janet Gilley and Mildred Gordon both had long-time, loyal secretaries. Gilley clearly maintained a formal relationship with hers. After forty years, they still used "Miss Gilley" and "Mrs. MacLeod" in their office communications, despite the fact that they often spent lunch hours together scouring antique shops in New Westminster.[52] Gordon had more of a "mother-daughter relationship" with her secretary, Ruth Masters, as well as a strong professional partnership.[53] They frequently travelled together and often socialized outside the office.[54]

As with decisions to enter law, ideology and expediency combined to keep most of the early women lawyers out of court work. Some explicitly stated that court work, especially criminal law cases, was not acceptable. Janet Gilley thought, for example, that it was entirely inappropriate to associate with people involved in the criminal justice system and she was quite horrified when one of her nephews acted as a prosecutor for a while; often asking, "Surely you don't want to make a career in criminal law?"[55] For other women, criminal law was

---

48 Bell, above note 7 at 5.
49 See Dorothy E. Chunn and Joan Brockman, "'She Never Did Anything by Halves': Mildred Elizabeth Louise Gordon" (2003) 61 The Advocate 725 ["She Never Did Anything by Halves"].
50 Interview #1, above note 23.
51 Interview #10, above note 36 and Interview #11 conducted by Brockman and Chunn (13 July 1997).
52 "She Never Did Anything by Halves," above note 49.
53 Interviews #1 and #2, above note 23.
54 *Ibid.*
55 Interview #9 conducted by Brockman and Chunn (10 July 1997).

time-consuming and simply did not pay enough. Ann Sutherland was able to specialize in criminal law because her lawyer-brother, John Sutherland, with whom she shared a house and an office, practised corporate law and earned enough money to support both of them.[56] In contrast, Viola DeBeck (McCrossan), who articled with Sutherland, liked criminal law but she was forced to diversify her practice to earn enough money to support herself.[57]

Almost all of the women did the "bread and butter" legal work — wills, estates, probate, and real estate transactions. Mildred Gordon specialized in land work; "she did park documents and covenants and easements and things with a thoroughness that stood the test of time."[58] A number of the women in our study also did family law, mainly divorces (which involved "the private investigator setup").[59] Mabel Miller's "really active legal career, which spanned about twenty years" started shortly after her husband's premature death in 1952. She had carried on his practice throughout his illness and when he died he left her with a divorce case that forced her to appear in court,[60] but shortly thereafter she joined a corporate firm and worked in the area of trusts for the rest of her career.[61] However, she did not go to that firm because she could practise corporate law but rather because her husband had articled there.[62] "And . . . so, one might say that more than seeking that type of law, she fell into it. She also was a very non-confrontational type of person and I think that she felt that she wouldn't be particularly at home in litigation."[63]

Several of the women in our study spent periods of time working as legal research assistants or legal secretaries, usually to accommodate the careers of husbands or other male relatives. According to one informant, Mabel Morris (Miller) was often at her husband's office "assisting" him:[64] "I don't believe she really had clients of her own or had a separate practice at all."[65] When his health declined, Stanley Miller sent a letter to the Law Society of British Columbia, explaining that he paid her fees so that she could carry on the practice if anything happened to him.[66] Similarly, Mildred Gordon worked as

---

56   Interview #8 conducted by Brockman and Chunn (30 June 1997).
57   Interview #14 conducted by Brockman and Chunn (21 May 1998) [Interview #14].
58   Interview #10, above note 36.
59   Ibid.
60   "Lawyer's Widow Appears as Counsel" *Vancouver Sun* (7 February 1953) 5.
61   Interview #4, above note 9.
62   Ibid.
63   Ibid.
64   Letter to Joan Brockman and Dorothy Chunn (22 July 1996).
65   Interview #4, above note 9.
66   Letter from Stanley Miller to the Law Society (24 November 1952), Law Society File M00604, File n. 108-8.

a legal secretary for one of her brothers in the Yukon where she met and married an Episcopalian minister. When they moved to California, she was not qualified to practise law in that jurisdiction and she spent ten years helping him with his work before they divorced.[67] Viola DeBeck left law before being called after she married her principal, George McCrossan, in 1922. She bore three children and resumed work in her husband's office in 1940. He was the city solicitor for the city of Vancouver and for many years she was in charge of special work for the city's legal department but was not officially working as a lawyer.[68]

A number of the women in our study who left law because of conformity to normative femininity or to accommodate the careers of male relatives had to become self-supporting because of a divorce from or death of a husband. As discussed above, some but not all were able to return to legal practice. After ten years out of law, Mildred Gordon returned to Canada "pretty much broke" after her divorce. The Law Society told her she had "all the qualifications," that there was need for a lawyer in the Comox/Courtenay areas on Vancouver Island, and suggested that she set up a practice there. "So she did. I think she borrowed a few hundred dollars from somebody to open her office [in Courtenay]" and resumed practice "in a very, very modest way."[69]

Likewise, the untimely death of her husband transformed Mabel Morris into a single mother with a twelve-year-old daughter at home and "it was necessary for her to ... go back to work."[70] She was "grateful" that she had her training because the thrust of her life had always been her family, "never her career, and ... not because that was forced on her in any way."[71] When she contracted cancer, Morris could not afford to take an extended time off work; she started radiation and resumed work in a month. "Sometimes she would be so weak from the radiation that she would have to lean against the building," but a chaise was put in her office so she could lie down for an hour, which "protected her a little."[72]

For women who did have to support themselves and/or children, not doing court work might have helped to ease the strain of the dual day. A job that was more cut and dried, more nine-to-five, may have been an important factor in helping those who did continue to practise or who dropped out and

---

67 Telephone interview conducted by Chunn (27 June 1997). Interviews #1 and #2, above note 23.
68 Interview #14, above note 57.
69 Telephone interview conducted by Chunn (27 June 1997), above note 67.
70 Interview #4, above note 9.
71 Ibid.
72 Ibid.

returned, to balance lawyering with care responsibilities related to children and parents. Unlike their male counterparts who did not have to endure the dual day, most of the pioneer women who were called had abbreviated careers and those who stayed in law for any length of time did not move up in the profession to the same extent as men. Interestingly, some of the women in our study felt that they did not experience discrimination or that any discrimination was from other women. For others such as Mildred Gordon, "that's the way things were and she didn't make a big issue of it."[73]

FORMAL GENDER EQUALITY AND THE LEGAL PROFESSION

WHAT DIFFERENCE DID WOMEN'S access to the legal profession make? After all, they constituted a mere handful of those who studied, qualified, and practised law in British Columbia during the early twentieth century. Viewed retrospectively, the entry of women to the legal profession in 1912 arguably can be seen as both a pragmatically driven and a symbolically important event. As we have discussed elsewhere, the decision of the Conservative government to override the intransigence of the Law Society and legislate the entry of Mabel French into the profession was intensely political.[74] It was similar to decisions in other jurisdictions that gave women access to the legal profession but also reflected the particular historical and cultural context of the "West beyond the West" during the early twentieth century.[75] Politicians and other elites were fixated on the question of how to build a strong, white settler-society and they feared the growing strength of organized feminism (and socialism) in the province.[76] Feminists and their allies wanted suffrage. Conservatives refused to accede to their demands, but the introduction and enactment of a bill that gave women the right to study and practise law was a strategic move in an election year that probably helped them get re-elected.[77]

Nonetheless, what was purely a pragmatic decision on the part of Conservative politicians had unanticipated consequences. The women who followed Mabel French into the legal profession during the subsequent two decades did help to entrench the idea that women could learn and practise

---

73 Interview #1, above note 23.
74 "A New Order of Things," above note 3 at 387.
75 Jean Barman, *The West Beyond the West: A History of British Columbia* (Toronto: University of Toronto Press, 1991).
76 Ibid. See also Chris Clarkson, *Domestic Reforms: Political Visions and Family Regulation in British Columbia, 1862–1940* (Vancouver: UBC Press, 2007).
77 "A New Order of Things," above note 3 at 385.

law as well as any man. And those who stayed in law for any length of time often left a gendered footprint through their everyday work with clients if not within the profession or on the national stage. Mildred Gordon made house calls, often to provide legal assistance to women who were widowed and had never learned to drive, and in many cases it was *pro bono* work for women who were left with few resources.[78] Ann Sutherland offered similar legal expertise to marginalized women who had been criminally charged with prostitution-related offences and even picked up her clients on the way to court.[79]

In the last analysis, however, there is ample evidence that formal equality in law is a necessary but not sufficient step towards the achievement of inter- and intra-gender equality.[80] As Morgan found, the women who followed Ontario's first women lawyer, Clara Brett Martin, into the legal profession were few in number and legal education at Osgoode Hall was not transformed to reflect the new gender order.[81] Our study findings support Morgan's conclusions. Even symbolically, "masculinism" continued in as much as the language on the Law Society's certificates of accreditation was not changed from "he" to "she" when the recipient was a woman. Indeed, this practice was mentioned by a number of our interviewees. As one put it, "[t]he Law Society couldn't be bothered to make the change."[82] The class and racial tilt of the legal profession in British Columbia was also little changed when women gained access to law. Although some less affluent women were able to article and qualify, all of the twenty-three women called before 1930 and the two who started during that time and were not called until later were white and middle or upper class.

Perhaps most importantly, there was no modification of the male model of legal education and practice to accommodate the lived experiences of women. The worldview of the white, middle-class male was the entrenched "norm" and therefore even white, middle-, and upper-class women (and later

---

78 Interview #1, above note 23.
79 Interview #3, above note 8.
80 See, for example, Carol Smart, *Feminism and the Power of Law* (London: Routledge, 1989); Brenda Cossman and Judy Fudge, eds., *Privatization, Law and the Challenge to Feminism* (Toronto: University of Toronto Press, 2002); Elizabeth Sheehy, ed., *Adding Feminism to Law: The Contributions of Justice Claire L'Heureux-Dubé* (Toronto: Irwin Law, 2004); Fay Faraday, Margaret Denike, and M. Kate Stephenson, *Making Equality Rights Real: Securing Substantive Equality under the Charter* (Toronto: Irwin Law, 2006); Dorothy E. Chunn, Susan B. Boyd, and Hester Lessard, eds., *Reaction and Resistance: Feminism, Law, and Social Change* (Vancouver: UBC Press, 2007).
81 Morgan, "An Embarrassingly and Severely Masculine Atmosphere," above note 2.
82 Interview #2, above note 23. Interviews #5 and #15 conducted on 16 August 1996 and 17 June 1998 respectively, contain the same observation.

racialized men and women) were judged by that standard and the onus fell on them to "be the same as" their male counterparts.[83] This expectation of women meant, of course, that they had to manage the dual burden of lawyering by day and fulfilling their caregiving and other domestic responsibilities after their "real" work was done. As discussed earlier, few did or wanted to do so.

Perhaps not surprisingly, the women who did manage to stay the course were often described by our interviewees as very bright, capable women. One said of "Pat" Rennie: "The thing that impressed me most about her was ... she really was very clever and the way she thought and she was so logical ... she was ... very demanding, she didn't ... suffer fools gladly."[84] In a similar vein, Kathryn Bradshaw's daughter described her mother as "remarkable" and went on to make the general observation that women in law at that time "had to be exceptional ... to be accepted they would have to just be that much better than ... their contemporaries."[85]

The demands of the dual day were, and still are, considerable. One or two of the early women lawyers did meet the challenge, however. "Pat" Rennie, who had wife-work to perform but no children or elders under her care, not only practised law but also worked successfully in the traditionally male domains of the military and law.[86] Other women managed to stay in law by making a trade-off; in order to accommodate their domestic responsibilities they settled for earning a living rather than trying to move up in their profession. Mildred Gordon, for example, had no children, but as the only daughter in her family she had to assume the care of her ailing mother for ten years at the same time that she was trying to build her practice.[87] When approached to apply for a judgeship, she thought it would be a great honour but declined to apply because of work and family responsibilities.[88] Likewise, her close friend, Mabel Morris (Miller), found herself with sole responsibility for a minor child when her husband died. While she made partner in her firm, she

---

83 A similar finding was made by Mary Jane Mossman in her study of first women lawyers around the world. Most of the women realized that they had to accept law on "the same terms as men" preventing them from challenging the formidable male culture that existed and excluded them from many aspects of practice; *The First Women Lawyers*, above note 1 at 281–84.
84 Interview #16 conducted by Brockman and Chunn (11 August 1998) [Interview #16].
85 Interview #7, above note 17.
86 Interview #16, above note 84.
87 Interview #1, above note 24.
88 Interview #2, above note 23.

turned down all offers that would have allowed her to "move up" in the legal profession or in public life — for instance, to a judicial or political position.[89]

Clearly, the demands of the dual day still control many women (and some men) entering the legal profession in the current context who cannot or will not fit themselves into work structures that are still reflective of the historically male mould of legal education and practice.[90] Like the pioneer women-lawyers discussed in this paper, their contemporary counterparts often feel as if they are stepping "into the rough of things," albeit in a different way and in a different time.[91]

---

89 Interview #4, above note 9.
90 See, for example, Margaret Thornton, *Dissonance and Distrust: Women in the Legal Profession* (New York: Oxford University Press, 1996); Joan Brockman, *Gender in the Legal Profession: Fitting or Breaking the Mould* (Vancouver: UBC Press, 2001); Jean Leiper, *Bar Codes: Women in the Legal Profession* (Vancouver: UBC Press, 2006); Elizabeth Sheehy and Sheila McIntyre, *Calling for Change: Women, Law, and the Legal Profession* (Ottawa: University of Ottawa Press, 2006).
91 As Jean Whiteside, one of the women in our study, stated in a 1925 interview, "[W]omen are not accustomed to getting out into the rough of things for themselves and it is going to take much to overcome that weakness but it will come." Bell, above note 7 at 5.

APPENDIX A: WOMEN CALLED TO THE BAR IN BRITISH COLUMBIA 1912–1930, BY YEAR OF CALL

1912   French, Mabel Penery

1916   Paterson, Edith Louise (Read)

1918   Kitchen, Gladys

1919   Lalonde, Leonie Cathrine
       Ringland, Muriel Lina (Bland)

1920   Cruickshank, Lilian Elizabeth
       Sutherland, Christy Ann

1921   Cartwright, Hilda Sophia
       Agar, Annie Jane

1922   Bradshaw, Kathryn Reade
       McKay, Jessie Evelyn Winnifred

1923   Watson, Bessie Lamont
       Seaton, Eveleen Eunice
       Beck, Marion Elma

1924   Gilley, Janet Kathleen
       Whiteside, Jean Kennedy (Drew)

1925   Mackie, Dorothy Maude
       Rennie, Sarah (Curtis)

1926   Brown, Saddie

1927   Morris, Mabel Irene (Miller)
       Gordon, Mildred Elizabeth Louise
       Dunsmore, Barbara Robertson

1930   Crane, Hazel Victoria

1938   Frost, Florence Katherine, started in 1924

1953   McCrossan, Viola Vivan (DeBeck), trained 1917–1920

APPENDIX B: WOMEN WHO ENROLLED BETWEEN 1912 AND 1930, BUT WERE NEVER CALLED TO THE BAR

Bristow, Ethia May: Vancouver; enrolled 22 March 1920; principal: William Joseph Baird.

Burne, Mary Evelyn: Kelowna (Mat. University of Toronto); enrolled 1921; principal: Edwin Clyde Weddell.

Chalmers, Annie Jean: Vancouver; enrolled 1928; principal: Matthys Adolph Van Roggen.

Copping, Muriel D: Vancouver; examined 8 December 1913.

Elliott, Jessie Bruce: Vancouver (B.A. McGill); enrolled 8 December 1919; principals: Henry Irvine Bird; J.B.H. Shoebotham 1920.

Ewen, Blanche Chris: Vancouver; 8 December 1919.

Grant, Muriel Helena: New Westminster (Mat. UBC); enrolled 28 December 1922; principal: J.P. Grant.

Horn, Laira Maurine: Vancouver; enrolled 11 December 1922; principal: J.A. Russell.

Strangland, Louella Margaret: New Westminster (B.A. UBC); enrolled 8 December 1930; principal: David Whiteside.

Tolmie, Carolyn May: Victoria (Mat. UBC); enrolled 11 December 1922; principal: John Ronald Green.

Turner, Jean Fay: Nelson (B.A., Toronto); enrolled October 1924; principal: Hilda S. Cartwright.

Wallace, Janet May: Victoria (Mat. UBC); enrolled June 1927; principal: Harold Arthur Beckwith.

Weinberg, Jeanette: Vancouver (B.A., UBC); enrolled December 1927; enrolled again in 1930; principal: Arthur Howard Fleishman.

Wooler, Effie Lovice: Victoria (B.A., Toronto); enrolled 5 September 1917; principal: G.H. Barnard.

Source: Law Society Fonds, Students' Roll Book 1880–1941, Vancouver, Legal Archives of British Columbia (File 355-2).

CHAPTER 14

"A Revolution in Numbers": Ontario Feminist Lawyers in the Formative Years 1970s to the 1990s

CONSTANCE BACKHOUSE*

THE TORONTO *GLOBE & MAIL* called it a "heated exchange," and an "ugly lecture room row."[1] On 14 November 1977, the bar admission class at Osgoode Hall erupted into unprecedented protest as women students took heated issue with sexist course materials distributed during the final stage of their professional licensing examinations. Albert Strauss, a well-known real estate lawyer with more than twenty years of practice under his belt, was lecturing to a class of several hundred students that morning, in a course called "Law Office Administration."[2] The topic was legal secretaries. His written text advised new lawyers to post "help wanted" ads: "[Seeking] a beautiful, young and confidential secretary .... Unless very beautiful, you should be able to take short-hand on machine dictation ... you should be a whiz at making

---

* I am indebted to my research assistants: Megan Reid, Sabina Mok, and Carly Stringer, for their help. I am also indebted to the University of Ottawa, the Law Foundation of Ontario, the Social Sciences and Humanities Research Council of Canada, the Bora Laskin Human Rights Fellowship, the Jules and Gabrielle Léger Fellowship, and the Trudeau Fellowship, for financial assistance.
1 Margaret Mironowicz, "Bar Admission Students Snap at Bra Remark, 'Sexist Text'" Toronto *Globe & Mail* (15 November 1977) 16 [Mironowicz].
2 Albert A. Strauss was called to the Ontario bar in 1956 and practised as the managing partner of the Strauss & Cooper law firm from 1956 to 1995, where he specialized in real estate law. From 1995 to 1998, he served as in-house counsel for the Lawyers' Professional Indemnity Company. He received a CBAO Distinguished Service Award in 1988, a Law Society Medal in 1991, and an Award for Excellence in Real Property from the CBAO in 2001. See Canadian Bar Association — Ontario News Release "CBAO Recognizes Albert Strauss as Recipient of 2001 Award for Excellence in Real Property" (1 February 2001).

good coffee ...." The text included pointers about ways to get "extra hours out of office staff free of overtime pay."

A group of women students had arrived to class early that morning, and seated themselves in the front row. As the lecture began, they peppered Albert Strauss with questions about what they critiqued as "sexist" and "manipulative" course content. A heavyset, gruff-looking man with stooped shoulders and bushy eyebrows, Strauss stood his ground, refusing to concede any point. One woman stood up, strode down to the instructor's podium, ripped the offending pages out of her loose-leaf text, and threw them into a dustbin near the front door as she exited the room. Strauss called out: "[Y]ou can send [the pages] back along with your brassieres.... Or any other garment." The room exploded into laughter and hissing as uneasy students tried to determine which side to take. Another female student followed, tossing her pages onto Strauss's lectern as she exited. "I guess she's not wearing a bra," Strauss exclaimed. Marilou McPhedran, a twenty-six-year-old bar ad student, commandeered Strauss's microphone to register a formal protest. "This is a very questionable approach as to how to treat legal secretaries," she asserted, adding that the attitude of the instructor was "inexcusable."[3]

The class split into factions, with some "appalled" by Strauss's comments and others opposed to the "confrontational" tactics of the women.[4] More women and a few men voted with their feet as they quit the classroom. When Strauss followed, he was surrounded by a group of angry students demanding an apology. He refused, later justifying his position with some rancour:

> If you're going to be destructive and sarcastic and critical, then you've got to be able to take it as well as give it out. When you get a student who tears up paper and throws it in your face, I don't think that's very constructive. If these people are going to be lawyers, well, good luck to them. I've got better things to do for the lousy pennies I get than to take abuse.[5]

The incident might have ended there, except that two women bar admission students, Diana Majury and I, decided to call the press. Together we walked over to the barristers' lounge at the courthouse to use the free phone. Diana Majury's recollection is that although we had no permission to be in the barristers' lounge, we wanted to save the dime for the phone call and to have a bit more

---

3   Mironowicz, above note 1.
4   Carole Curtis recalls that the majority of the men in the audience were "totally allied with Strauss, with what he said and how he behaved." She recollects that McPhedran became the "flashpoint," characterized as "hysterical." Interview with Carole Curtis (6 July 2007) in Toronto.
5   Mironowicz, above note 1.

privacy. Mostly, however, she recalls it as "part of the act of rebellion — claiming space." Thinking back, she mused: "How appropriate it was to have launched the press from inside the male barristers' lounge!"[6] My recollection is that I took on the role of alerting the press because some years earlier I had worked for one of Ralph Nader's public interest law firms in Washington, D.C., where I had watched American lawyers skilled at handling press strategies. I phoned a young female reporter at the *Globe and Mail*, whose byline I had been following for some time, and who I thought might be supportive of feminist issues, and told her about the story. Reporter Margaret Mironowicz was amazed to learn that the entire debacle could be viewed that afternoon on the videotape that was used to teach the overflow half of the bar admission students.[7]

Mironowicz agreed to come down to Osgoode Hall and observe the fracas first-hand.[8] Reminiscing, Diana Majury said she could still visualize making that phone call: "I was just awestruck that you did it, and that she was going to come. It was unbelievable to me that we would get media coverage, and that you seemed to just assume we would get it, and that it happened. In those days they liked those stories!"[9] Reflecting further on why we were successful with the press, she added:

> I guess we were seen as a novelty... we were seen as hip. The men who cat-called in that room would have been seen as the losers, not us. That's why the press was sympathetic. It was the energetic, bright young women who were leading in a way people wanted to go. You might feel sorry for Strauss but he did represent the old school that was stuck, boring, resistant. We were the new wave.[10]

---

6   Interview with Diana Majury (10 July 2007) Lumsden, Saskatchewan.
7   Unbeknownst to us, the bar admission director had met with his staff over lunch to discuss whether to play the video that afternoon or yank it. In the end, they chose to let Strauss make a second in-person appearance, and then replayed the lecture on video.
8   Reflecting on the event recently, Margaret Mironowicz wrote:

> The whole episode of Albert Strauss setting off that feminist storm in his lecture room was a classic example of how everything was ready to explode at that time. Clark Davey [the managing editor of the *Globe and Mail*] wanted the women's stories on the front page, and as the Seventies unrolled, and women's issues became everyone's issues, for the first time in everyone's lives in Canada, it was simply the job of the newspaper to not just keep abreast of issues, but to lead the way. My own consciousness truly did not know what to make of this new world, as I ran to record it. Now, I can see... that we were all part of something huge that has swept the planet over the past 30 years. My part was to have had the privilege of reporting on it, and having contact with such feminist brains.

(from e-mail correspondence to the author from Margaret Mironowicz (13 and 18 August 2007)).
9   Interview with Diane Majury, above note 6.
10 *Ibid.*

The headline the *Globe and Mail* editors attached to the article, "Bar Admission Students Snap at Bra Remark, 'SexistText,'" was less than auspicious and probably pleased neither Mironowicz, the feminist students, nor the Law Society. But the article itself was outstanding. Mironowicz cited all of the sexist passages from Strauss's text and quoted several of the protesters, including Beth Symes, who stated that the materials were "more than just in bad taste" especially at a time when "new lawyers were being forced to set up their own practices because of the tight job market." Barbara Jackman was quoted as "really surprised" to find "this kind of stuff" in the course. Jeff House, a supportive male student, added that another instructor had given them "pointers on how to do well in the trial situation," by "hiring an articling student with, excuse me but this is how he put it, with big tits and getting her sitting right up there close to the jury." Contacted for his comments, Strauss remained intransigent. "I don't propose to take a public platform and grovel," was his last word.[11]

The spectacle took on more visibility when NDP opposition leader Stephen Lewis stepped into the fray. Speaking to reporters outside the legislature the next day, Lewis characterized Strauss's behaviour as "sexist and worthy of an 11-year-old." Lewis added that Strauss "simply should not be teaching such a class." In the face of the escalating pressures, Albert Strauss was forced to reconsider. Accompanied by bar admission director George Collins-Williams, he returned to class the next morning and explained that he had meant the remarks "in a light-hearted way" but now realized that this had been "hurtful." He did not actually equate the text or his comments with "sexism," but he promised to "review" the material in the future.[12]

The "Albert Strauss affair" was one of the first public manifestations of the confrontation between the growing force of the second-wave feminist movement and the legal profession in Ontario. Some women lawyers may have identified with feminism decades earlier, but prior to the 1970s, most embraced a "primary identity as *lawyers*, ungendered." As Mary Jane Mossman characterized it, women lawyers from earlier generations seem to have preferred to "eschew connections with the women's movement in favour of

---

11 Mironowicz, above note 1.
12 "Law Lecturer Apologizes to Students" Toronto *Globe & Mail* (16 November 1977) 15. Several letters to the editor followed. Nanci Nickle from West Hill wrote on 22 November 1977 to suggest that if Strauss had "better things to do for the lousy pennies" perhaps he should consider working "at a brassiere factory." John Swaigen wrote the same day to point out that sexist comments had been made when he was a student at the bar ad in 1974, and that previous complaints had been "swept under the rug": "Law Students" Toronto *Globe & Mail* (22 November 1977) 7.

strictly professional identities."[13] Then, as Supreme Court of Canada Judge Rosalie Abella has dubbed it, there was a "revolution in numbers."[14] While the number of male law students across Canada doubled between 1962 and 1980, female law students increased twenty-four times.[15] A critical mass of women was entering law, and the new women had very definite ideas of how the profession should change to accommodate the new gender realities.

The context of the era gave an incendiary impetus to the swelling numbers of women in law. The week before the bar admission protest, American feminist Charlotte Bunch had addressed a full auditorium at the University of Toronto's Innis College, demanding a "radical restructuring of the whole patriarchal order." Nellie's battered women's shelter in Toronto was clamouring for funding. Girls were fighting for the right to play hockey. Letters to the editor bemoaned sexist humour in the *Globe and Mail*'s daily feature "Your Morning Smile." Rape crisis workers in London, Ontario were expressing outrage over police-sponsored educational films that advised women "not to resist" sexual attackers, a message they complained was dangerously incorrect. November 5th had witnessed a dramatic "national day of protest" against violence against women, with hundreds of women marching along Yonge Street. That night demonstrators were arrested for disrupting traffic in front of a Toronto cinema that was showing a "snuff film," depicting the sexualized murder of female actresses. Toronto columnist Dick Beddoes responded with vitriol, harping about the "shrill women" whose tactics he labeled "tunnel-visioned flailing at the world." He ventured that their "crusade against violence" might "emasculate men." Joanne Kates's column in the *Globe and Mail* summed it up more positively: the women's movement was "up on its feet and marching."[16]

---

13   Mary Jane Mossman, *The First Women Lawyers: A Comparative Study of Gender, Law and the Legal Profession* (Oxford: Hart, 2006) at 21 [Mossman]. An example of a woman who was clearly an exception to this generalization was Margaret Hyndman, whose trailblazing work on behalf of women distinguished her remarkable legal career. Even she, however, was reluctant to take on a gendered identity. She was quoted in 1949 in *Maclean's* in McKenzie Porter, "The Legal Lady" *Maclean's* 62:14 (15 July 1949) at 15, 22–24: "Only the fact that I am a lawyer matters. That I am a woman is no consequence."
14   As quoted in Mossman, *ibid.* at 10.
15   Mossman, *ibid.* at 2, quoting Canadian Bar Association, *Touchstones for Change: Equality, Diversity and Accountability — The Report on Gender Equality in the Legal Profession* (Ottawa: Canadian Bar Association, 1993) at 25; D.A.A. Stager with H.W. Arthurs *Lawyers in Canada* (Toronto: University of Toronto Press, 1990) at 159–60 [*Lawyers in Canada*].
16   "Your Morning Smile" Toronto *Globe & Mail* (2 November 1977) 1; "Board Halts Film Giving Rape Advice" Toronto *Globe & Mail* (15 November 1977) 16; "Letters to the Editor: Sexist Jokes" Toronto *Globe & Mail* (15 November 1977) 6; Dick Beddoes

SECOND-WAVE FEMINISM AND THE SCOPE OF THIS STUDY

AS AUSTRALIAN FEMINIST WRITER Dale Spender has noted, as long as there has been sexist oppression, there have been feminist resisters.[17] However, there have been certain decades when the feminist movement has emerged with exceptional power, clarity, and cohesion. Historians have characterized the women's movement that developed in the late 1960s and 1970s as a "second wave" of feminism, the strongest showing of forces for gender equality since the "first wave" of feminist suffrage and temperance advocates held forth in the late nineteenth and early twentieth centuries.[18] The second wave manifested itself across a wide spectrum, as women demanded equal opportunities in electoral politics, education, the media, the family, health and welfare, the labour market, sports, and the arts.[19] The history of the second

---

"Shrill Women Getting Worse" Toronto *Globe & Mail* (16 November 1977) 8; Joanne Kates "Snuffing Snuff" Toronto *Globe & Mail: Fanfare* (16 November 1977) 8; "Girls in Hockey" Toronto *Globe & Mail* (16 November 1977) 7.

17 Dale Spender, *Women of Ideas and What Men Have Done to Them* (London: Routledge & Kegan Paul, 1982) at 7.

18 For an introduction into the literature regarding the genesis and nature of both first and second waves of the Canadian women's movement, see Alison Prentice *et al.*, *Canadian Women: A History* (Toronto: Harcourt Brace Jovanovich, 1988). See also the Clio Collective, *Quebec Women: A History* (Toronto: Women's Press, 1987). The release in 1970 of the Report of the Royal Commission, *The Status of Women in Canada* (Ottawa: Information Canada, 1970) is often taken as a marker for the commencement of the second wave. The genesis for this renewed wave of feminism has been attributed in part to the sexism embedded in the hippie counterculture and anti-Vietnam war movements that had swept North America in the 1960s.

19 For some description of the wider second wave Canadian feminist movement, see Angela Miles and Geraldine Finn, *Feminism in Canada: From Pressure to Politics* (Montreal: Black Rose Books, 1982); Maureen Fitzgerald, Connie Guberman, and Margie Wolfe, *Still Ain't Satisfied: Canadian Feminism Today* (Toronto: Women's Press, 1982); Penney Kome, *The Taking of Twenty-Eight: Women Challenge the Constitution* (Toronto: Women's Press, 1983); Roberta Hamilton and Michele Barrett, *The Politics of Diversity: Feminism, Marxism and Nationalism* (Montreal: Book Center, 1986); Jeri Dawn Wine and Janice L. Ristock, *Women and Social Change: Feminist Activism in Canada* (Toronto: James Lorimer, 1988); Nancy Adamson, Linda Briskin, and Margaret McPhail, *Feminist Organizing for Change: The Contemporary Women's Movement in Canada* (Toronto: Oxford University Press, 1988); Peta Tancred-Sheriff, ed., *Feminist Research: Prospect and Retrospect* (Montreal: McGill-Queen's University Press, 1988); Sandra Burt, Lorraine Code, and Lindsay Dorney, eds., *Changing Patterns: Women in Canada* (Toronto: McClelland & Stewart, 1988); Constance Backhouse and David H. Flaherty, *Challenging Times: The Women's Movement in Canada and the United States* (Montreal: McGill-Queen's University Press, 1992); Linda Carty, ed., *And Still We Rise: Feminist Political Mobilizing in Contemporary Canada* (Toronto: Women's Press, 1993); Gayle

wave has yet to be fully researched and written, but there has been even less exploration of how second-wave feminism flowered within the legal profession.[20] This article is my first attempt to begin to chronicle some of that history for Ontario.

Many questions need to be explored. What factors facilitated the creation of a "wave" of Ontario feminist lawyers during these years? Why did so many feminists choose law as their profession? How did law schools and the legal profession react to their presence? How did feminists attempt to reshape legal education and the practice of law to accommodate their needs? How did their feminism influence the law reform projects they undertook? The feminist lawyers from this era appear to have worked "collectively" on many projects, with overlapping relationships and activities that created a powerful "cohort" situated to demand change. Why and how did that happen? What was it like to be a feminist in law during these decades? Did feminist lawyers exercise a disproportionate influence upon the wider Canadian feminist movement and, if so, was this beneficial or problematic? Did their efforts produce documented change?

For the purposes of this article, I am using a very broad definition of "feminism" to encompass a politics that has the capacity to recognize gender inequality, analyze the problems that result, and work for change. Philosophers have distinguished between many strands of feminism, including liberal feminism, socialist feminism, radical feminism, cultural feminism, ecofeminism, and postmodern feminism, among others. I would include all of these within my understanding of feminism. I also recognize that gender cuts across boundaries of race, class, ethnicity, religion, language, sexual identity, and disability. Activists who seek equality on these other critical forefronts, who recognize that gender equality is also a serious variable in the pursuit of social justice, would fit within my expansive definition of feminism as well.

This research is based upon forty-five interviews with women who graduated from law school after 1970.[21] Although the focus is on their activities in On-

---

MacDonald, Rachel L. Osborne, and Charles C. Smith, eds., *Feminism, Law, Inclusion: Intersectionality in Action* (Toronto: Sumach Press, 2005); Judy Rebick, *Ten Thousand Roses: The Making of a Feminist Revolution* (Toronto: Penguin, 2005).

20 Little has been written on the Canadian history of feminist lawyers, although there is an extensive literature on the wider question of the status of women lawyers within the Canadian profession. The early publications dealt primarily with gender exclusively, while later research began to incorporate more diversity issues such as race, ethnicity, and other variables. For examples, see Appendix B.

21 Thirty-two (71 percent) graduated between 1970 and 1979. Twelve (27 percent) graduated between 1980 and 1988. One (2 percent) who went to law school as a mature student and whose age puts her within this same cohort, graduated in 1993.

tario, the interviewees migrated to central Canada from a remarkable diversity of regions across Canada and beyond.[22] Some no longer live in Ontario, but all were active in feminist legal work in Ontario during portions of the thirty-year period, from a number of locations: Toronto, Ottawa, Kingston, Hamilton, London, Windsor, Sudbury, and Manitoulin Island. Thirty-nine (87 percent) would self-define as "white," while six (13 percent) would define as African-Canadian, Japanese-Canadian, Chinese-Canadian, or Aboriginal.

All would place themselves within the definition of feminism I have outlined above, and all have devoted large portions of their careers and lives to feminist legal work over the last thirty years. The forty-five women represent only a small cross section of the much larger community, selected to illustrate the range of the cohort with respect to geographic distribution, career paths, and intersectional diversity based on class, ethnicity, race, age, linguistic heritage, disability, and sexual identity. The number of interviews could have been multiplied ten times or more, and still I would not have begun to tap the depth of the feminist legal community. I have been part of this feminist legal community from the 1970s, as an activist, a writer, and a law professor, and have been personally involved in some of the work described by the interviewees and so have taken the liberty of adding my own voice to the data.[23]

The feminist lawyers in this sample have had extraordinary lives that exemplify the remarkable range of careers that legal credentials can offer those who seek to change the world. One practises law as a sole practitioner on M'Chigeeng Reserve on Manitoulin Island; another practises out of her home basement. Some have practised in small all-female firms. Others have practised in small mixed-gender firms, midsized firms, and megafirms on Bay Street. Their areas of practice include family law, labour and employment law,

---

22 They were born in Fredericton, Montreal, Sherbrooke, Arvida, Sudbury, Blind River, Ottawa, Perth, Kingston, Peterborough, Toronto, Hamilton, London, St. Thomas, Windsor, Winnipeg, Neepawa, Wolseley and North Battleford, Lethbridge, Detroit (Michigan), Urbana and Evanston (Illinois), Belfast (Northern Ireland), Bombay (India), Graz (Austria), and Christchurch (New Zealand).

23 The list of interviewees follows: M. Elizabeth Atcheson, Constance Backhouse, Nancy L. Backhouse, Beverley Baines, Susan Boyd, Margaret Buist, Emily Carasco, Mary Cornish, Andrée Coté, Carole Curtis, Brettel Dawson, Linda Silver Dranoff, Mary Eberts, Marlys Edwardh, Susan Elliott, Susan Eng, Mary Lou Fassel, Shelley Gavigan, Phyllis Gordon, Shirley Greenberg, Susan Hare, Patricia Hennessy, Barbara Jackman, Martha Jackman, Frances Kiteley, Kathleen Lahey, Diana Majury, Peggy Mason, Judith McCormack, Elizabeth McIntyre, Marilou McPhedran, Maureen McTeer, Renate Mohr, Patricia Monture, Maryka Omatsu, Kim Pate, Jane Pepino, Denise Réaume, Harriet Sachs, Joanne St. Lewis, Elizabeth Sheehy, Elizabeth Shilton, Beth Symes, Susan Vella, Geraldine Waldman. I am greatly indebted to these women, who were uniformly generous and flexible in scheduling the interviews despite the many demands on their time.

immigration and refugee law, Aboriginal law, administrative and constitutional law, civil litigation, tax law, municipal law, criminal law, human rights law, disability law, feminist law, and general practice. Some have worked for the federal and provincial governments in litigation, management, and policy analysis in domestic and international capacities. One has served as an ambassador to the United Nations.

A number have become legal academics, teaching in law schools, interdisciplinary departments of law, sociology, and native studies. One worked in-house for a university. Some have run community legal clinics, others have run for political office (NDP as well as Progressive Conservative), and still others have headed feminist and social welfare advocacy organizations. Several have served as Law Society benchers, and one achieved the highest position in the bar when she was elected as Treasurer of the Law Society of Upper Canada. One has left law to become a novelist, another to pursue art-making; one has become a feminist philanthropist, and a few have retired. Some were appointed as adjudicators and chairs of administrative tribunals, and others have sat as judges on the Ontario Court of Justice and the Superior Court of Justice.

This paper represents only the preliminary stage of this research and is limited to examining how these women came to decide to become lawyers and the multiple influences that shaped their feminist politics. Although all have consented to be quoted by name, I have chosen to attach names to the quotations only rarely, when the particular events being chronicled involved specific women whose identity is important to the public record. Otherwise, I have used quotations without identifying interviewees by name because many women experienced similar things, and their analysis was often interconnected. In the main, this is a *collective history*.

A "WAVE" OF FEMINIST LAWYERS

IS IT ACCURATE TO describe the Ontario feminist lawyers as constituting a "wave" between the 1970s and the 1990s, in a force and strength that has been unparalleled before or since? All the interviewees agreed that the size of the feminist legal community was unprecedented, a point that is hard to debate given the small number of women called to the bar prior to 1970. There was not universal agreement with the proposition that the community has ebbed in strength after 2000, but none disagreed with the characterization of feminist lawyers as a "wave" during the thirty years under examination. Asked why and how the "wave" came to be, the women offered a number of observations.

First, they spoke to the "revolution in numbers," the fact that previous women lawyers had constituted only a "sprinkling," whereas the 1970s began to see women entering the profession in dramatically increasing numbers, offering women the first opportunity to come together as a cohesive group. At the end of the Second World War in 1945, only 3.7 percent of those called to the Ontario bar were female. By 1960, this figure had dropped to 3 percent. In 1970, the number had inched up only to 4.3 percent. By 1975, marked progress was discernible, with women reaching an unprecedented 10.4 percent. Numbers rose steadily thereafter, reaching 27.2 percent in 1980, 36.8 percent in 1985, 39.8 percent in 1990, 47.6 percent in 1995, and 48.4 percent in 2000 (for full data, see Appendix A).[24]

Several interviewees also stressed, conversely, that it was an important factor that the 1970s and 80s never saw complete gender parity in the law schools, something that did not come until the 1990s.[25] They described their cohort of women as "a critical mass" but not a "majority." "There weren't so many of us that we got washed away in a sea of women lawyers," noted one. "We knew who we were, we knew who our comrades-in-arms were; there was a way in which you could be more cohesive." Another said: "The mission was fueled by our minority status. We were beleaguered by that minority status, but not so beleaguered that you could just barely keep body and soul together." Still another described it as a situation where "we had a combination of people with the same orientation and a growing momentum, but there were not so many of us as to make it unmanageable or impossible to coordinate. It was in many ways the perfect storm."

Some added that it was also relevant that women still felt somewhat anomalous in law school. "We were the group that was referred to as 'lawyer-

---

24 The data in Appendix A were specially compiled by Susan Lewthwaite, Research Coordinator, Corporate Records and Archives, Law Society of Upper Canada for this research. Earlier research has cited inconsistent statistics, and Susan Lewthwaite took this opportunity to run programs from member databases and barristers rolls, double-checking every individual where gender was not apparent from the name. It would appear that these numbers are the definitively accurate Ontario figures. The wider Canadian data show higher percentages of women, largely due to the fact that the Quebec civil law profession saw its female component increase earlier than the common law provinces. In 1945, 4.4 percent of the law students in Canada were female; in 1960 5.1 percent; in 1970 12.7 percent; in 1980 38.2 percent; and in 1985 45.7 percent. See Statistics Canada, *Survey of Higher Education and Universities: Enrolment and Degrees*, cited in *Lawyers in Canada*, above note 15 (Toronto: University of Toronto Press, 1990) Table 4.3 at 96–97.
25 John Hagan and Fiona Kay, *Gender in Practice: A Study of Lawyers' Lives* (New York: Oxford University Press, 1995) at 11; Brian M. Mazer, "An Analysis of Gender in Admission to the Canadian Common Law Schools from 1985–86 to 1994–95" (1997) 20 Dal. L.J. 135.

ettes.' We stuck out like sore thumbs. Going to law school wasn't what women did then." Several contrasted that to today, where a woman's decision to go to law school has become "a choice like any other." "Most of the women we went to law school with went because we wanted to change the world, to rearrange where women fit." "Thinking of law school as a woman in the 1970s was such an unusual aspiration that it set you apart. We were serious people. We knew we were different and special." One noted that second-wave feminism was still so novel that everything we did gave us a sense of "being the first" to advocate for specified changes. "We were the first large group in law. We knew we were just there by the skin of our teeth. Five years earlier, we couldn't have done any of it. That gave us a sense of both belonging and of being new. There was a feistiness about being there."

Although not all of the interviewees agreed, many believe that the wave slowed in speed sometime during the 1990s. A number noted that the discrimination women experience now is "subtler," and "harder to pinpoint." One added:

> The gender barriers hit us in the face more directly, like, for example, being sexually harassed by a senior male counsel, or hearing ignorant statements in law school from male profs, or having people tell you that you're not going to be a serious lawyer because you're a woman. Today, the barriers are just that much more underground, and it takes longer to realize what is happening, to understand the causation.

"Few women today have the same experience we did of sitting in a room with our mouths hanging open at the level of sexism being displayed," observed one. Another suggested that the feminist work now is "harder, picking up the shards and ruins of the work we did, restoring and repairing in a social and economic climate that is harsher than ours was."

A necessary part of the creation of a wave of feminist lawyers is also that there be sufficient women who identify as feminist. I asked the interviewees how they came to identify with feminism, the politics that combined with the unprecedented numbers to create a movement. Some defined themselves as feminist from a very young age, while others did not so identify until university years. Some who described themselves as "late bloomers" did not adopt feminist politics until several years after they finished their professional education. Some came into the women's movement after they had spent time on the left, in socialist and Marxist-Leninist circles, in the student revolution, in communes, in the American civil rights movement, the Black power movement and other anti-racist activism, French-language rights work, and from the lesbian community. Several ascribed their feminism to the influence of their families — often their grandmothers, mothers, or sisters. Many learned about feminism through subscriptions to feminist periodicals such as *Ms Magazine,* and the Canadian counterparts like *Broadside, Upstream, Women Heathsharing.* One spoke about the importance of the very name, *Ms Magazine*: "Ms was a real breakthrough for me. I hated being 'Miss.' 'Ms' made it easy to identify as a feminist, to insist on it." Most spoke about reading the books of the brilliant French, American, Australian, and English writers of the 1970s and 80s.[26] "There was a very visible feminist leadership that I think galvanized the wave," said one.

A number spoke about discovering feminism through the work of the wider anti-violence movement, as they learned about sexual assault, battering, sexual harassment, child sexual abuse, prostitution, and pornography. Others became converted in consciousness-raising groups, or through programs run by women's organizations like the YWCA, which addressed women's job skills, career planning, and family breakdown. Some started in the reproductive rights movement, working for access to birth control and abortion. One ascribed her feminism to the influence of powerful nuns who pressed their young students in Catholic girls' schools to excel, while another

---

26 Books mentioned included Simone de Beauvoir, *The Second Sex* (New York: Alfred E. Knopf, 1952); Betty Friedan, *The Feminine Mystique* (New York: Dell, 1963); Kate Millett, *Sexual Politics* (Garden City, NY: Doubleday, 1970); Germaine Greer, *The Female Eunuch* (London: Paladin, 1970); Shulamith Firestone, *The Dialectic of Sex* (New York: Morrow, 1970); Robin Morgan, *Sisterhood Is Powerful* (New York: Vintage, 1970); and *Going Too Far* (New York: Vintage, 1978); Susan Brownmiller, *Against Our Will: Men, Women and Rape* (New York: Simon and Schuster, 1973); Andrea Dworkin, *Our Blood: Prophecies and Discourse on Sexual Politics* (New York: Harper and Row, 1976) and *Right Wing Women* (New York: Perigee, 1983); Mary Daly, *Gyn/Ecology: The Metaethics of Radical Feminism* (Boston: Beacon Press, 1978); Gloria Steinem, *Outrageous Acts and Everyday Rebellions* (New York: Holt, Rinehart & Winston, 1983); Marilyn Frye, *The Politics of Reality* (Freedom, CA: Crossing Press, 1983); Angela Y. Davis, *Women, Race and Class* (New York: Vintage, 1983); Audre Lorde, *Sister Outsider* (Trumansburg, NY: Crossing Press, 1984); Catherine A. MacKinnon, *Sexual Harassment of Working Women* (New Haven: Yale University Press, 1979). MacKinnon was the only lawyer on this list, although it was her first book on sexual harassment that was referred to in this collection of early literature. Her later books, focused more upon feminist legal issues, would come some years later: see for example, *Feminism Unmodified* (Cambridge: Harvard University Press, 1987) and *Towards a Feminist Theory of the State* (Cambridge: Harvard University Press, 1989). Commenting on the lack of Canadian names in this lineup, some noted that the Canadian feminist movement was less of a "star" system; the leading feminists here tended to share the limelight rather than become individual icons. "We had leaders, but there was a sense that we were in it together. The leaders weren't out on their own. It was a time of collectives — that was the politic. The women who were the leaders of our generation knew they needed the rest of us."

described the Catholic Church as a negative force, becoming a feminist in reaction to the "bigoted, patriarchal, hypocritical" religion in which she had been raised. One explained that she became a feminist "because I came out as a lesbian, and began to immerse myself in women-positive culture."

Several explained turning to feminism as they reacted with surprise and outrage over individual and systemic sexist practices and attitudes that impeded their life plans. One spoke of her great pride in arriving at Yale University to pursue a graduate degree in English, only to be dismissed by a sexist male faculty adviser who told her that "as a married woman," she was not going to be "much use as a scholar." She added:

> My chosen field was English, I wanted to be the best, to get into the best graduate school, and here I was at Yale, at the pinnacle, and it was just awful. It caused me to readjust all of my thinking about what success meant, and where as an ambitious, high-achieving woman I would fit into the world. It made me a card-carrying feminist.

Another lost her career path as a graduate mathematician when her male professor fell in love with her. "I wasn't interested in him, but I realized what a delicate situation it was. I couldn't just say 'shove off.'" She rebounded into the job market only to have a prospective employer offer her a substantially lower salary than what she knew were the going rates. When she asked why, the recruiter replied: "Oh, that's the salary we offer to men, we offer a different salary to women."

Several described destructive experiences of sexual harassment from male professors or employers as the turning point. One recalled experiencing the "click" when she was pursuing her graduate law degree in Texas. "A group of women were organizing to protest the Portia Contest, a beauty contest among women law students. I listened to the language these women were using, the passion, and I just knew in my gut that the beauty contest was offensive and wrong. I didn't have the proper vocabulary, but they had read the books, and they spoke so well." Some attributed their conversion to nasty run-ins with sexist male law students or lawyers. And for some, an unexpected breakup with a male partner was the "great eye-opener." One described having had her consciousness raised over a short-lived marriage that left her divorced with an infant. Another one added, "I'm a little shy over the fact that I can relate so much of this back to the end of a relationship with a man."

Another explained what it felt like to join the Women Against Violence Against Women anti-pornography collective in New York City while she was at graduate school:

> It was really incredible. I went on those tours where feminists led other women through the Times Square pornography district to bear witness to what was going on. There I was, trying to write about pornography, and my male thesis supervisor kept telling me there was absolutely nothing to say. It was a time of dawning understanding for me when everything came together."

One attributed some of it to "the arrogance and absolutism of youth," laughing somewhat ruefully as she reminisced:

> I thought I was unquestionably right, and anybody who didn't agree with me was wrong and an asshole and they should be publicly denounced, made to look like an asshole, and it only was a question of having the courage to do that. It was my failing if I wasn't doing it, and what was more, I should be doing it at every opportunity.[27]

Many spoke about how wonderful it was to work collectively with other interesting women. "I was happy just to be with these really energetic, smart, committed women." "I loved being in the company of these women, the presence of brilliant women was an enormous inspiration." Others drew attention to the "notion of acting collectively," a principle that sat at the heart of the women's movement at the time. "That brought women together in groups to work for constitutional equality, equal pay, and so forth. The guy lawyers weren't collecting in groups, they were mostly individually pursuing their own careers." Some spoke about the safety that came with numbers.

> You knew you were all under threat, but you didn't feel in immediate peril yourself. We had the confidence, the safety net, that sticking our heads out wouldn't mean we'd be knocked off at the knees. Part of it was knowing that there were like-minded women, and the synergy of having enough of us around to realize that you wouldn't just be standing on your own.

Such sentiments were echoed repeatedly:

> It was a time to celebrate victories and commiserate in defeats, because you had this conviction that what you were doing was right, and it was shared. It wasn't a Joan of Arc kind of thing, it was shared.

---

27 The interviewee continued with a further reflection on how much her thinking had changed: "I now think I'm the asshole half the time, I never am confident I'm right, everything is way more complicated than I ever thought, and nobody's a total asshole, and it's systemic, so why would you hurt and berate an individual? But this sort of makes it problematic to produce visible, punchy, newsworthy actions."

Others said:

> When you wanted to change something, in those days you had to have a group or a committee. We would see each other in the hallways, we'd call a meeting, we'd phone everyone we knew, we'd do up flyers, we'd hold community forums, we'd network and organize to demand action. I think what we were trying to do was less socially acceptable than today, so you needed other people around for support.

And:

> The women who had gone before had left guideposts and ideas. The first women university teachers, lawyers, judges bore the brunt of their beliefs so much more than we did. We had a huge advantage, just in our numbers. Even if our classmates and colleagues weren't as feminist as we were, they were fellow travelers in some sense, and they agreed with large parts of what we did. We were not just personally engaged, but engaged as a group.
>
> I had the sense that I could go out on any limb and I wouldn't be alone. If I marched out there, somebody else would be marching out with me, even if I chose to go first.

In summary, many factors facilitated the creation of a "wave." Numbers were critical. It mattered that this female cohort was dramatically bigger in size than those who came before, and it mattered that women had not yet achieved numerical parity. The feminists recognized their anomalous status and were exhilarated that they were the "first" group to be able to demand gender equity. The novelty and freshness of the work, along with the "collective ethic" of the era, cemented them together as a defined group. The wider feminist movement, discernible throughout Canadian society, bolstered and gave impetus to the women in law, and the jaw-dropping, unrefined level of sexism that surrounded them provided an essential catalyst. The interviewees were in unanimous agreement that their cohort of women lawyers constituted a wave. One summed up the feeling: "I remember being at a Persons' Day breakfast, listening to Gloria Steinem, and seeing the young women around me so taken up by her energy. You got caught up in it. And you became part of it whether you had planned to or not. It literally felt like a wave. We were simply swept up in it."

BEGINNINGS AND MOTIVATIONS

WHO WERE THE WOMEN who made up the feminist lawyer cohort, and what brought them to law school? Although most law students come from the middle and upper classes, many with lawyers in their family backgrounds, this was surprisingly not the case for most of the feminist lawyers in this study. Only seven (15 percent) had lawyers in their family, and of these only two (4 percent) had lawyer-fathers (one of whom was a stepfather).[28] Twenty-six (58 percent) described themselves as part of the first generation in their families to go to university. Their fathers were farmers, welders, boiler-makers, typesetters, meat packers, hunters and trappers, restaurateurs, construction contractors, draftsmen, dry cleaners, factory workers, warehousemen, journalists, high school teachers, salesmen, department store managers, branch managers of trucking companies, public radio producers, military employees, and public servants. Nineteen (42 percent) were not the first generation to attend university and reported fathers with occupations such as businessmen, accountants, veterinarians, architects, ministers, engineers, professors, publishers, and doctors. Although most of the interviewees' mothers worked inside the home, many had held traditional women's jobs prior to having children: as secretaries, typists, bookkeepers, nurses, hairdressers, teachers, waitresses, salesclerks, physiotherapists, public servants, librarians, social workers, pharmacy assistants, and factory workers. One mother ran a dress shop, another managed a tearoom, and another had been an alderman. Only one had been a professional: a professor of sociology.

Asked about how they came to apply for law school, a number of the interviewees stressed that it might never have happened if birth control and abortion had not become significantly more accessible, allowing women to plan for a career along with a family. Many also attributed their motivation to widened occupational horizons resulting from postwar economic optimism. "I think we had expectations ... and we hit the right side of the economic curve," concluded one. "Government, universities [and] law firms were all expanding." A number spoke about demographics: "We were part of the excitement of the baby boom generation. That inspired confidence, insubordination, new ways of behaving." "You had a whole generation of women who were going through post-secondary education, walking around with our eyes open, seeing areas in which there was flagrant gender-based injustice. We felt obligated to try and work to make it better." "There was a relaxing of the men-

---

28 Two had older brothers who became lawyers, and one of these also had an uncle in law. One had a dead uncle who had been a judge, and one had an alcoholic grandfather whose legal career had ended in disgrace. One reported with glee that her grandfather's brother had been the lawyer who hired Clara Brett Martin, Canada's first female lawyer, as an articling student. However, she noted that she had known nothing of this when she decided to go to law school, and that she "certainly didn't become a lawyer because there was any kind of family tradition."

tal prison that the culture had been trying to fasten on women's heads since the end of World War II." "We were situated to be able to imagine a different way of being female. We could access spaces previously designated as male-only." One contrasted her situation to her mother's generation, pressured to leave behind paid labour positions to become housewives after the soldiers returned from the war. "Our generation was asking why girls shouldn't be allowed to do whatever boys did. Maybe we were living our mothers' pent-up dreams."

Parental influences played a role for some. A number explained that their mothers had been key to their decision to attend law school, because they had scoffed at their daughters' earlier ideas about becoming teachers, nurses, or writers, insisting that they think much more grandly about their future careers, and emphasizing that it was critical to strive for financial independence. One laughingly recalled: "I think my mother put a tape recording under my pillow saying 'you will be a lawyer.'" Another had a stepmother who had worked as a law librarian and urged her to think about law. Some had fathers who were equally supportive, but others had fathers who were dubious. One interviewee's father dismissed his daughter's plans, saying, "Who'd go to a woman lawyer?" Several of the Asian interviewees mentioned that their communities actively discouraged young people from entering law. "Our cultures don't think of law as a good profession, like medicine or life sciences, where there is a chance you might find a cure for cancer. They think lawyers defend guilty people." Some deliberately defied parental advice not to pick law.

One interviewee attributed her decision to the influence of an older sister, who had worked in the American civil rights movement and then in Appalachia: "I decided to become a lawyer because I wished to work in social justice fields like my sister." A few pointed to strong role models outside their families, who inspired them to enroll. One listed Judy LaMarsh, a woman she had admired in high school, as the motivating influence: "I thought she was absolutely great. She was a woman lawyer, and so I thought that must be a very good thing to be."[29] Another was inspired by a female don in residence at Glendon College, who was an articling student. One linked her decision to Karl Jaffey, a lawyer and NDP municipal politician in Toronto, for whom she had interned. "He did good work and he was smart, and he made it seem like it was a useful kind of degree. When he said I should become a lawyer, I decided to do it." One recalled that Clayton Ruby, a leftist lawyer, had spoken at the "alternative" free school that she attended and had taken the students

---

29 For information on this remarkable woman, who was called in the 1940s, see her autobiography: *Memoirs of a Bird in a Gilded Cage* (Richmond Hill, ON: Pocket Books, 1970).

on a tour of the courts and introduced them to a couple of ex-convicts. "I was intrigued. I thought law could be oriented to social justice." Another explained that her father had extolled F.R. Scott: "He felt law was a site of power. I wanted to be a poet, and my father said you can be both a lawyer and a poet, like F.R. Scott."

"I wanted to be Ralph Nader," was one woman's explanation. Another had met Murray Fraser, then the dean of law at the University of Victoria, who encouraged her to go into law. One had spoken with a young female law professor, who urged her to enroll (remarkably, it turns out this was me, although it is a conversation I do not remember). One was a devotee of Perry Mason, and another of Della Street. The latter explained: "I'd watched Perry Mason, and thought Della Street was the power behind the throne." Still another chose Nancy Drew. "Nancy was a private detective, and for some reason I didn't think being a detective would work for me, so I decided to become a lawyer, like Nancy Drew's father." Another spoke of a role model whose career she did not want to follow. Although she explained that she was Protestant, she greatly admired a particular Catholic nun who had left the convent after Vatican II and was working in a very poor neighbourhood. "I thought, it's all very well to be a social worker, living in community with people, but you've also got to have somebody who knows how to address legal problems. So I headed off to law school to change the world."

Many described having excelled in undergraduate studies in fields such as History, Political Science, Sociology, and English Literature. Their professors were nurturing and supportive, and under different circumstances, they would have gone on to do graduate work in these disciplines. But many were told by their professors that there were very few jobs in universities, and that they would do better to look to professions like law. "My profs said normally they would say go on to graduate school, but don't do it unless you're rich (which I wasn't), because they couldn't guarantee a job." Others spoke of frustrated desires to go to medical school. "I wanted to be a doctor, but I was poor in sciences and math," was voiced more than once. One explained that her desire to become a professor of religious studies was thwarted when her professor critiqued her less-than-thorough study methods and told her she was "a bullshit artist" with excellent advocacy skills who "needed to go to law school."

Still another, previously a university mathematics instructor, explained that her husband was transferred to Kingston, where she could not find a job: "So then I decided to get a trade," she quipped. "They didn't have dentistry at Queen's, so I went into law." Another went into law school after she abandoned the idea of becoming a politician. One chose law because she had been frustrated as a sales clerk. "I worked at the Bay where all the managers were male, and they seemed half-witted, with nothing better to do than to harass lowly sales clerks like me. It seemed obvious that one needed some sort of certification to lift yourself above the crowd." Still another left her previous career for distinctly feminist reasons:

> I had been a legal secretary, so I knew what law entailed. And I got involved with the women's movement in Ottawa. Women had nothing but complaints about their doctors and lawyers. I saw the dire need for professionals who had sensitivity to women. I decided it was something I could do.

A surprising number revealed that their decision to apply had been a spur-of-the-moment thing, with little foresight and no understanding of what a legal education and a law career entailed. Someone they knew was writing the LSAT, and they decided to sign up as well. "One of my friends was running off to write his LSAT, and I said 'what are those?' He explained, and I went too" said one. "It was a bit of a fluke," said another. "I just applied, but I knew nothing about what I was getting into." "I had formed the view that you had to be brilliant to be in the legal profession," said another. "But when I was in my last year of undergrad, all kinds of people were writing the LSAT who were not brilliant. They were all men, not a single woman. I decided I was as smart as those guys, and if they could do the LSAT and get in, so could I." It was a common sentiment: "In undergrad, I hung around with a group of drunken, party-boy jocks, almost all of whom went to law school. I thought, 'I can do that!'" Another added: "There was this guy who dumped me who thought he was more clever than I was, and he wanted to go to law school. He wrote the LSAT and didn't do very well. I wanted to demonstrate I could do better, so I wrote the LSAT." One characterized law as a "default option." "I didn't go to law school necessarily intending to become a lawyer," said another; "I went because I didn't know what else to do."

Some ascribed their interest in law to pure defiance. "I went to law school for no other reason than to pick something that women weren't supposed to do," said one. "I had no vision of acquiring tools or opportunities. I just knew I wasn't going to be a teacher or a social worker or a nurse. I thought 'I'm going to be something important, something women aren't supposed to be.'" Another echoed this sentiment: "Why law school? Girls didn't do it! And so I wanted to." Another spoke of deliberately casting about for the most challenging, most difficult professional program she could find.

> I knew I was smart, and I wanted to compete in the toughest program I could get into. I went to school with a woman classmate who was always pissing

off the guys by boasting that she was smarter than they were. She stunned them when she went into law school right after two years of undergraduate. I thought, that's a woman I'd like to emulate.

A few described a desire for independence, financial and otherwise, as key to their decision. One explained that she just wanted to make a lot of money to support her working-class family, that she had "no altruistic goals" when she started. Another described it as a "conscious decision that I wanted to be self-employed. I guess I never wanted anyone to be in charge of me. I didn't grow up with a burning ambition to be a lawyer, but to be accountable to myself, not bossed around by others." But most saw their chance to go to law school as an instrument for problem solving or had wider objectives to "change the world." One had been part of a feminist coalition fighting for the decriminalization of abortion, which she said made her "very interested in law." One impoverished interviewee had had to sign up for premium assistance during undergraduate in order to get OHIP health coverage. "There was so much red tape, I said geez, you just about have to be a lawyer to be poor in this province. So I thought, that's a good idea! And I applied to Western law school." Another had become involved in an unsuccessful union-organizing campaign in an earlier job and concluded that "if I wanted to be effective as a woman activist, I needed to be more credentialed than the guys. Law was obviously one way to get more credentialed."

One had attended the only French working-class public high school in Toronto as an anglophone, long before French immersion became common. "It had a huge impact on me," she said; "I wanted to do something to protect minority language rights." Another had gone to an alternative free school in Toronto, where she became interested in a course on law. One said she wanted to "act on behalf of people who were chronically under-represented." "I'd been on the student council at the University of Windsor, I was politically active," said another. "I thought law would give me the skills to be able to help people." One had worked as a parliamentary intern, where she watched debates about capital punishment, abortion, and other "hot button issues": "It seemed to me I should get legal training, so I could make a contribution to the important issues in society." One had worked with the American Indian Movement and been politically active in First Nations' communities. She wanted to learn more about the legal system that was oppressing her peoples. Similar sentiments motivated another Aboriginal woman back in Canada: "I knew what was happening to Aboriginal people, with the police and the courts. It was about getting the power to make a difference." One of the racialized interviewees took her first legal degree in Uganda, choosing that profession for "independence" in a climate where Idi Amin was getting ready to expel all of the Asians from the country.

Overall then, as a group the Ontario feminist lawyers came from less prosperous families than their male counterparts, and the majority were first-generation university graduates without lawyers in the family. Their motivations in selecting law were diverse. They identified such factors as increasing reproductive autonomy, postwar economic optimism, the demographic force of the baby boomer generation, parental and sibling influence, inspirational male and female role models, frustrated career paths in other fields, a desire for independence, defiance over sexist treatment, and feminist/anti-racist and other social reform objectives.

FUTURE RESEARCH

WHAT HAPPENED WHEN THIS turbulent, insubordinate, ambitious, free-wheeling cohort of women hit the law school milieu? "Some pretty heavy lifting," was the retort of one interviewee. The first members of the cohort to enter law school experienced a brick wall of resistance, with deans, faculty, and male students openly dismissive of their very presence. All of the interviewees, even those who came to law school a decade or more after the earliest entrants in the group, reported that sexism, racism, and homophobia ran rampant inside the classroom and in extra-curricular activities. Female and racialized students were openly demeaned, and their career prospects publicly belittled. Women students were sexualized, and their status as sex objects was given substantially more prominence than their academic credentials. Those who needed accommodation for pregnancy and child-care responsibilities were castigated for having dared to imagine that they could combine parenting with a legal career.

Future articles will document what happened to the second-wave feminists in law school, and how they resisted the discriminatory treatment. Their initial individual, sporadic acts of resistance combined humour with anger, and clandestine information-sharing with open complaint. The women tried to introduce feminist ideas into law schools by pasting cartoons to bulletin boards, writing feminist columns in campus newspapers, and raising complaints about sexism and racism in law texts, classroom lectures, and exams. They used techniques of gossip, confrontation, police tips, petitions, and student electoral politics to try to stem the sexual harassment from faculty and fellow students alike. But these were isolated *ad hoc* responses that rose and declined based upon the courage and imagination that individual women could muster. It would take more sustained action to make a significant difference.

Second-wave feminists soon turned to more concerted, organized resistance and wider community initiatives. They organized women and the law conferences, caucuses, and national organizations. They lobbied for the creation of feminist law seminars, and the hiring of more female law professors. When they observed the newly hired feminist law professors being mistreated in the classroom, some attempted to intervene collectively to stop unfair behaviour. They fund-raised to create public legal education programs and educational materials for women. They campaigned for family law reform, and attempted to redesign their student community legal clinics to address unmet needs of female clients. Some ran anti-racism hotlines, staffed the barricades at Oka, and lobbied for the inclusion of Aboriginal perspectives within legal education. Collective strategies appear to have resulted in substantially more progress.

The final stage of this research will document what happened when this remarkable cohort of feminists sought to obtain articling positions and came up against sexist lawyers and judges, and what they went on to do in practice. Some consciously set up all-female practices, designed to provide an alternative, feminist law firm culture and to service women clients. Others blended into existing male-dominated legal settings and worked within these firms for feminist change. Still others worked far removed from traditional professional structures, using their feminism and legal skills to make change from outside. Many interviewees believed that feminist lawyers became some of the most influential activists within second-wave Canadian feminism. While none would accept the premise that their feminist activities have brought about a truly gender-equal or racially equal society, most would agree that many positive changes ensued.

They founded the Women's Legal Education and Action Fund (LEAF). They became the forefront of activism in areas such as the repatriation of the constitution, *Charter* litigation, violence against women, rape law reform, sexual harassment, pay equity, employment equity, women in trade unions, family law reform, same-sex marriage and lesbian rights, compensation for child sexual abuse survivors, refugee rights, tax law reform, disability law reform, anti-racist litigation and redress campaigns, international women's issues, disarmament, poverty law reform, women prisoners' rights, reproductive rights, Aboriginal women's rights, and the reshaping of legal education and research to become more inclusive of gender, race, Aboriginality, class, and sexual identity.

Also left to future stages of this research will be a fuller analysis of the multiple fissures and divisions that beset feminism and the impact that had upon feminist lawyers, and an attempt to explore what the future decades might hold for the women in this wave, and the feminists who follow.

ACTIVISM IN COLLECTIVITY: WHAT WAS IT LIKE TO BE A FEMINIST LAWYER IN THIS ERA?

THIS ARTICLE WILL CLOSE with some discussion of the collective nature of their feminist endeavours, and the *joie de vivre* of being a feminist in law during the second wave. The interviewees indicated that their power and influence came largely from their collaborative working relationships, that the sum was greater than the constituent parts. It was in part an outgrowth of the politics of second-wave feminism that stressed the importance of collectivity. It was in part due to the perceived danger of the work they tried to do, a desire for greater safety in numbers. And it was in part due to the sheer energy that so many drew from the community of feminists. "We knew we were part of a grand movement," said one. "It was totally exhilarating." "There was a vibrancy about feminism, it was inspirational." "Those times were fantastic. We lived through the most exciting times anyone could ever imagine."

"I had this sense that I could do anything and be who I wanted to be in the world. And that I had women who would be like me, I wasn't going to be an odd ball. It was a real sense that we are changing the world around us. If twenty of us get on the battering ram, we will break that wall down." Another emphasized her sense that feminist lawyers "could achieve enormous change. There were different ways to go, and no right answer. It wasn't like building on the past, it was a steep learning curve. We were impassioned, incredibly driven to find the right path." "It felt so positive," said one, "just a flooding of analysis and ideas being put out there by engaged women, on the move wherever they were." "I don't want to gloss over the differences," said another. "The core issues we felt passionate about were not identical, but there was sufficient independence and flexibility to think differently, to be who we were, and still be part of the community." "You never felt like you were just a cog in the wheel; you felt like you were respected, that you were part of large scale reform. It was gratifying."

"We worked with women from every province, we went on speaking tours all across Canada, to speak in church basements, to trade unionists, to women's institutes, to farm wives, to bar associations, at universities, to anybody who would listen. The reception was overwhelming." "Part of what we enjoyed so markedly was a sisterhood. Everything was the work of many hands." "It's been so rewarding to be even a very, very small part of the feminist movement," said another. "Were we always right? Were we inclusive enough? Probably not, but we had a view of the world we wanted to live in, and set out to make parts of that happen." "We were multi-taskers," said another. "We moved from one issue to the next, we lobbied, we litigated, we fund-raised, we tried to make change within law schools, law firms, the government. We were very skilled and adaptive." "Maybe we were reckless," ventured another. One described it as "emotionally draining" and "difficult at times," but "always passionate and endlessly stimulating." "We had a vision of how we were going to be lawyers," said one. "And there was a synergy in terms of friendship. We'd have lunches and dinners together, we'd travel together, we'd share information, and talk about everything — about sex, politics, everything. If there was a crisis, people dropped everything to help each other."

Many emphasized the humour that infused the intensity of emotions: "What made us laugh? Each other, ourselves, the assholes. The humour was the flip-side of the anger, that fiery passion that moved us into action. We laughed until we cried, falling off our chairs, which is pretty funny because we took ourselves very damn seriously." "Humour is a survival technique," said another. "It's a way of getting perspective, of managing incongruent realities. God knows, *we* were often the incongruent realities. Humour was essential equipment." One reminisced about the hilarity of feminist gatherings staged to showcase "the Feminist Fantasy of the Future" where women arrived rigged out in spectacular costumes. Another recalled the delightfully sarcastic guerilla tactics, and the "Barefoot and Pregnant Award." "We knew how to throw great parties," said another. "We mixed food, wine, work, and friendship. I can't think of a better way to work." Another said: "There was never an issue so serious that it didn't somewhere involve at least a couple of bottles of wine and a potluck. We worked like dogs in serious meetings, then somebody would say, 'we need a laugh, my house on Sunday night, potluck at 6 pm.'" Another summed it up: "We knew how to have fun. It was laugh or kill yourself."

"The feminist community's motto was 'live life to the fullest.' We did everything hard — we worked hard, played hard, laughed hard," said another interviewee. "The hub of activity was wonderful. But we always took the time to have lunch, to share, to make it a community." "I love that quote, 'If I can't dance, I can't be part of your revolution.'" "I loved those crazy songs and the wonderful wit." "There were so many meetings where we had impromptu celebrations." "To live and work in a feminist legal community is about as good as it gets."

APPENDIX A: WOMEN CALLED TO THE BAR IN ONTARIO, 1945-2000

Year	Total No. Called	No. Women Called	%
1945	54	2	3.7
1946	51	6	11.8
1947	103	3	2.9
1948	226	9	4.0
1949	236	5	2.1
1950	199	7	3.7
1951	217	8	3.7
1952	99	2	2.0
1953	218	2	0.9
1954	249	6	2.4
1955	226	7	3.1
1956	225	3	1.3
1957	249	7	2.8
1958	247	9	3.6
1959	294	12	4.1
1960	269	8	3.0
1961	58	1	1.7
1962	304	12	3.9
1963	245	10	4.1
1964	257	7	2.7
1965	235	6	2.6
1966	282	7	2.5
1967	286	6	2.1
1968	348	11	3.2
1969	397	20	5.0
1970	444	19	4.3
1971	455	35	7.7
1972	498	20	4.0
1973	690	50	7.2
1974	715	53	7.4
1975	816	85	10.4
1976	850	109	12.8

Year	Total No. Called	No. Women Called	%
1977	945	153	16.2
1978	1009	192	19.0
1979	1074	275	25.6
1980	1077	293	27.2
1981	1080	327	30.3
1982	1045	345	33.0
1983	990	338	34.1
1984	1025	338	32.9
1985	1050	386	36.8
1986	1111	419	37.7
1987	1139	467	41.0
1988	1173	500	42.6
1989	1183	491	41.5
1990	1221	486	39.8
1991	1196	494	41.3
1992	1270	529	41.7
1993	1225	542	44.2
1994	1280	589	46.0
1995	1226	583	47.6
1996	1295	585	45.2
1997	1182	564	47.8
1998	1264	602	47.6
1999	1219	560	45.9
2000	1280	620	48.4

Credit: *Law Society of Upper Canada*

APPENDIX B: CHRONOLOGICAL LIST OF HISTORICAL SOURCES ON WOMEN AND THE LAW

Cameron Harvey, "Women in Law in Canada" (1970) 4 Man. L.J. 9

Linda Silver Dranoff, "Women as Lawyers in Toronto" (1972) 10 Osgoode Hall L.J. 177

Lynn Smith, Marylee Stephenson, and Gina Quijano, "The Legal Profession and Women: Finding Articles in British Columbia" (1973) 8 U.B.C.L. Rev. 137

Barry D. Adam, "Stigma and Employability: Discrimination by Sex and Sexual Orientation in the Ontario Legal Profession" (1981) 18 Canadian Review of Sociology and Anthropology 216

Marie Huxter, "Survey of Employment Opportunities for Articling Students and Graduates of the Bar Admission Course in Ontario" (1981) L. Soc'y Gaz. & Guardian Gaz. 2; 169

Barry Adam and Douglas Baer, "The Social Mobility of Women and Men in the Ontario Legal Profession" (1984) 21 Canadian Review of Sociology and Anthropology 21

John Hagan, Marie Huxter, and Patricia Parker, "Class Structure and Legal Practice: Inequality and Mobility among Toronto Lawyers" (1988) 22:1 Law & Soc'y Rev. 9

David Stager and David Foot, "Changes in Lawyers' Earnings: The Impact of Differentiation and Growth in the Canadian Legal Profession" (1988) 13:1 Law and Soc. Inquiry 71

David Foot and David Stager, "Intertemporal Market Effect on Gender Earnings Differentials: Lawyers in Canada 1970–1980" (1989) 21 Applied Economics 1011

Joan Brockman, "Encountering the Barriers and/or Moving On: A Survey of Former Members of the Law Society of British Columbia" (Report, Law Society of British Columbia's Subcommittee on Women in the Legal Profession, 1990)

John Hagan, "Gender and the Structural Transformation of the Legal Profession in the United States and Canada" in Maureen Hallinan, David Klein, Jennifer Glass, eds., *Changes in Societal Institutions* (New York: Plenum Press, 1990) at 49

John Hagan, "The Gender Stratification of Income Inequality among Lawyers" (1990) 68 Social Forces 835

Joan Brockman, "Identifying Barriers: A Survey of Members of the Law Society of British Columbia" (Report, Law Society of British Columbia's Subcommittee on Women in the Legal Profession, 1991)

John Hagan, Marjorie Zatz, Bruce Arnold et al., "Cultural Capital, Gender, and the Structural Transformation of Legal Practice" (1991) 25 Law & Soc'y Rev. 239

Fiona M. Kay, "Transitions in the Ontario Legal Profession: A Survey of Lawyers Called to the Bar between 1975–1990" (Toronto: Law Society of Upper Canada, 1991)

Ejan Mackaay, "L'État de la profession d'avocat au Québec en 1991: résumé des principales conclusions du sondage général des members du barreau" (Un rapport au Barreau du Québec, 1991)

Jean E. Wallace, "Why Lawyers Decide to Quit Their Jobs: A Study of Job Satisfaction and Organizational Commitment among Calgary Lawyers" (Report, Alberta Law Foundation, 1991)

Joan Brockman, "Bias in the Legal Profession: Perceptions and Experiences" (1992) 3 Alta. L. Rev. 747

Joan Brockman, "Gender Bias in the Legal Profession: A Survey of Members of the Law Society of British Columbia" (1992) 17 Queen's L.J. 91

Joan Brockman, "'Resistance by the Club' to the Feminization of the Legal Profession" (1992) 7 C.J.L.S. 47

Joan Brockman and Dorothy Chunn, eds., *Investigating Gender Bias: Law, Courts and the Legal Profession* (Toronto: Thompson Educational, 1993)

Canadian Bar Association, *Touchstones for Change: Equality, Diversity and Accountability* (Ottawa: Canadian Bar Association, 1993)

Joan Brockman, "Leaving the Practice of Law: The Wherefores and the Whys" (1994) 32 Alta. L. Rev. 116

Fiona M. Kay and John Hagan, "Changing Opportunities for Partnership for Men and Women Lawyers during the Transformation of the Modern Law Firm" (1994) 32 Osgoode Hall L.J. 413

John Hagan and Fiona Kay, *Gender in Practice: A Study of Lawyers' Lives* (New York: Oxford University Press, 1995)

Fiona M. Kay and John Hagan, "The Persistent Glass Ceiling: Gendered Inequalities in the Earnings of Lawyers" (1995) 46 British Journal of Sociology 279

John Hagan and Fiona Kay, "Hierarchy in Practice: The Significance of Gender in Ontario Law Firms" in Carol Wilton, ed., *Inside the Law: Canadian Law Firms in Historical Perspective* (Toronto: University of Toronto Press, 1996) at 530

Fiona M. Kay, Nancy Dautovich, and Chantelle Marlor, "Barriers and Opportunities within Law: Women in a Changing Legal Profession" (Report to the Law Society of Upper Canada, 1996)

Fiona M. Kay, "Flight from Law: A Competing Risks Model of Departures from Law Firms" (1997) 31 Law & Soc'y Rev. 301

Fiona M. Kay and John Hagan, "Raising the Bar: The Gender Stratification of Law Firm Capitalization" (1998) 63 American Sociological Review 728

Fiona M. Kay and John Hagan, "Cultivating Clients in the Competition for Partnership: Gender and the Organizational Restructuring of Law Firms in the 1990s" (1999) Law & Soc'y Rev. 101

Joanne St. Lewis and Benjamin Trevino, *Racial Equality in the Canadian Legal Profession: The Challenge of Racial Equality; Putting Principles into Practice* (Ottawa: Canadian Bar Association, 1999)

Joanne St. Lewis and Benjamin Trevino, *Virtual Justice: Systemic Racism and the Canadian Legal Profession* (Ottawa: Canadian Bar Association, 1999)

Linda Hill *et al.*, "Lawyers with Disabilities: Identifying Barriers to Equity, a Report of the Disability Research Working Group of the Equity and Diversity Subcommittee" (Vancouver: Law Society of British Columbia, 2000)

Fiona M. Kay and Joan Brockman, "Barriers to Gender Equality in the Canadian Legal Establishment" (2000) 8 Fem. Legal Stud. 169

Joan Brockman, *Gender in the Legal Profession: Fitting or Breaking the Mould* (Vancouver: University of British Columbia Press, 2001)

Michael Ornstein, *Lawyers in Ontario: Evidence from the 1996 Census* (Toronto: Law Society of Upper Canada, 2001)

Gerry Ferguson and Kuan Foo, "Addressing Discriminatory Barriers Facing Aboriginal Law Students and Lawyers" (Vancouver: Law Society of British Columbia, 2002)

Merril Cooper, Joan Brockman, and Irene Hoffart, *Final Report on Equity and Diversity in Alberta's Legal Profession* (Calgary: Law Society of Alberta, 2004)

Fiona M. Kay, "Turning Points and Transitions: Women's Careers in the Legal Profession" (Toronto: Law Society of Upper Canada, 2004)

Fiona M. Kay, Cristi Masuch, and Paula Curry, "Diversity and Change: The Contemporary Legal Profession in Ontario (Report to the Law Society of Upper Canada, Toronto, September 2004)

Michael Ornstein, "The Changing Face of the Ontario Legal Profession, 1971–2001" (Report to the Law Society of Upper Canada, Toronto, October 2004)

Joan Brockman, "An Update on Gender and Diversity in the Legal Profession in Alberta, 1991–2003" in Elizabeth Sheehy and Sheila McIntyre, eds., *Calling for Change: Women, Law, and the Legal Profession* (Ottawa: University of Ottawa Press) at 237

Fiona M. Kay, Christi Masuch, and Paula Curry, "Growing Diversity and Emergent Change: Gender and Ethnicity in the Legal Profession" in Elizabeth Sheehy and Sheila McIntyre, eds., *Calling for Change: Women, Law, and the Legal Profession* (Ottawa: University of Ottawa Press, 2006) at 203

Jean McKenzie Leiper, *Bar Codes: Women in the Legal Profession* (Toronto: University of Toronto Press, 2006)

Noteworthy Sources that Explore the History of Feminist Lawyers Specifically

Sherene Razack, *Canadian Feminism and the Law: The Women's LEAF & the Pursuit of Equality* (Toronto: Second Story Press, 1991)

Elizabeth Sheehy and Sheila McIntyre, eds., *Calling for Change: Women, Law, and the Legal Profession* (Ottawa: University of Ottawa Press, 2006)

List of Contributors

Eric M. Adams is a Professor of Law at the University of Alberta. His publications include "Canada's 'Newer Constitutional Law' and the Idea of Constitutional Rights" (2006) 51 McGill L.J. 435 and "Ghosts in Court: Jonathan Belcher and the Proclamation of 1762" (2004) 27 Dal. L.J. 321.

Constance Backhouse is a Professor of Law and University Research Chair at the University of Ottawa. Her published works include *Carnal Crimes: The Legal History of Sexual Assault Trials in Canada, 1900–1975* (Toronto: Irwin Law, 2008); *The Heiress versus the Establishment: Mrs. Campbell's Campaign for Legal Justice* (Vancouver: UBC Press, 2004), co-authored with Nancy Backhouse; *Colour-Coded: A Legal History of Racism in Canada, 1900–1950* (Toronto: University of Toronto Press, 1999); and *Petticoats and Prejudice: Women and Law in Nineteenth-Century Canada* (Toronto: Women's Press/Osgoode Society, 1991).

D.G. Bell is a Professor of Law at the University of New Brunswick. His published works include *Early Loyalist Saint John: The Origin of New Brunswick Politics, 1783–86* (Fredericton: New Ireland Press, 1983, rev. ed. 2007); and *Legal Education in New Brunswick: A History* (Fredericton: University of New Brunswick, Faculty of Law, 1992).

Joan Brockman is a Professor of Criminology at Simon Fraser University. Her published works include *Gender in the Legal Profession: Fitting or Breaking the Mould* (Vancouver: UBC Press, 2001); and *Investigating Gender Bias: Law, Courts and the Legal Profession* (Toronto: Thompson, 1993), which she edited with Dorothy E. Chunn.

Mélanie Brunet, Ph.D., is a Sessional Lecturer in the Department of History at the University of Toronto. Her doctoral thesis was entitled "Becoming Lawyers: Gender, Legal Education, and Professional Identity Formation in Canada, 1920–1980."

Dorothy E. Chunn is a Professor of Sociology and Anthropology at Simon Fraser University. Her published works include *Women, Madness and the Law: A Feminist Reader* (London: Cavendish/Glasshouse, 2005), which she edited with Wendy Chan and Robert J. Menzies; *Regulating Lives: Historical Essays on the State, Society, the Individual and the Law* (Vancouver: UBC Press, 2002), which she edited with John McLaren and Robert J. Menzies; *Contesting Canadian Citizenship: Historical Readings* (Toronto: Broadview, 2002), which she edited with Robert L. Adamoski and Robert J. Menzies; and *From Punishment to Doing Good: Family Courts and Socialized Justice in Ontario 1880–1940* (Toronto: University of Toronto Press, 1992).

Hamar Foster is a Professor of Law at the University of Victoria. His published works include *Let Right Be Done: Calder, Aboriginal Title, and the Future of Indigenous Rights* (Vancouver: UBC Press, 2007), which he edited with Heather Raven and Jeremy H.A. Webber and *British Columbia and the Yukon* (Toronto: Osgoode Society, 1995), which he edited with John McLaren.

Donald Fyson is a Professor of History at Université Laval. His published work includes *Magistrates, Police and People: Everyday Criminal Justice in Quebec and Lower Canada, 1764–1837* (Toronto: University of Toronto Press, 2006).

Jean-Philippe Garneau is a Professor of History at Université du Québec à Montréal. His publications include "Une culture de l'amalgame au pretoire: les avocats de Québec et l'élaboration d'un langage juridique commun" (2007) 88:1 Canadian Historical Review 113 and "Une masquerade de Jurisprudence Françoise?" *Normes juridiques et pratiques judiciares du Moyen Age à l'époque contemporaine* (Dijon, Oct. 2006).

Philip Girard is a Professor of Law at Dalhousie University. His published works include *The Supreme Court of Nova Scotia, 1754–2004* (Toronto: University of Toronto Press, 2004), which he edited with Jim Phillips and Barry Cahill; and *Bora Laskin: Bringing Law to Life* (Toronto: University of Toronto Press, 2005).

Jeffrey Haylock, a third-year LL.B. student at Dalhousie University, holds an Honours B.A. in history and linguistics from Trinity College at the University of Toronto and an M.Phil. in linguistics from Queens' College, Cambridge. He will be pursuing graduate studies in law beginning in the fall of

2009. His paper on the recruitment practices of large Halifax law firms in the early twentieth century is scheduled for publication in the upcoming issue of the Dalhousie Law Journal.

Susan Lewthwaite, Ph.D., is a Research Coordinator at Corporate Records and Archives, Law Society of Upper Canada and a Sessional Lecturer in the Criminology Program at Woodsworth College, University of Toronto. Her published work includes Jim Phillips, Susan Lewthwaite, and Tina Loo, eds., *Essays in the History of Canadian Law, vol. V. Crime and Criminal Justice* (Toronto: University of Toronto Press, 1994).

Christopher Moore is an author and legal historian. His publications include *McCarthy Tétrault: Building Canada's Premier Law Firm 1855–2005* (Vancouver: Douglas & McIntyre, 2005); and *The Law Society of Upper Canada and Ontario's Lawyers, 1797–1997* (Toronto: University of Toronto Press, 1997); he is also a columnist for *The Law Times* (Toronto).

Jim Phillips is a Professor of Law at University of Toronto, and Editor-in-Chief of Osgoode Society for Legal History. His published works include *A History of Canadian Legal Thought: Collected Essays, R.C.B. Risk* (Toronto: University of Toronto Press, 2006), which he edited with G. Blaine Baker; *The Supreme Court of Nova Scotia, 1754–2004* (Toronto: University of Toronto Press, 2004), which was written with Philip Girard and Barry Cahill; and *Crime and Criminal Justice: Essays in the History of Canadian Law*, vol. V (Toronto: Osgoode Society, 1994), which he edited with Susan Lewthwaite and Tina Merrill Loo.

W. Wesley Pue is a Professor of Law at the University of British Columbia, and Editor of the *Law and Society Series*, UBC Press. His published works include *A History of British Columbia Legal Education* (Vancouver: Faculty of Law, University of British Columbia, 2006); and *Lawyers and Vampires: Cultural Histories of Legal Professions* (Oxford: Hart, 2003), which he edited with David Sugarman.

Deidré Rowe Brown is a Ph.D. candidate at OISE, University of Toronto and executive assistant to the Treasurer of the Law Society of Upper Canada. Her thesis is entitled, "Setting a Precedent: The Owen Sound Women Teachers' Association, 1918–1928."

Index

Abella, Rosalie, 269
Aboriginal justice, 228–32, 237–38
Abraham Lincoln argument, 41, 43
Act for the Better Regulating the Practice of the Law, An, 4, 14
Act to Make Better Provision for the Administration of Justice in the Unorganized Tracts of Country in Upper Canada, An, 235
Adams, Eric M., 173, 295
Aikins, James, 84, 108
Aitkins, Sir James, 40
Allen, Maureen O'Mullin, 95, 97
Almon, William, 169
Amiro, Delmar, 96
Anderson, May Gladys, 94
Anger, Harry, 174
Arab, Edward Francis, 92, 96
Archambault, Joseph-Papin, 52
Arnup, John, 25, 174, 190
Atlantic Charter, 188

Backhouse, Constance, 13, 194, 218, 219, 265, 266, 267, 295
Baker, G. Blaine, 16, 107
Baldwin, Robert, 20, 105
Baldwin, William Warren, 17, 18, 20, 21, 24, 105
Baldwin Range, 22
Bartleman, James, 13
Battle of the Standard, 31
Baxter, John, 40, 41, 43, 44
Beaubien, Benjamin, 136, 137
Beck, J.M., 166
Bédard, J., 137
Beddoes, Dick, 269
Bell, David G., 31, 295
Bender, F.-X., 137
Bennett, R.B., 56, 57, 111
Bingley, William, 169
Bissett, F.W., 96, 97
Blake, Edward, 110
Blowers, Sampson Salter, 167
Boehmer, Lola, 66
Bolsu, Petrio, 199
Borden, Henry, 174
Borden, Robert, 78, 85, 88, 230
Bothwell, Robert, 173
Boulton, John, 20
Bowering, Marilyn, 225

Bradshaw, Kathryn, 248, 249, 253, 260
Brawn, Dale, 76, 82, 83, 86
Brennan, Francis Patrick, 204
Brenton, James, 162, 164
Brockman, Joan, 245, 295
Brown, Albert J., 111
Brown, George, 236
Brown, Saddie, 250
Brown, Walter James, 221
Brunet, Elise, 13
Brunet, Mélanie, 49, 154, 296
Bunch, Charlotte, 269
Bureaucratic dictatorship, 175

Cahill, Barry, 81
Campney, Ralph, 112
Canadian Bar Association (CBA), 179
Carey, Thomas, 145
Cartwright, Hilda, 250
Cartwright, John, 178
Cause lawyering, 225
Champoux, Gonzague, 156
Chapman, Richard, 53
Chapter authors
    Adams, Eric M., 173, 295
    Backhouse, Constance, 265, 295
    Bell, David G., 31, 295
    Brockman, Joan, 245, 295
    Brunet, Mélanie, 49, 296
    Chunn, Dorothy E., 245, 296
    Foster, Hamar, 225, 296
    Fyson, Donald, 141, 296
    Garneau, Jean-Philippe, 129, 296
    Girard, Philip, 75, 296
    Haylock, Jeffrey, 75, 296
    Lewthwaite, Susan, 193, 297
    Moore, Christopher, 103, 297
    Phillips, Jim, 161, 297
    Pue, W. Wesley, 1, 297
    Rowe Brown, Deidré, 13, 297
    Watt, Steven, 129
Chitty, Joseph, 177
Chitty, Robert Michael Willes, 175–90
Choquette, Philippe-Auguste, 155

Chrétien, Jean, 65
Chunn, Dorothy E., 245, 296
Churchill, Winston, 188
Clark, Bruce, 239
Clark, J.M.M., 234
Cohen, Leonard, 241
Cole, Curtis, 80
Collins-Williams, George, 268
Commission Sylvestre, 143
Constitutional rights, 173–90
    Atlantic Charter, 188
    bureaucratic dictatorship, 175
    conclusions, 189–90
    Defence of Canada Regulations
        (DOCR), 180–81
    report on constitutional bill of rights,
        185–88
    Special Committee on Civil Liberties,
        184–85
    War Measures Act, 173, 175, 180
    WPTB, 174, 175
Contempt, 168–69
Contributors. *See* Chapter authors
Copland, John James, 93
Covert, Frank, 90
Cowichan Petition, 229
Cronkite, F.C., 48
Cross, E. Lionel, 93, 193-223
    articling, 197
    birth, 195
    cricket, 221
    criminal cases, 198–200
    disbarred, 222
    early years, 195
    Ku Klux Klan, 218–21
    military service, 196
    Oakville KKK incident, 219–20
    Rationalist Society, 200–1
    religion, views on, 215–16
    social consciousness, 217–18
    Sterry cases, 202–15
    writer, as, 215
Cruickshank, Bessie, 252
Culture de l'amalgame, 153

Index

Cumberland, Frederic William, 23

Dalhousie Law School/University of New Brunswick Law School, 31–48
   Abraham Lincoln argument, 41, 43
   gain and loss, 43–45
   Halifax, 1933, 45–48
   raising the standard, 39–43
   special students, 35–37
   undergraduates, 37–39
Daniels, Ronald J., 118
Darrow, Clarence, 207
Davis, Delos, 95
Davis, E.P., 110
Davis, George, 93
De Blois, Rodolphe, 143, 144
Debating, 64
DeBeck, Viola, 250, 256, 257
Defence of Canada Regulations (DOCR), 180–81
Deschamps, Isaac, 162, 163, 167, 168, 169, 171
Desrivieres, Eugene, 152
Diefenbaker, John, 189
Donahoe, Richard, 96
Doran, Burke, 70
Doyle, Ernest F., 89
Dresner, Josephine, 94
Drysdale, Arthur, 85
Dumas, Alexandre, 135
Dunsworth, Marjorie, 94

Earle, Allen, 36
Edmonds, Henry Lovekin, 250
Ewart, John, 18

Fairclough, Ellen, 69
Falconbridge, J.D., 39
Farris, J.W., 111
Fasken, David, 111
Ferguson, Howard, 65
Finucane, Bryan, 163
Fish, Frances, 93, 94
"Flaming Youth," 156

Flavelle, Sir Joseph, 107
Fleming, Donald M., 53, 54, 55, 56
Foster, Hamar, 225, 296
Fowler, Robert, 174
Fraser, Murray, 282
French, Mabel, 38, 245, 249
Friedson, Eliott, 112
Frost, Florence Katherine, 250
Frye, Northrup, 4
Fyson, Donald, 141, 296

Galanter, Marc, 2
Gallagher, Mary, 66
Garneau, Blanche, 147
Garneau, Jean-Philippe, 129, 153, 296
Gavazzi, Alessandro, 142
Gavazzi riot, 142–143, 145
Gilley, Janet, 247, 249, 250, 252, 254, 255
Girard, Philip, 7, 15, 19, 75, 296
Godfrey, John, 110
Goffe, Rowland Parkinson, 92, 93
Gordon, Donald, 174
Gordon, Mildred, 250, 251, 252, 255, 256, 257, 258, 259, 260
Green, Nathan, 96, 97
Greenberg, Michael, 96
Greenwood, Murray F., 129
Griffith, J. Eaglan, 92, 93, 96, 196
Gros village, 147–49
Groulx, Lionel, 59
Harris, Robert, 88

Hay, Douglas, 169
Haylock, Jeffrey, 75, 296
Heighington, Wilfrid, 56
History of the Canadian Legal Profession, The, 13
Holmes, Benjamin Mulberrry, 170
Howe, Clarence Decatur, 174
Hunter, Rainey, 63

Jackman, Barbara, 268
Jackson, E.S., 221–22
Jaffey, Karl, 281

Jamieson, James, 25

Kanigsberg, Robert, 97
Kates, Joanne, 269
Kelly, Peter, 239
Kerr, James, 136
Keskinen, William, 199
Khattar, George, 92
Khattar, Simon, 92
Kilbourn, William, 173
King's College. *See* Dalhousie Law School/University of New Brunswick Law School
Kitchen, Gladys, 250, 252
Kitz, Leonard A., 92, 96
Kogonock, John, 199
Kolish, Evelyn, 129
Ku Klux Klan, 218–21

Lachance, Arthur, 155
Lacroix, J.D., 137
L'affaire Blanche Garneau, 147
Lafleur, Eugene, 110
Laine, Martti, 199
Lalonde, Leonie, 248, 249, 250, 251, 252, 253
LaMarsh, Judy, 281
Landreville, Leo, 96
Landry, René Wilfrid Émilien, 92, 96
Lane, Henry Bower, 22
Langelier, Charles, 155
Lapointe, Ernest, 173
Large law firms. *See* Megafirms
Larson, Magali, 112
Lash, Zebulon, 107
Laurier, Wilfrid, 228, 230
Law Society of Upper Canada, 4, 15, 17, 22
Lawson, J. Earl, 54, 55
Lazarovitz, Sadie, 97
Lesage, Jean, 155, 156
Lewis, Stephen, 268
Lewthwaite, Susan, 193, 297
Ligoure, C.C., 196
Linklaters, 123

Loyalist lawyers, 161–72

Macaulay, Leopold, 66
MacDonald, David A., 250
MacDonald, Vincent, 84
Macdonnell, Allan, 235, 236
Mackay, J. Keiller, 58
Mackenzie, Emelyn, 94
MacKenzie, Gavin, 13
Mackenzie King, William Lyon, 64, 88, 188
Mackie, Dorothy, 251, 253
Macklaier, William, 112
Maclean, Ann Eileen, 95
Macpherson, Jean Chisholm, 95
MacRae, Donald, 40, 42, 44
Maddin, Mary Olive, 94
Maguire, John, 143, 145
Maitland, Sir Peregrine, 17
Majury, Diana, 266, 267
Maloney, Arthur, 58
Mansfield, Lord, 169
Marchildon, Greg, 81
Margolian, Samuel, 96
Martin, Clara, 38, 95
Masters, Ruth, 255
Matthew, Beverley, 111
McCarthy, D'Alton, 110, 173, 175, 184
McCarthy, Leighton, 112
McCarthy Tétrault, 119–22
McCrea, Charles, 66
McCrossan, George, 250, 257
McDiarmid, F.A., 251
McDougall, Gordon, 112
McInnes, Caroline, 94
McKay, Winnifred, 250
McKenna-McBride Agreement, 231
McKinney, David, 205, 210
McPhedran, Marilou, 266
McRuer, J.C., 66
Megafirms, 103–26
    centralized decision-making, 122–23
    conclusion, 124–26

corporate law firms without corporate structures, 107–9
firm/client link being personal, 112
foundation dates of law firms, 106
geographical expansion, 117–18
large firm in history, 104–5
Linklaters, 123
McCarthy Tétrault, 119–22
modernization, 113–15
19th-century form of large law firm, 109–13
origins of corporate law, 105–7
profit-per-partner (PPP), 117, 124
second transformative moment (1980–2000), 115–19
structural change, 119–24
team practice, 122
up-or-out system, 110
Meighen, Arthur, 64
Mellish, Humphrey, 88
Menzies, James Mellon, 240
Miller, Mabel, 248, 249, 252, 256, 257, 260
Miller, Stanley, 256
Millidge, Thomas, 165
Mills, Gertrude, 94, 97
Mironowicz, Margaret, 267, 268
Mockridge, Harold, 111
Model parliament, 61–64
Monette, Gustave, 184
Monk, James, 136
Moore, Christopher, 7, 17, 19, 20, 21, 24, 86, 103, 297
Morin, Emile, 143–44
Morin Inquiry, 155
Morris, Mabel, 248, 249, 252, 256, 257, 260
Mossman, Mary Jane, 38, 268
Mulroney, Brian, 65
Murphy, Edward J., 206, 211–12

Nelson, Robert L., 109, 112, 113, 123
Nisga'a Petition, 229, 231
Normand, Slyvio, 154

Oakville KKK incident, 219–20

Ogden, D., 137
O'Hearn, W.J., 91
Oliver, John, 232
O'Meara, Arthur Eugene, 225–41
  Aboriginal justice, 228–32, 237–38
  Cowichan Petition, 229
  lawyer and advocate, as, 232–35
  McKenna-McBride Agreement, 231
  Nisga'a Petition, 229, 231
  psychologizing the man, 235–36
O'Meara, Frederick Augustus, 226
O'Meara, Robin, 237
O'Meara, Thomas, 226, 236
O'Mullin, Maureen, 95, 97
Ontario Securities Act, 114
Osgoode Conservative Club, 58
Osgoode Hall, 3, 13–28
Osler, B.B., 110
Osler, H.S., 111

Panet, Narcisse, 137
Parr, Sir John, 165, 166
Paterson, Edith, 249, 254
Pearson, John, 202
Pemberton, Jeremy, 163
Phillips, Jim, 13, 161, 297
Pink, Irving, 96
Pitt, B.J. Spencer, 93
Political clubs, 65–67
Politicians, 49–71
  debating, 64
  model parliament, 61–64
  natural, 50–60
  other pursuits, 70
  political clubs, 65–67
  women, 67–69
Pottier, Vincent, 87, 92, 96
Power, John J., 91
Profit-per-partner (PPP), 117, 124
Public office. *See* Politicians
Pue, W. Wesley, 1, 13, 75, 84, 297
Purtill, Merle Marcella, 95, 97

Quebec, 129–157

 Commission Sylvestre, 143
criminal justice as anti-modern phenomenon, 149–51
culture de l'amalgame, 153
domestication of judicial establishment, 151–56
"Flaming Youth," 156
Gavazzi riot, 142–43, 145
gros village, 147–149
l'affaire Blanche Garneau, 147
Morin Inquiry, 155
penal justice, 141–157
Quebec City municipal court scandal,
 143–44, 146
Recorder's Court, 145
years following *Quebec Act of 1774*,
 129–39
Quebec City municipal court scandal,
 143–44, 146

Rationalist Society, 200–1, 209
Read, John, 43, 83–84
Recorder's Court, 145
Reid, J., 137
Rennie, Sarah "Pat," 252, 260
Riddell, William R., 110
Ringland, Muriel, 251
Risk, R.C.B., 190
Robinette, J.J., 175
Robinson, John Beverley, 16, 17, 18
Robson, H.A., 6
Robson, Hugh, 84
Roe, Walter, 14
Rogers, Tecumseh Sherman, 88
Roosevelt, Franklin, 188
Rosenblum, Charles, 91
Ross, D., 137
Rowe Brown, Deidré, 13, 297
Royal Securities Corporation (RSC), 77
Ruby, Clayton, 281
Russell, Benjamin, 84
Russell, Finley, 250
Russell, Joe, 249
Russell, Robert Henry, 145

Ryan, Lionel, 96

Saint John Law School. *See* Dalhousie
 Law School/University of New
 Brunswick Law School
Scott, Duncan Campbell, 232, 236
Scott, F.R., 282
Scott, Thomas, 16
Seaton, Eveleen, 249
Secretan, Charles, Jr., 145
Sewell, S., 137
Shaw, George Bernard, 213
Sheffman, Abraham, 96
Sing, John, 203
Singer, Ephraim Frederick, 196
Smith, Bob, 250
Smith, Sidney, 84
Special Committee on Civil Liberties,
 184–85
Special students, 35–37
Spence, Wishart, 174
Spender, Dale, 270
St. Catherine's Milling case, 233
St-Laurent, Louis, 88
Steel, Aileen, 63
Sterns, Jonathan, 162–72
Sterry, Ernest Victor, 202–15
Stewart, James McGregor, 89, 90
Storm, William G., 23
Strachan, Ian, 55
Strachan, John, 17
Strange, Thomas, 163, 171
Strauss, Albert, 265, 266, 268
Stringer, Isaac, 227
Sutherland, Ann, 248, 249, 256, 259
Sutherland, John, 256
Symes, Beth, 268

Talbot, Lance, 194
Tamaki, George, 96
Taschereau, Louis-Alexandre, 147
Taylor, William, 162–72
Theriault, Edward J., 92
Tilley, W. Norman, 111

To All Appearances a Lady (Bowering), 225
Tory, J.S.D., 111
Trudeau, Pierre, 176

University of New Brunswick. *See* Dalhousie Law School/University of New Brunswick Law School
Up-or-out system, 110
Urban bar, 75–102
    Acadian lawyers, 92
    big three, 81
    black lawyers, 92–93
    conclusion, 98–99
    diversity, 90–98
    Halifax, 77–78
    Halifax bar, 78–81
    Jewish lawyers, 91–92
    Lebanese-Christian lawyers, 92
    migration of lawyers westward, 79
    religion, 91–92
    role of Halifax law firms, 81–90
    rural-urban tensions, 86
    tables, 100–2
    women lawyers, 93–95

Van Wart, Beatrice, 66
Vertical Mosaic, The (Porter), 60
Viger, D.B., 137
Vipond, R.C., 190

Wade, F.C., 237
Waldo, Nathan, 206, 210
Wambolt, Grace, 63, 87, 94, 95
War Measures Act, 173, 175, 180
Ward-Whate, F.C., 217
Wartime Prices and Trade Board (WPTB), 174, 175
Watt, Steven, 129
Webber, Harry, 91
Weldon, Richard, 33, 61
Wells, H.G., 213
White, John, 16
White, Sir Thomas, 65

Whiteside, Arthur, 250, 252
Whiteside, Jean Kennedy, 248, 249, 253
Whitton, Charlotte, 69
Wilkes, John, 169
Williams, E.K., 84
Willis, John, 35, 190
Winn, Charles, 199
Women lawyers
    BC lawyers (1912–30), 245–63
    Nova Scotia lawyers, 93–95
    Ontario feminist lawyers, 265–94
Wood, Daniel, 170, 171
Woodsworth, J.S., 88
WPTB, 174, 175
Wright, Caesar, 25, 179, 188

Ying, Joseph, 202, 203

Zive, Aaron, 96